4

STORY & CHARACTER & FORMATION

Sumire Suō was a third-year at Ikari Kawaguchi Middle School. Despite her overwhelming talent as a winger, her summer comes to an end before she can accomplish anything... Not willing to see that talent go to waste, Suō's rival, Midori Soshizaki, approaches her and says, "Let's join the same team. I won't let you play alone."

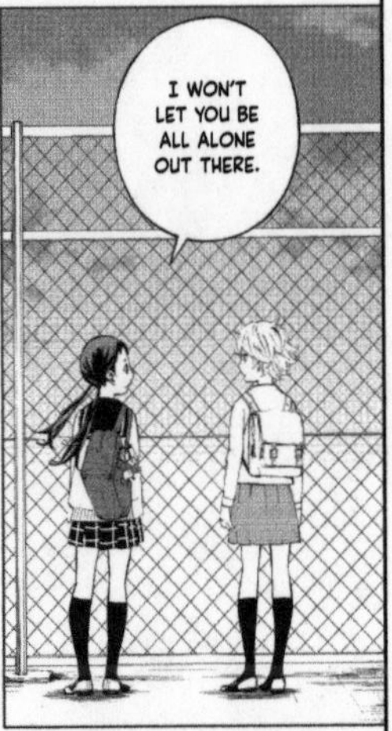
I WON'T LET YOU BE ALL ALONE OUT THERE.

So Suō chooses a school, and Soshizaki goes with her...to Warabi Seinan High School, a school with a weak team that everyone mocks as "the Wallabies." It was sympathy for Tase, a second-year who had been the only girl on her team to actually try, that led Suō to choose this school.

Soshizaki is stunned to end up on such a low-level team. However...there's another talented girl who has joined their ranks. Her name is Nozomi Onda, and she is unknown in the world of girls' soccer, because she played on the boys' team in middle school. But her talent is real. With 17 girls on the team and a sorry excuse for a coach, the Wallabies take their first step forward.

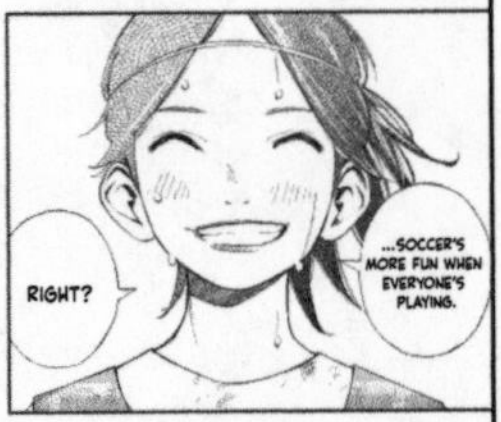
...SOCCER'S MORE FUN WHEN EVERYONE'S PLAYING.
RIGHT?

Then Warabi Seinan gets a new coach, as well. Her name is Naoko Nōmi, a legendary soccer athlete who played on Japan's national team. She has now retired and come back to her alma mater to coach. She uses her connections to arrange their first practice match—against the best high school girls' soccer team in Japan, Kunogi Academy.

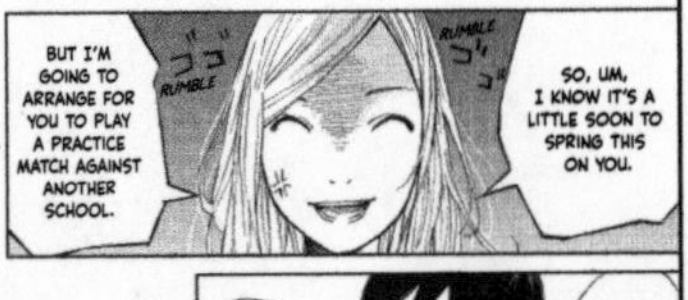
SO, UM, I KNOW IT'S A LITTLE SOON TO SPRING THIS ON YOU.
RUMBLE
RUMBLE
BUT I'M GOING TO ARRANGE FOR YOU TO PLAY A PRACTICE MATCH AGAINST ANOTHER SCHOOL.

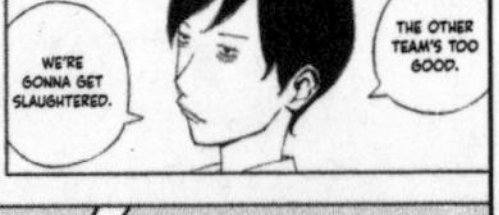
THE OTHER TEAM'S TOO GOOD.
WE'RE GONNA GET SLAUGHTERED.

The title of best of in Japan was well earned. After the first half, Warabi Seinan is losing 0-7. But Nozomi Onda's spirit is not broken. Her heart thrills at the high-level playing of Kunogi's team, and she even begins to shine brighter!!

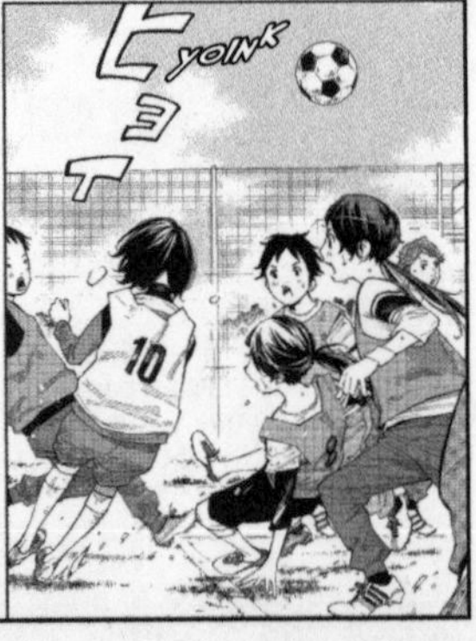
YOINK

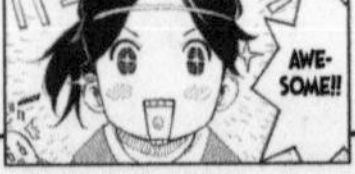
EHA
O BEE
AWE-SOME!!

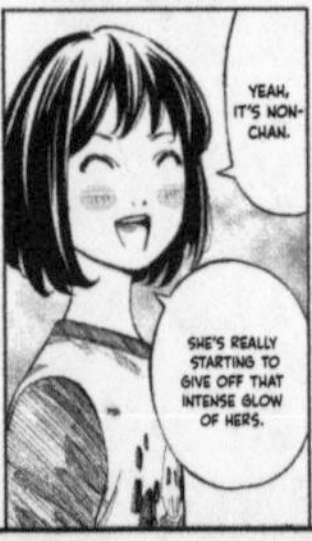
YEAH, IT'S NON-CHAN.
SHE'S REALLY STARTING TO GIVE OFF THAT INTENSE GLOW OF HERS.

Warabi Seinan High School Formation 4-1-4-1

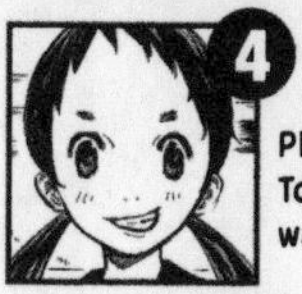
4

MIDORI SOSHIZAKI (1ST-YEAR)

Played defensive midfielder for Todakita Middle School, which was third in the nation.

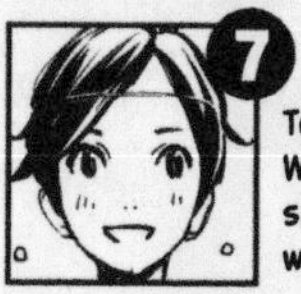
7

ERIKO TASE (2ND-YEAR)

Team captain. Core player for Warabi Seinan. A kind and responsible girl who sympathizes with others' struggles.

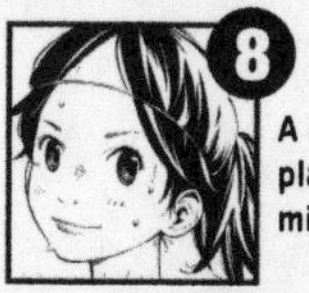
8

NOZOMI ONDA (1ST-YEAR)

A charismatic midfielder who played for a boys' team in middle school.

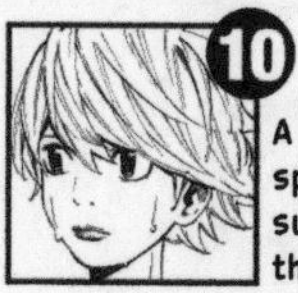
10

SUMIRE SUŌ (1ST-YEAR)

A winger with overwhelming speed. Upon Soshizaki's suggestion, the two go to the same high school.

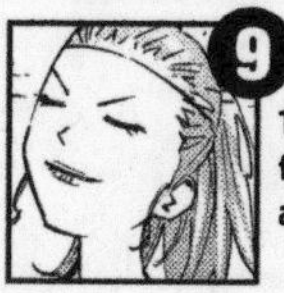
9

AYA SHIRATORI (1ST-YEAR)

The self-proclaimed center-forward, who's more loud and annoying than anything else.

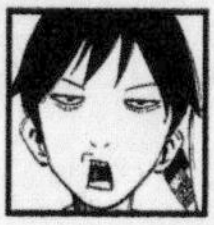

HEAD COACH: FUKATSU

Is always reading horse-racing magazines.

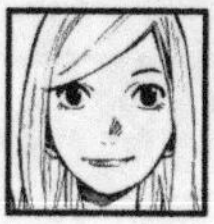

COACH: NAOKO NŌMI

A legend in Japanese girls soccer. Has now retired and become a coach.

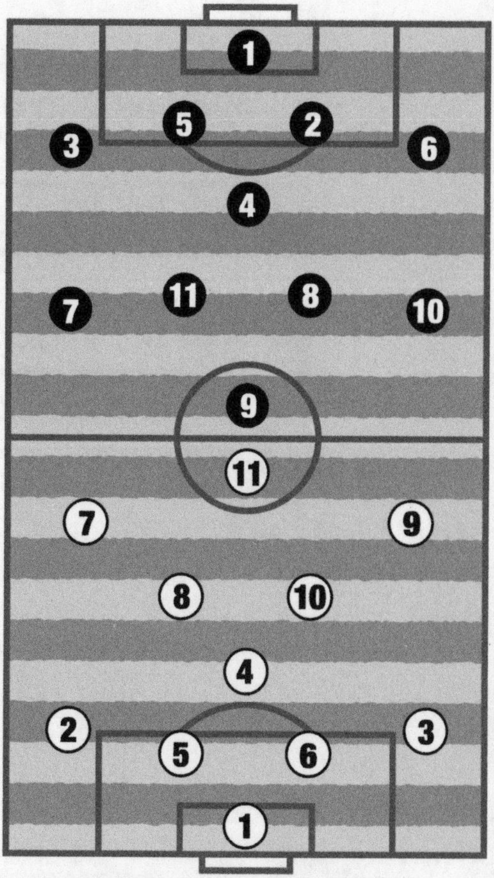
1
5
2
3
6
4
11
8
7
10
9
11
7
9
8
10
4
2
3
5
6
1

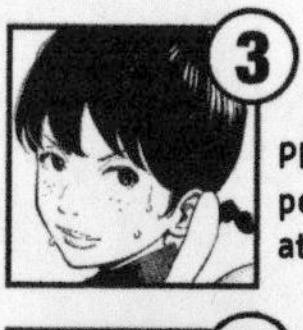
3

MAO TSUKUDA (1ST-YEAR)

Played on the U-17 team. A powerful wing back who excels at offense and defense.

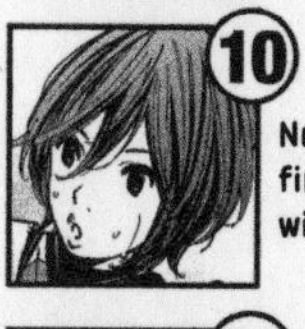
10

HARUNA ITŌ (1ST-YEAR)

Number 10 on Kunogi Academy's first-year team. Good friends with Tsukuda.

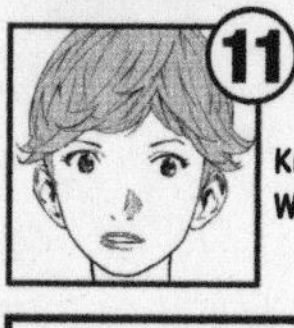
11

MIZUKI KAJI (2ND-YEAR)

Kunogi Academy's star player. Was captain of the U-15 team.

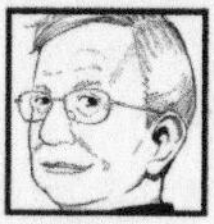

HEAD COACH: KENROKU WASHIZU

Famed commander of Kunogi Academy's high school girls' soccer team, the best team in Japan.

Kunogi Academy Formation 4-1-2-3

CONTENTS

12. THE GATES OF HELL — 05

13. THE THREE FIENDS OF WARABI SEINEN — 51

14. THE FRONTIER — 99

15. LOVESICK — 145

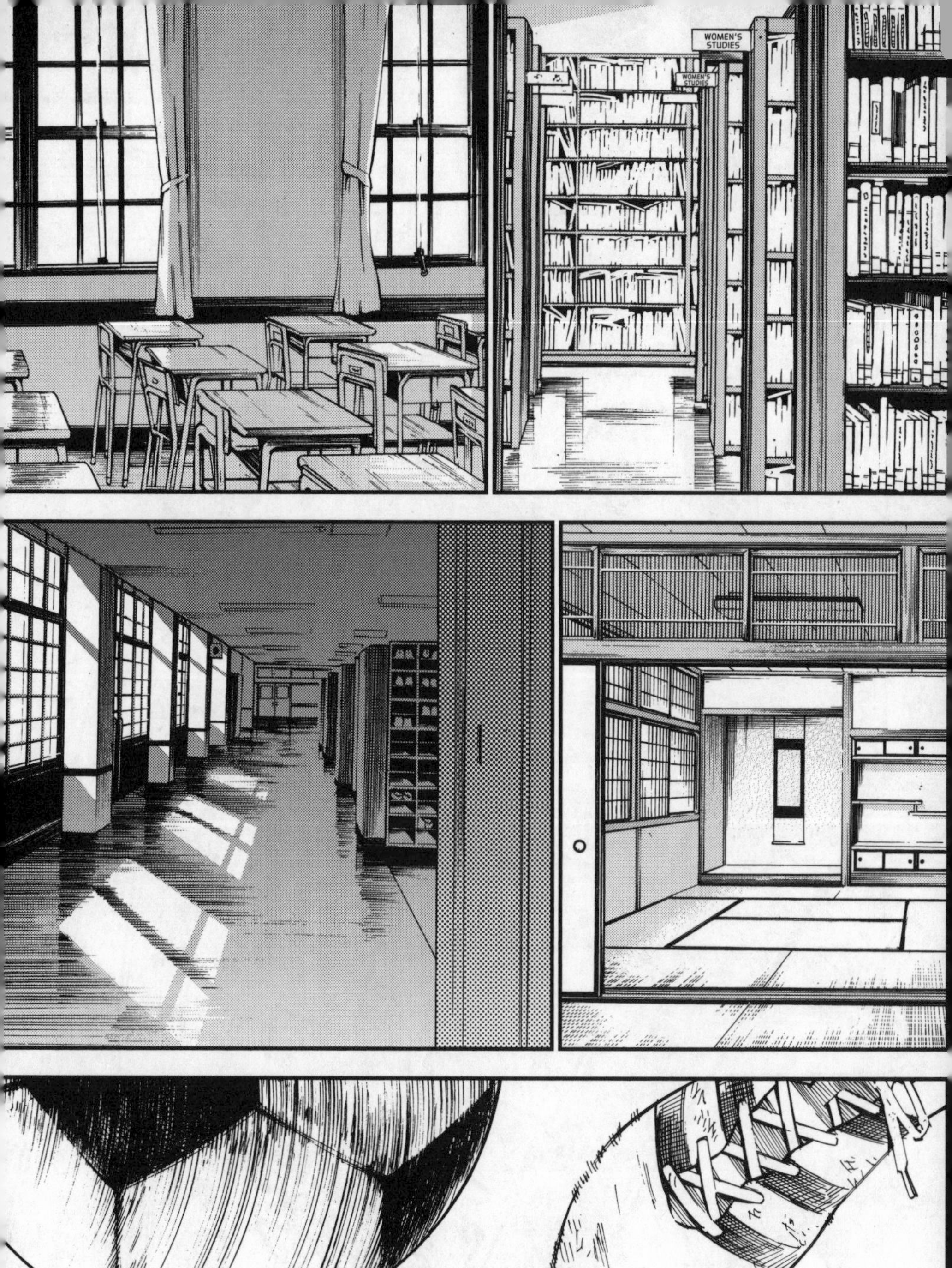
WOMEN'S STUDIES
WOMEN'S STUDIES

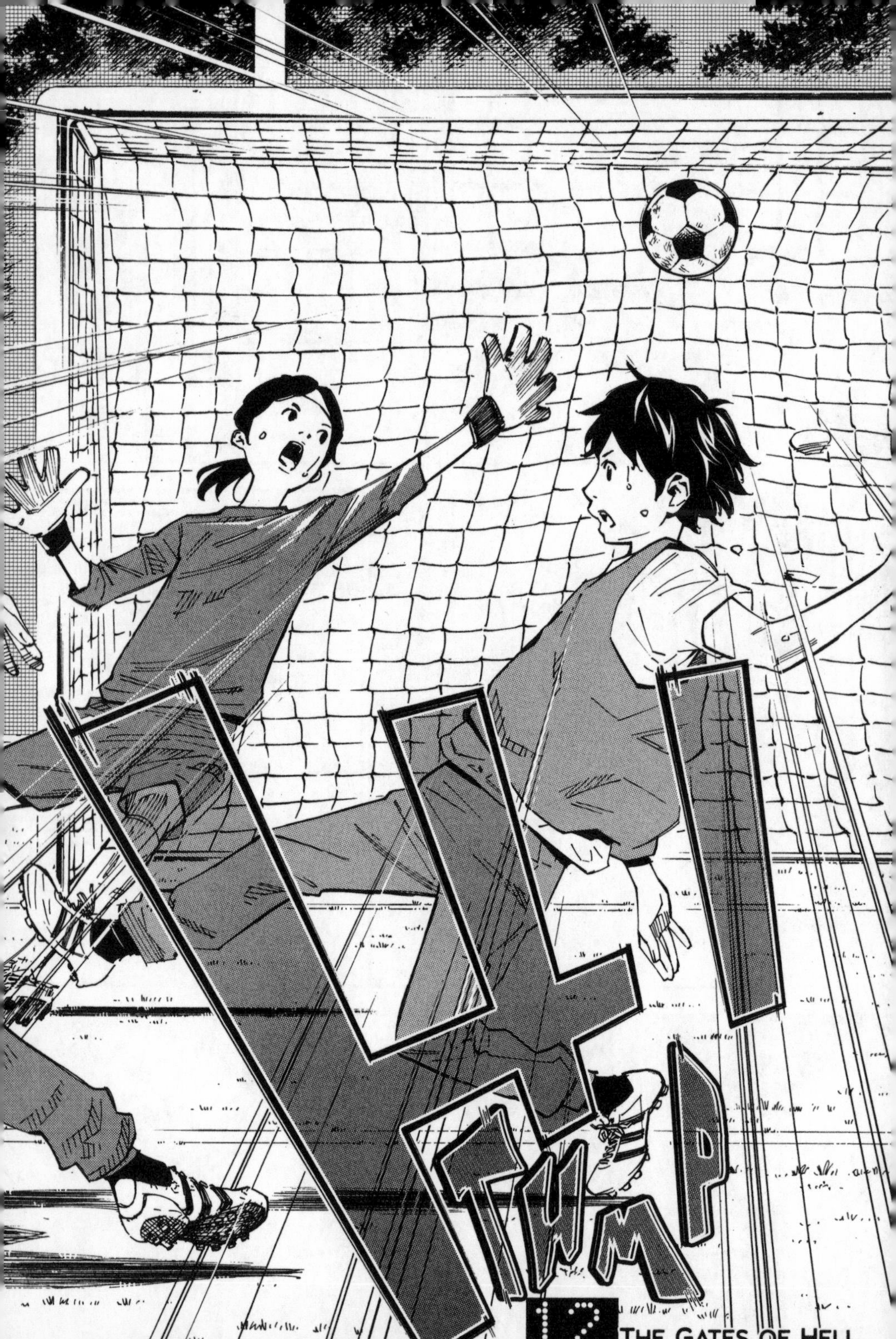
THUMP

12. THE GATES OF HELL

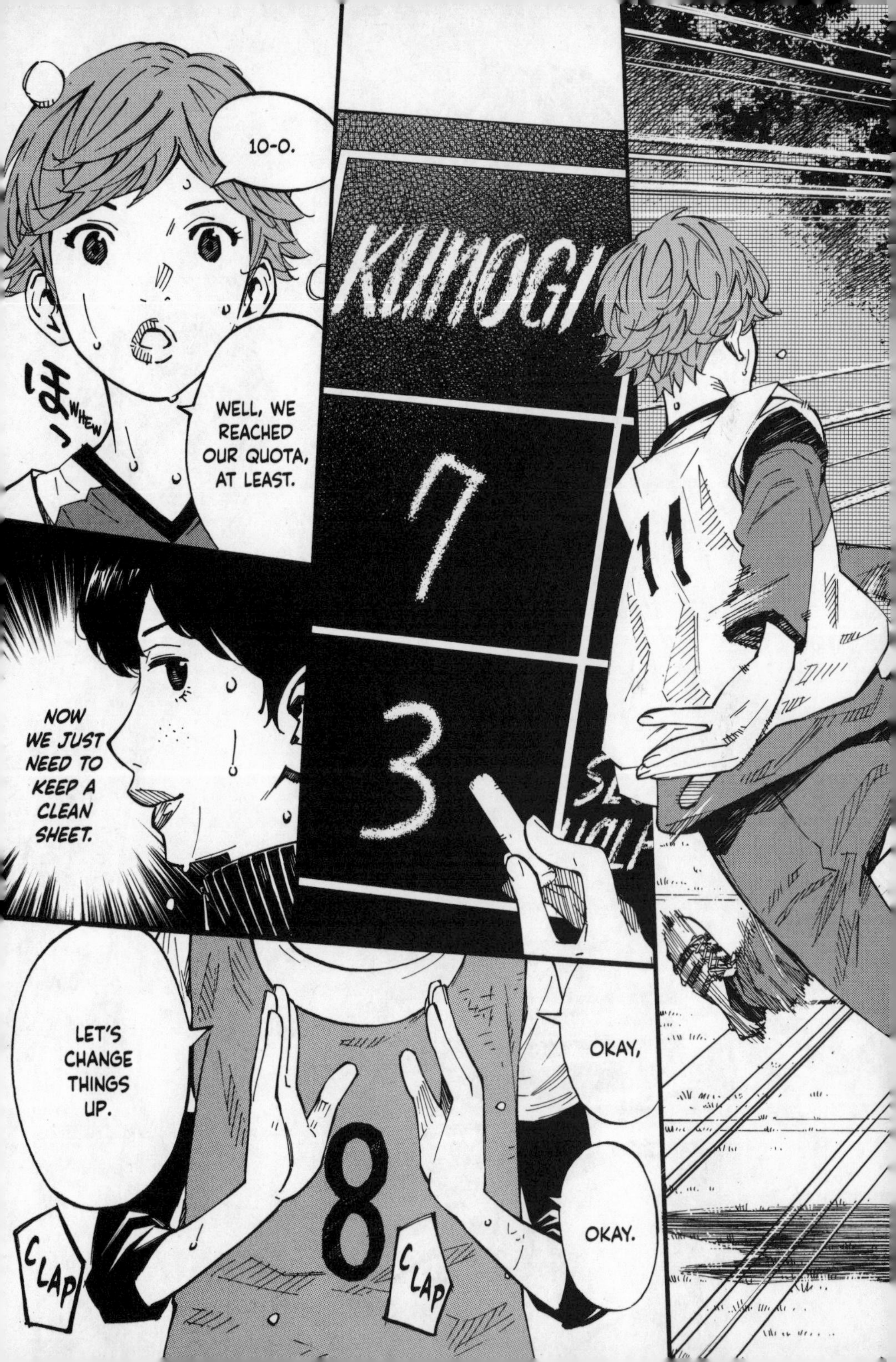
KUNOGI
7
3
10-0.
ほっ
WHEW
WELL, WE REACHED OUR QUOTA, AT LEAST.
NOW WE JUST NEED TO KEEP A CLEAN SHEET.
OKAY,
OKAY.
LET'S CHANGE THINGS UP.
CLAP
CLAP

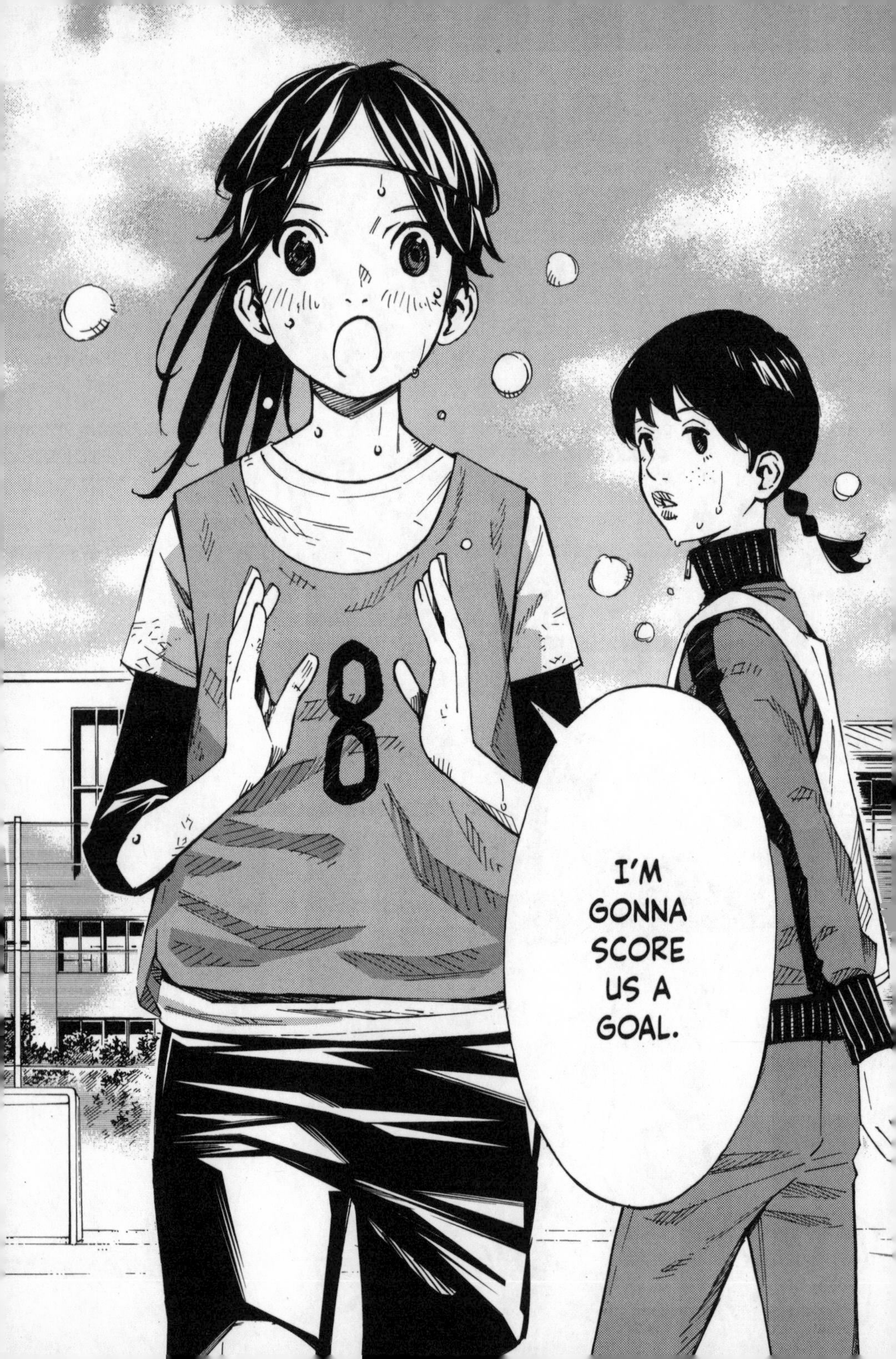
I'M GONNA SCORE US A GOAL.

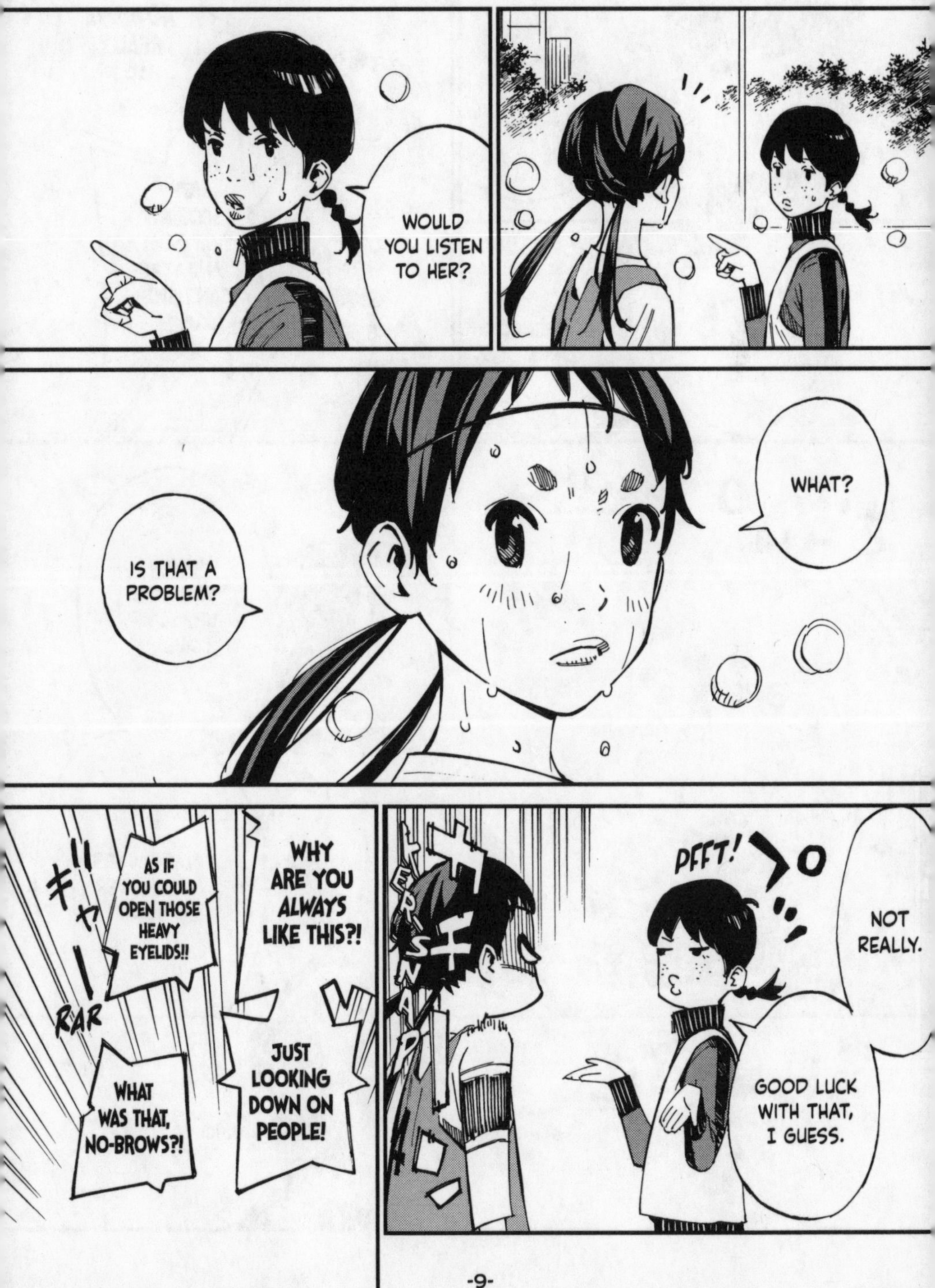

WOULD YOU LISTEN TO HER?
WHAT?
IS THAT A PROBLEM?
PFFT!
NOT REALLY.
GOOD LUCK WITH THAT, I GUESS.
WHY ARE YOU ALWAYS LIKE THIS?!
AS IF YOU COULD OPEN THOSE HEAVY EYELIDS!!
JUST LOOKING DOWN ON PEOPLE!
WHAT WAS THAT, NO-BROWS?!
ギャー
RAR

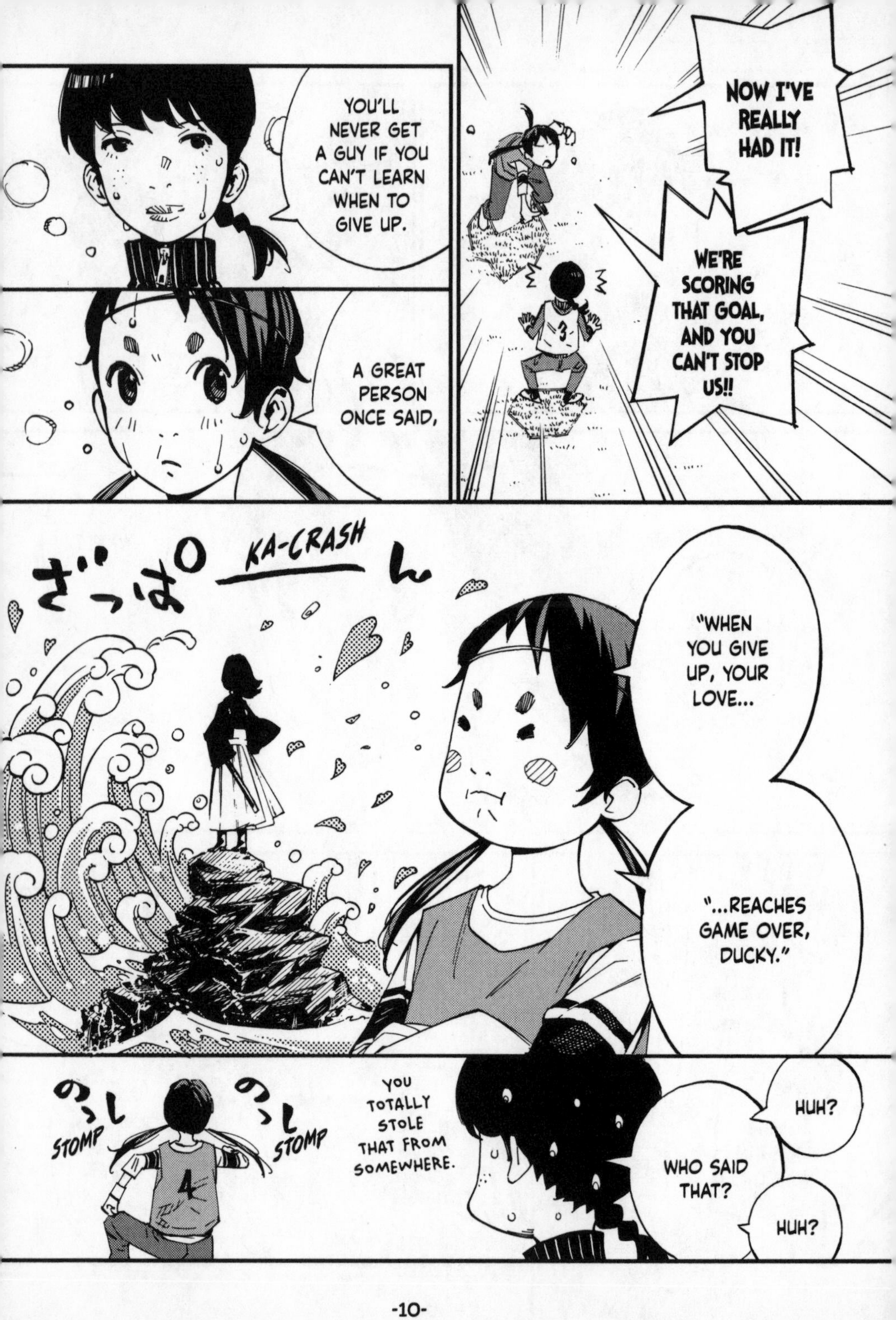
NOW I'VE REALLY HAD IT!
WE'RE SCORING THAT GOAL, AND YOU CAN'T STOP US!!
YOU'LL NEVER GET A GUY IF YOU CAN'T LEARN WHEN TO GIVE UP.
A GREAT PERSON ONCE SAID,
"WHEN YOU GIVE UP, YOUR LOVE...
"...REACHES GAME OVER, DUCKY."
ざっぱーん
KA-CRASH
HUH?
WHO SAID THAT?
HUH?
YOU TOTALLY STOLE THAT FROM SOMEWHERE.
のっし
STOMP
のっし
STOMP

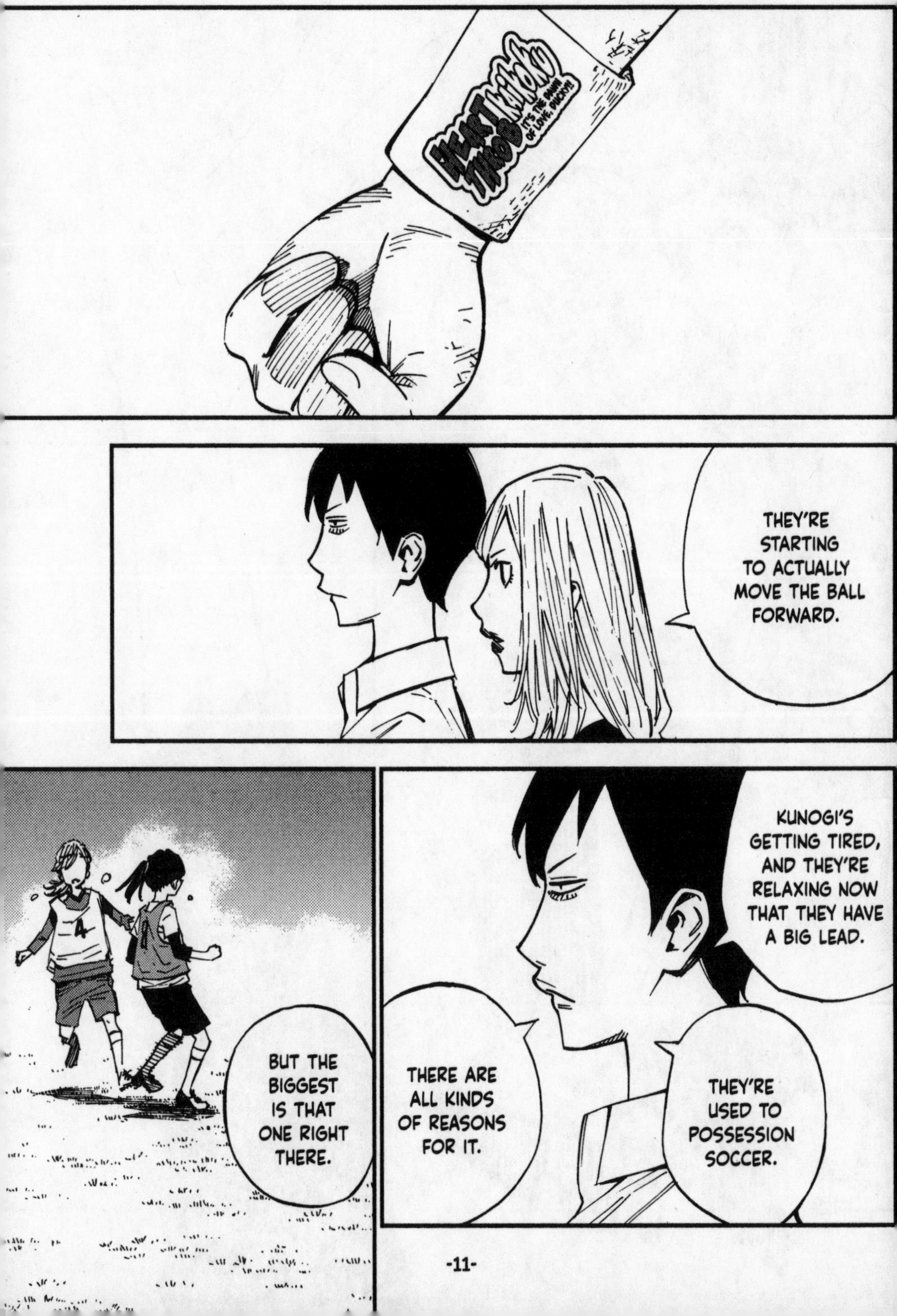
HEART THROB
IT'S THE DAWN OF LOVE, DUCKY!!
THEY'RE STARTING TO ACTUALLY MOVE THE BALL FORWARD.
KUNOGI'S GETTING TIRED, AND THEY'RE RELAXING NOW THAT THEY HAVE A BIG LEAD.
THEY'RE USED TO POSSESSION SOCCER.
THERE ARE ALL KINDS OF REASONS FOR IT.
BUT THE BIGGEST IS THAT ONE RIGHT THERE.

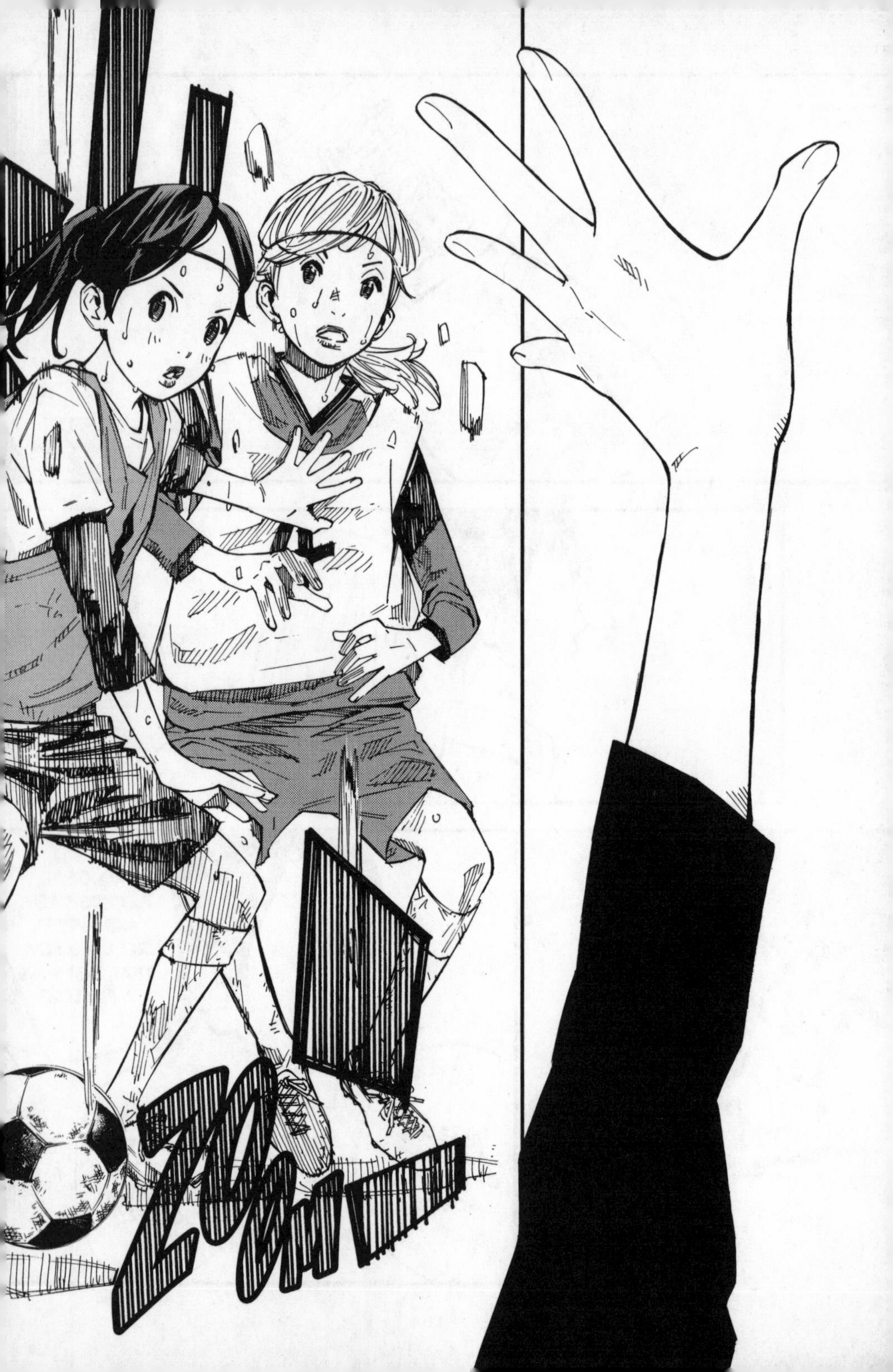

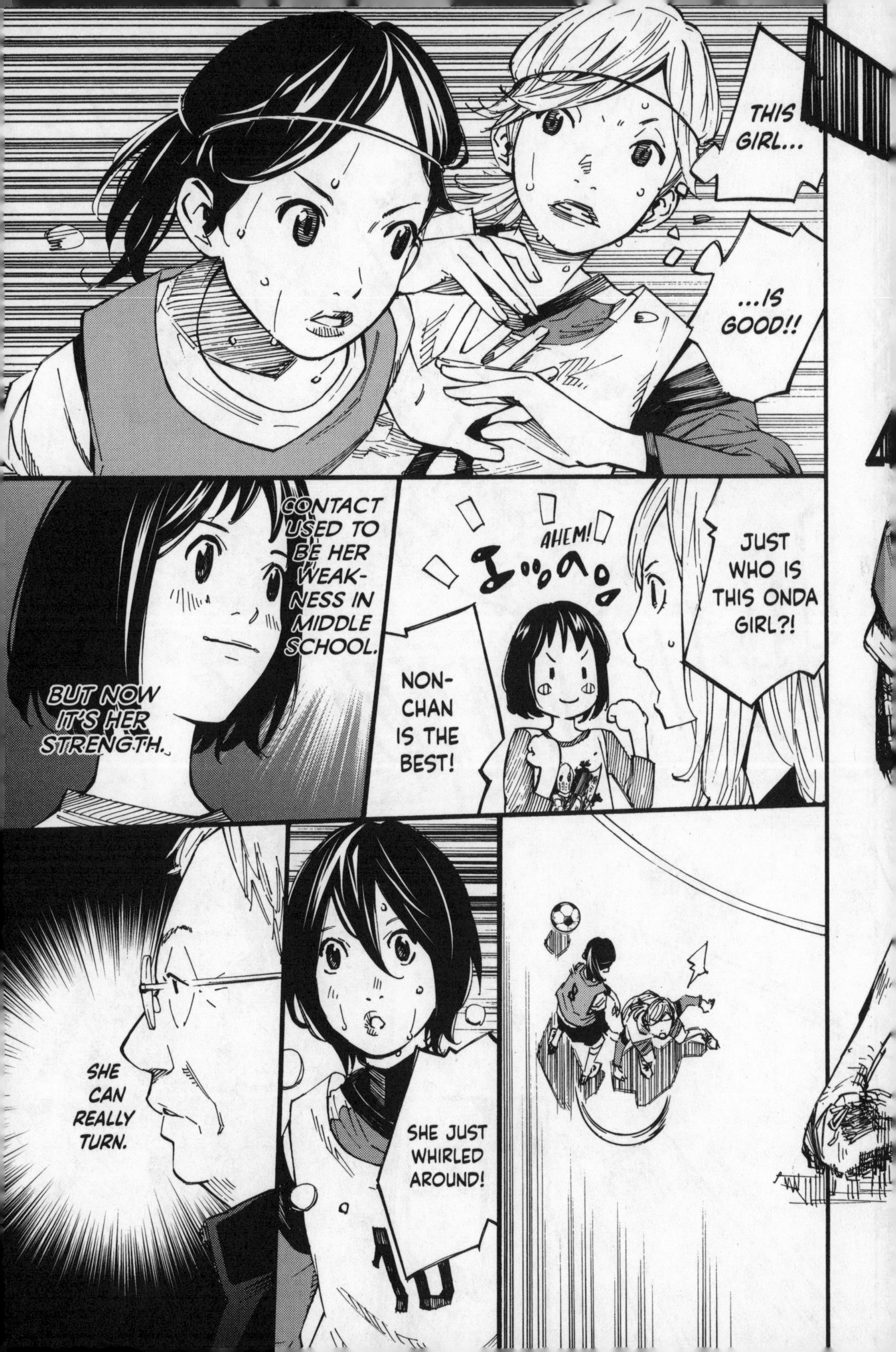
THIS GIRL...
...IS GOOD!!
JUST WHO IS THIS ONDA GIRL?!
AHEM!
NON-CHAN IS THE BEST!
CONTACT USED TO BE HER WEAKNESS IN MIDDLE SCHOOL.
BUT NOW IT'S HER STRENGTH.
SHE JUST WHIRLED AROUND!
SHE CAN REALLY TURN.

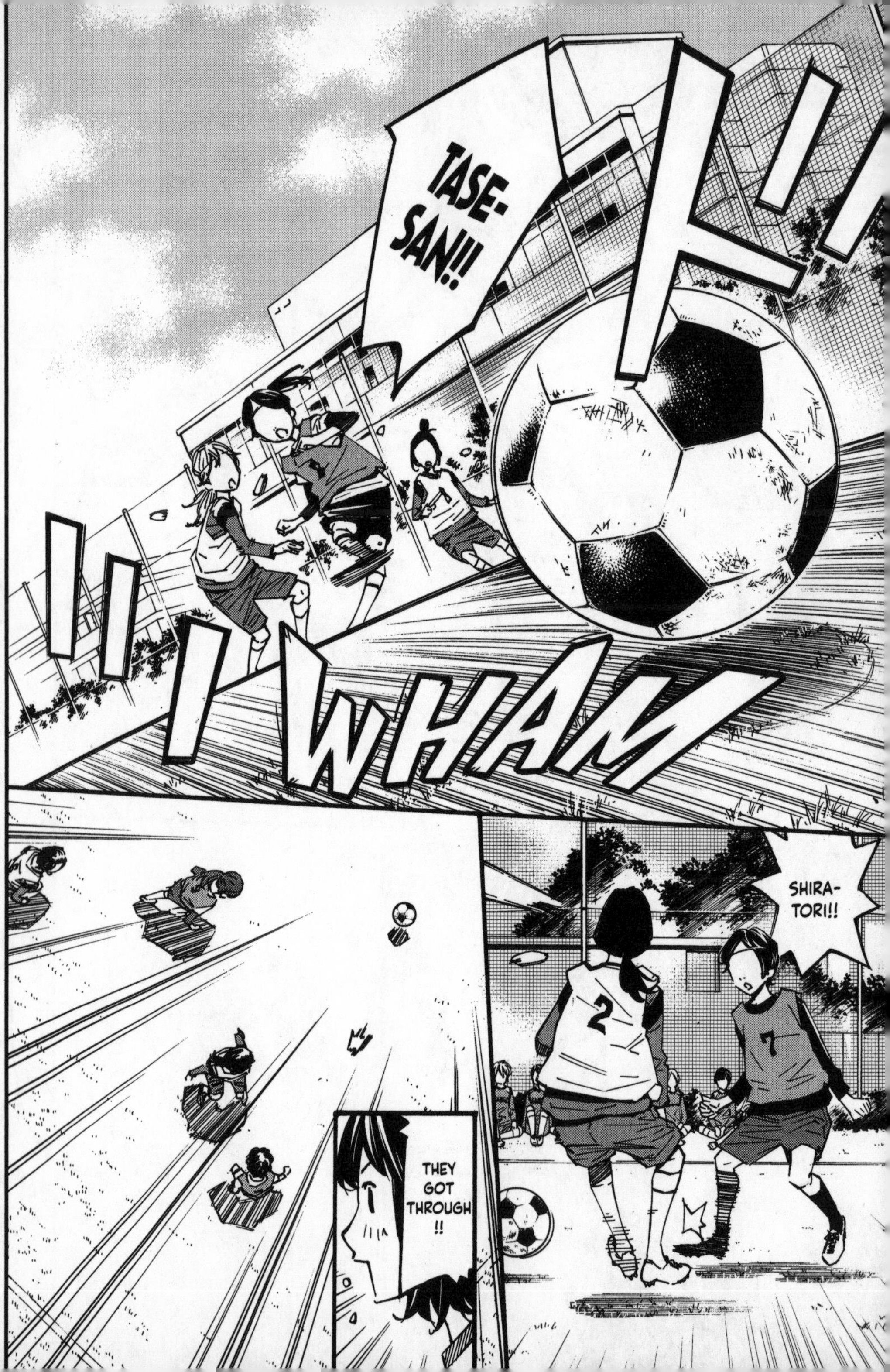
TASE-SAN!!
WHAM
SHIRA-TORI!!
THEY GOT THROUGH !!

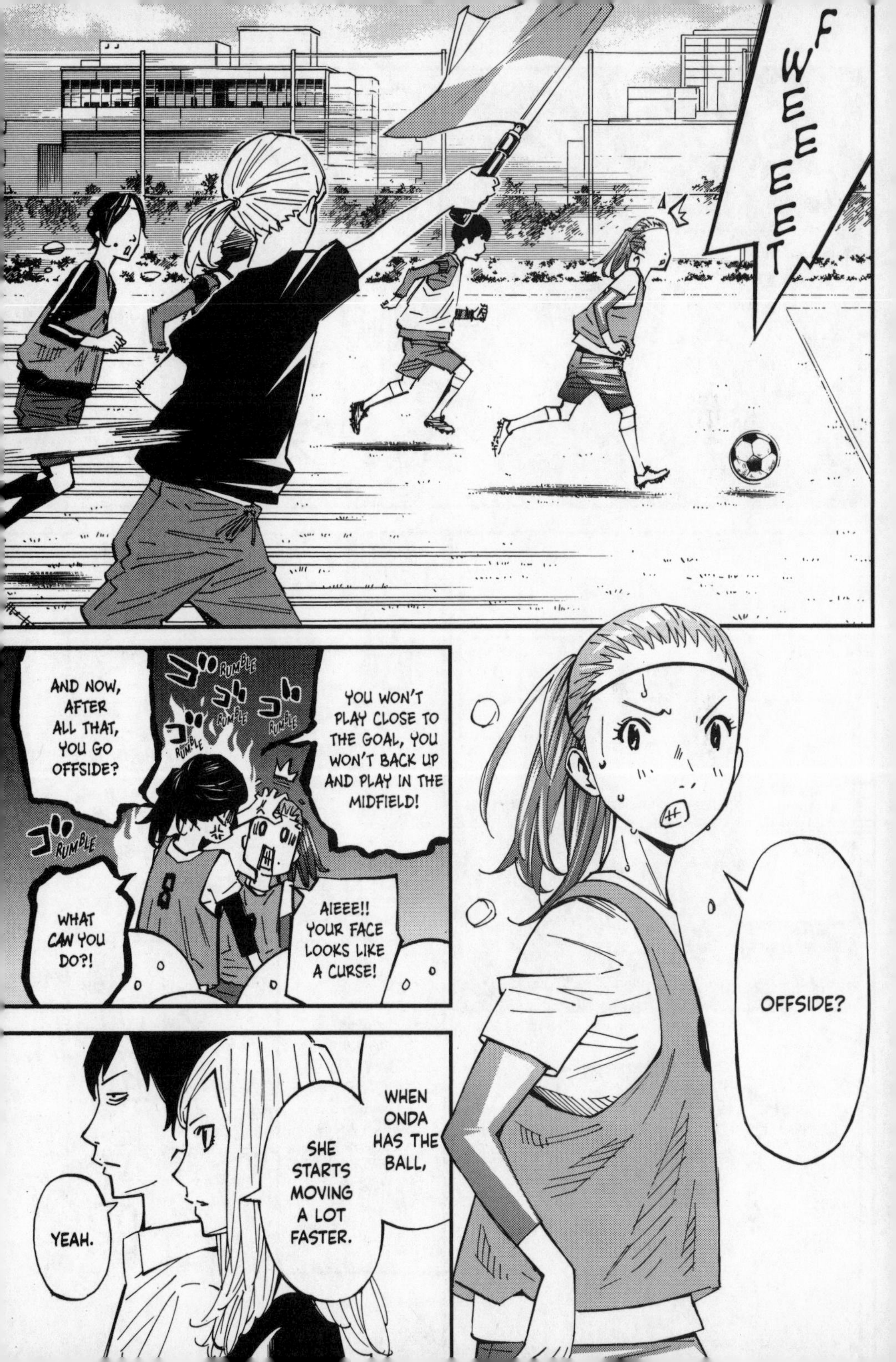
FWEEEET
OFFSIDE?
YOU WON'T PLAY CLOSE TO THE GOAL, YOU WON'T BACK UP AND PLAY IN THE MIDFIELD!
AND NOW, AFTER ALL THAT, YOU GO OFFSIDE?
RUMBLE RUMBLE RUMBLE RUMBLE RUMBLE
AIEEE!! YOUR FACE LOOKS LIKE A CURSE!
WHAT CAN YOU DO?!
WHEN ONDA HAS THE BALL,
SHE STARTS MOVING A LOT FASTER.
YEAH.

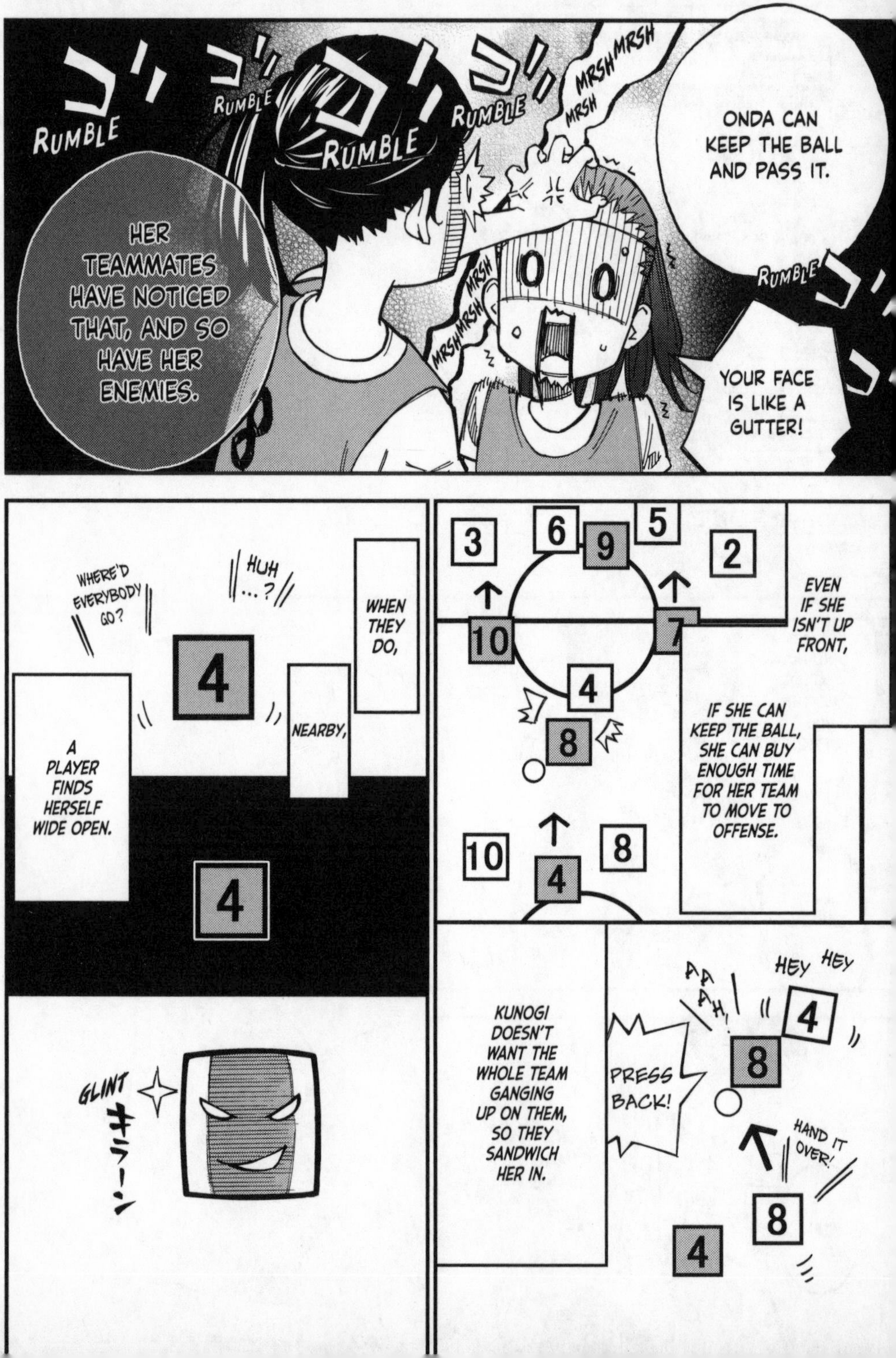
ONDA CAN KEEP THE BALL AND PASS IT.
RUMBLE
MRSH MRSH MRSH
RUMBLE
RUMBLE
RUMBLE
RUMBLE
YOUR FACE IS LIKE A GUTTER!
MRSH MRSH MRSH
HER TEAMMATES HAVE NOTICED THAT, AND SO HAVE HER ENEMIES.
3 6 9 5 2
10 7
4
8
10 4 8
EVEN IF SHE ISN'T UP FRONT,
IF SHE CAN KEEP THE BALL, SHE CAN BUY ENOUGH TIME FOR HER TEAM TO MOVE TO OFFENSE.
HEY HEY
AAAH!
4
8
HAND IT OVER!
8
4
PRESS BACK!
KUNOGI DOESN'T WANT THE WHOLE TEAM GANGING UP ON THEM, SO THEY SANDWICH HER IN.
WHEN THEY DO,
HUH...?
NEARBY,
WHERE'D EVERYBODY GO?
4
A PLAYER FINDS HERSELF WIDE OPEN.
4
GLINT
キラーン

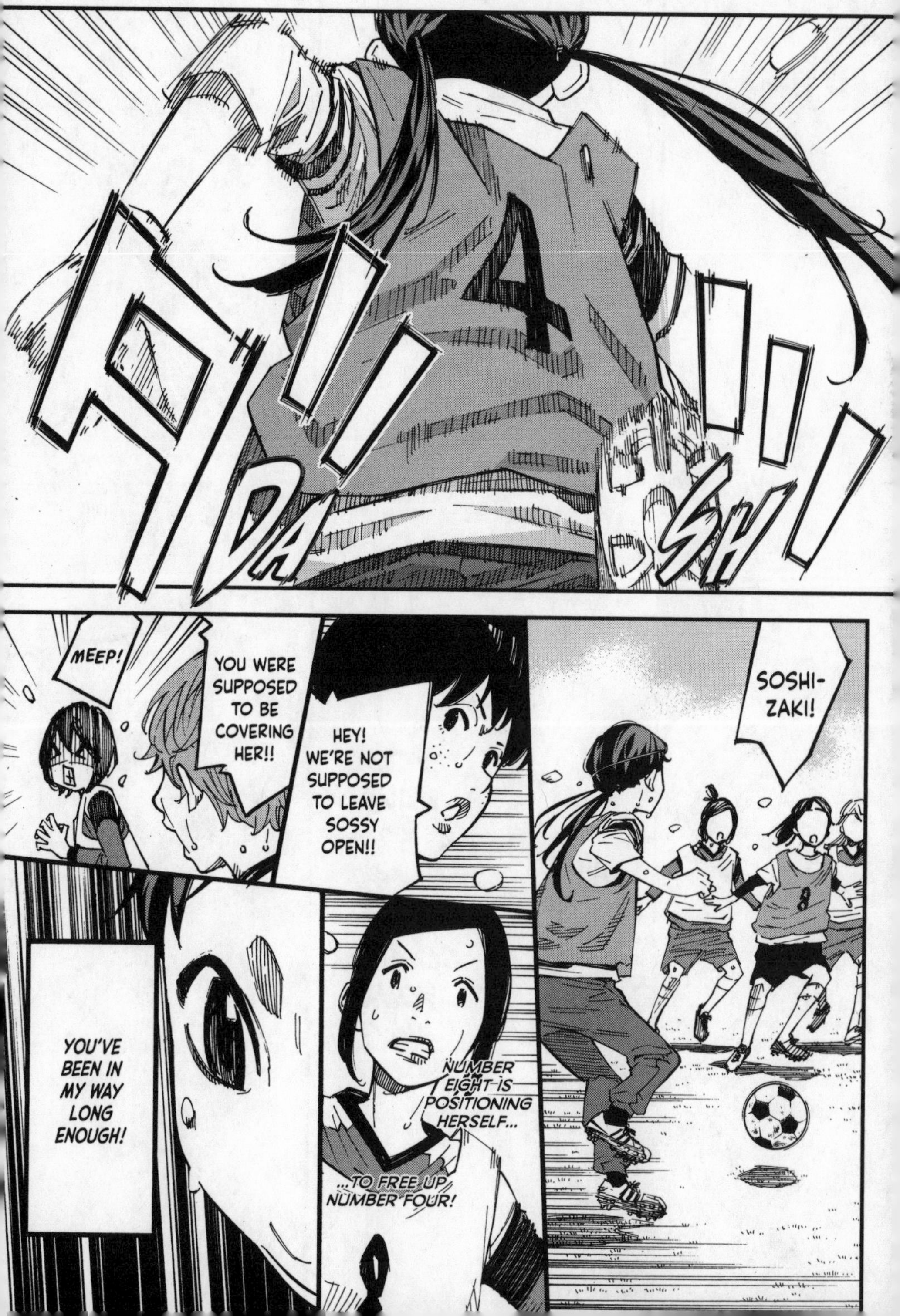
DA
SH
SOSHI-ZAKI!
HEY! WE'RE NOT SUPPOSED TO LEAVE SOSSY OPEN!!
YOU WERE SUPPOSED TO BE COVERING HER!!
MEEP!
NUMBER EIGHT IS POSITIONING HERSELF...
...TO FREE UP NUMBER FOUR!
YOU'VE BEEN IN MY WAY LONG ENOUGH!

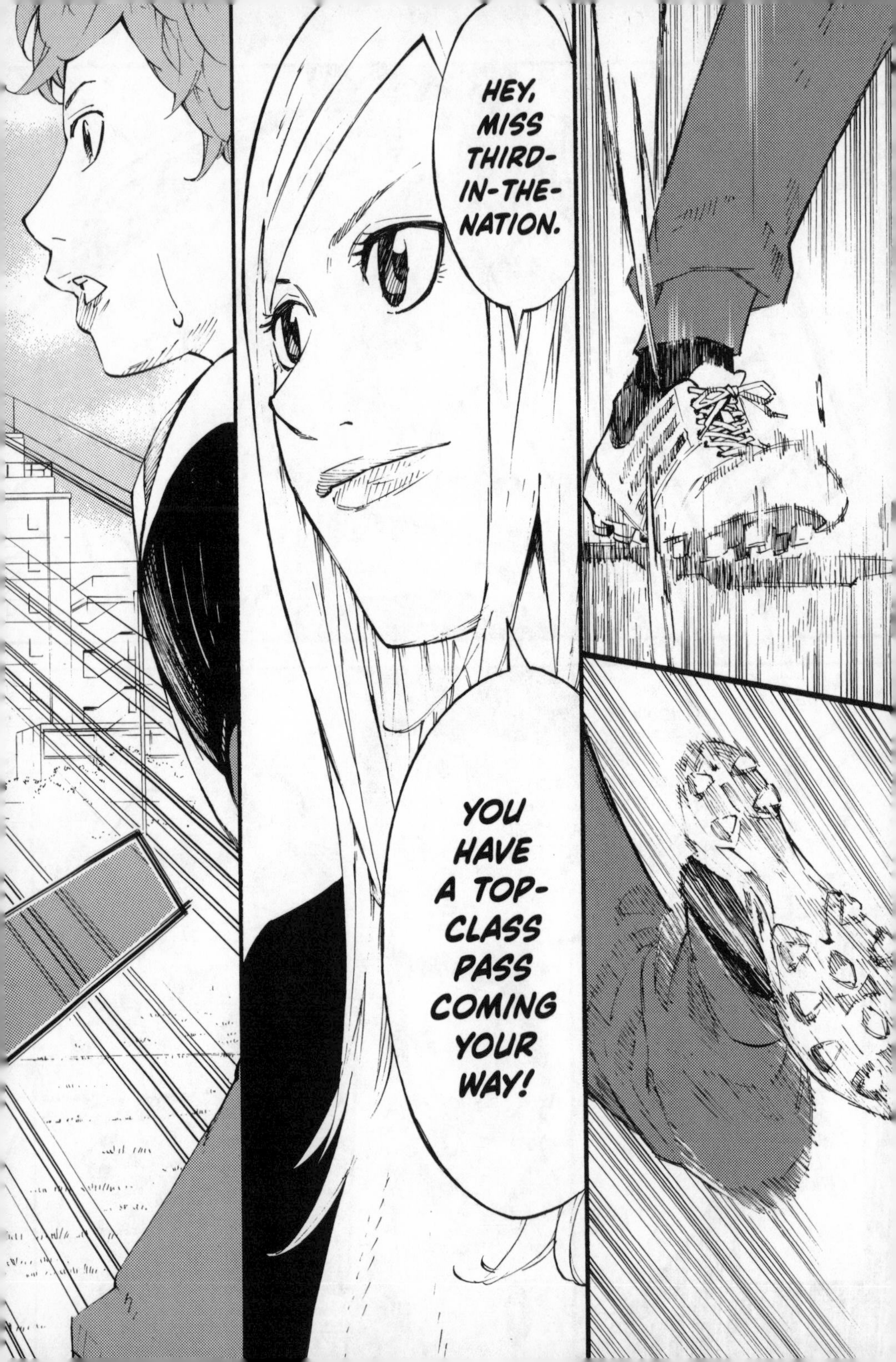
HEY, MISS THIRD-IN-THE-NATION.
YOU HAVE A TOP-CLASS PASS COMING YOUR WAY!

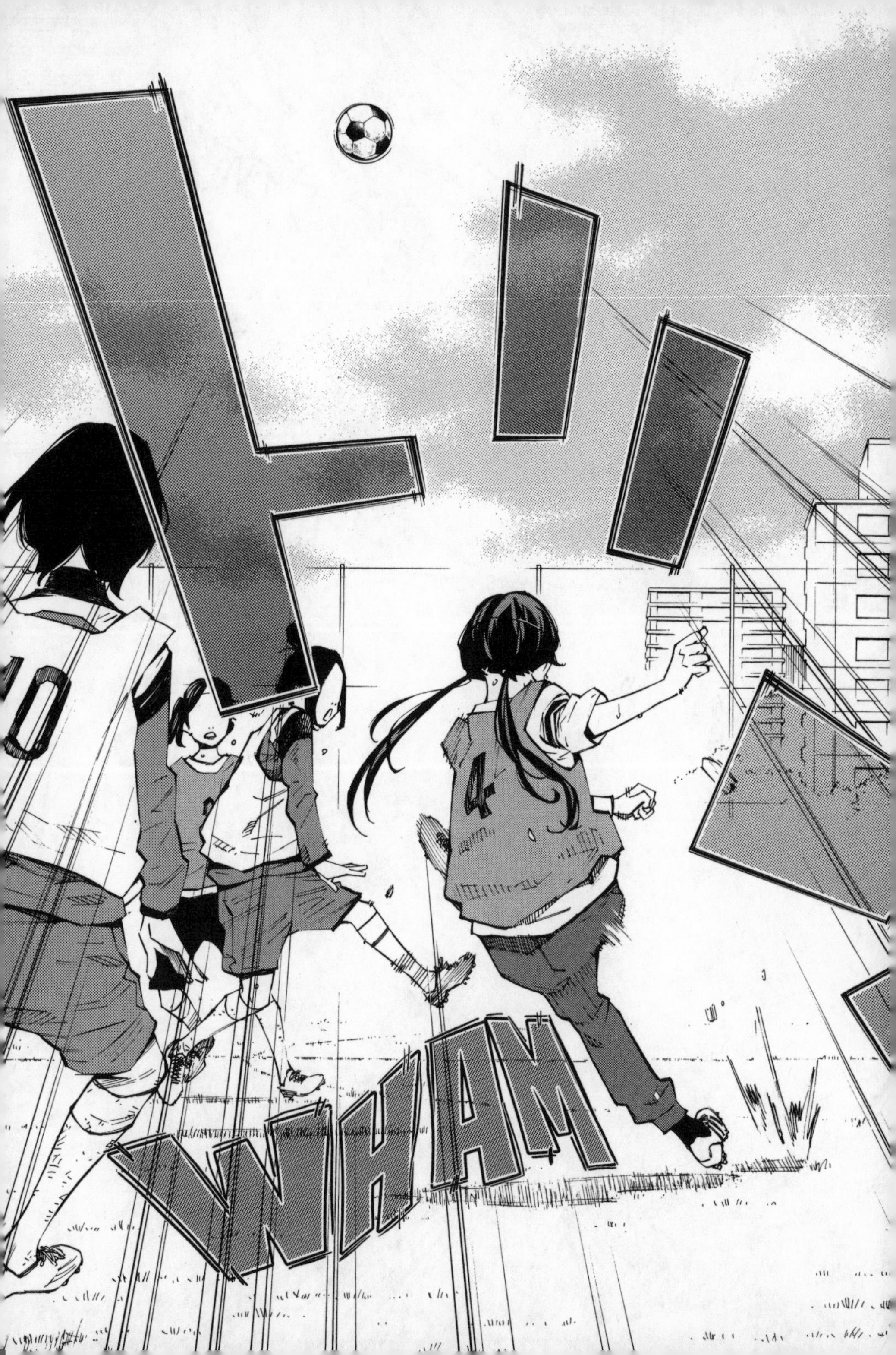
ド
WHAM

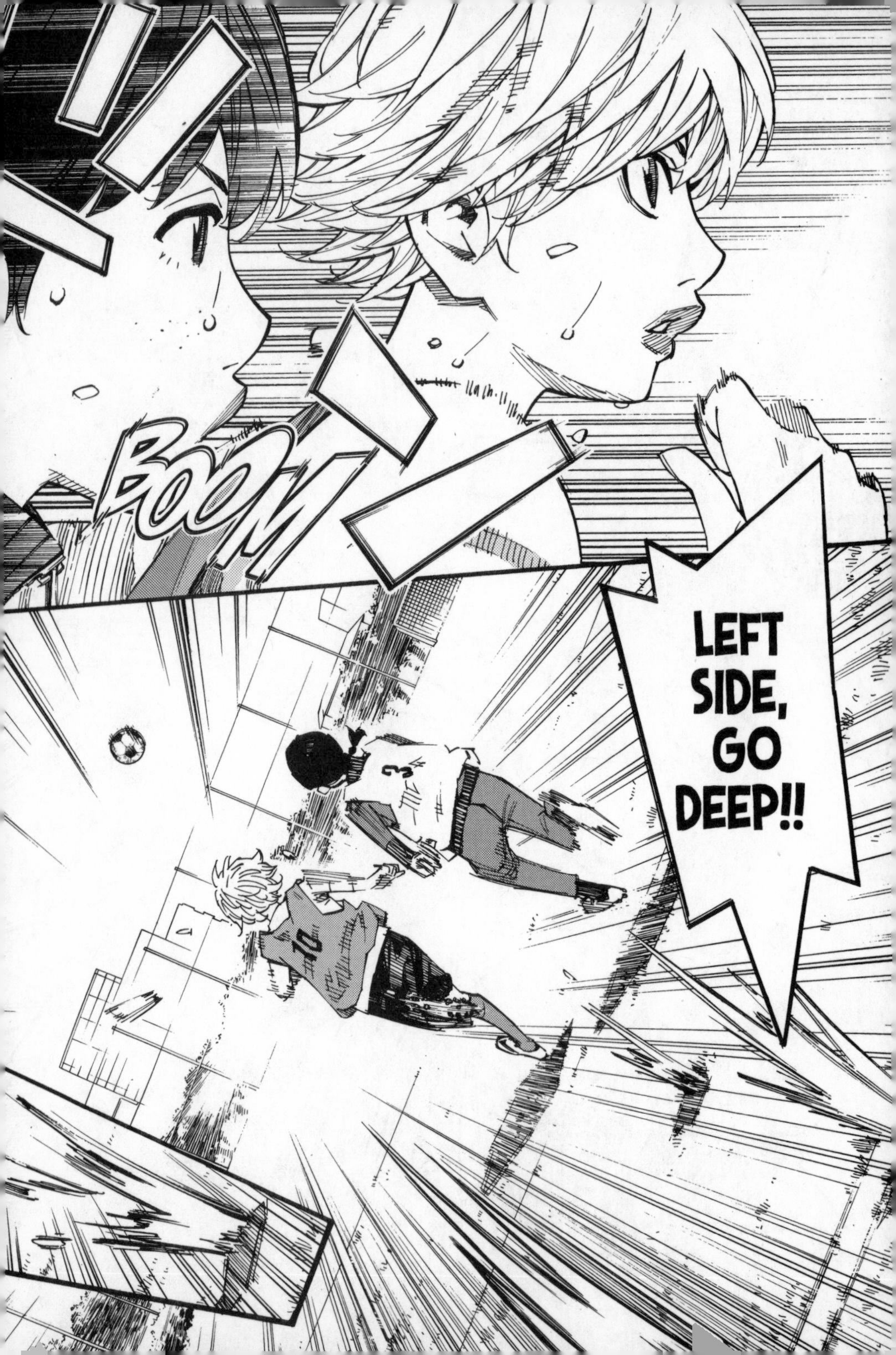
BOOM
LEFT SIDE, GO DEEP!!

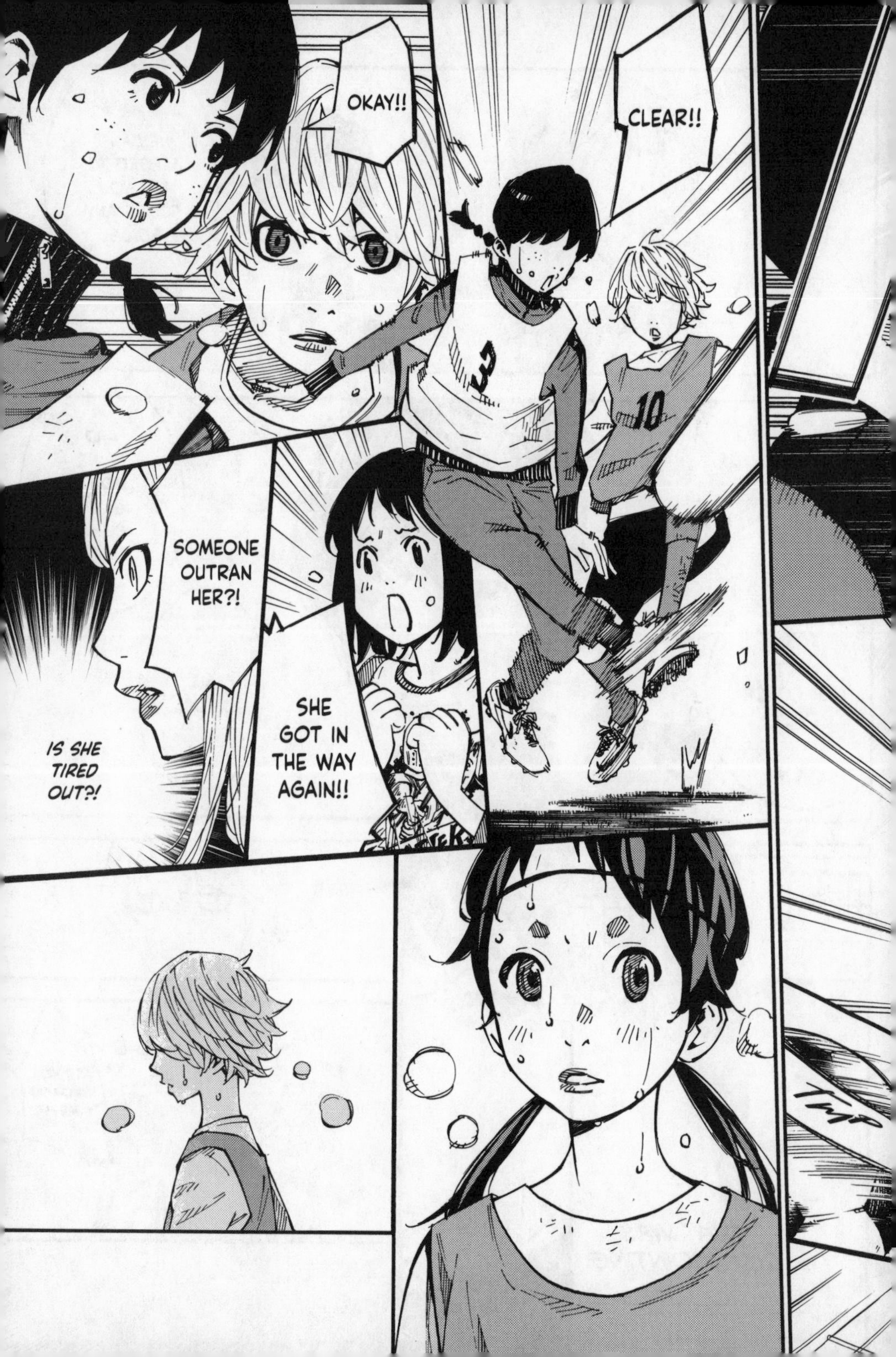
CLEAR!!
OKAY!!
SHE GOT IN THE WAY AGAIN!!
SOMEONE OUTRAN HER?!
IS SHE TIRED OUT?!

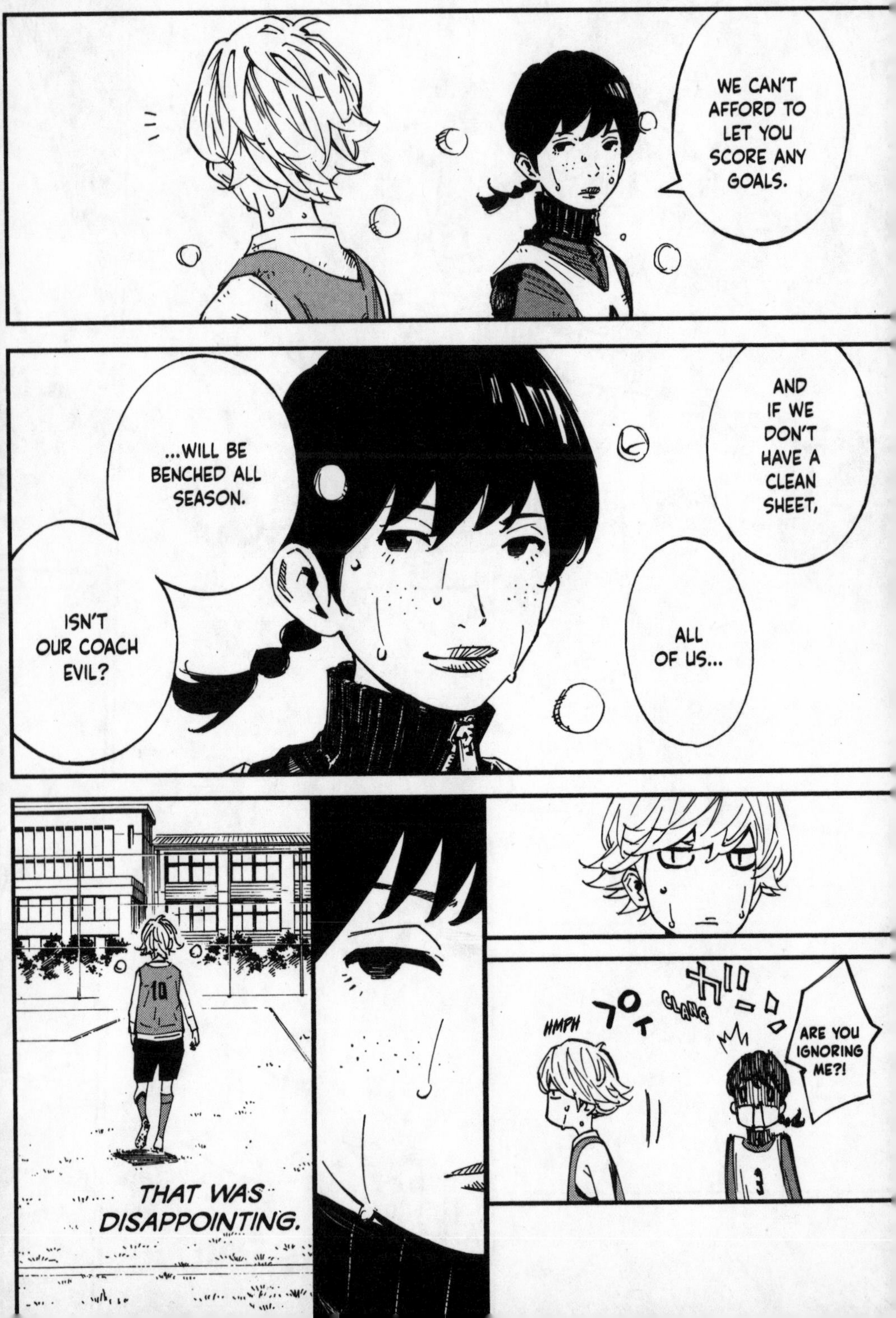
WE CAN'T AFFORD TO LET YOU SCORE ANY GOALS.
AND IF WE DON'T HAVE A CLEAN SHEET,
ALL OF US...
...WILL BE BENCHED ALL SEASON.
ISN'T OUR COACH EVIL?
ARE YOU IGNORING ME?!
CLANG
HMPH
THAT WAS DISAPPOINTING.

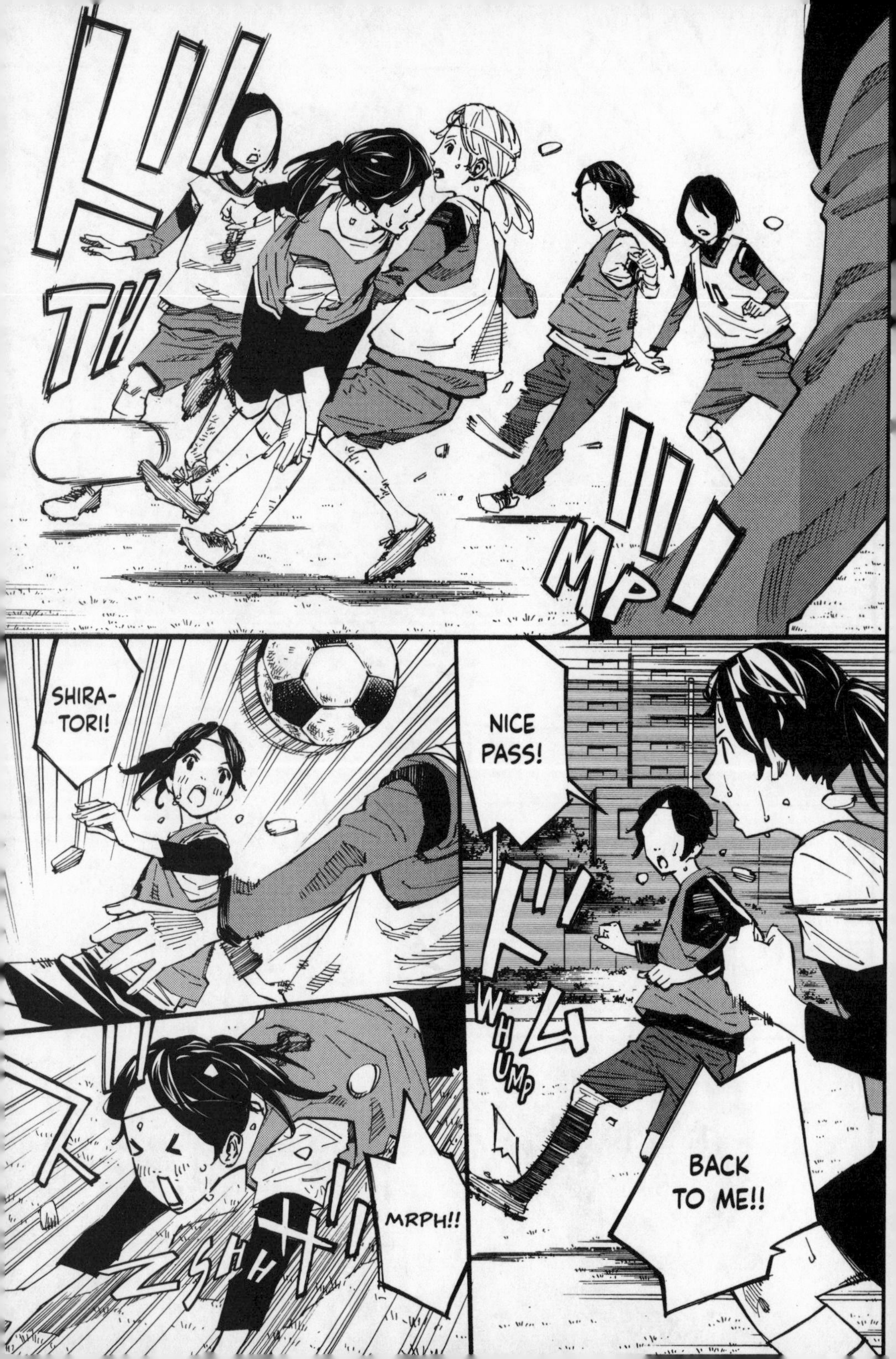
TH
MP
NICE PASS!
WHUMP
BACK TO ME!!
SHIRA-TORI!
MRPH!!
ZSHH

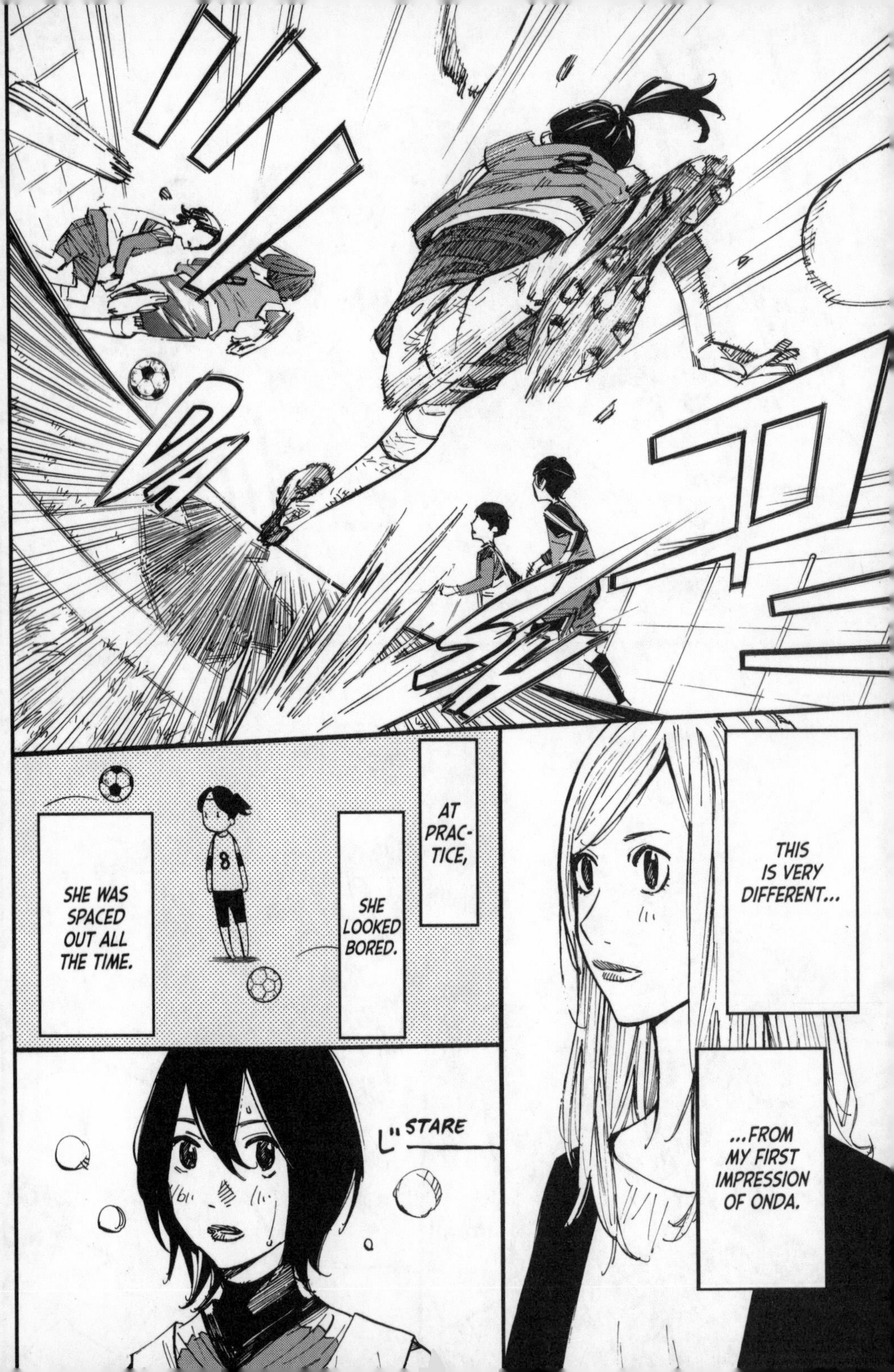
THIS IS VERY DIFFERENT...
...FROM MY FIRST IMPRESSION OF ONDA.
AT PRACTICE,
SHE LOOKED BORED.
SHE WAS SPACED OUT ALL THE TIME.
STARE

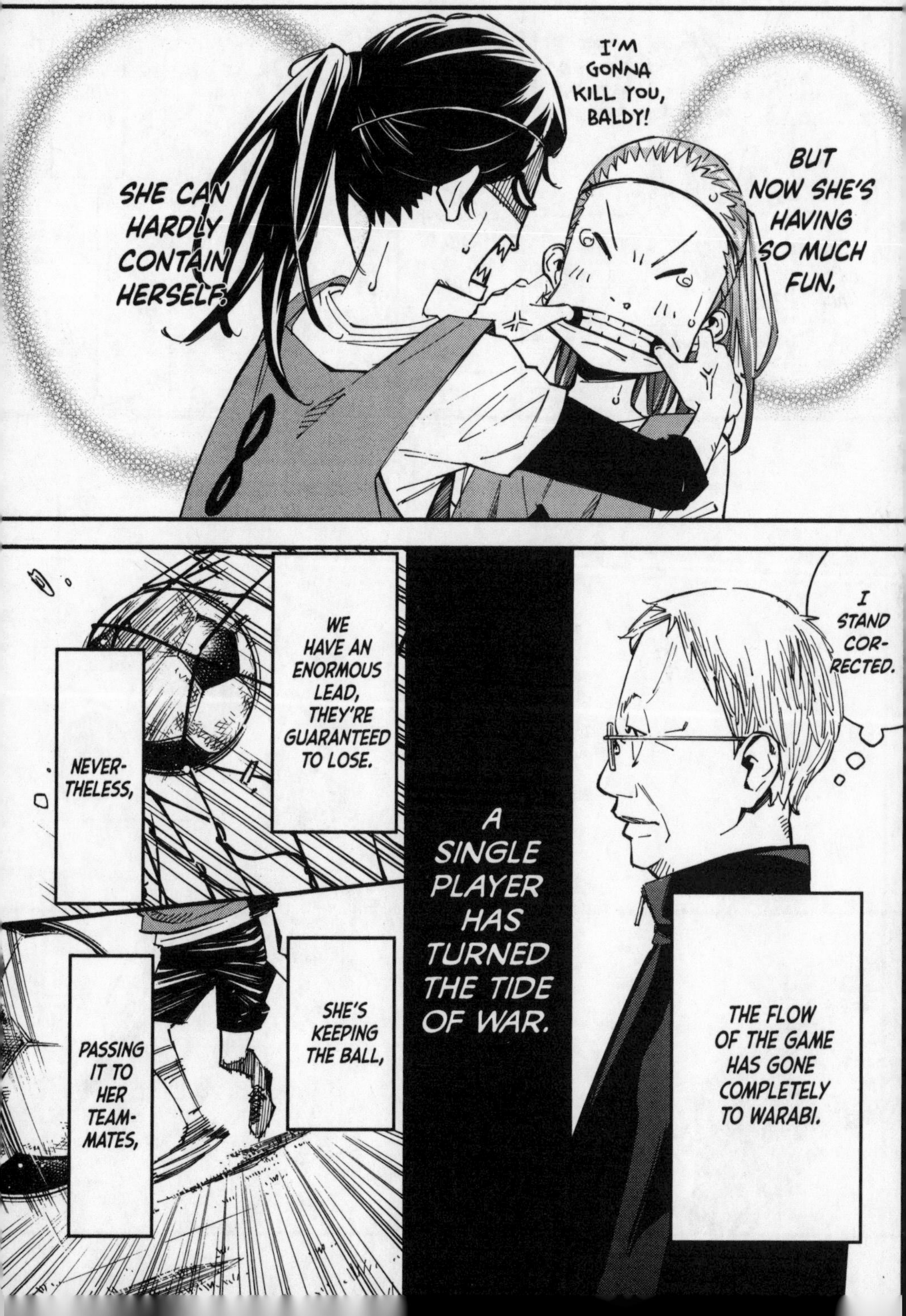
BUT NOW SHE'S HAVING SO MUCH FUN,
I'M GONNA KILL YOU, BALDY!
SHE CAN HARDLY CONTAIN HERSELF.
I STAND COR-RECTED.
THE FLOW OF THE GAME HAS GONE COMPLETELY TO WARABI.
A SINGLE PLAYER HAS TURNED THE TIDE OF WAR.
WE HAVE AN ENORMOUS LEAD, THEY'RE GUARANTEED TO LOSE.
NEVER-THELESS,
SHE'S KEEPING THE BALL,
PASSING IT TO HER TEAM-MATES,

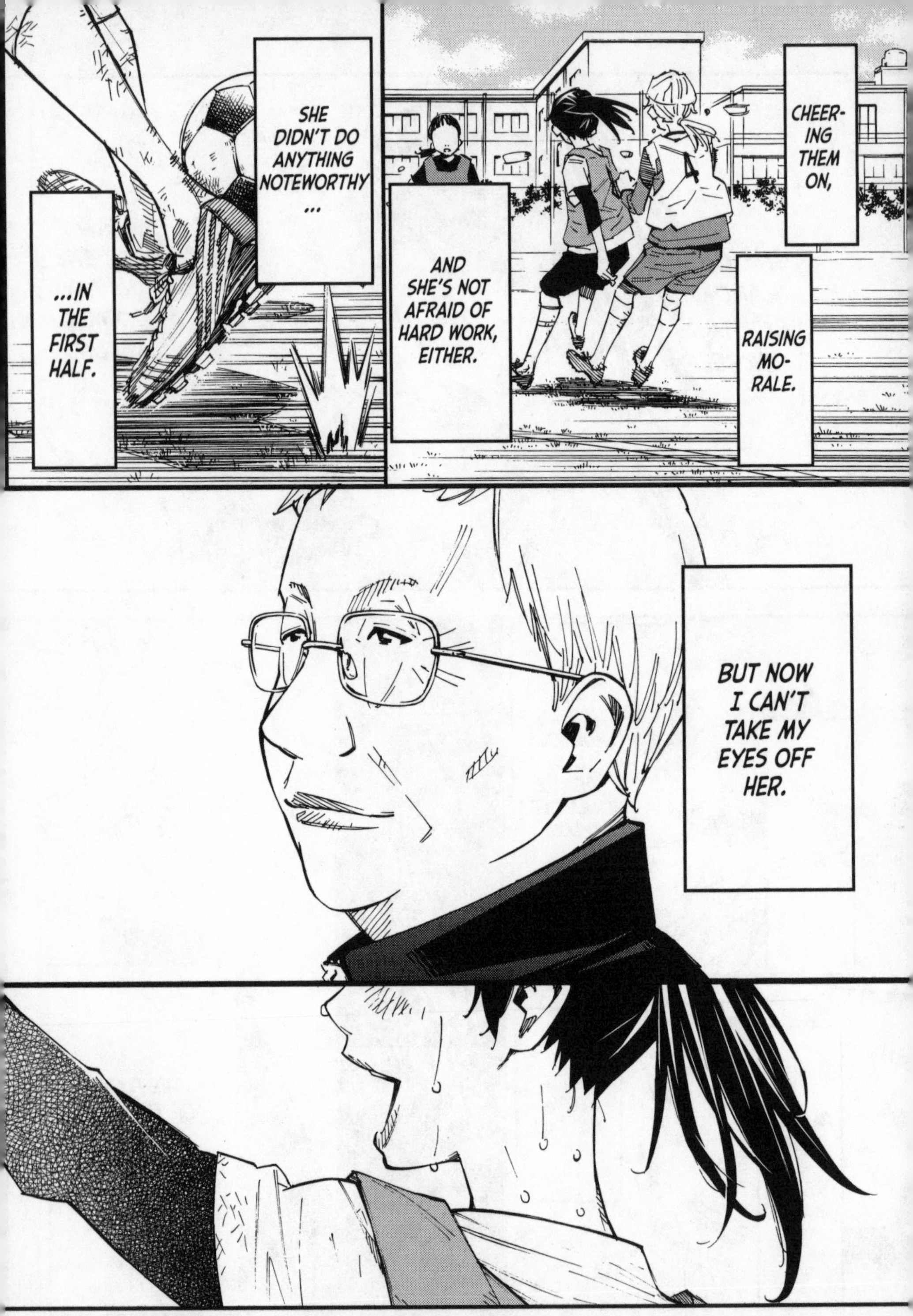
CHEERING THEM ON,
RAISING MORALE.
AND SHE'S NOT AFRAID OF HARD WORK, EITHER.
SHE DIDN'T DO ANYTHING NOTEWORTHY ...
...IN THE FIRST HALF.
BUT NOW I CAN'T TAKE MY EYES OFF HER.

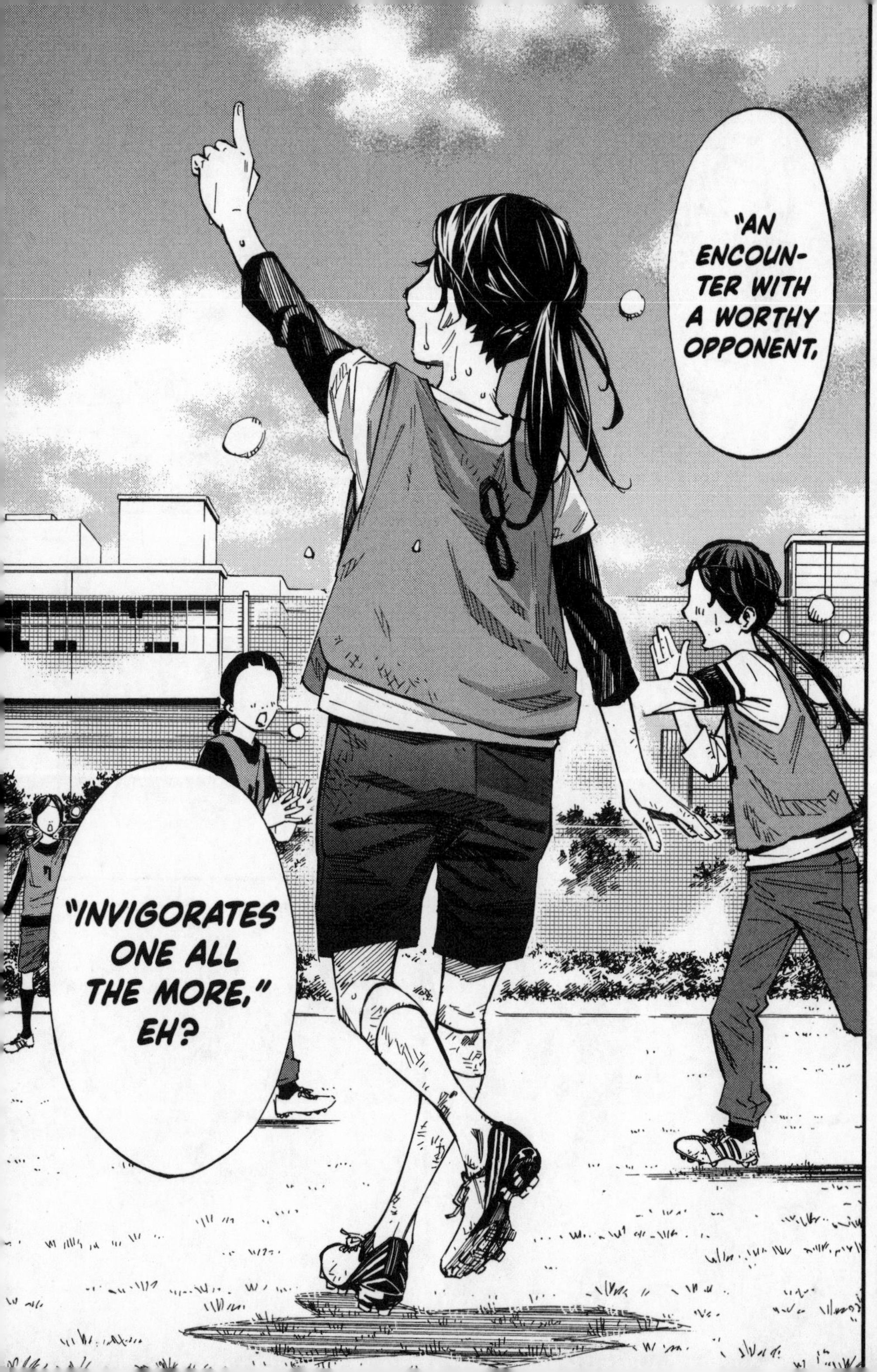
"AN ENCOUN-TER WITH A WORTHY OPPONENT,
"INVIGORATES ONE ALL THE MORE," EH?

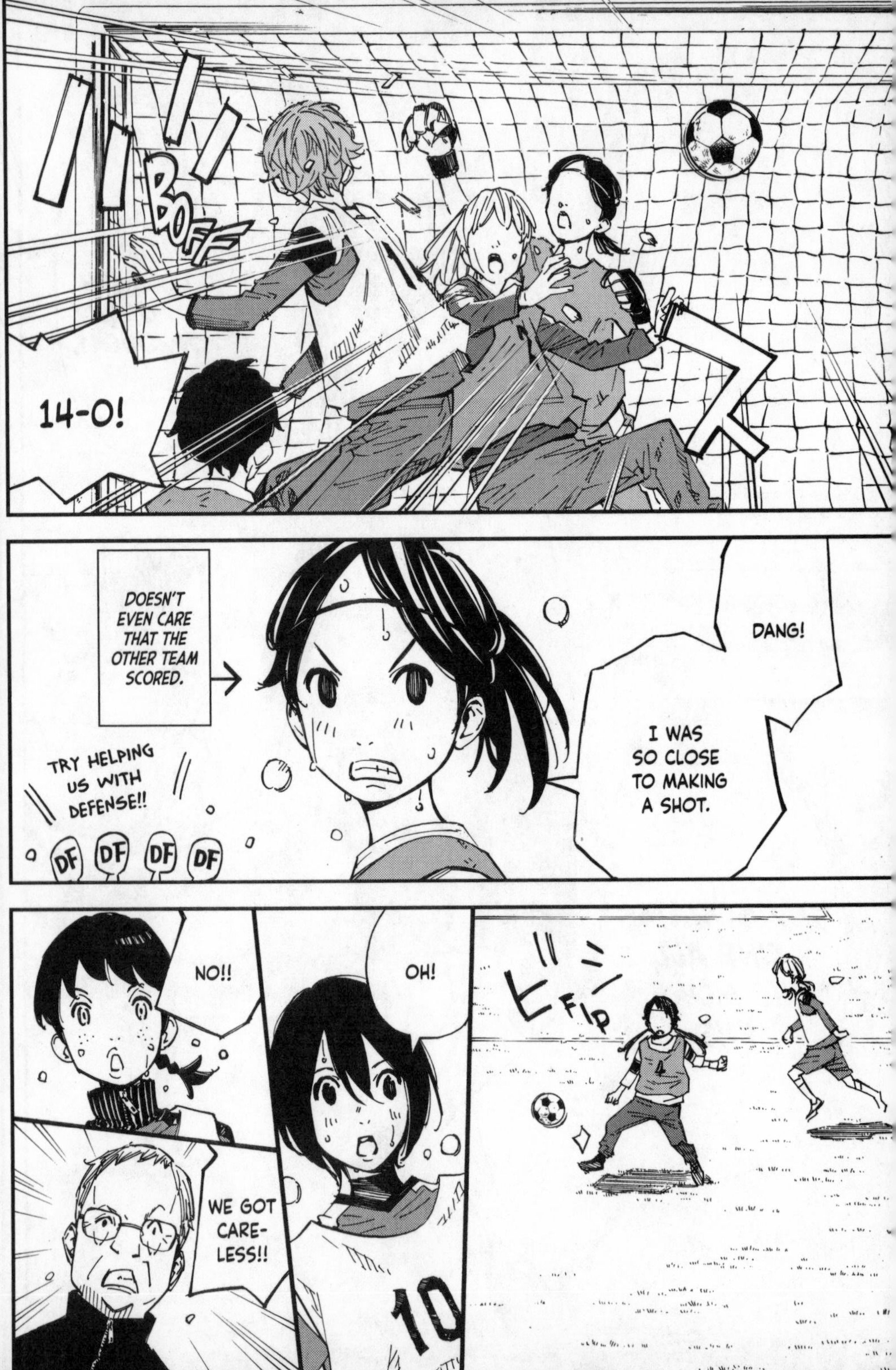
BOFF
14-0!
DANG!
I WAS SO CLOSE TO MAKING A SHOT.
DOESN'T EVEN CARE THAT THE OTHER TEAM SCORED.
TRY HELPING US WITH DEFENSE!!
DF DF DF DF
FLIP
OH!
NO!!
WE GOT CARE-LESS!!

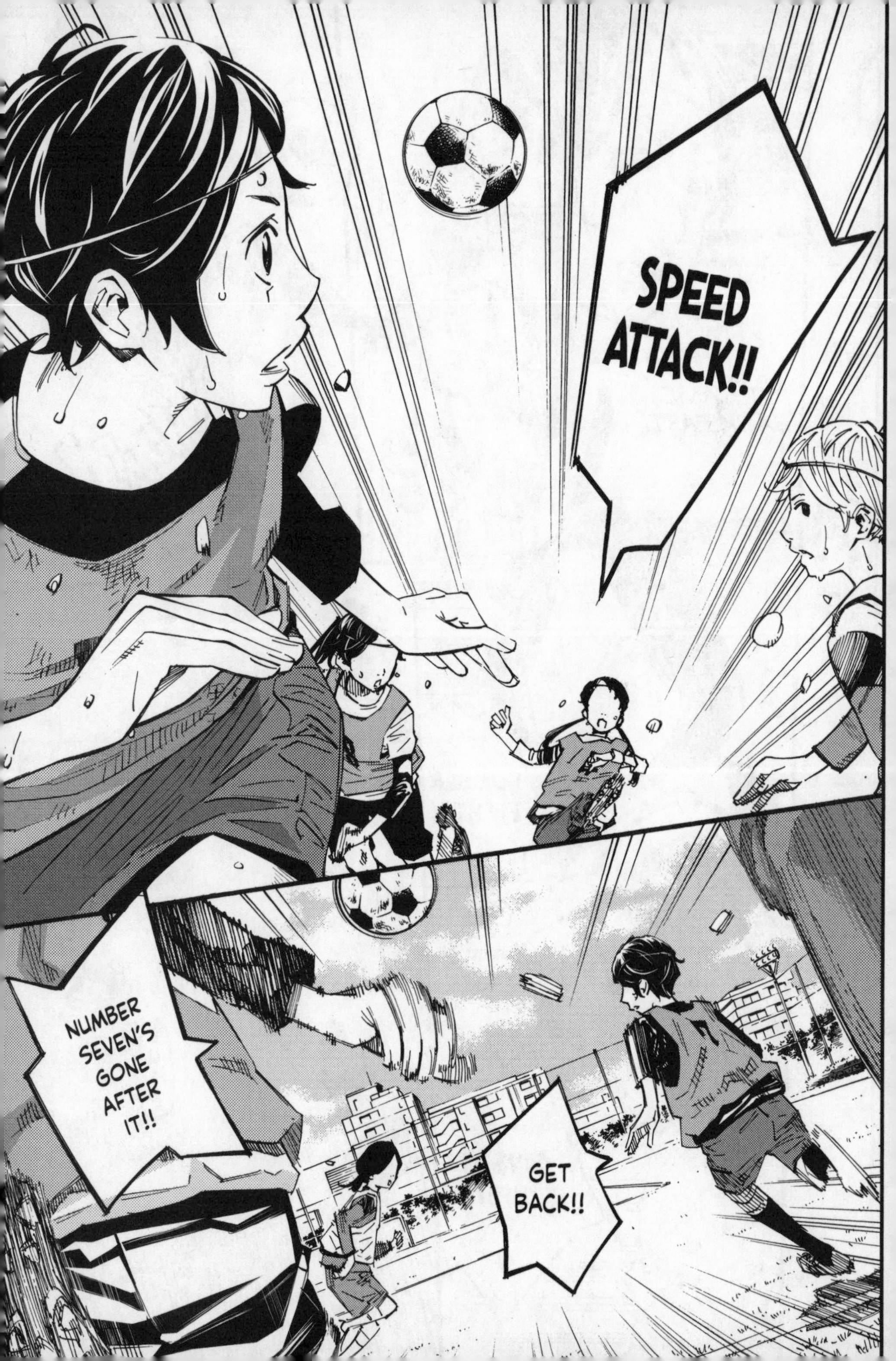
SPEED ATTACK!!
GET BACK!!
NUMBER SEVEN'S GONE AFTER IT!!

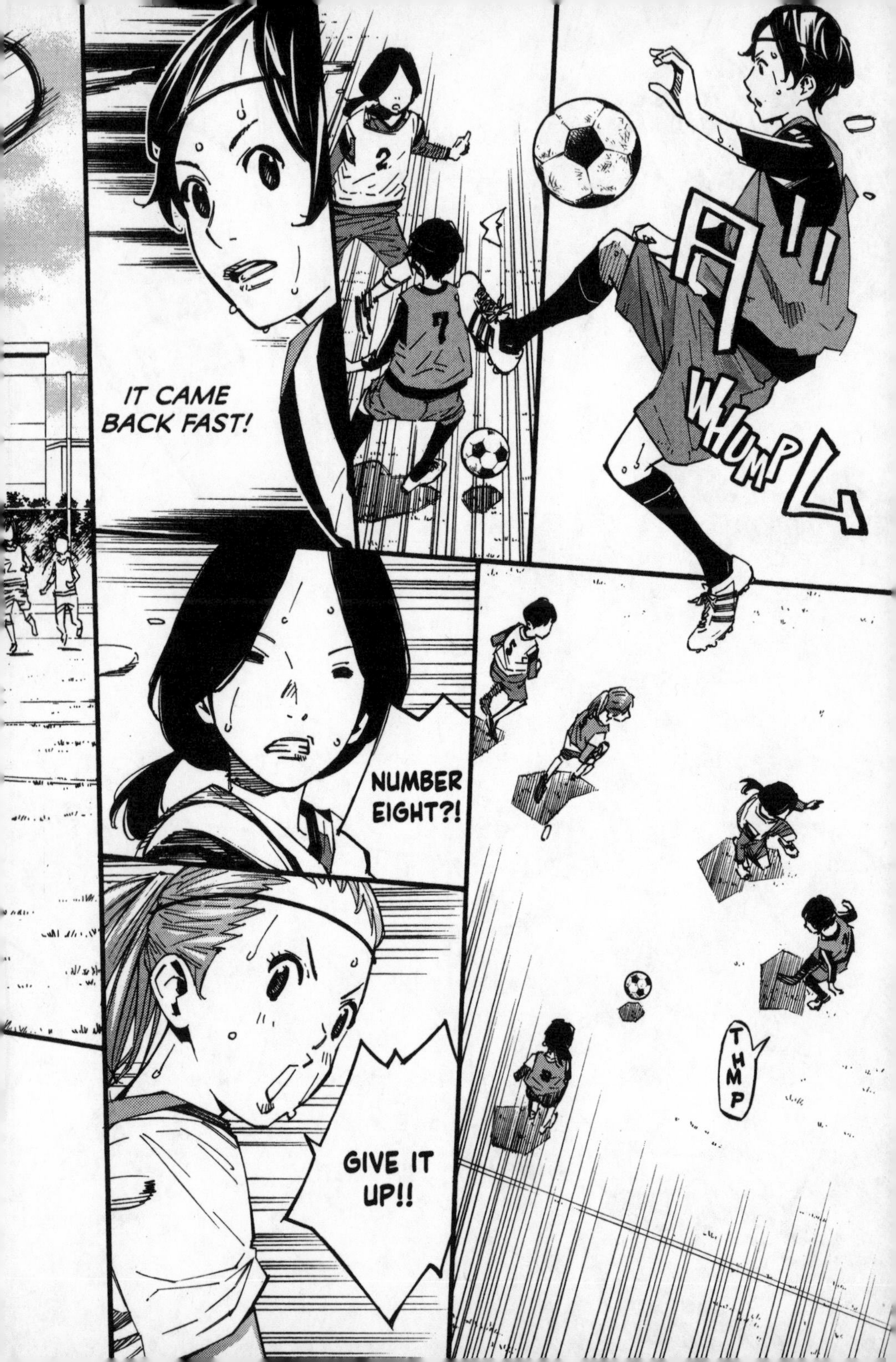
WHUMP
IT CAME BACK FAST!
THMP
NUMBER EIGHT?!
GIVE IT UP!!

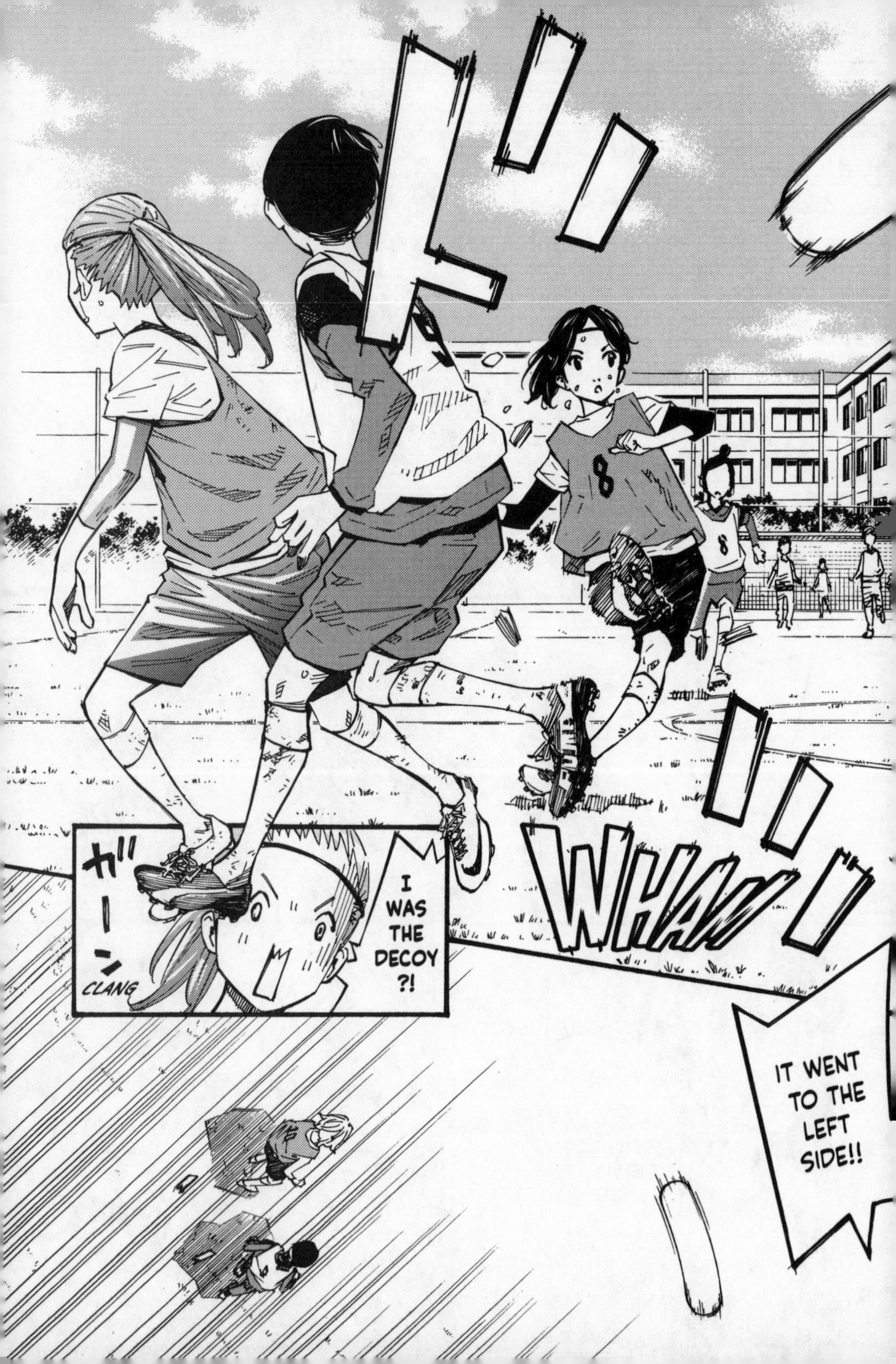
WHAM
I WAS THE DECOY ?!
ガーン
CLANG
IT WENT TO THE LEFT SIDE!!

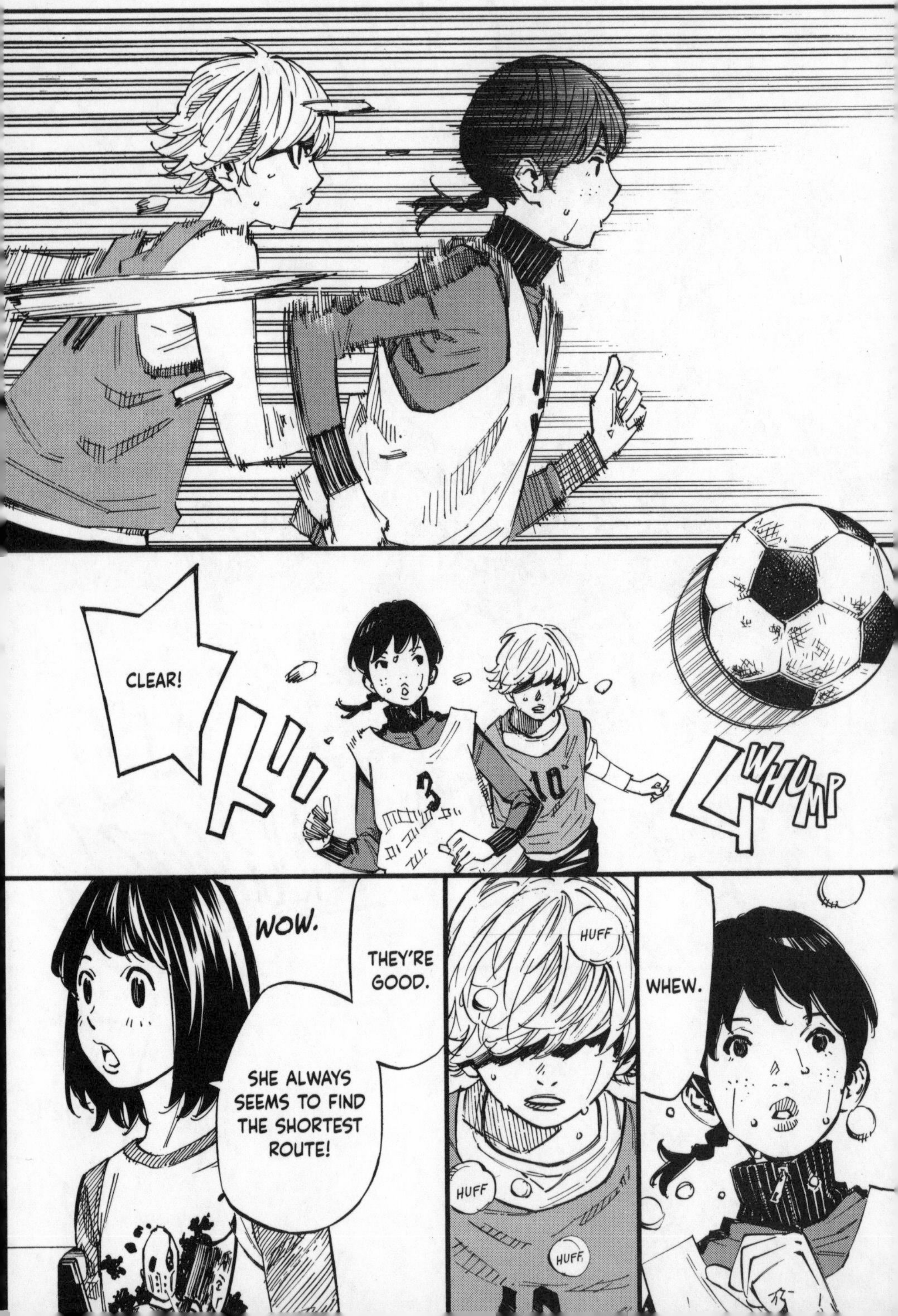
WHUMP
CLEAR!
WHEW.
HUFF
HUFF
HUFF
THEY'RE GOOD.
WOW.
SHE ALWAYS SEEMS TO FIND THE SHORTEST ROUTE!

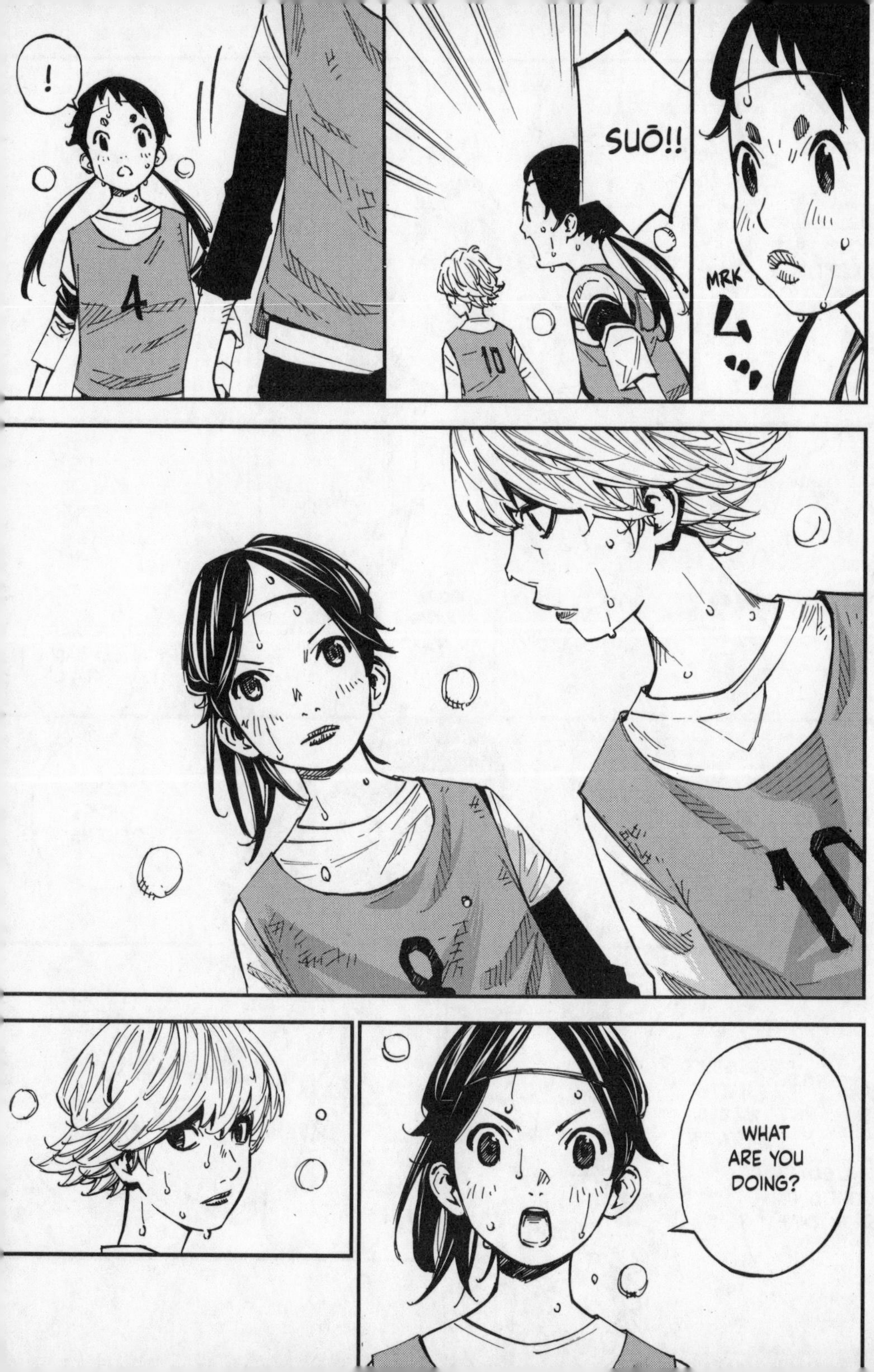
MRK
SUŌ!!
!
WHAT ARE YOU DOING?

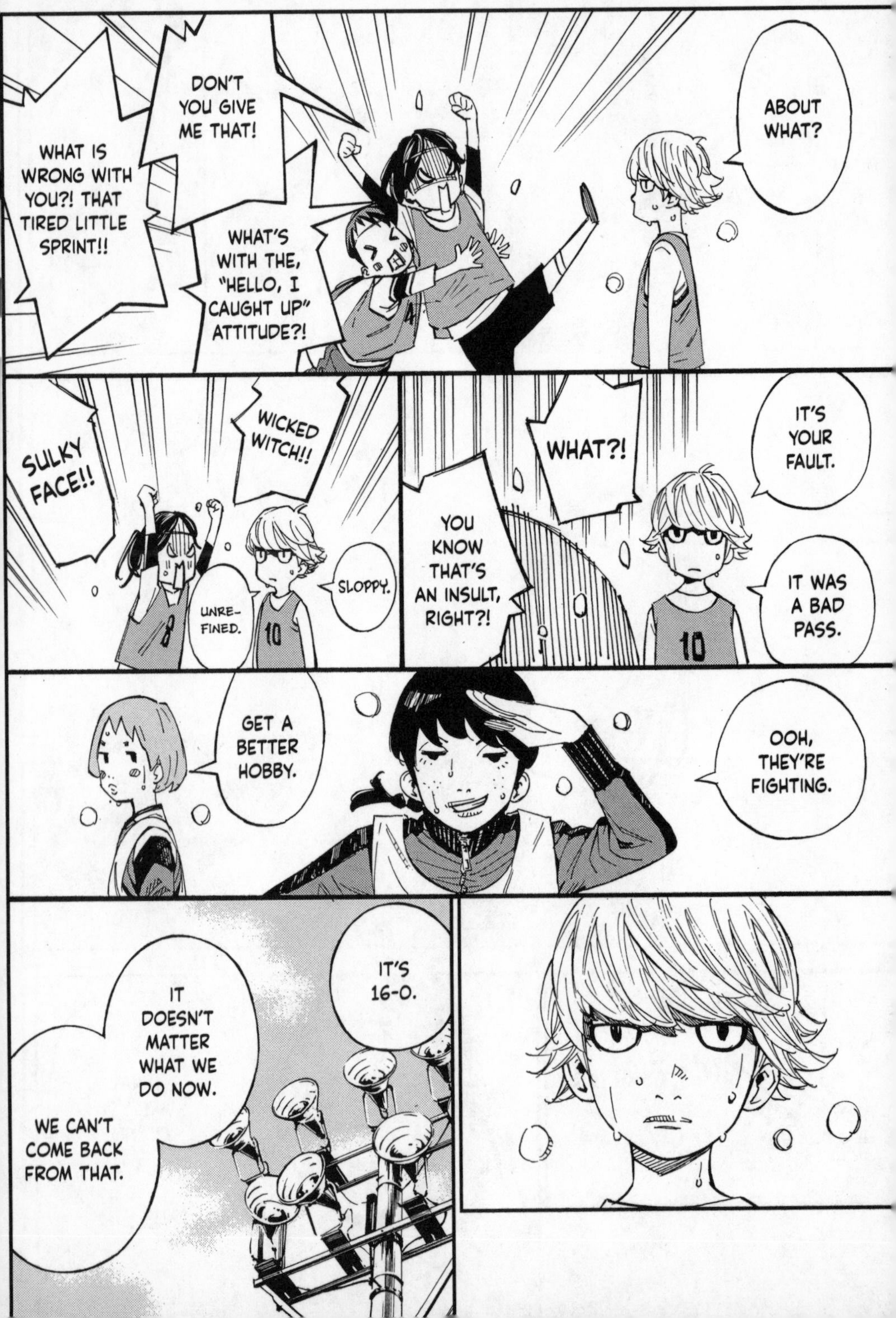
ABOUT WHAT?
DON'T YOU GIVE ME THAT!
WHAT IS WRONG WITH YOU?! THAT TIRED LITTLE SPRINT!!
WHAT'S WITH THE, "HELLO, I CAUGHT UP" ATTITUDE?!
IT'S YOUR FAULT.
WHAT?!
IT WAS A BAD PASS.
YOU KNOW THAT'S AN INSULT, RIGHT?!
WICKED WITCH!!
SULKY FACE!!
SLOPPY.
UNRE-FINED.
OOH, THEY'RE FIGHTING.
GET A BETTER HOBBY.
IT'S 16-0.
IT DOESN'T MATTER WHAT WE DO NOW.
WE CAN'T COME BACK FROM THAT.

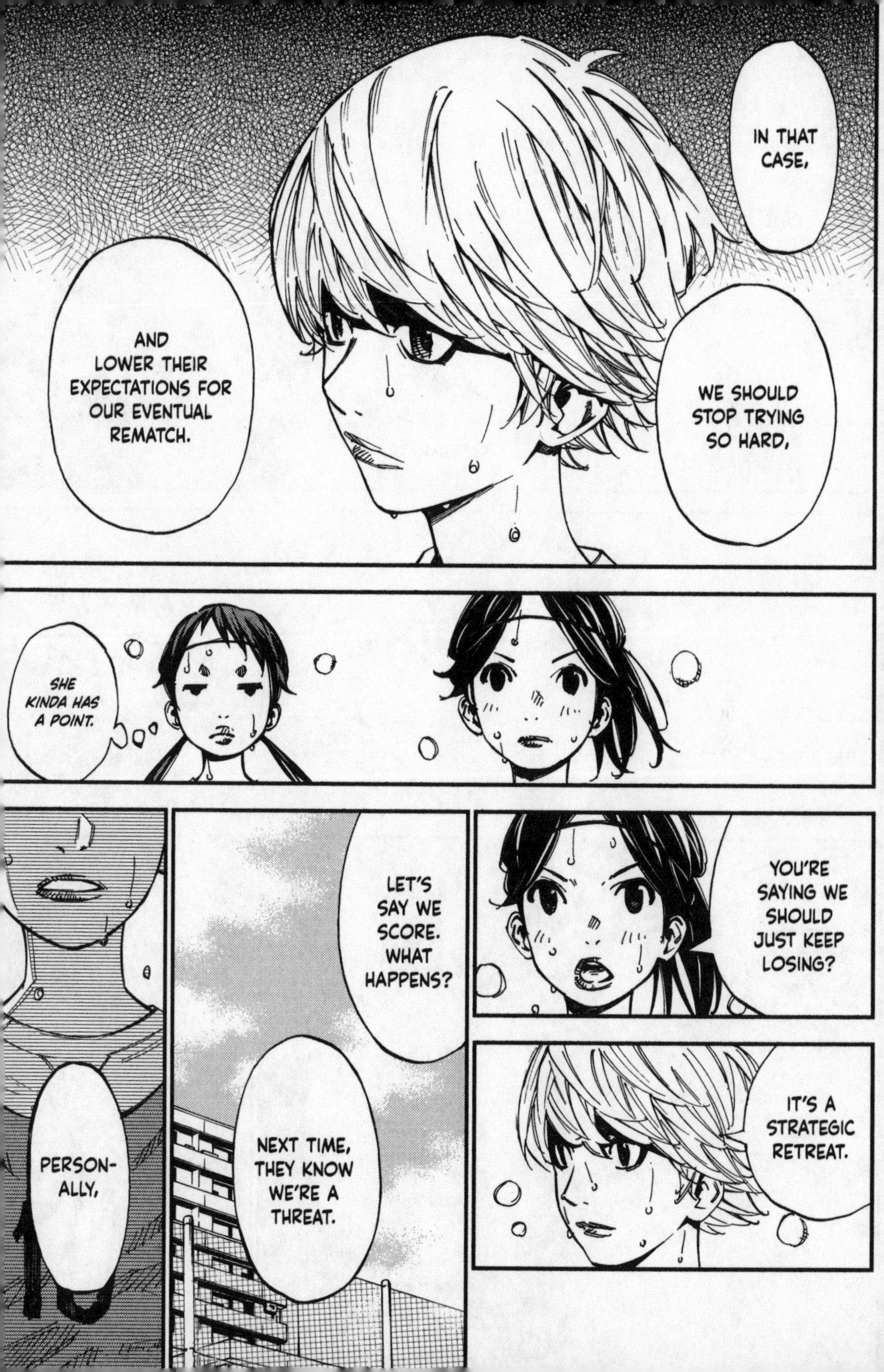
IN THAT CASE,
WE SHOULD STOP TRYING SO HARD,
AND LOWER THEIR EXPECTATIONS FOR OUR EVENTUAL REMATCH.
SHE KINDA HAS A POINT.
YOU'RE SAYING WE SHOULD JUST KEEP LOSING?
IT'S A STRATEGIC RETREAT.
LET'S SAY WE SCORE. WHAT HAPPENS?
NEXT TIME, THEY KNOW WE'RE A THREAT.
PERSON-ALLY,

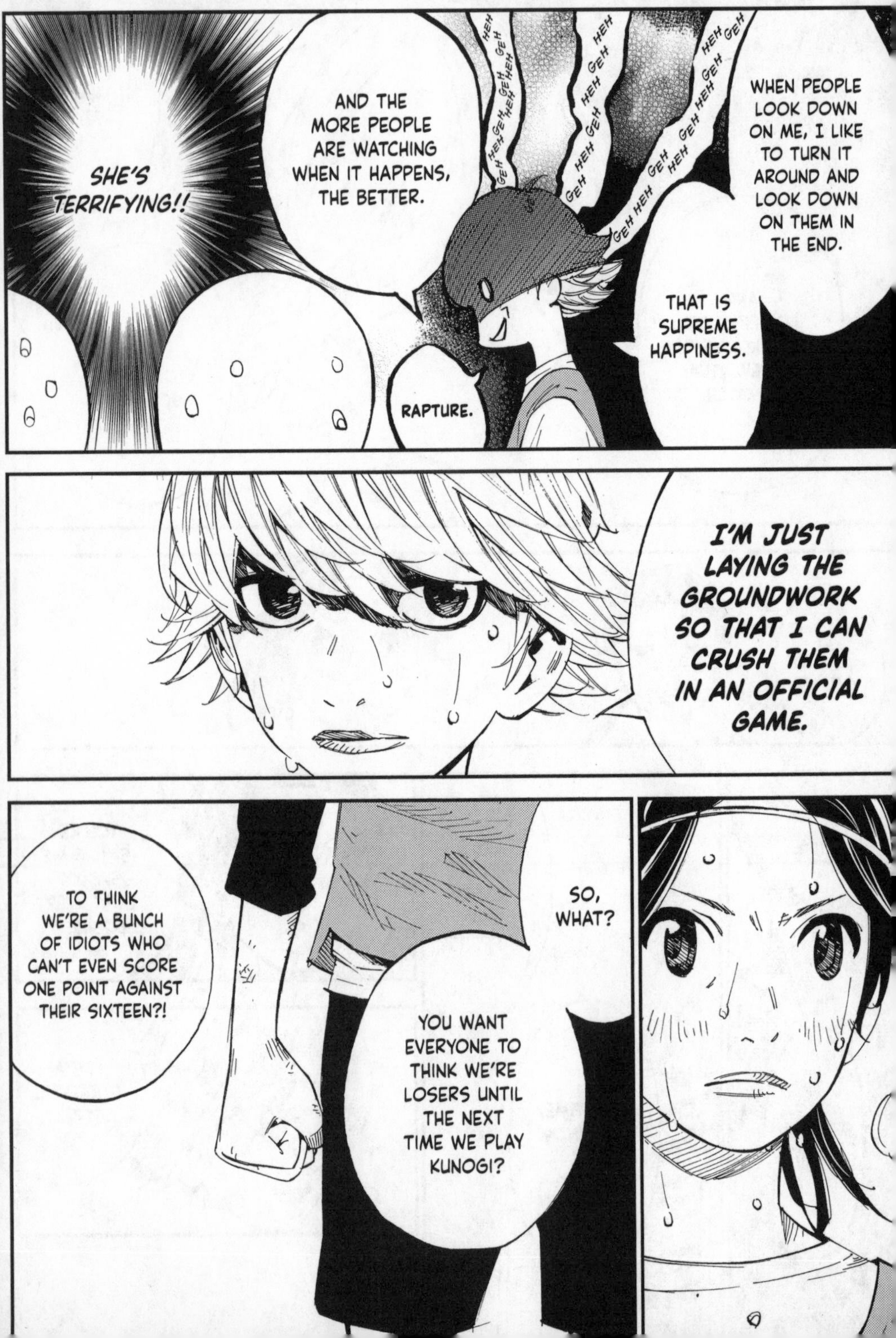
WHEN PEOPLE LOOK DOWN ON ME, I LIKE TO TURN IT AROUND AND LOOK DOWN ON THEM IN THE END.
THAT IS SUPREME HAPPINESS.
AND THE MORE PEOPLE ARE WATCHING WHEN IT HAPPENS, THE BETTER.
RAPTURE.
SHE'S TERRIFYING!!
I'M JUST LAYING THE GROUNDWORK SO THAT I CAN CRUSH THEM IN AN OFFICIAL GAME.
SO, WHAT?
YOU WANT EVERYONE TO THINK WE'RE LOSERS UNTIL THE NEXT TIME WE PLAY KUNOGI?
TO THINK WE'RE A BUNCH OF IDIOTS WHO CAN'T EVEN SCORE ONE POINT AGAINST THEIR SIXTEEN?!

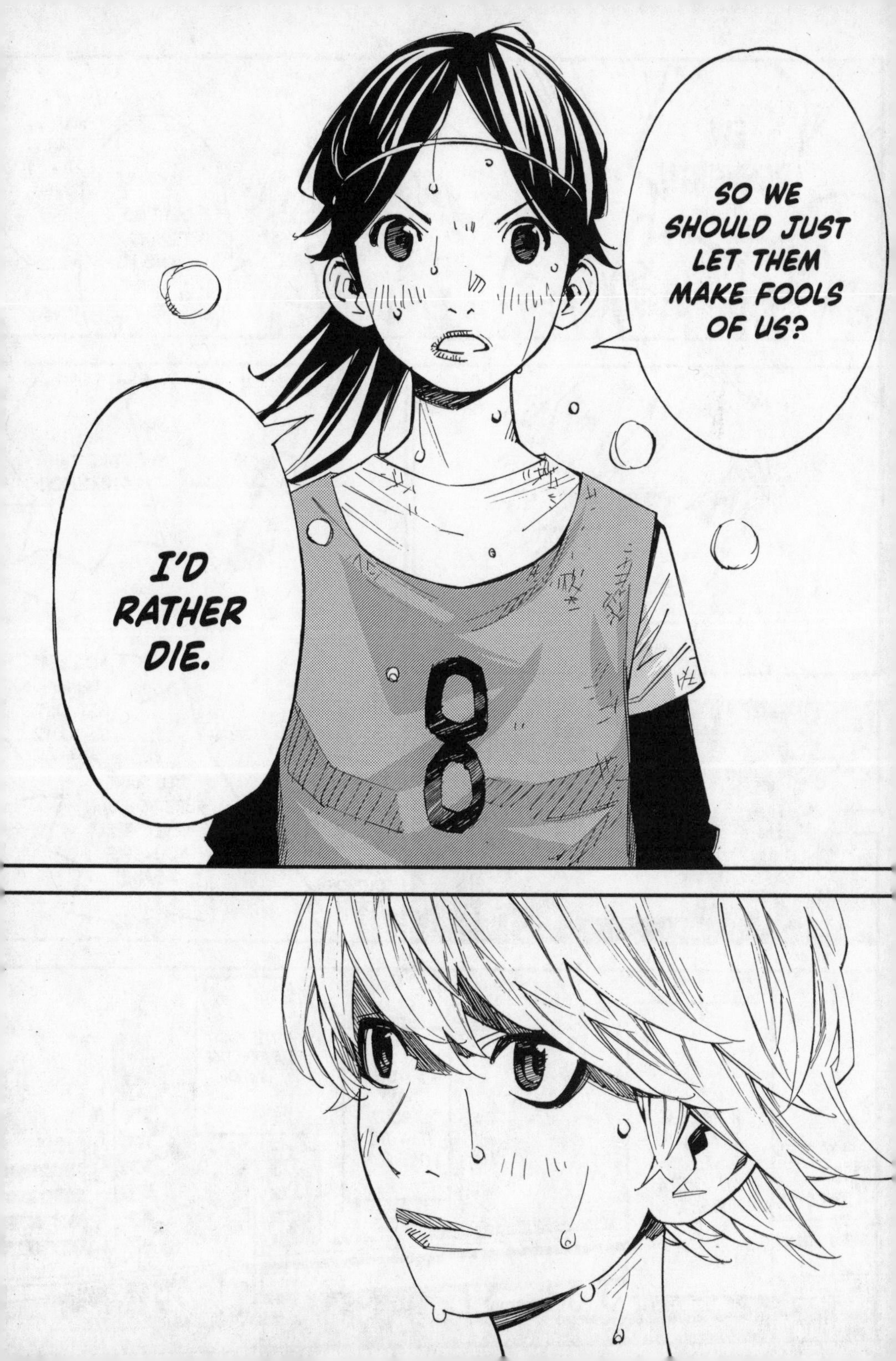
SO WE SHOULD JUST LET THEM MAKE FOOLS OF US?
I'D RATHER DIE.

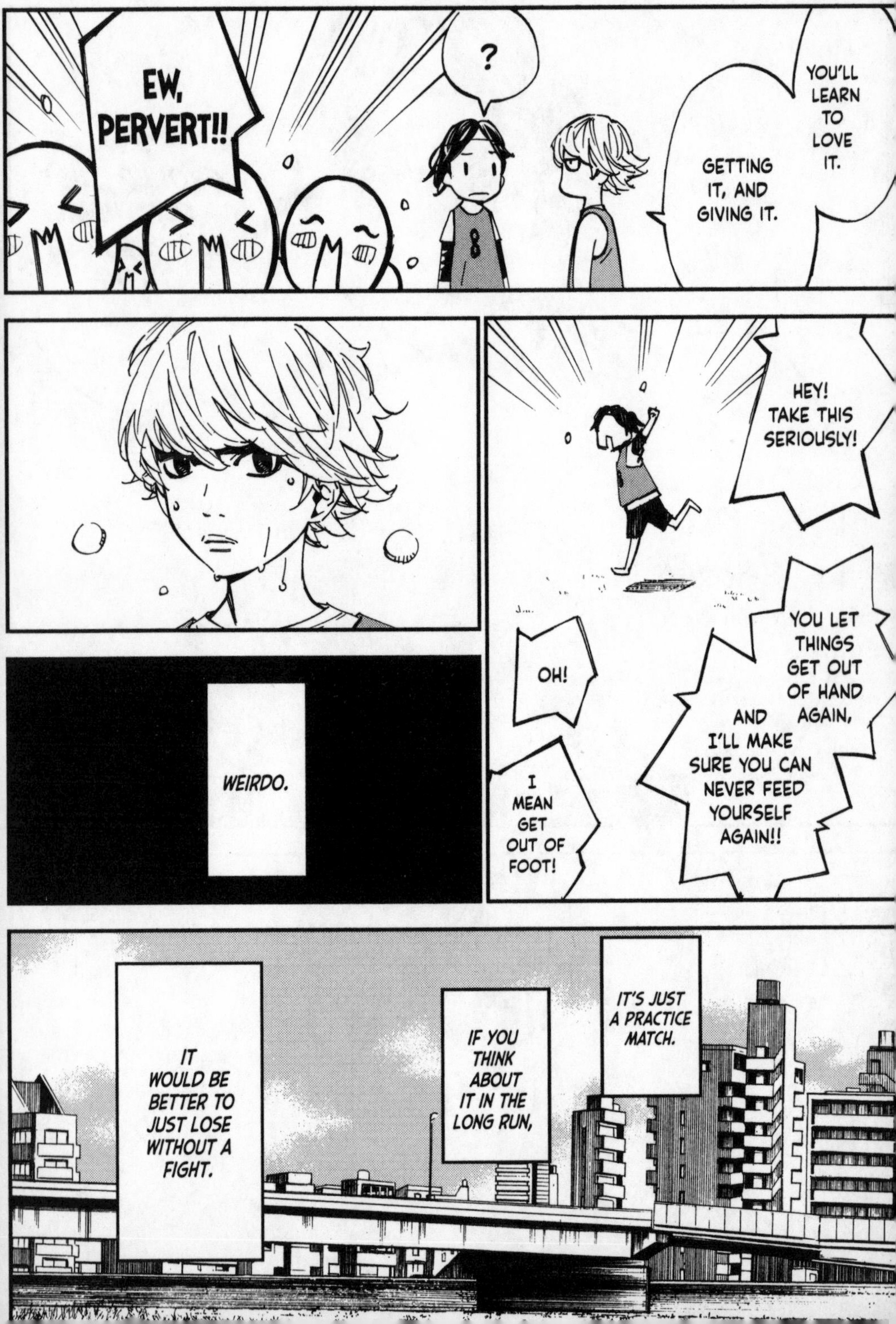
YOU'LL LEARN TO LOVE IT.
GETTING IT, AND GIVING IT.
?
EW, PERVERT!!
HEY! TAKE THIS SERIOUSLY!
YOU LET THINGS GET OUT OF HAND AGAIN,
AND I'LL MAKE SURE YOU CAN NEVER FEED YOURSELF AGAIN!!
OH!
I MEAN GET OUT OF FOOT!
WEIRDO.
IT'S JUST A PRACTICE MATCH.
IF YOU THINK ABOUT IT IN THE LONG RUN,
IT WOULD BE BETTER TO JUST LOSE WITHOUT A FIGHT.

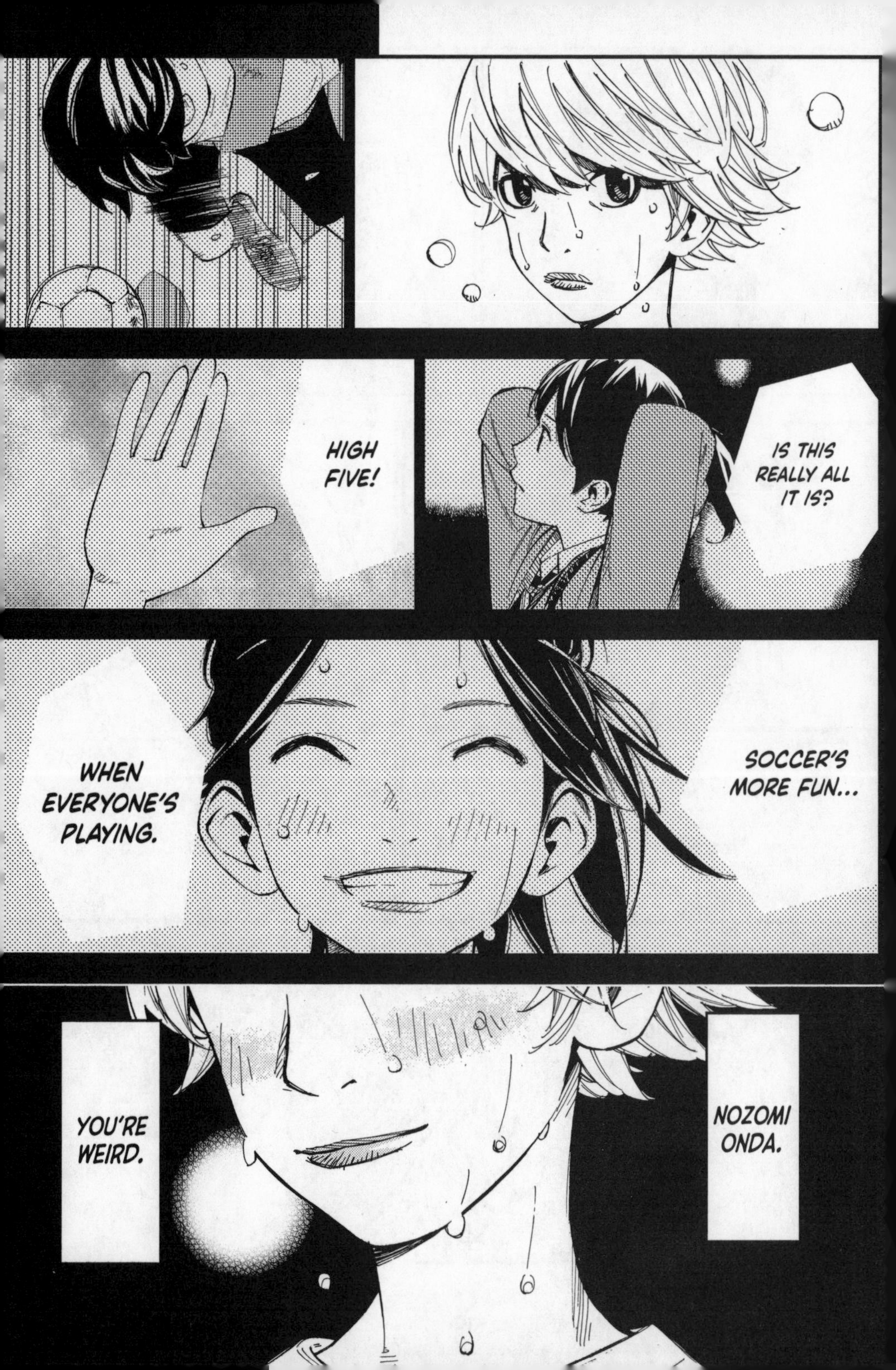
IS THIS REALLY ALL IT IS?
HIGH FIVE!
SOCCER'S MORE FUN...
WHEN EVERYONE'S PLAYING.
NOZOMI ONDA.
YOU'RE WEIRD.

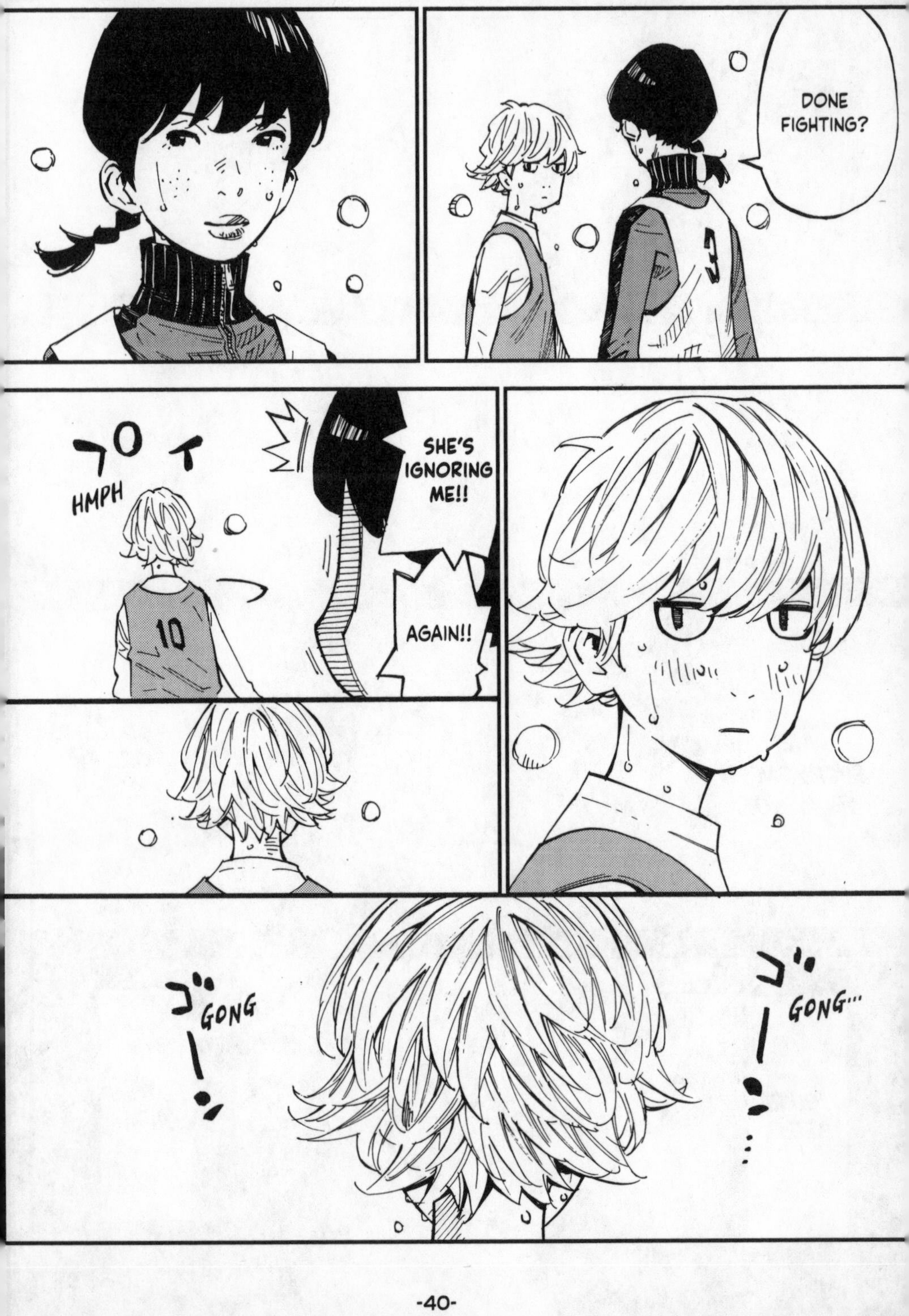
DONE FIGHTING?
SHE'S IGNORING ME!!
AGAIN!!
HMPH
GONG…
GONG

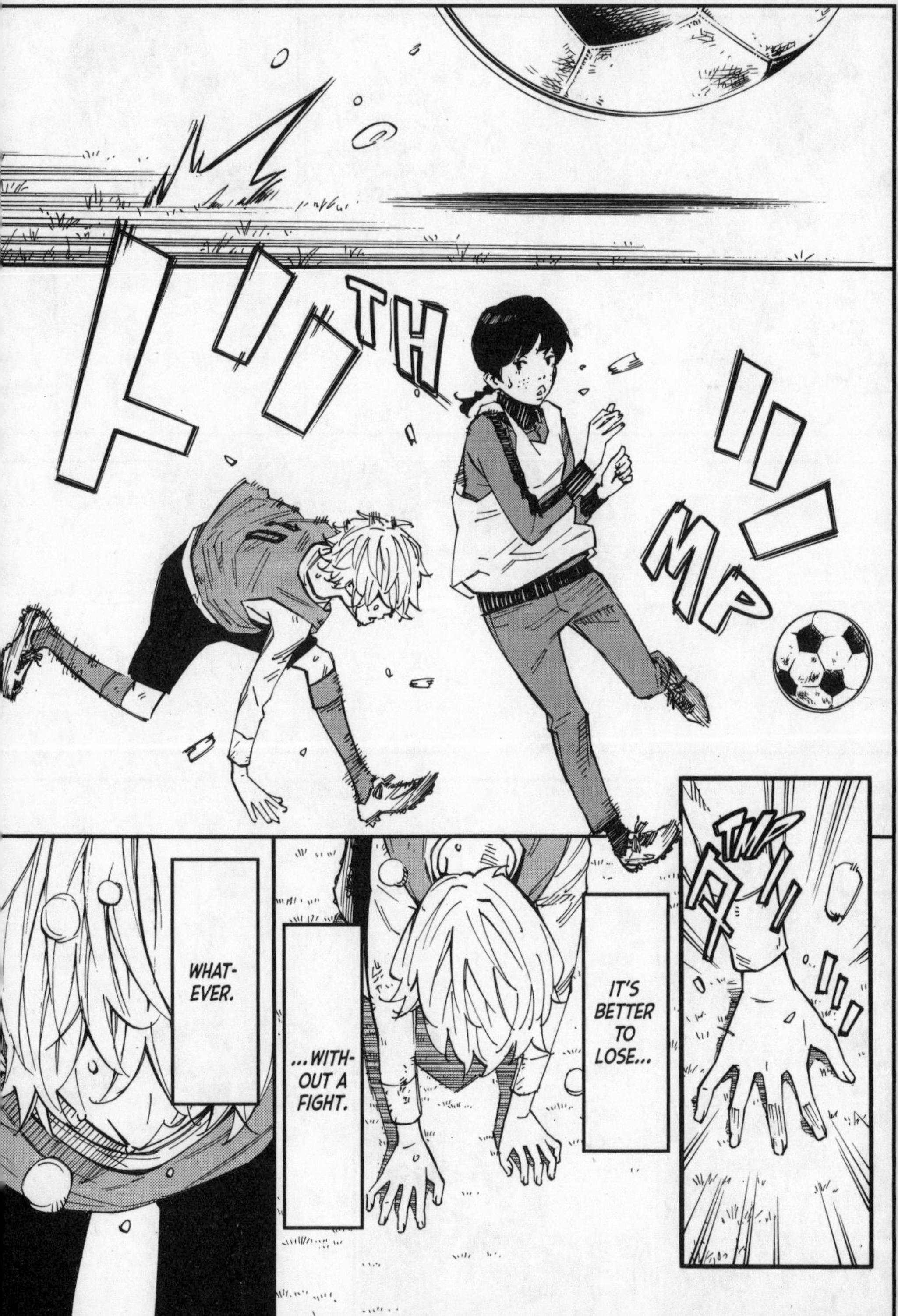
TH
MP
IT'S BETTER TO LOSE...
...WITH-OUT A FIGHT.
WHAT-EVER.

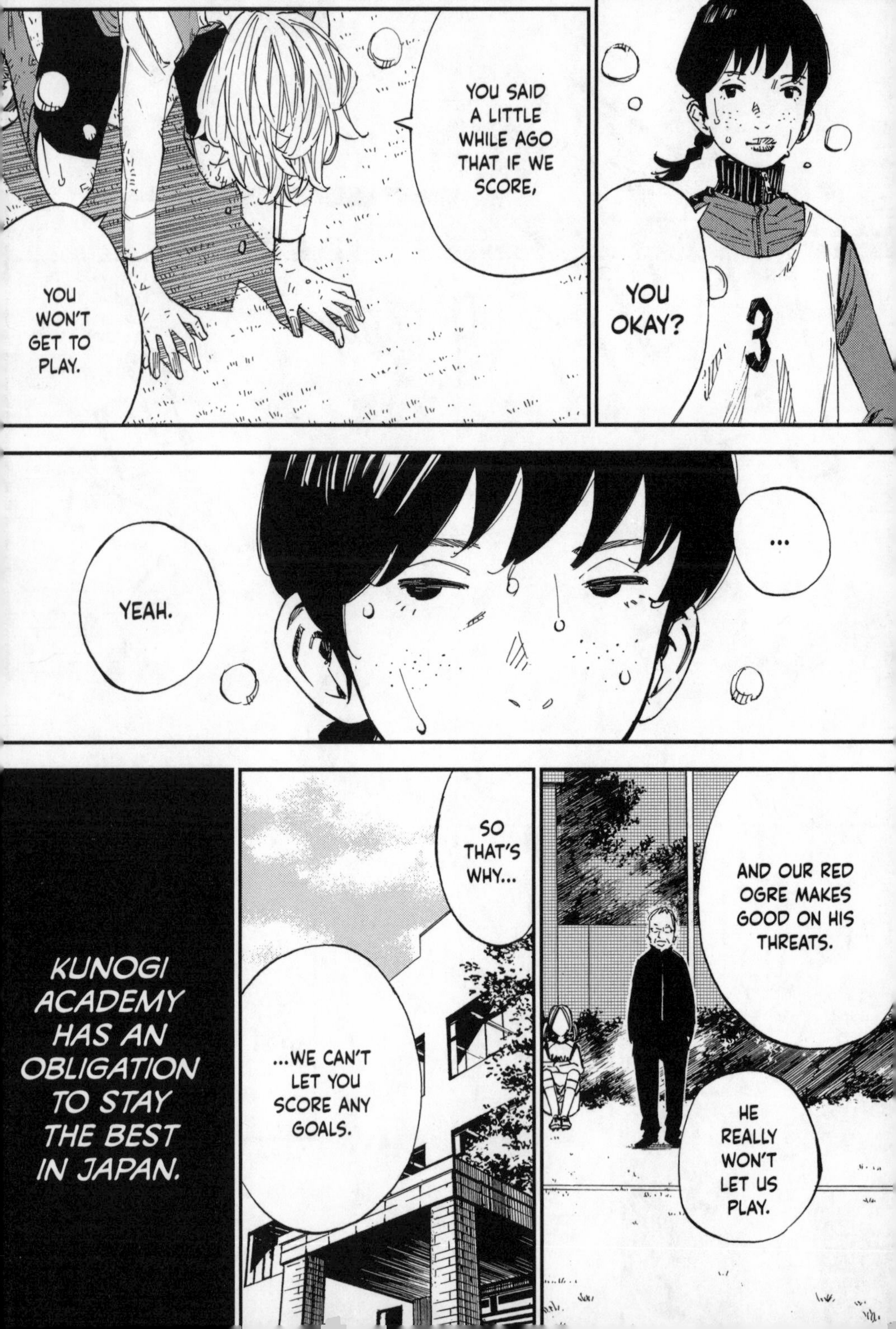
YOU OKAY?
YOU SAID A LITTLE WHILE AGO THAT IF WE SCORE,
YOU WON'T GET TO PLAY.
...
YEAH.
AND OUR RED OGRE MAKES GOOD ON HIS THREATS.
HE REALLY WON'T LET US PLAY.
SO THAT'S WHY...
...WE CAN'T LET YOU SCORE ANY GOALS.
KUNOGI ACADEMY HAS AN OBLIGATION TO STAY THE BEST IN JAPAN.

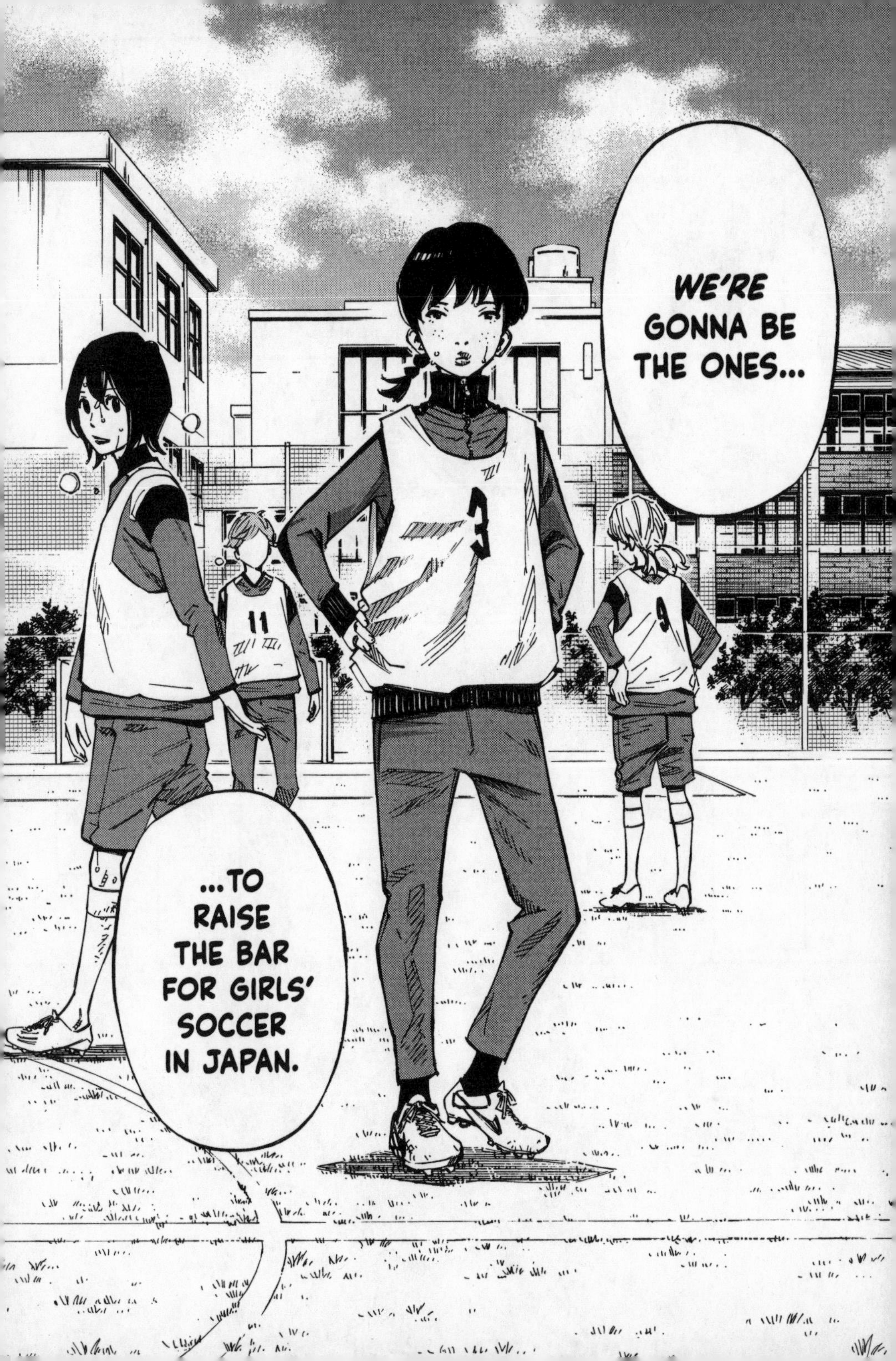
WE'RE GONNA BE THE ONES...
...TO RAISE THE BAR FOR GIRLS' SOCCER IN JAPAN.

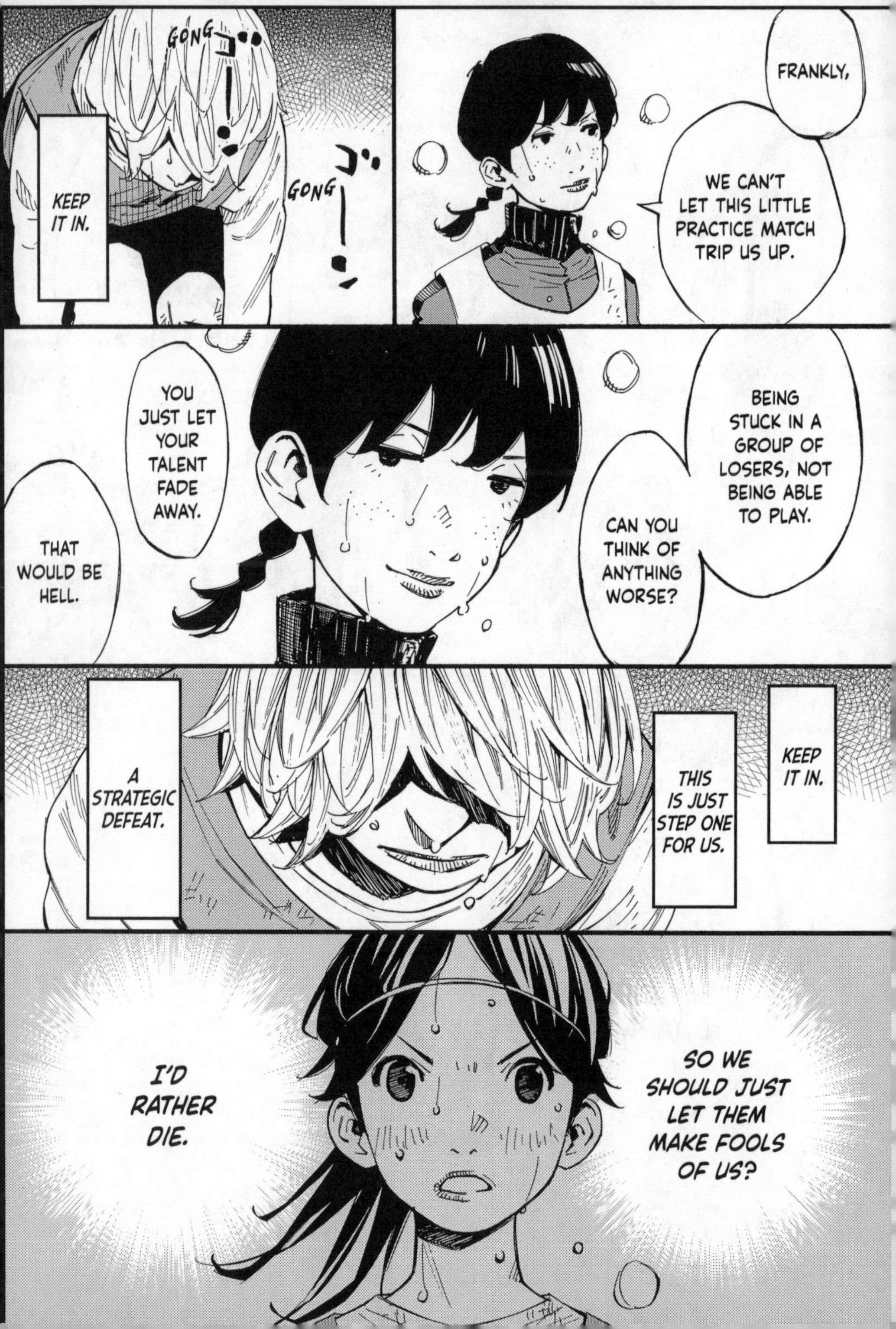
FRANKLY,
WE CAN'T LET THIS LITTLE PRACTICE MATCH TRIP US UP.
GONG
GONG
KEEP IT IN.
BEING STUCK IN A GROUP OF LOSERS, NOT BEING ABLE TO PLAY.
CAN YOU THINK OF ANYTHING WORSE?
YOU JUST LET YOUR TALENT FADE AWAY.
THAT WOULD BE HELL.
KEEP IT IN.
THIS IS JUST STEP ONE FOR US.
A STRATEGIC DEFEAT.
SO WE SHOULD JUST LET THEM MAKE FOOLS OF US?
I'D RATHER DIE.

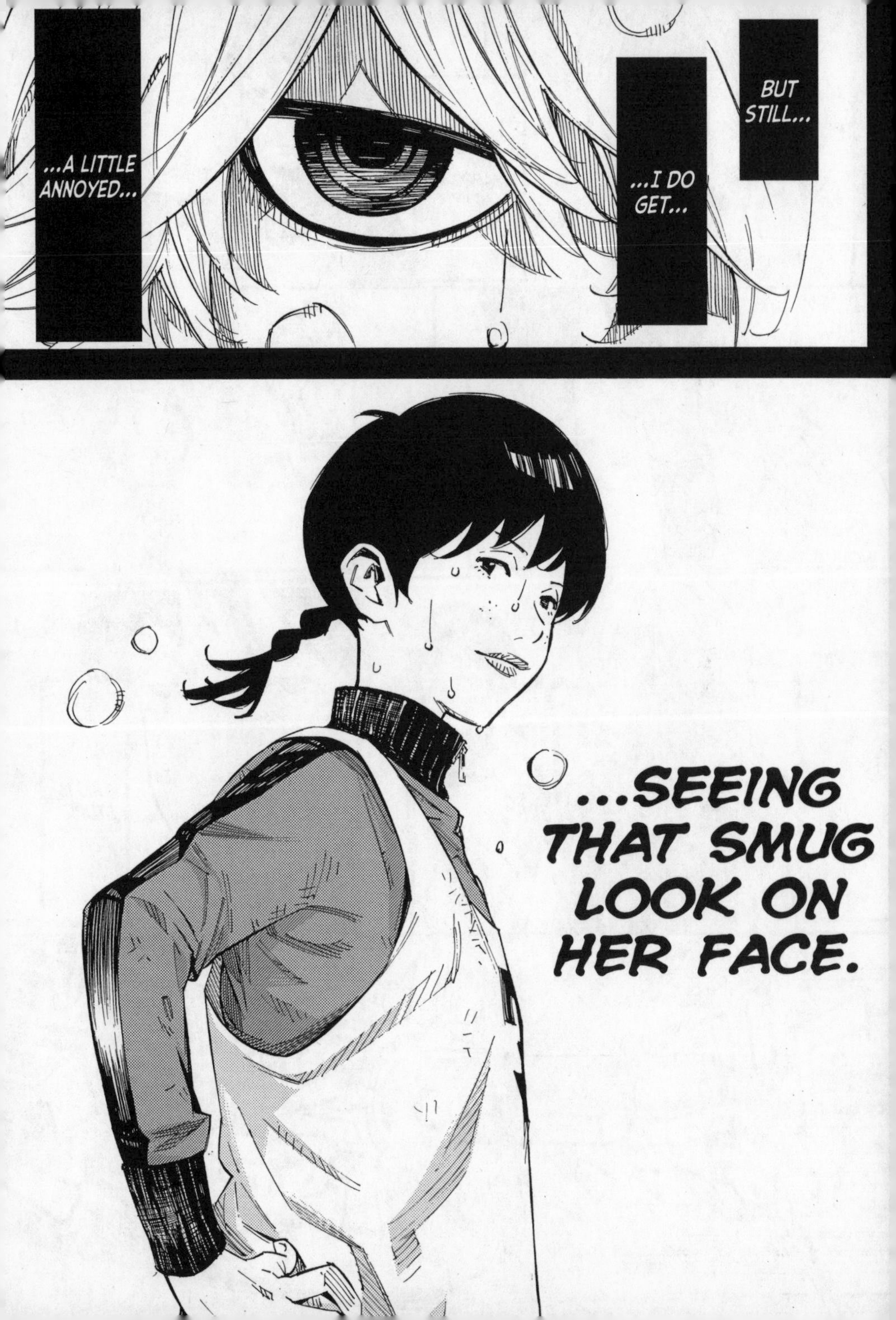
BUT STILL...
...I DO GET...
...A LITTLE ANNOYED...
...SEEING THAT SMUG LOOK ON HER FACE.

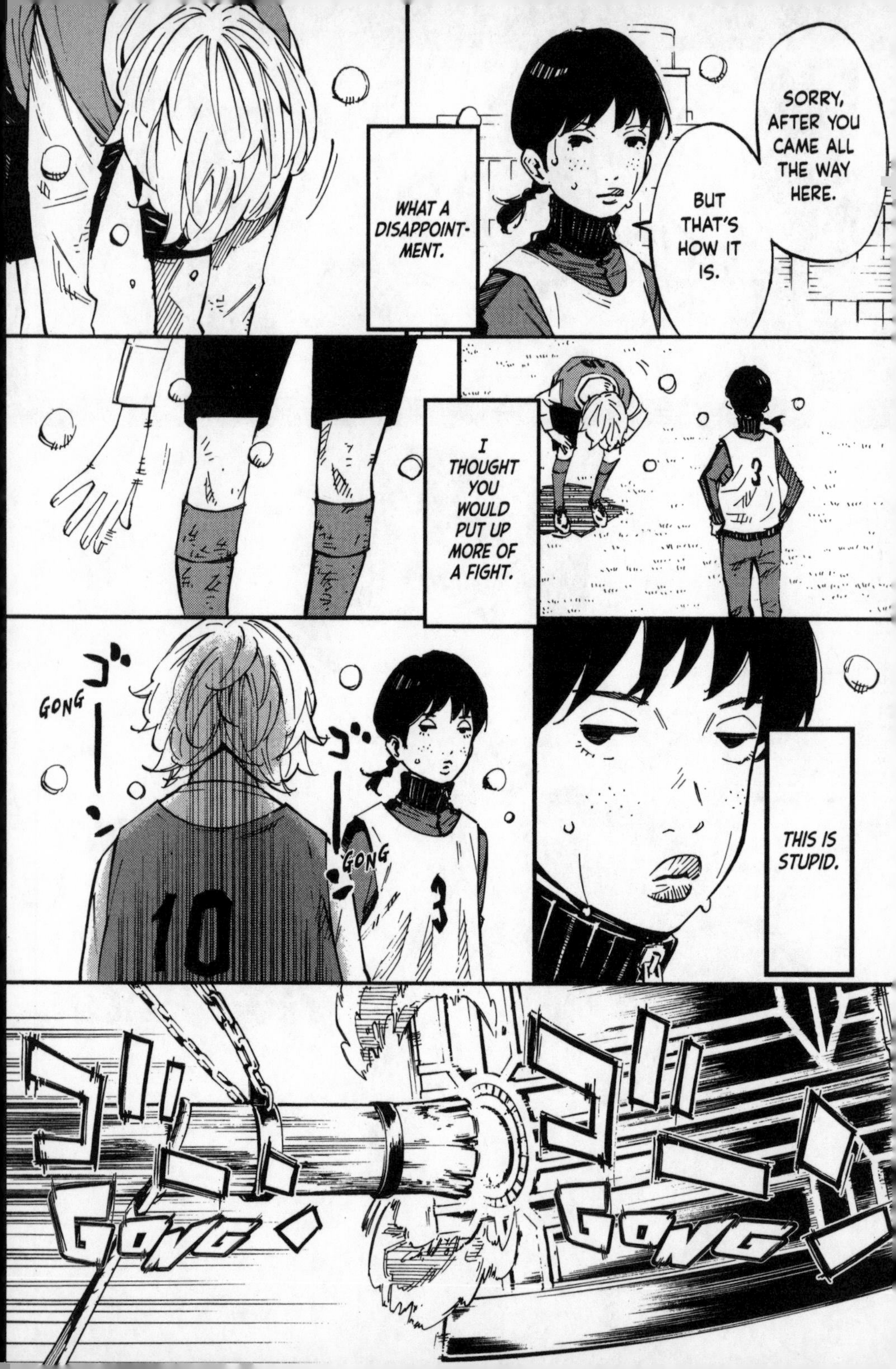
SORRY, AFTER YOU CAME ALL THE WAY HERE.
BUT THAT'S HOW IT IS.
WHAT A DISAPPOINT-MENT.
I THOUGHT YOU WOULD PUT UP MORE OF A FIGHT.
THIS IS STUPID.
GONG
GONG
GONG
GONG

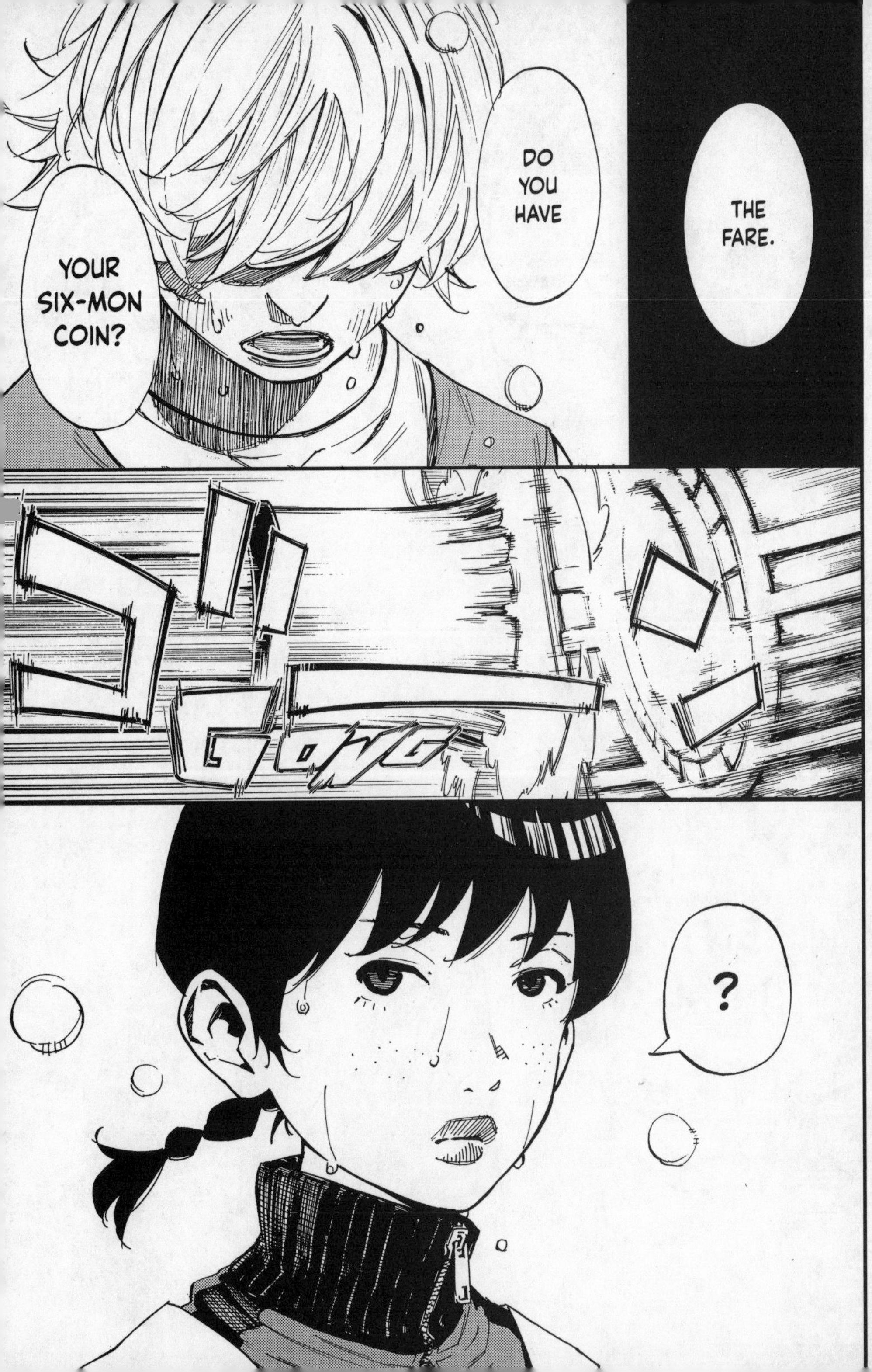
THE FARE.
DO YOU HAVE
YOUR SIX-MON COIN?
GONG
?

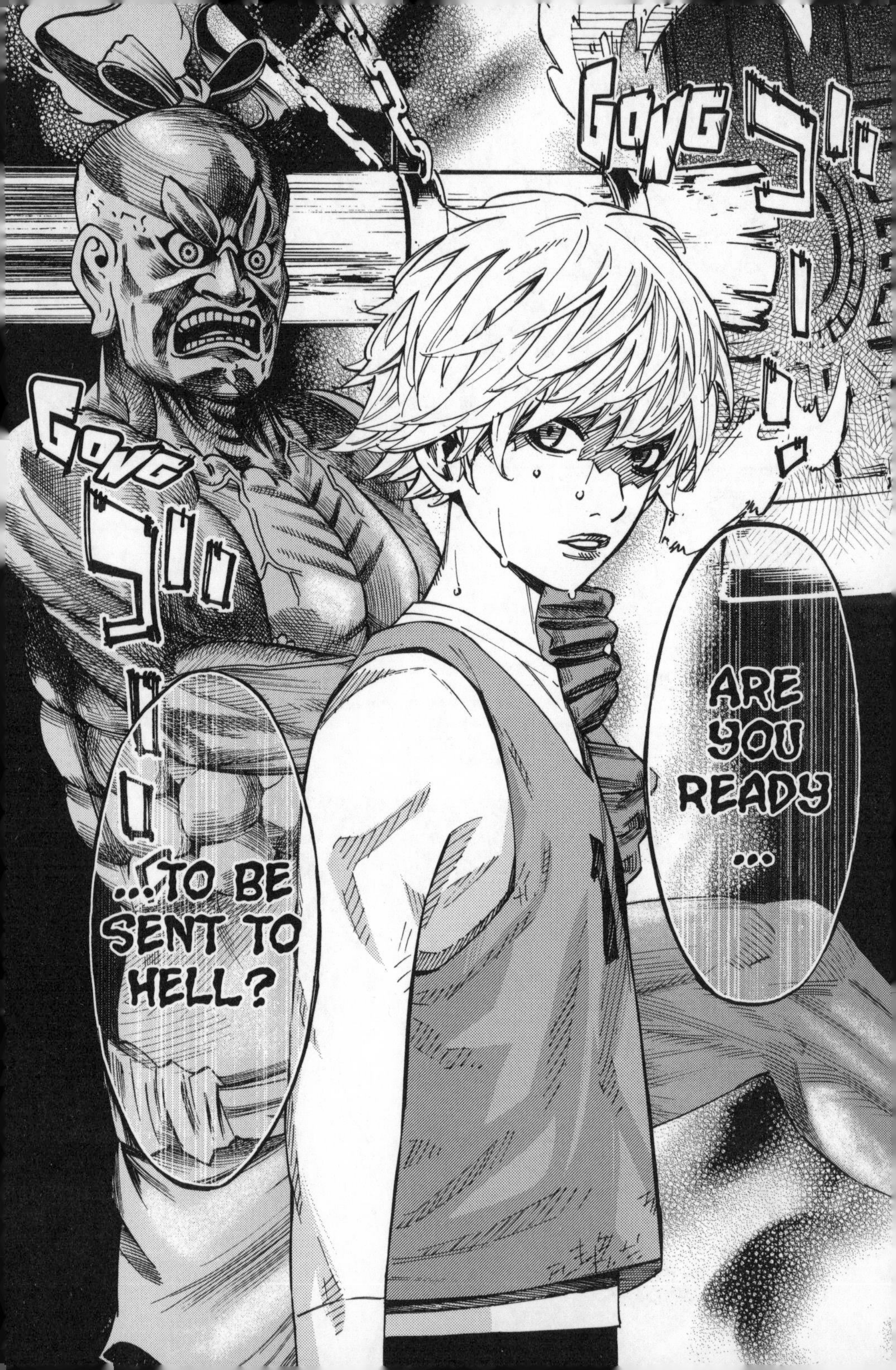
GONG
ARE YOU READY ...
GONG
...TO BE SENT TO HELL?

Farewell, My Dear Cramer

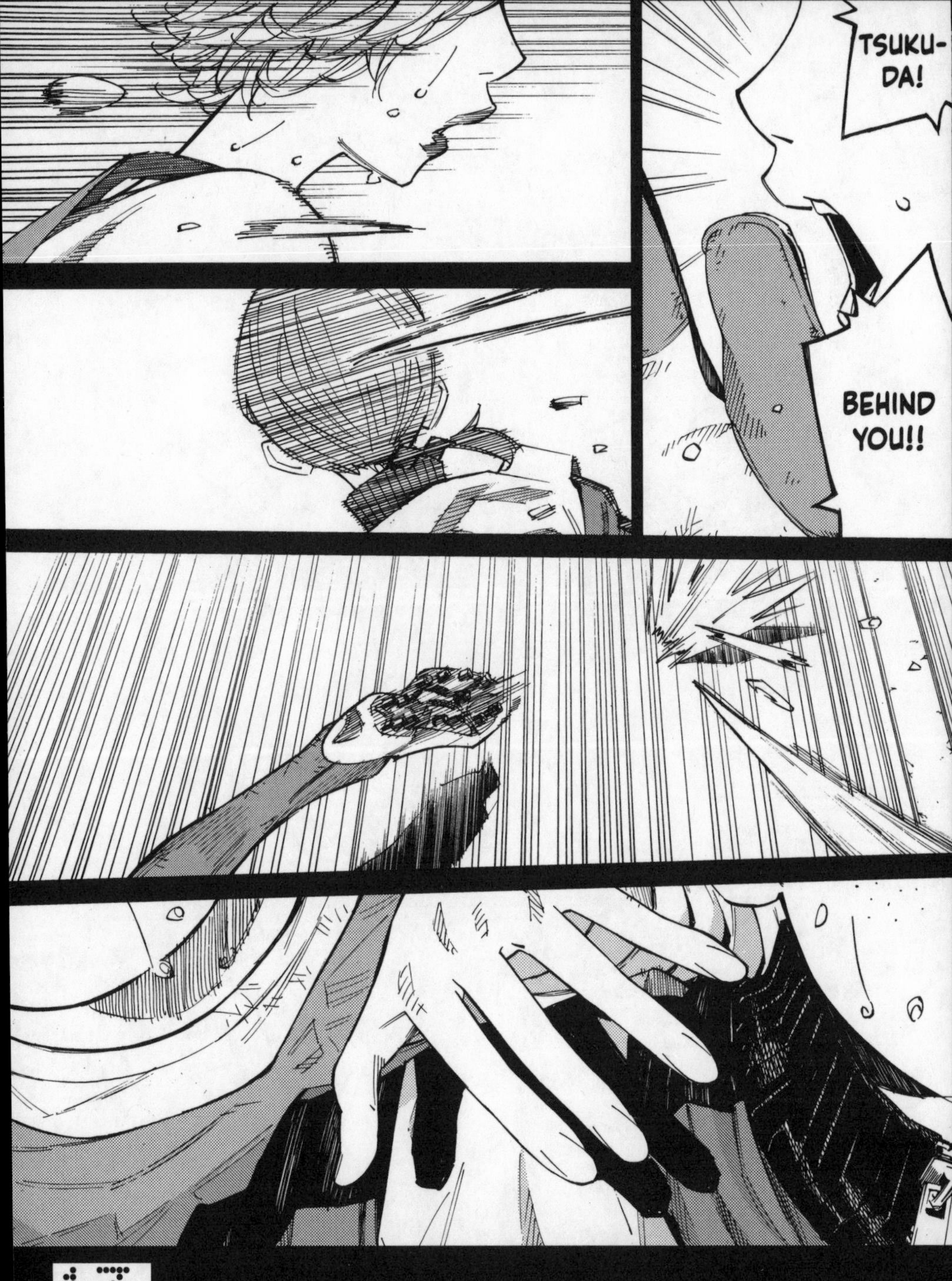
TSUKU-DA!
BEHIND YOU!!

13. THE THREE FIENDS OF WARABI SEINEN

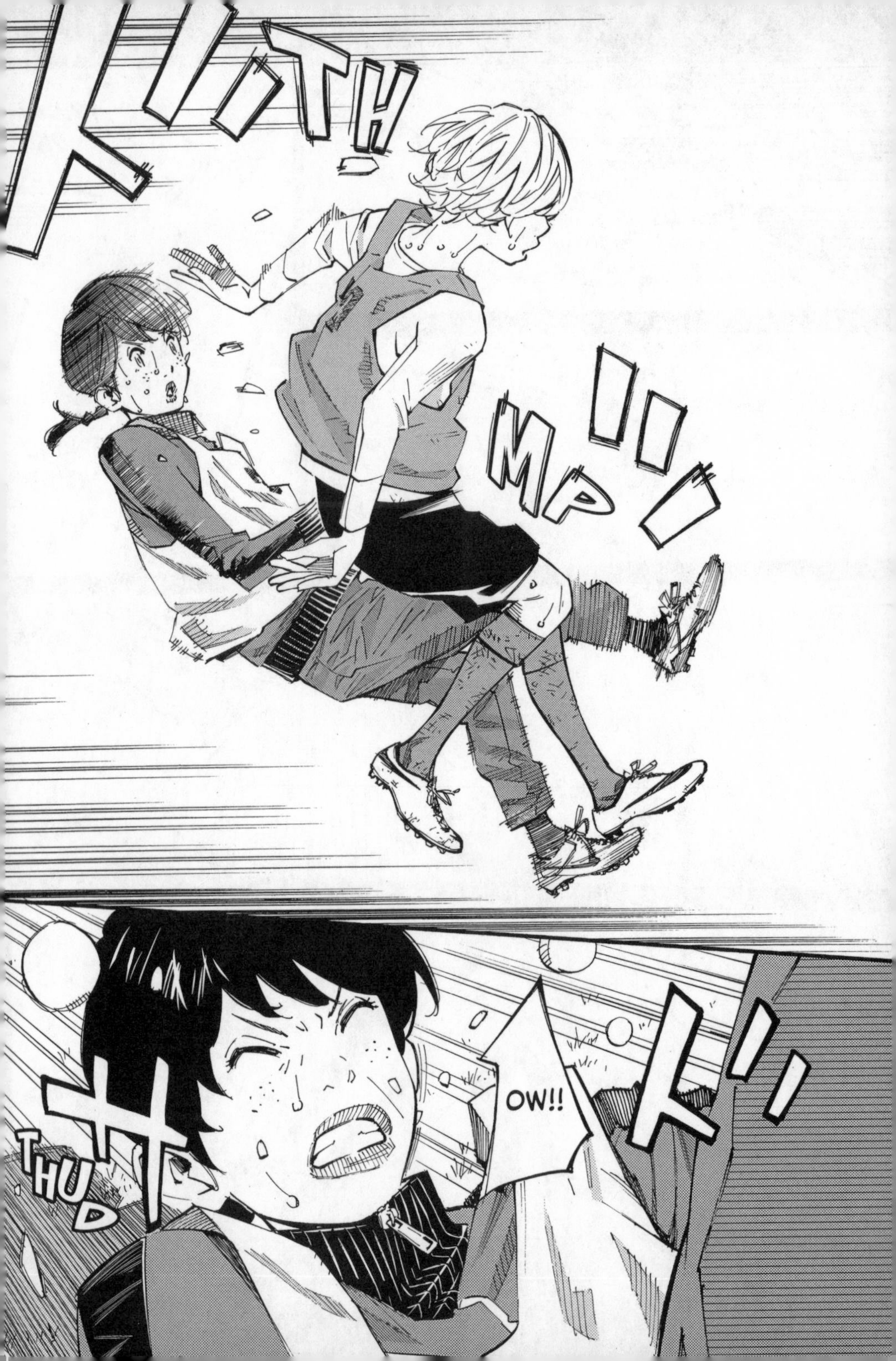
TH
MP
OW!!
THUD

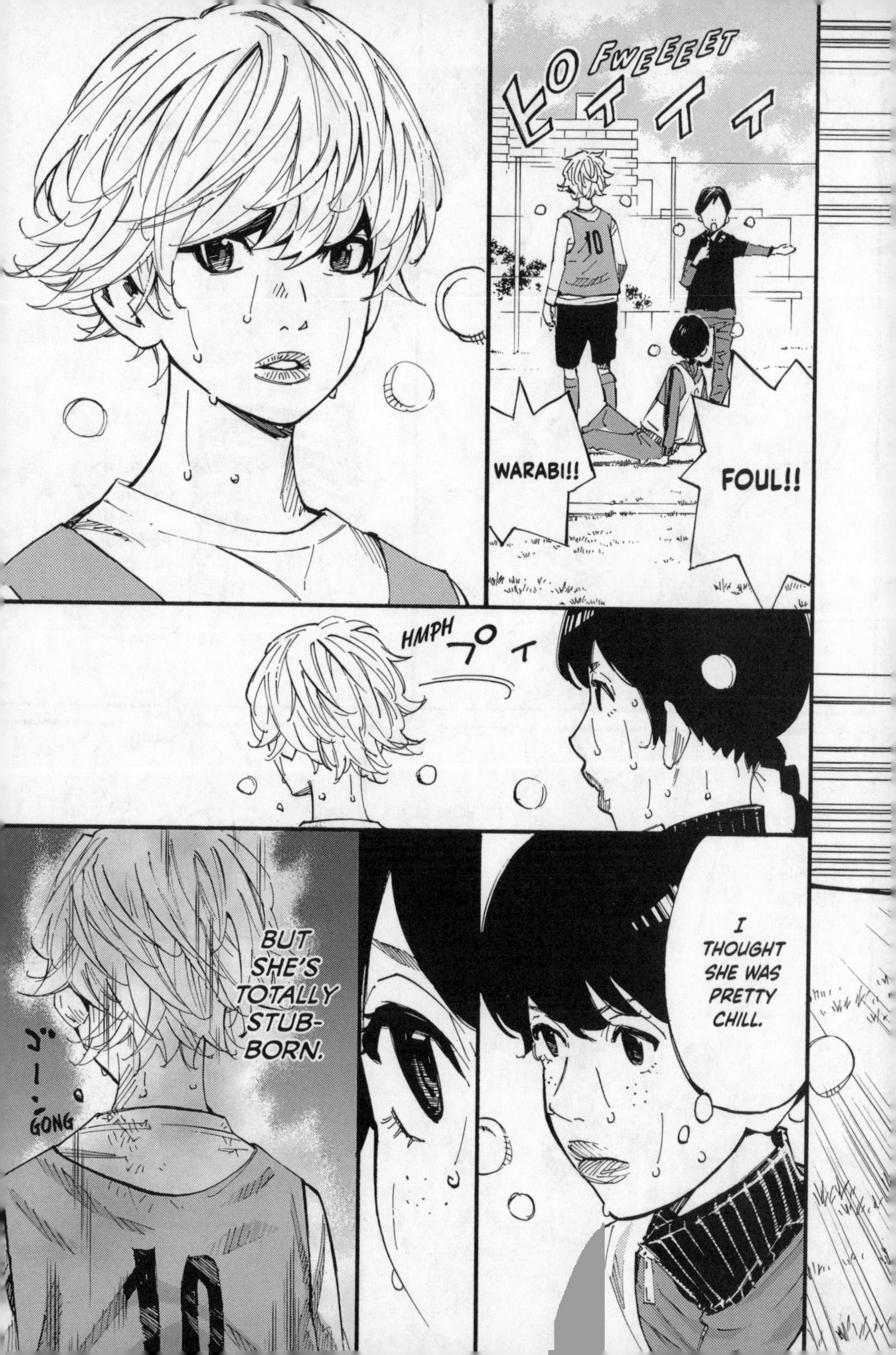
FWEEEEET
FOUL!!
WARABI!!
HMPH
I THOUGHT SHE WAS PRETTY CHILL.
BUT SHE'S TOTALLY STUBBORN.
GONG

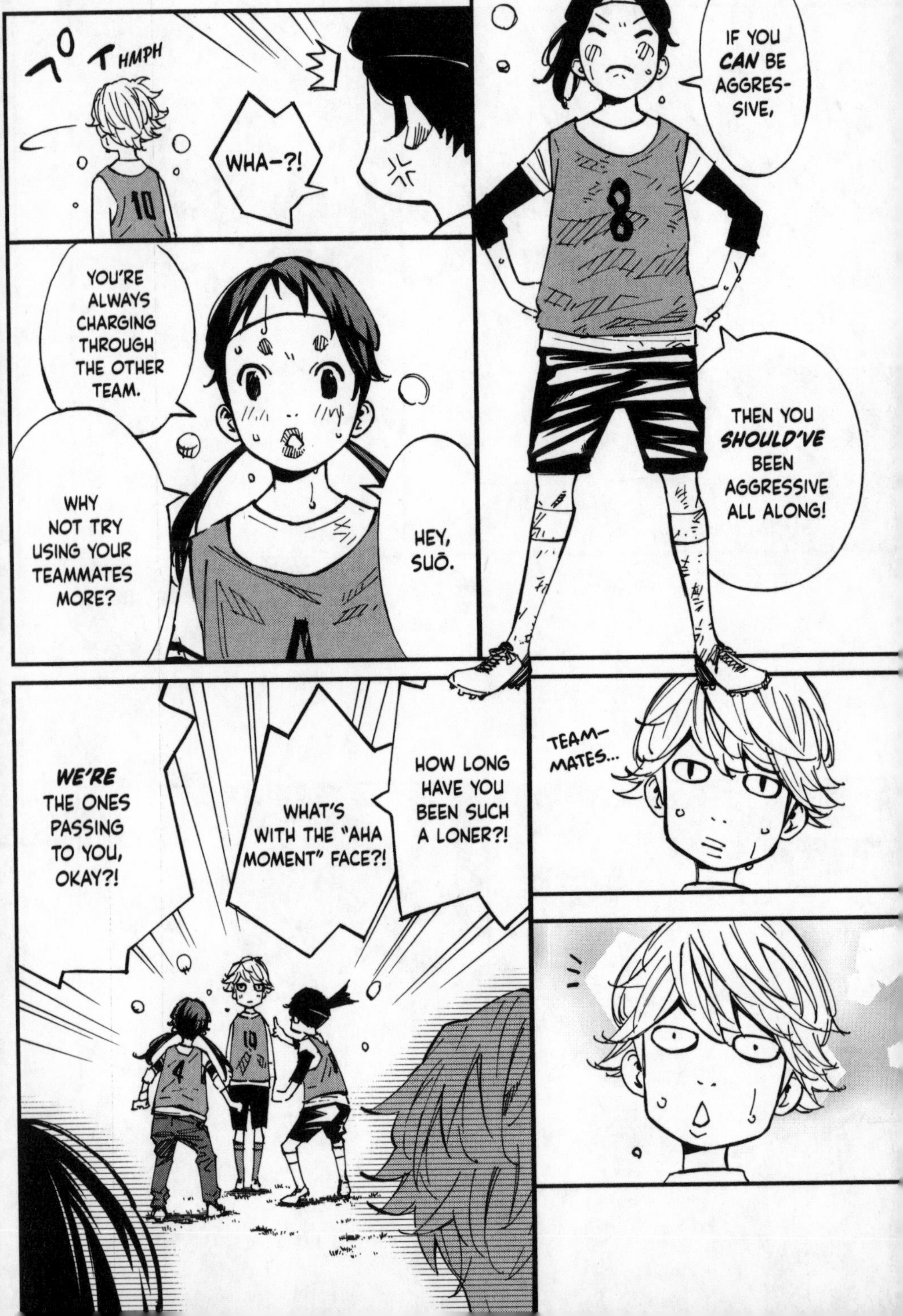
IF YOU CAN BE AGGRES-SIVE,
THEN YOU SHOULD'VE BEEN AGGRESSIVE ALL ALONG!
WHA-?!
THMPH
HEY, SUŌ.
YOU'RE ALWAYS CHARGING THROUGH THE OTHER TEAM.
WHY NOT TRY USING YOUR TEAMMATES MORE?
TEAM-MATES...
HOW LONG HAVE YOU BEEN SUCH A LONER?!
WHAT'S WITH THE "AHA MOMENT" FACE?!
WE'RE THE ONES PASSING TO YOU, OKAY?!

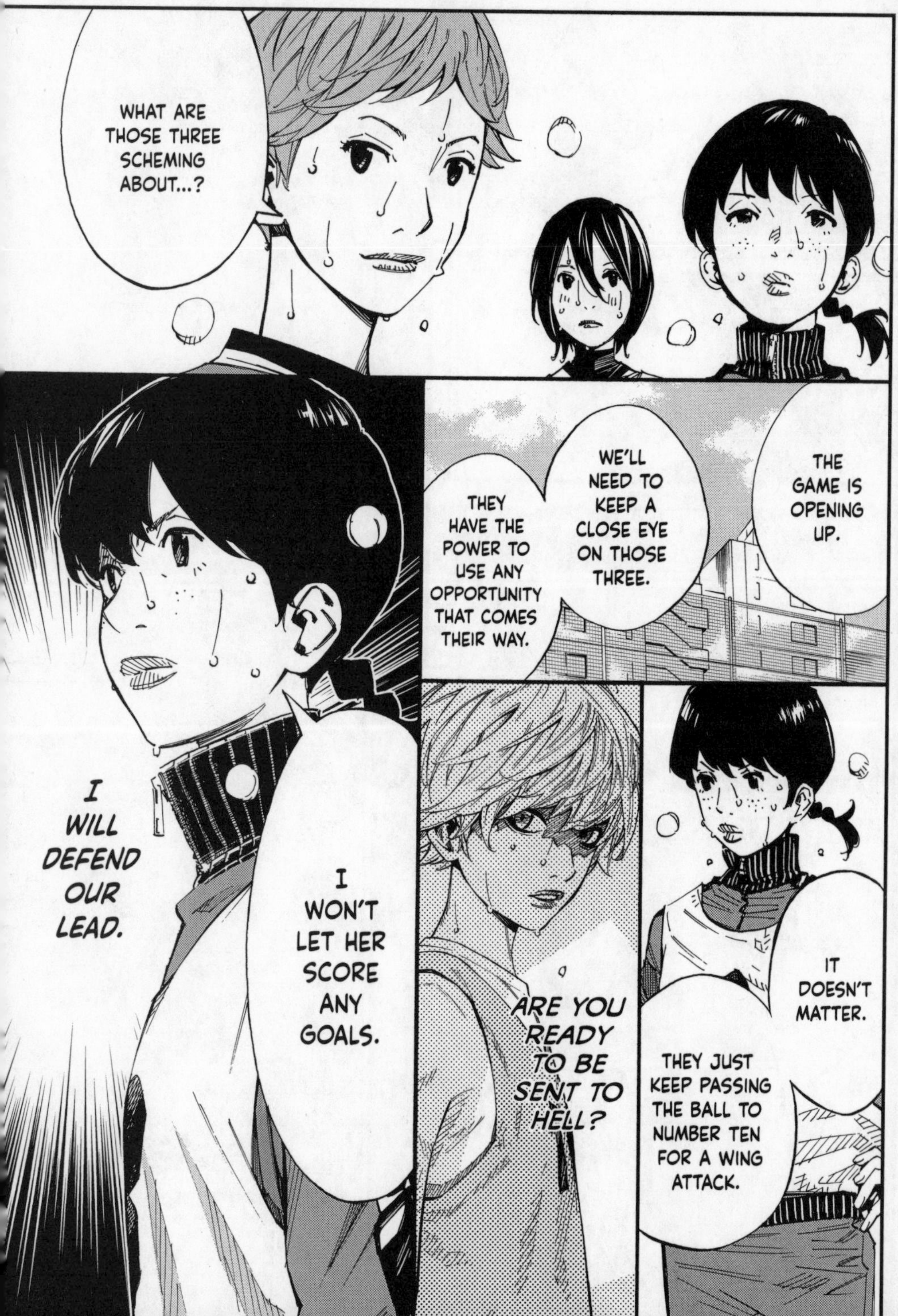
WHAT ARE THOSE THREE SCHEMING ABOUT...?
THE GAME IS OPENING UP.
WE'LL NEED TO KEEP A CLOSE EYE ON THOSE THREE.
THEY HAVE THE POWER TO USE ANY OPPORTUNITY THAT COMES THEIR WAY.
IT DOESN'T MATTER.
THEY JUST KEEP PASSING THE BALL TO NUMBER TEN FOR A WING ATTACK.
ARE YOU READY TO BE SENT TO HELL?
I WON'T LET HER SCORE ANY GOALS.
I WILL DEFEND OUR LEAD.

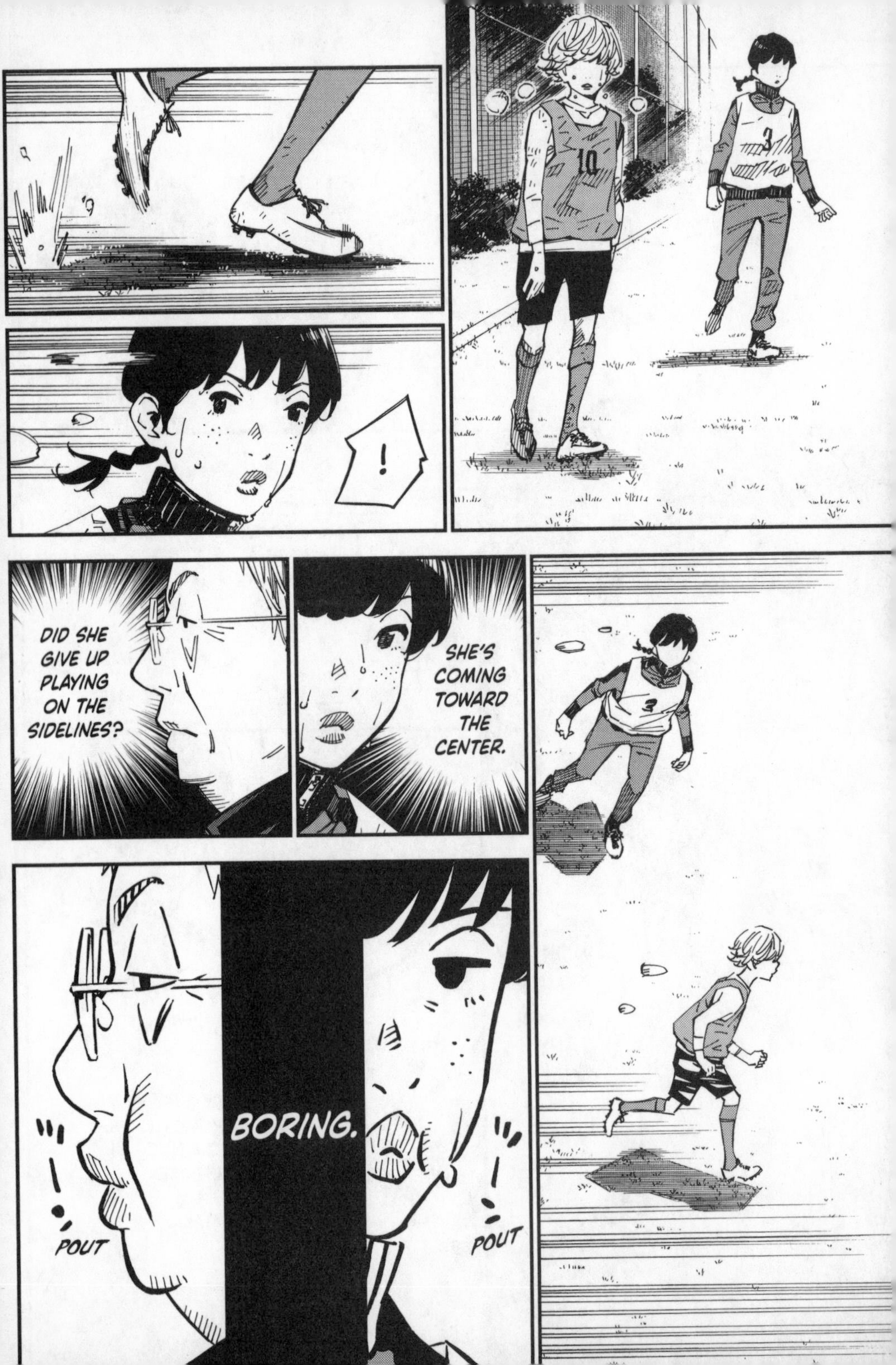
!
SHE'S COMING TOWARD THE CENTER.
DID SHE GIVE UP PLAYING ON THE SIDELINES?
POUT
BORING.
POUT

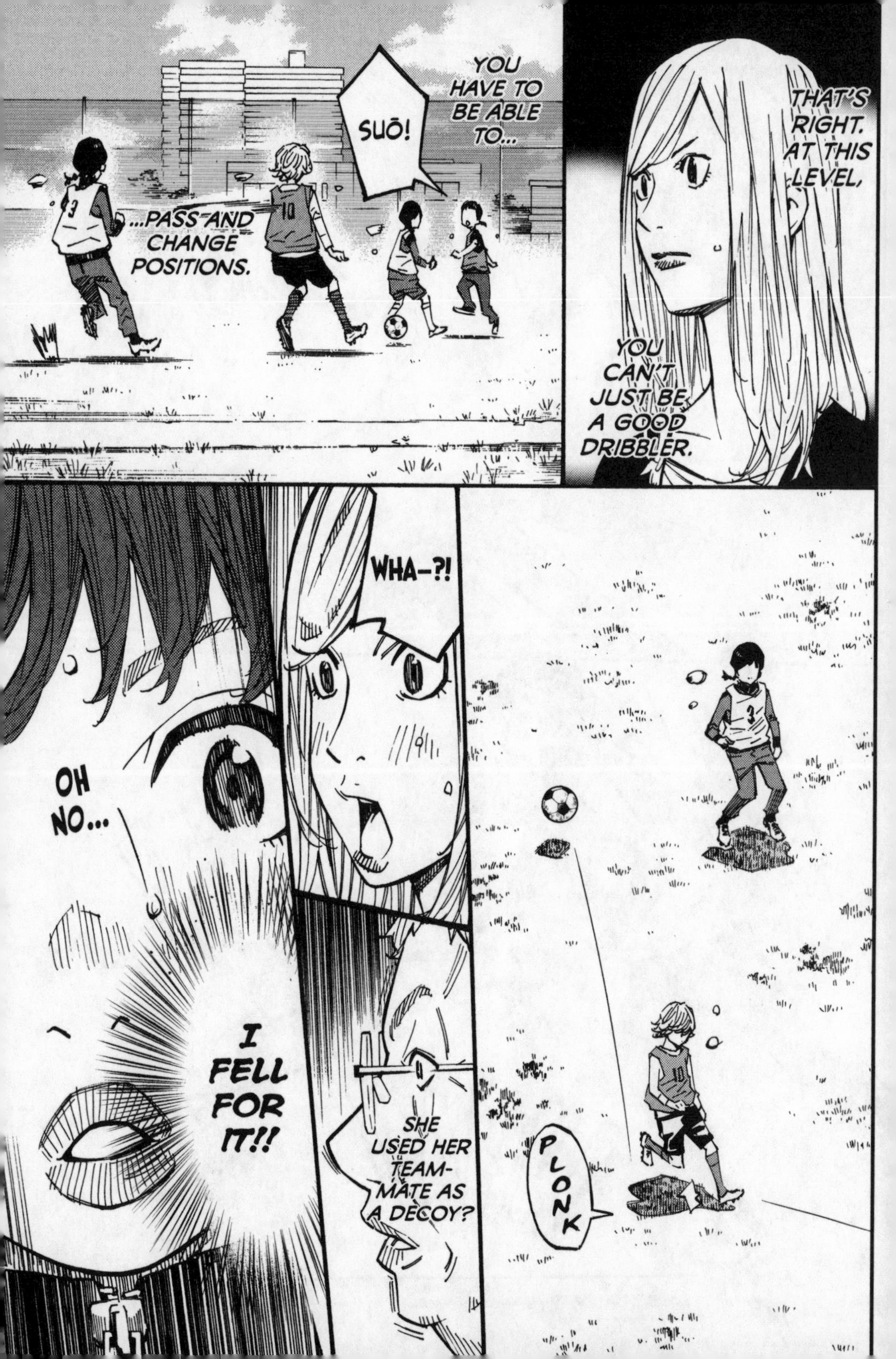
THAT'S RIGHT. AT THIS LEVEL,
YOU CAN'T JUST BE A GOOD DRIBBLER.
YOU HAVE TO BE ABLE TO...
SUŌ!
...PASS AND CHANGE POSITIONS.
PLONK
WHA-?!
SHE USED HER TEAM-MATE AS A DECOY?
OH NO...
I FELL FOR IT!!

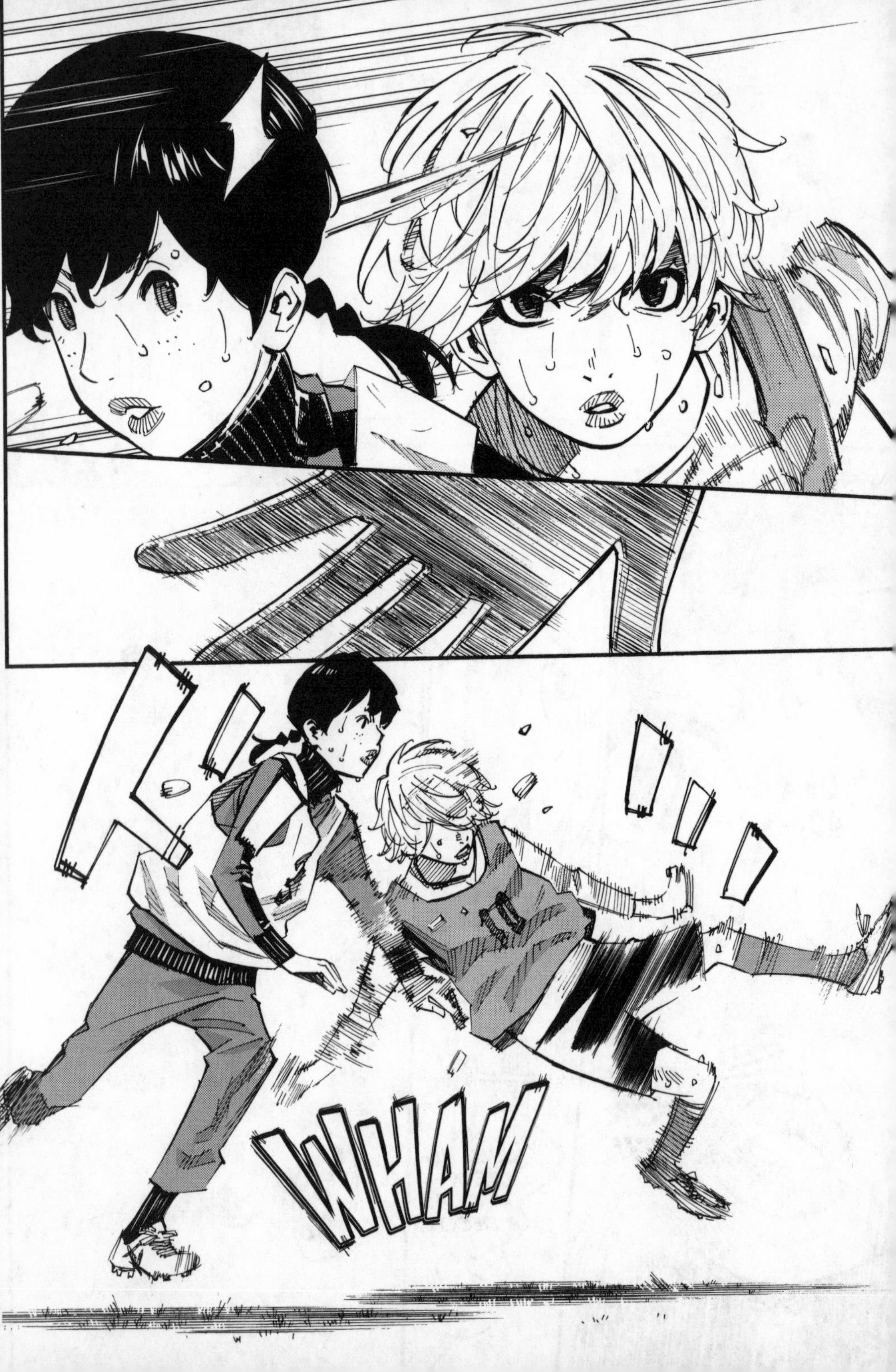
WHAM

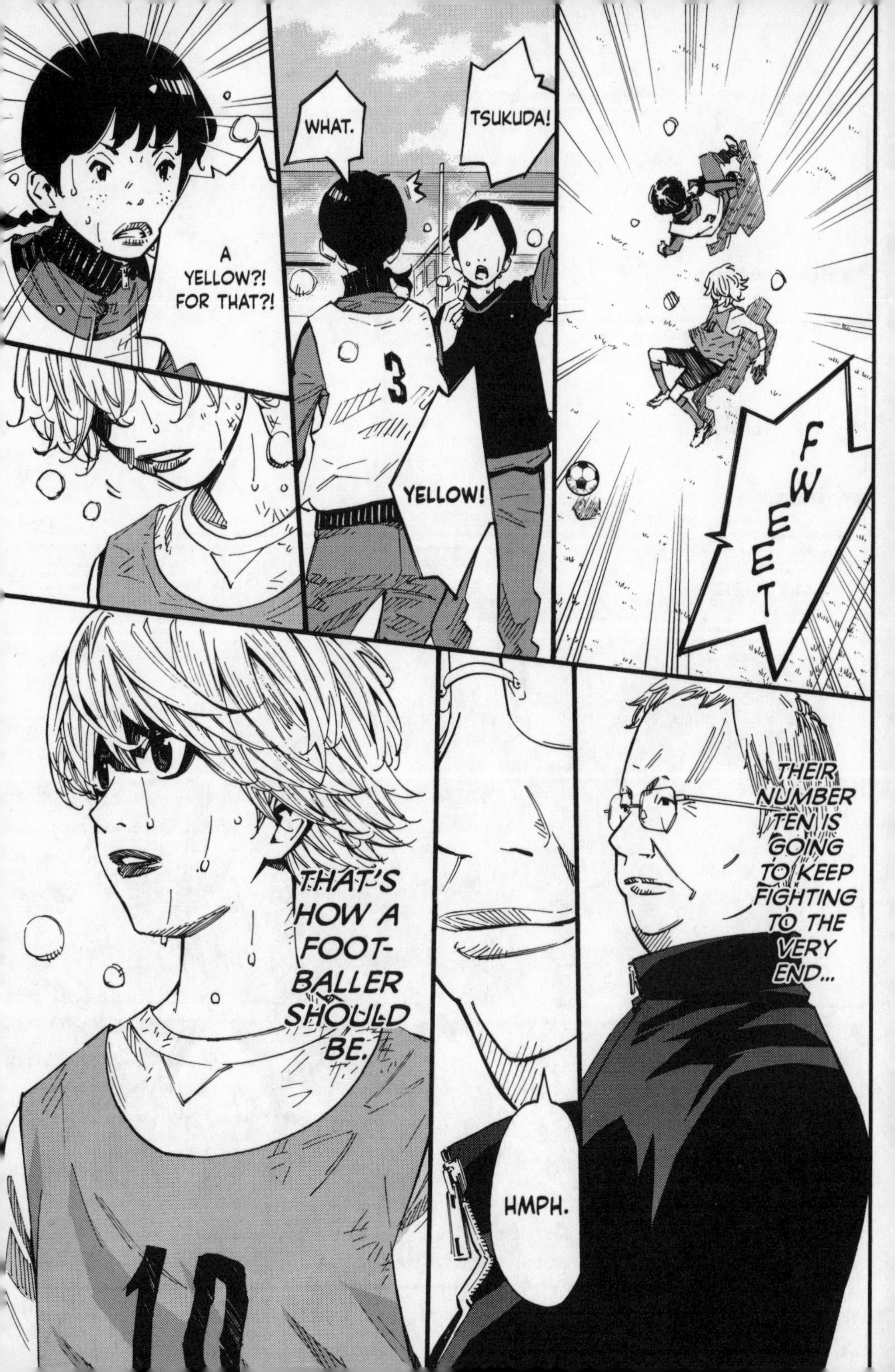
FWEET
TSUKUDA!
WHAT.
YELLOW!
A YELLOW?! FOR THAT?!
THEIR NUMBER TEN IS GOING TO KEEP FIGHTING TO THE VERY END...
HMPH.
THAT'S HOW A FOOT-BALLER SHOULD BE.

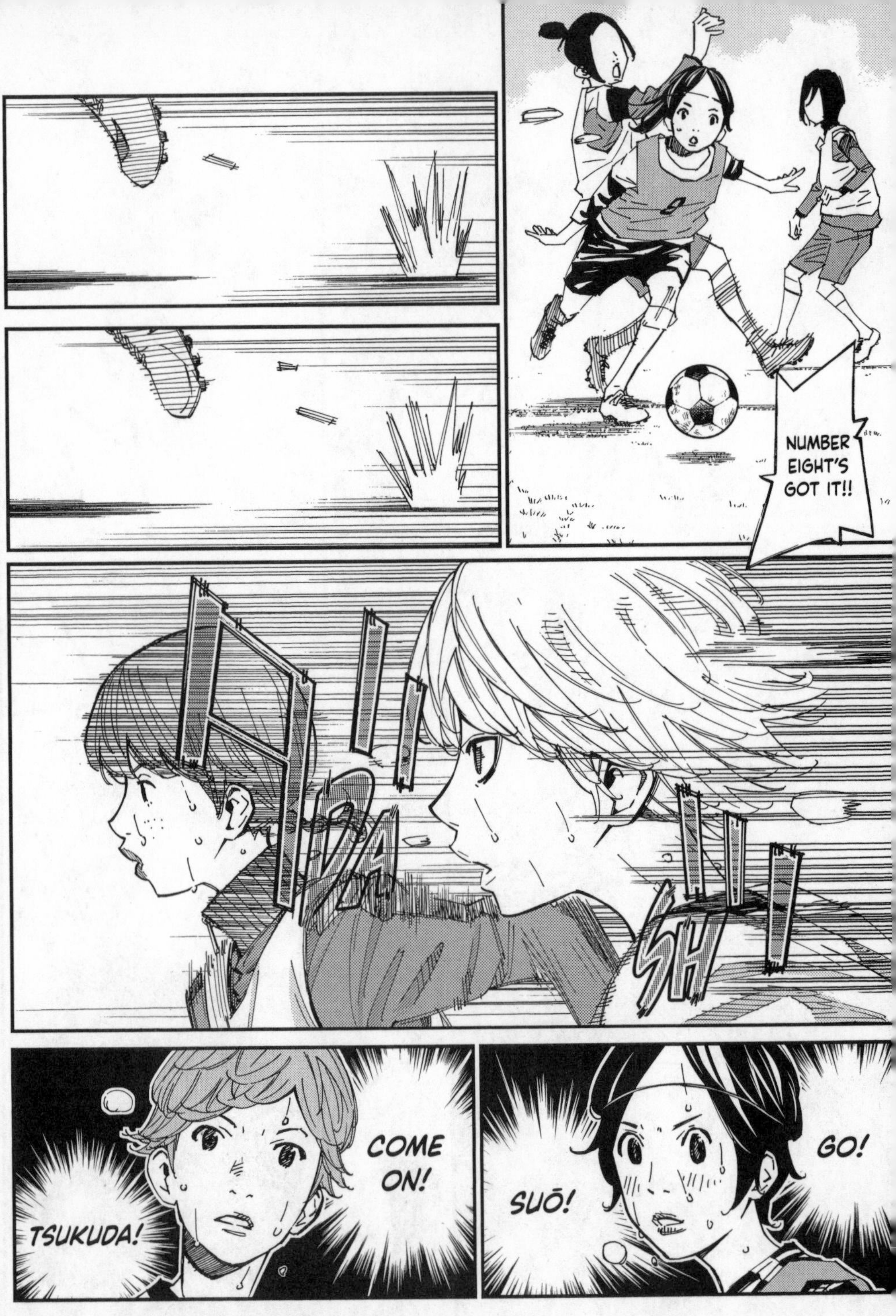
NUMBER EIGHT'S GOT IT!!
GO!
SUŌ!
COME ON!
TSUKUDA!

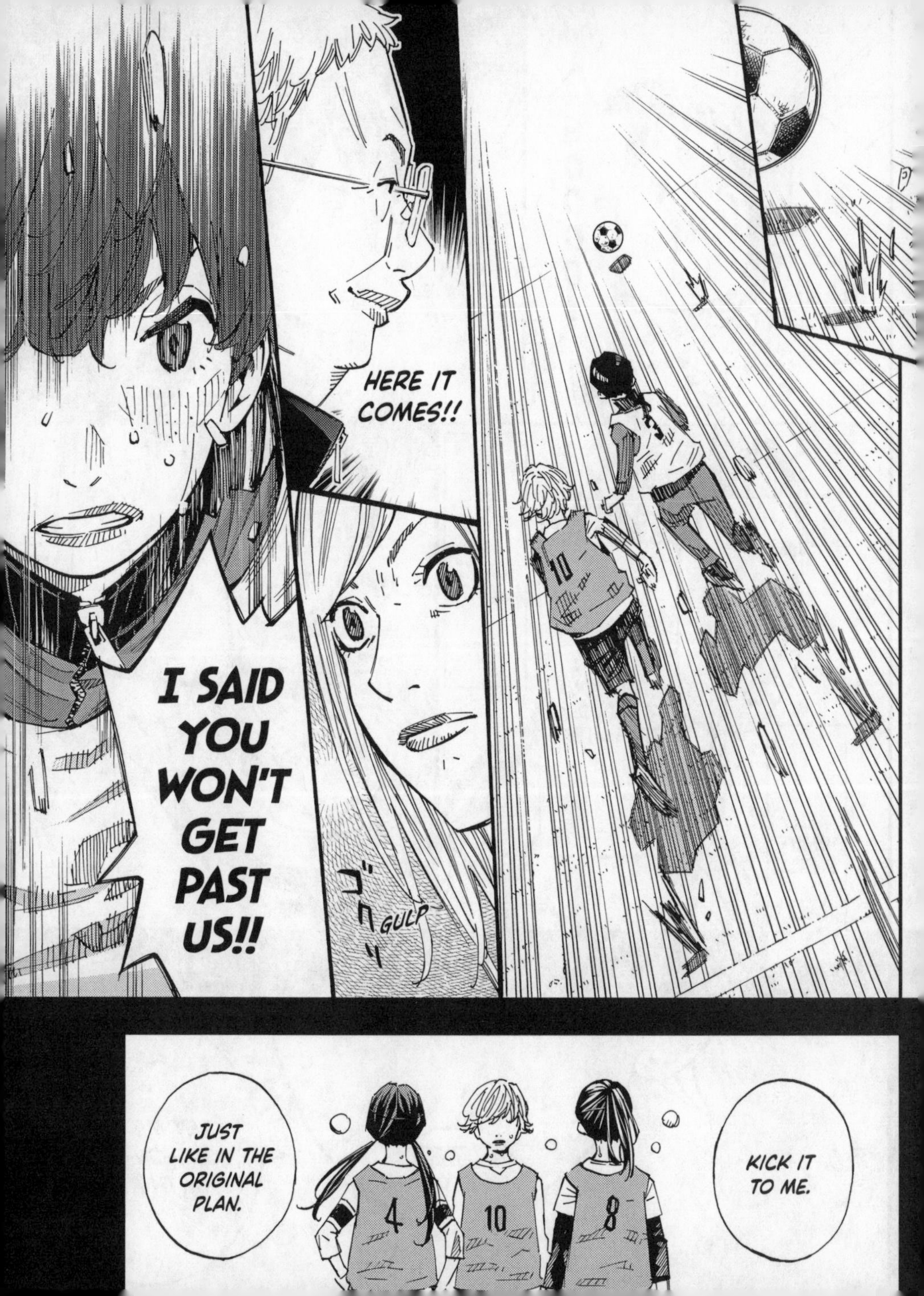
HERE IT COMES!!
GULP
I SAID YOU WON'T GET PAST US!!
KICK IT TO ME.
JUST LIKE IN THE ORIGINAL PLAN.

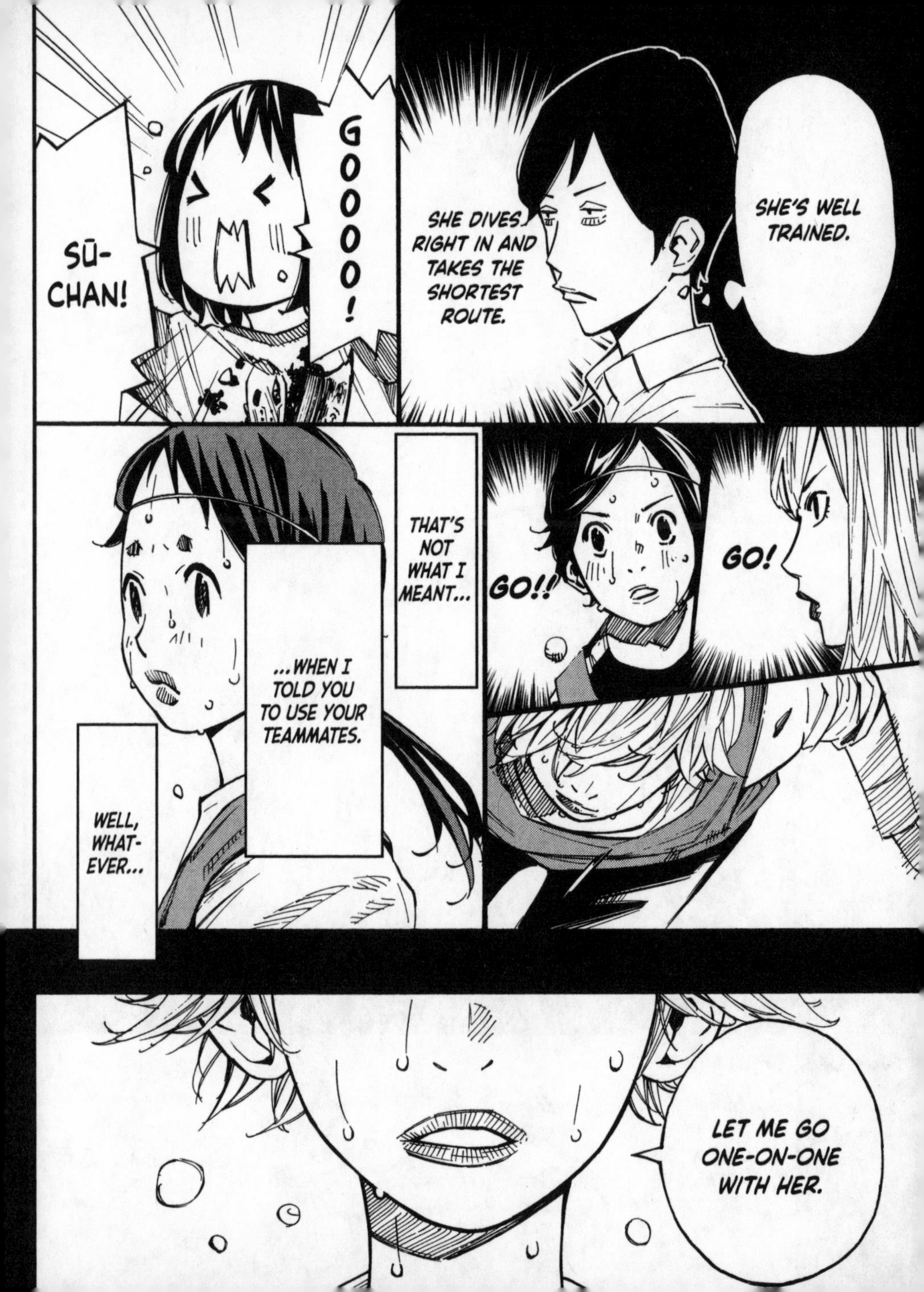
SHE'S WELL TRAINED.
SHE DIVES RIGHT IN AND TAKES THE SHORTEST ROUTE.
GOOOOO!
SŪ-CHAN!
GO!
GO!!
THAT'S NOT WHAT I MEANT...
...WHEN I TOLD YOU TO USE YOUR TEAMMATES.
WELL, WHATEVER...
LET ME GO ONE-ON-ONE WITH HER.

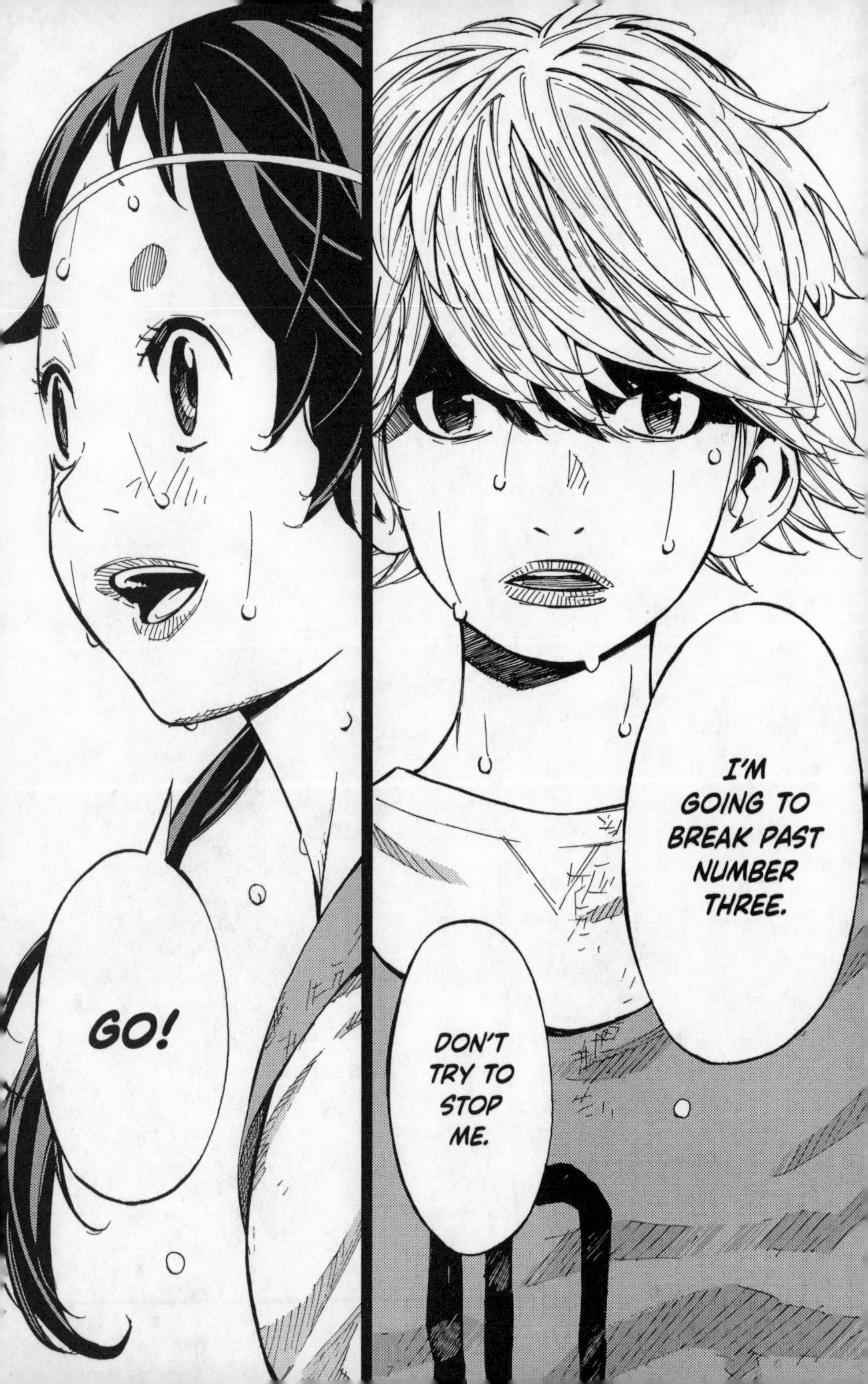
I'M GOING TO BREAK PAST NUMBER THREE.
DON'T TRY TO STOP ME.
GO!

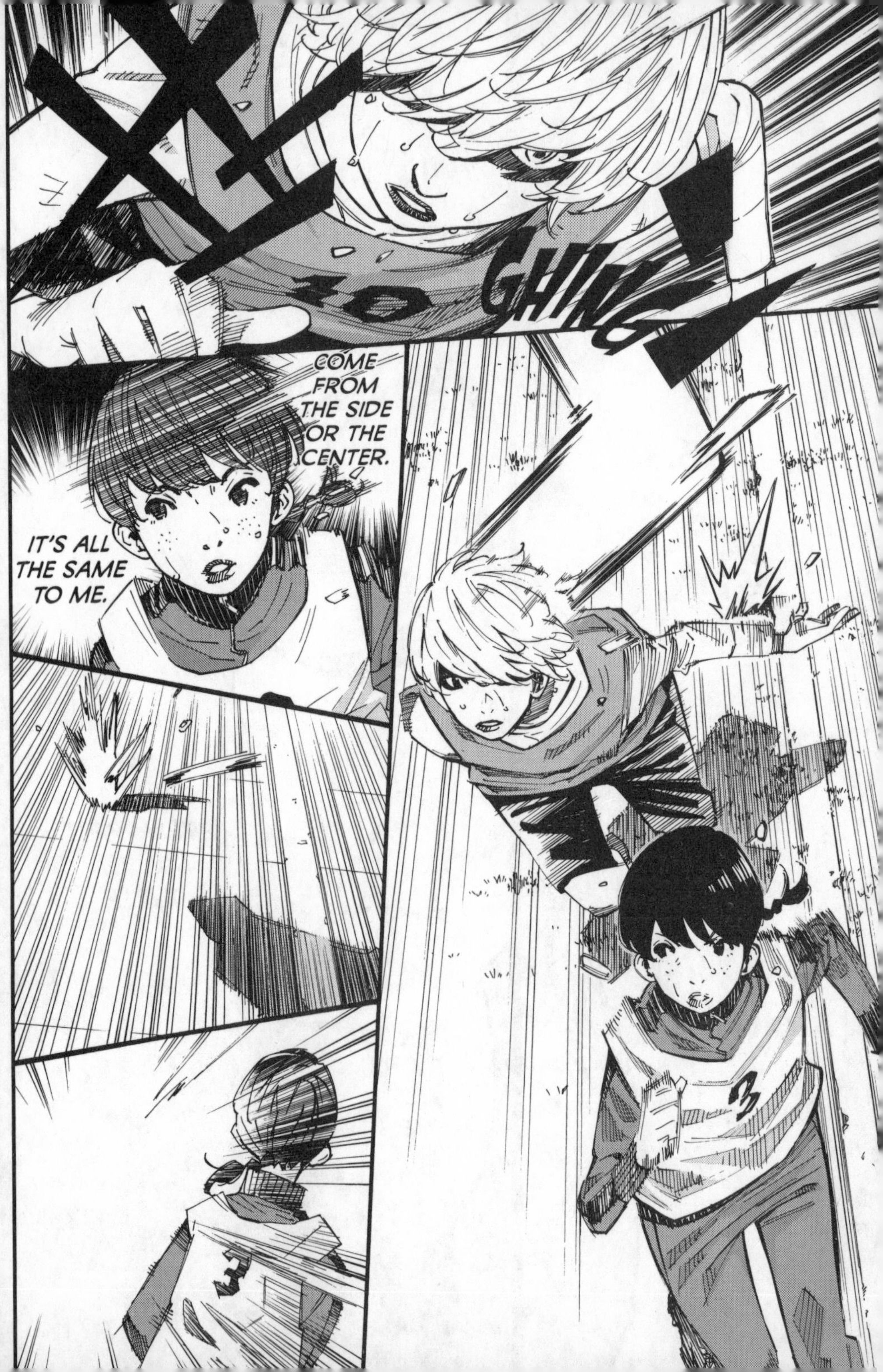
GHING
COME FROM THE SIDE OR THE CENTER.
IT'S ALL THE SAME TO ME.

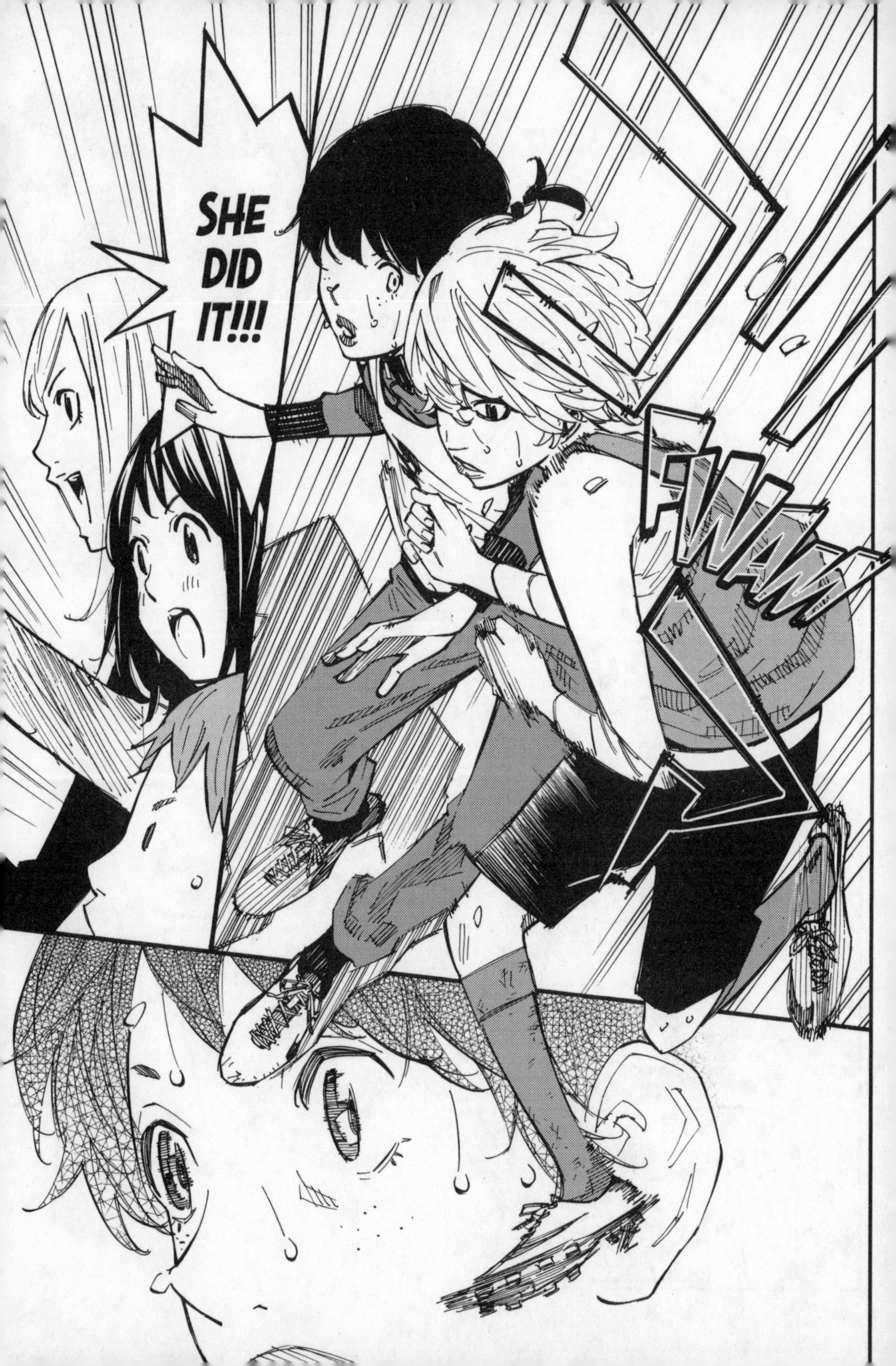
SHE DID IT!!!
FWAM

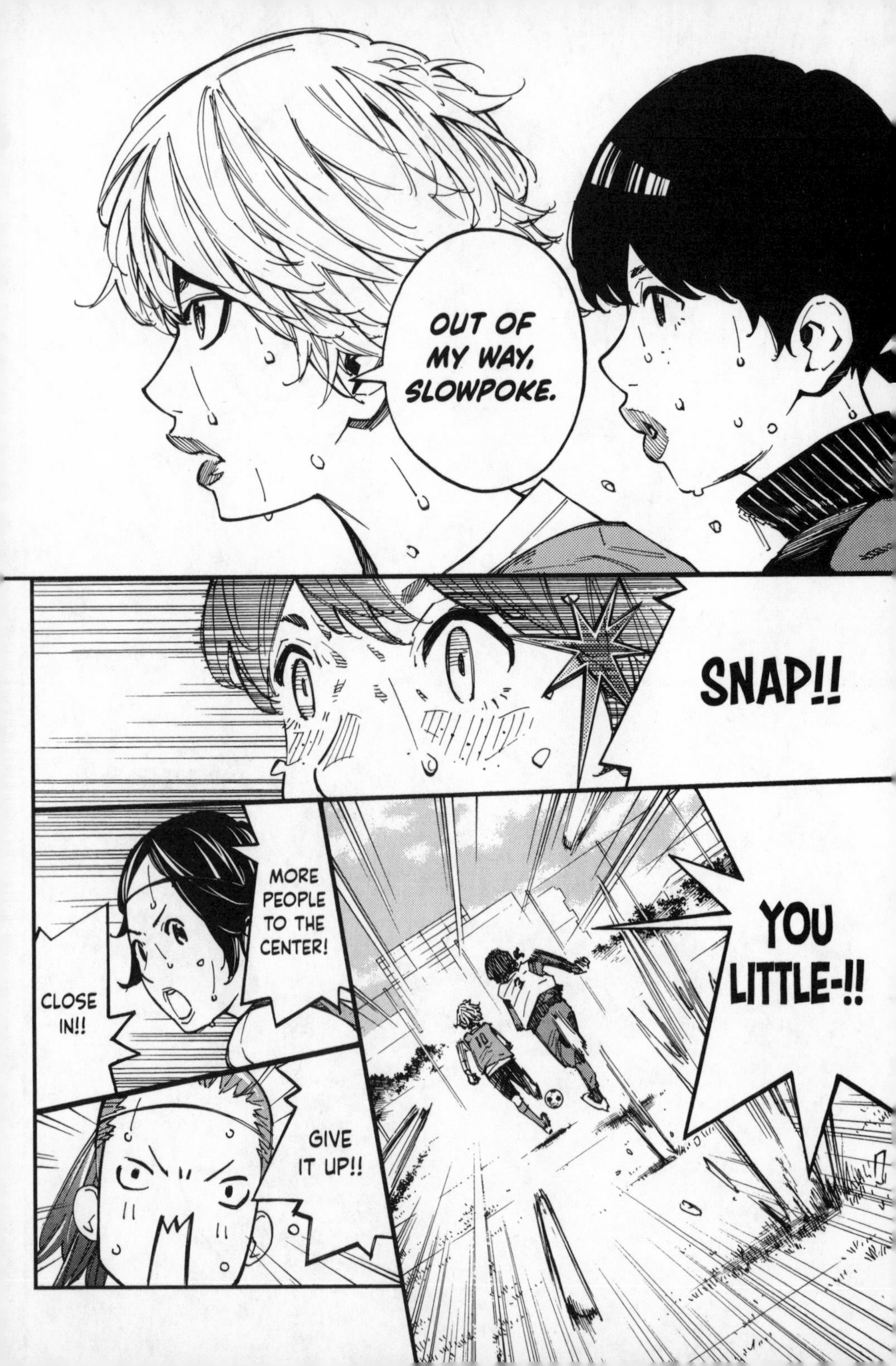
OUT OF MY WAY, SLOWPOKE.
SNAP!!
YOU LITTLE-!!
MORE PEOPLE TO THE CENTER!
CLOSE IN!!
GIVE IT UP!!

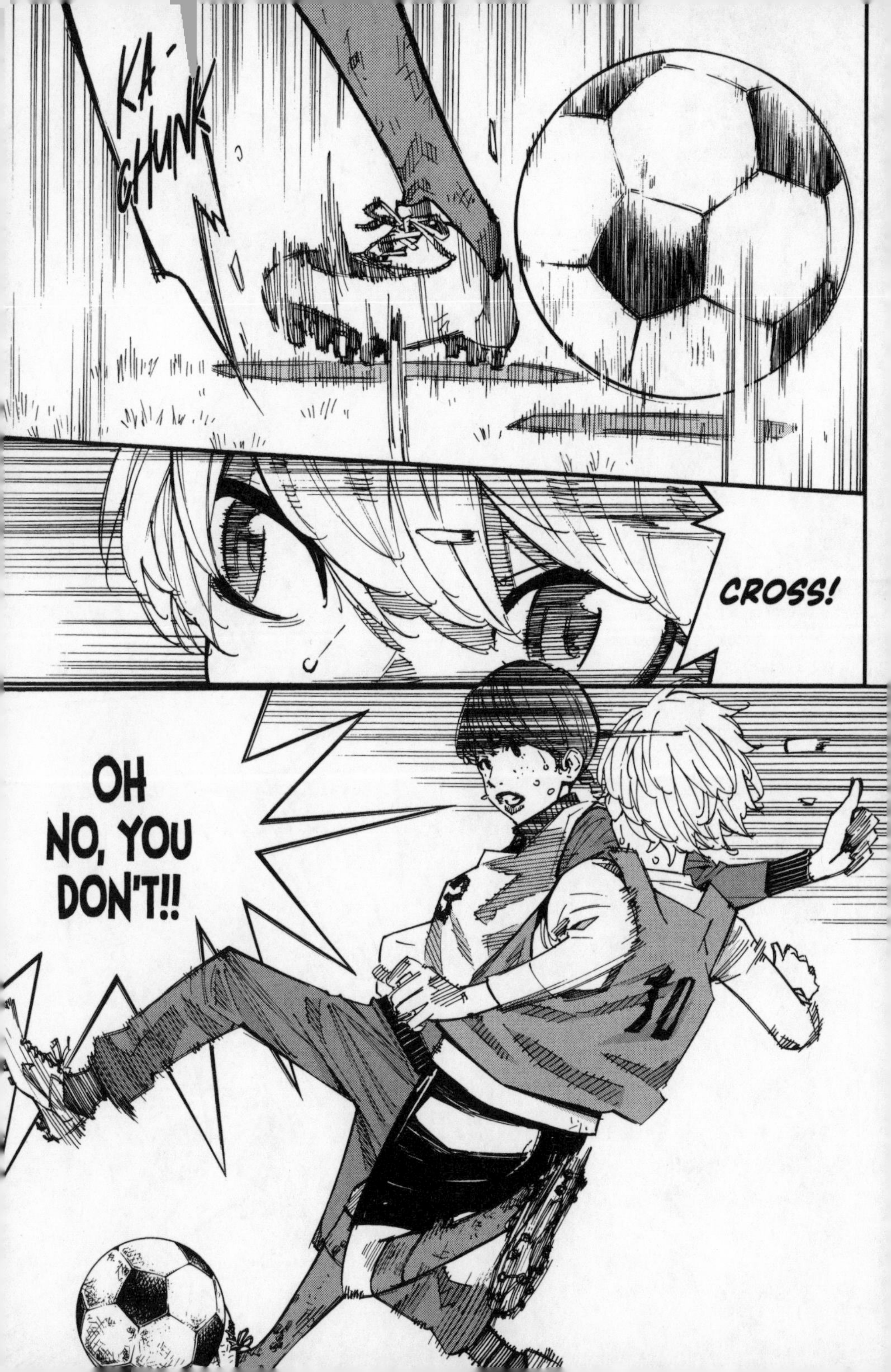
KA-CHUNK
CROSS!
OH NO, YOU DON'T!!

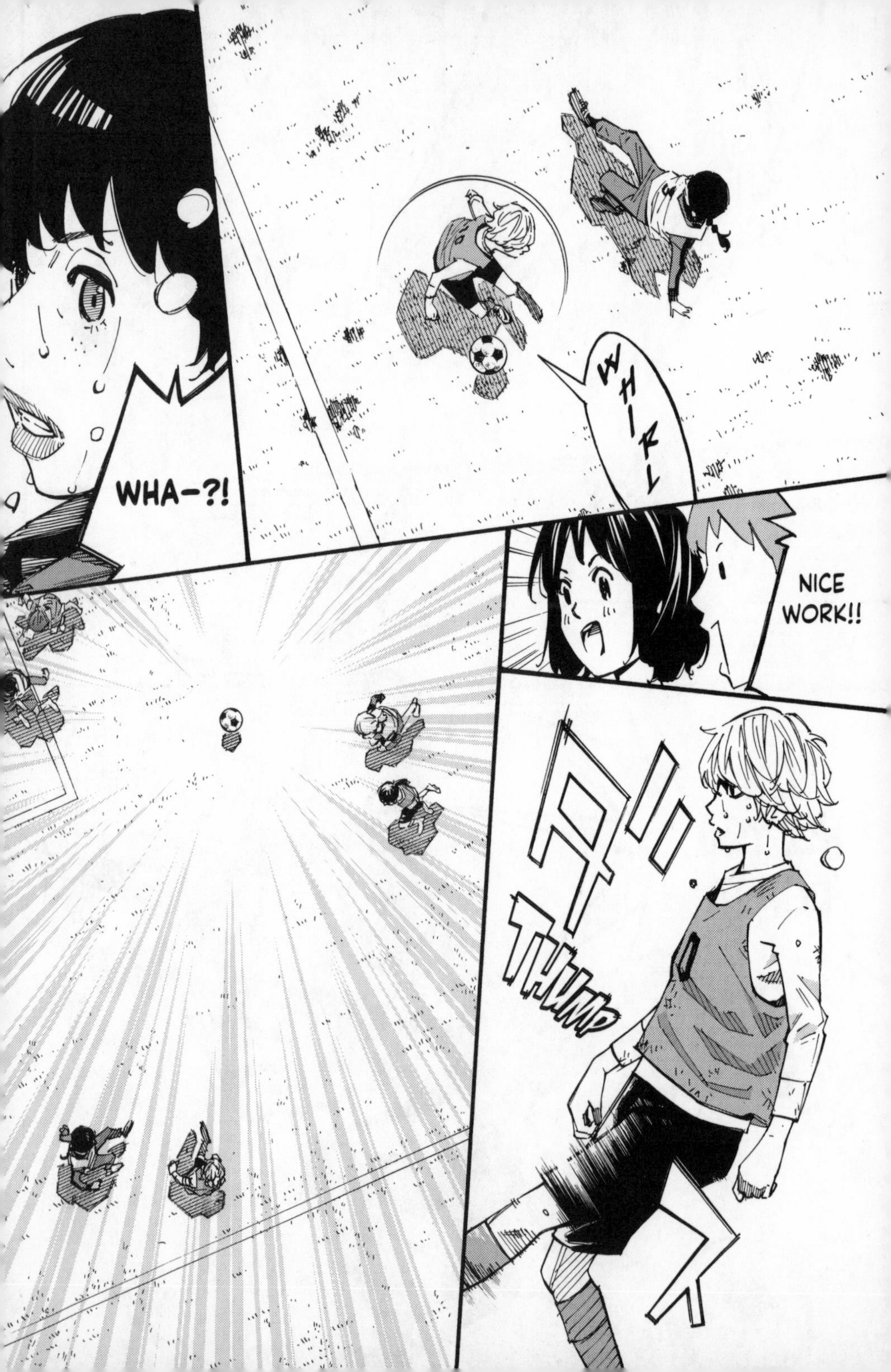
WHIRL
WHA-?!
NICE WORK!!
THUMP

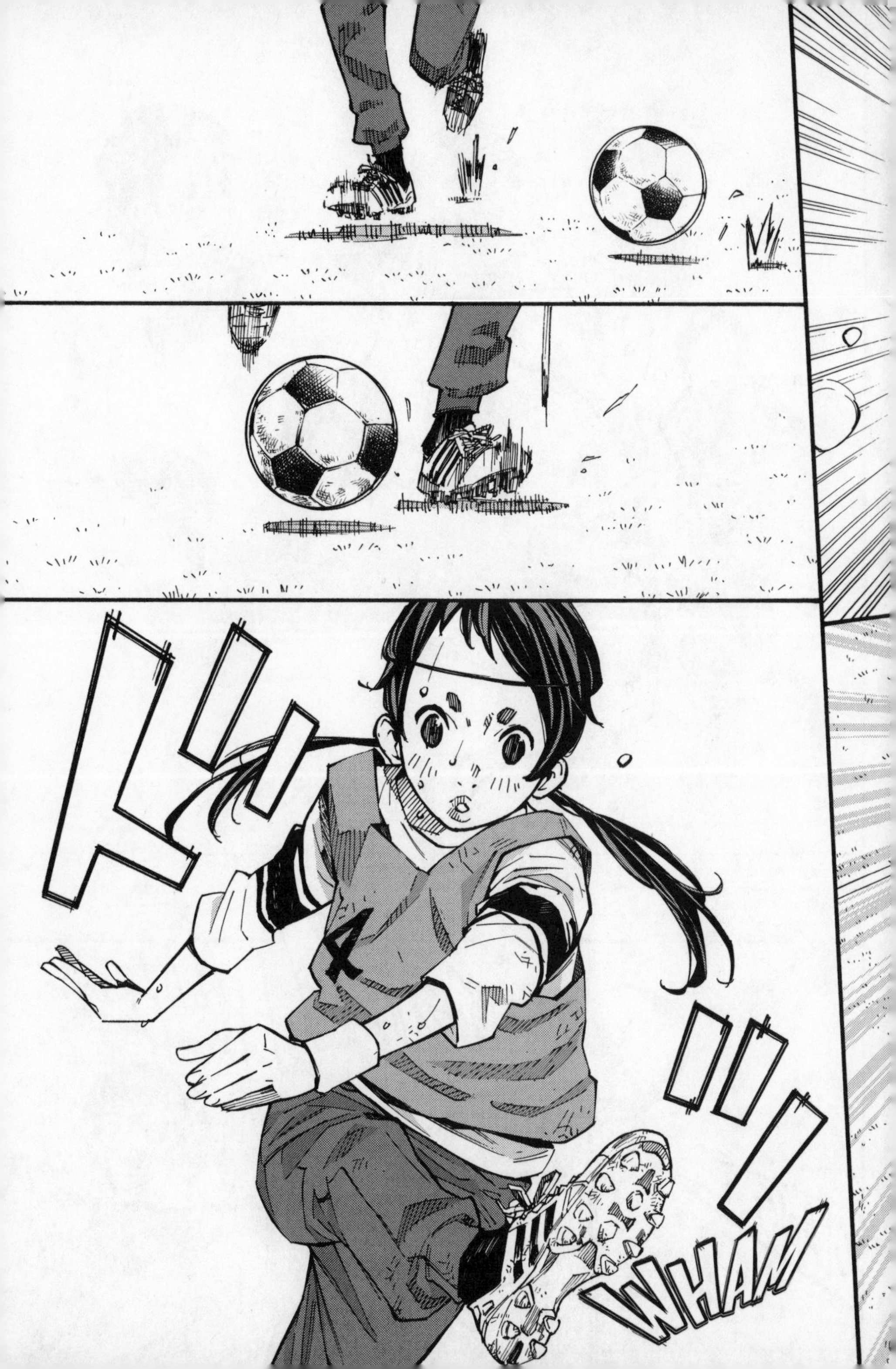
WHAM

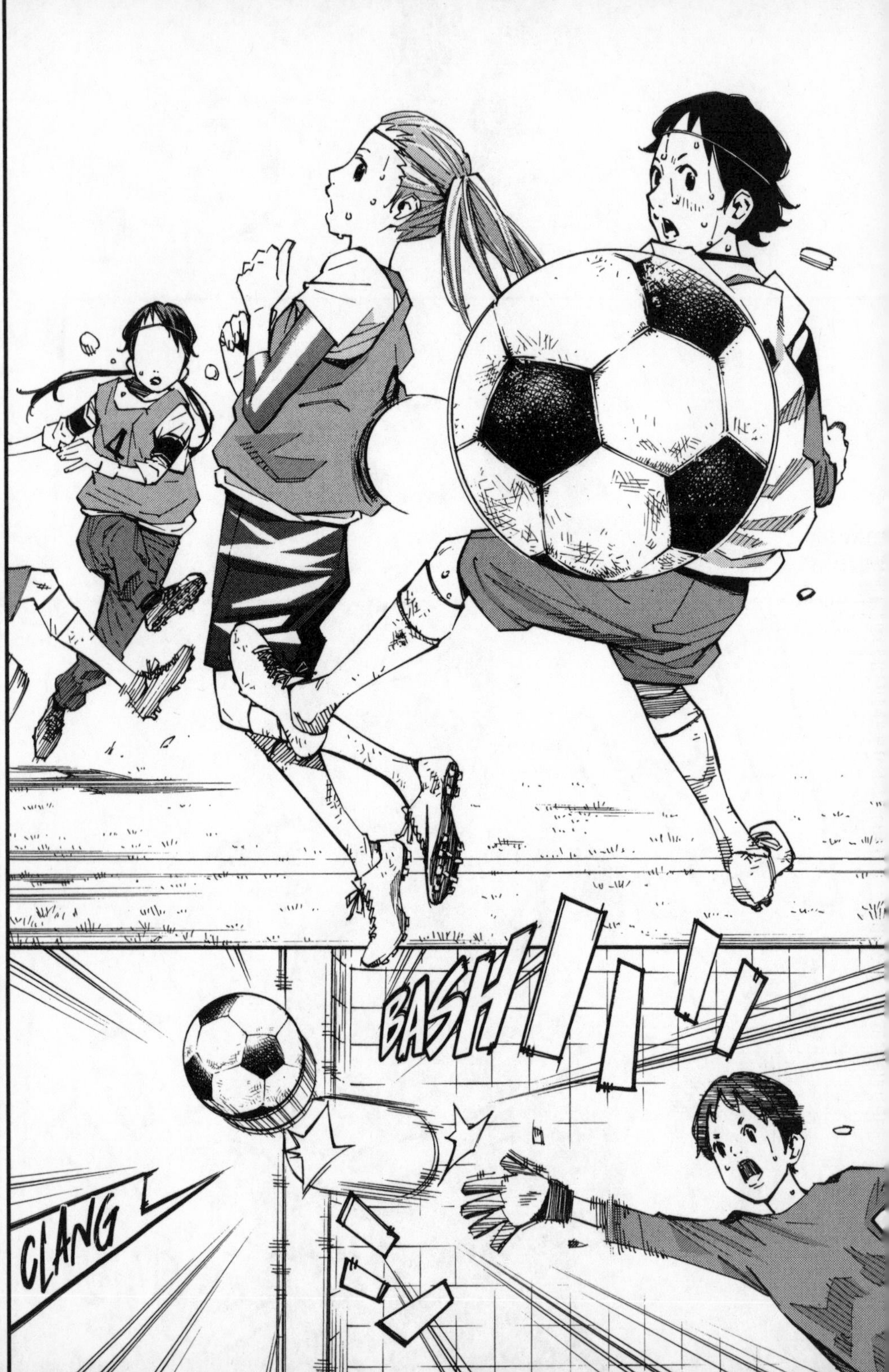
BASH!!!!
CLANG

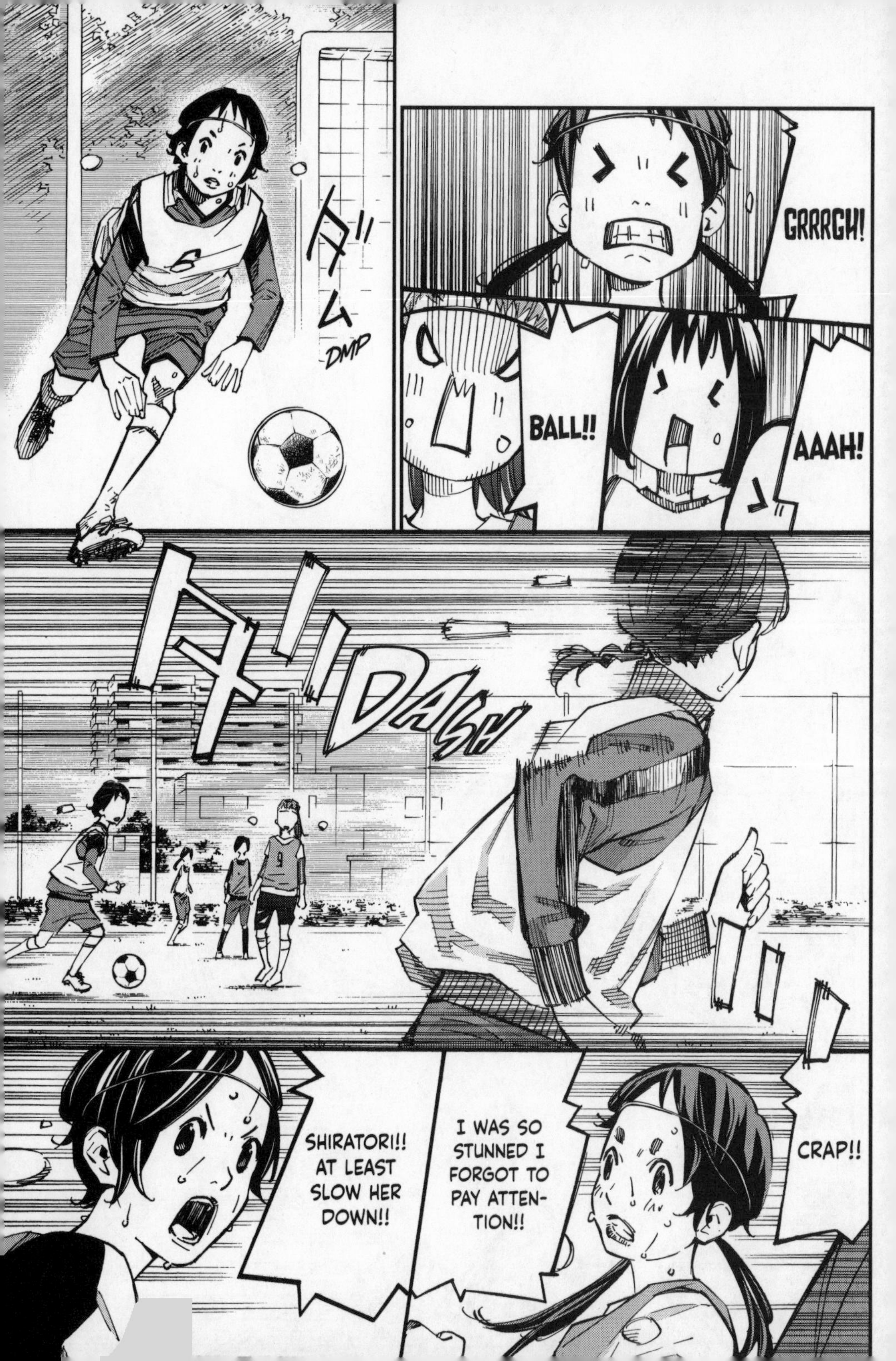
GRRRGH!
AAAH!
BALL!!
ダム
DMP
ダッ
DASH
CRAP!!
I WAS SO STUNNED I FORGOT TO PAY ATTEN-TION!!
SHIRATORI!! AT LEAST SLOW HER DOWN!!

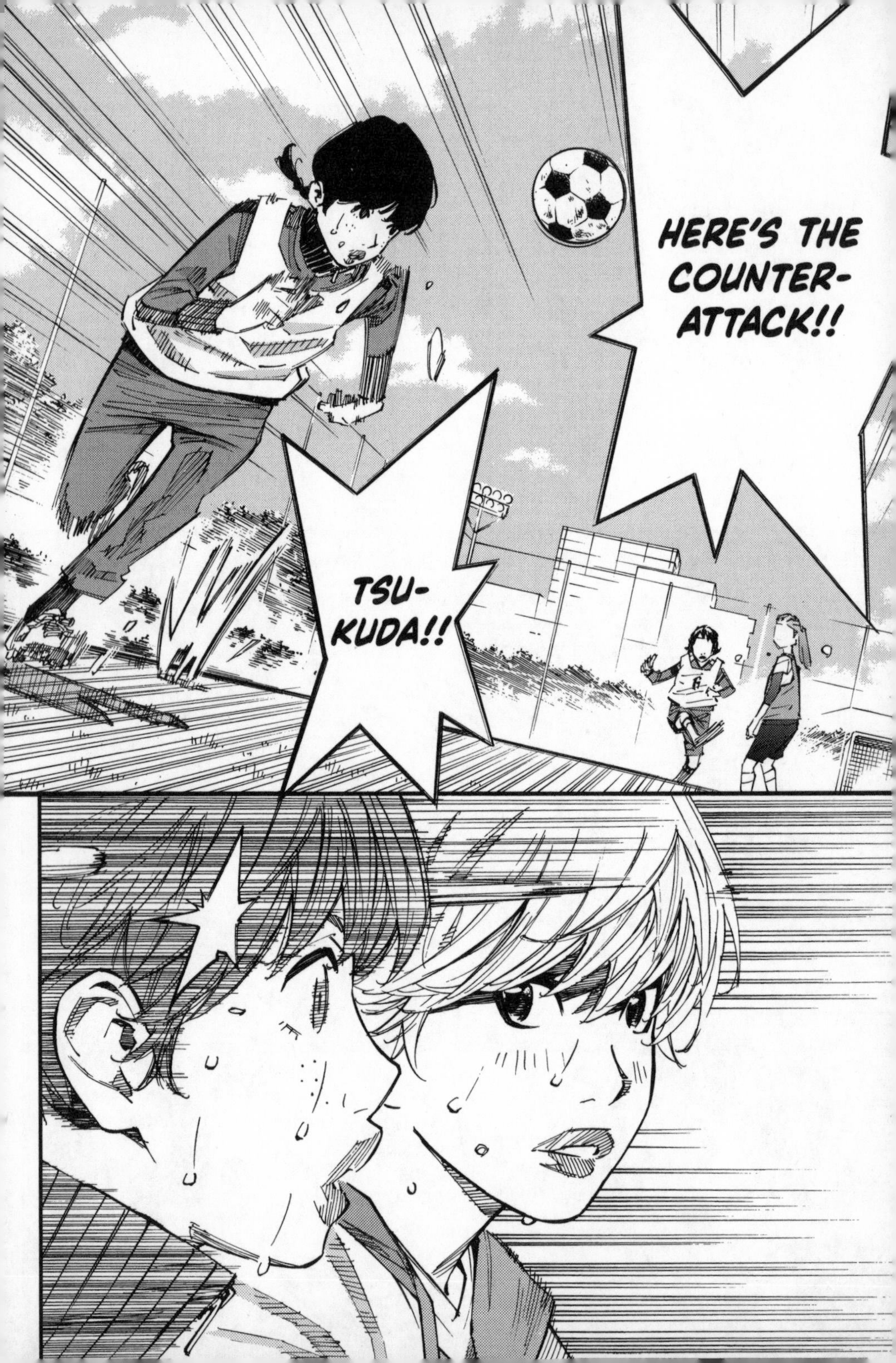
HERE'S THE COUNTER-ATTACK!!
TSU-KUDA!!

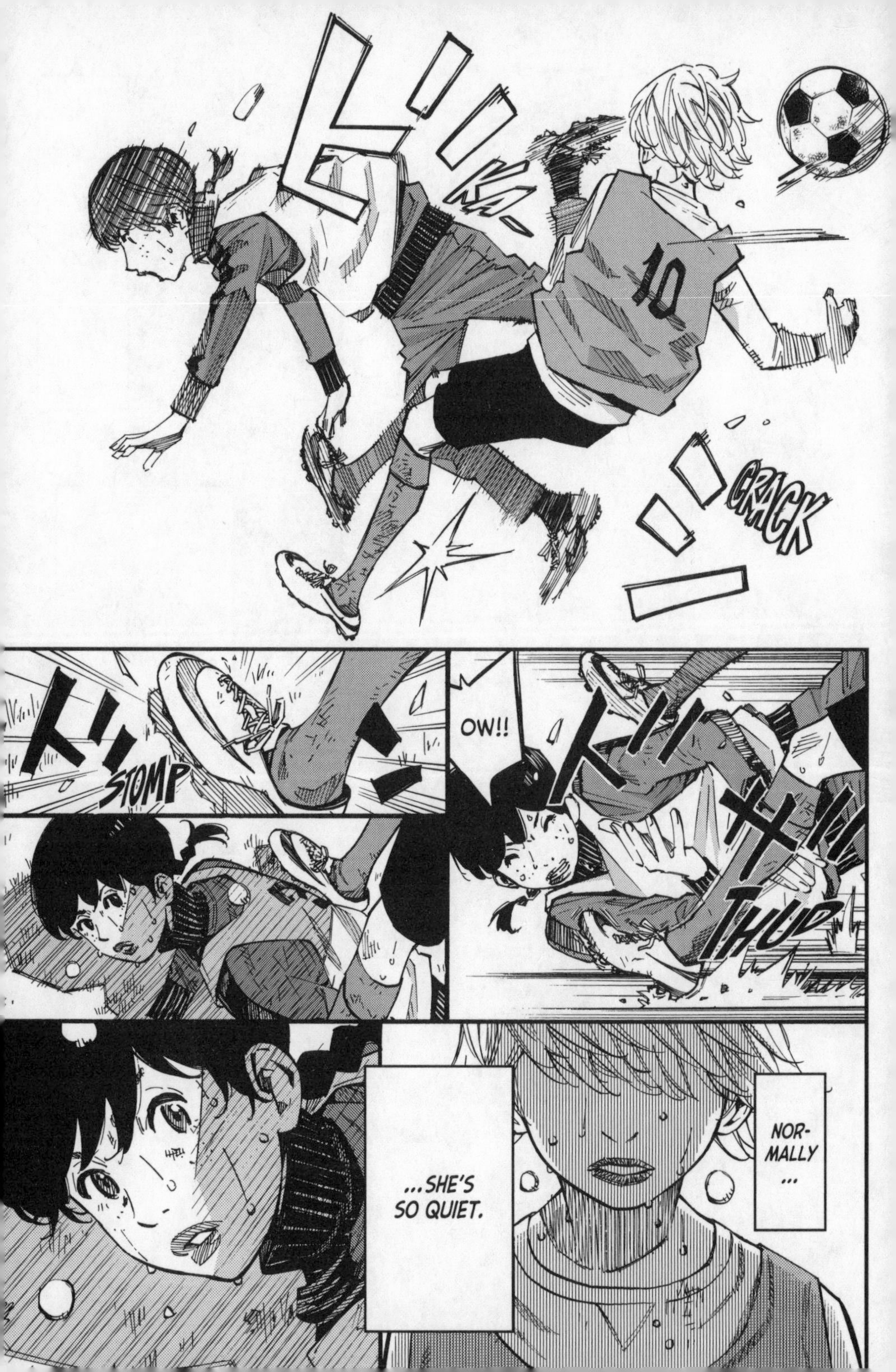
KA-
CRACK
OW!!
THUD
STOMP
NOR-
MALLY
...
...SHE'S
SO QUIET.

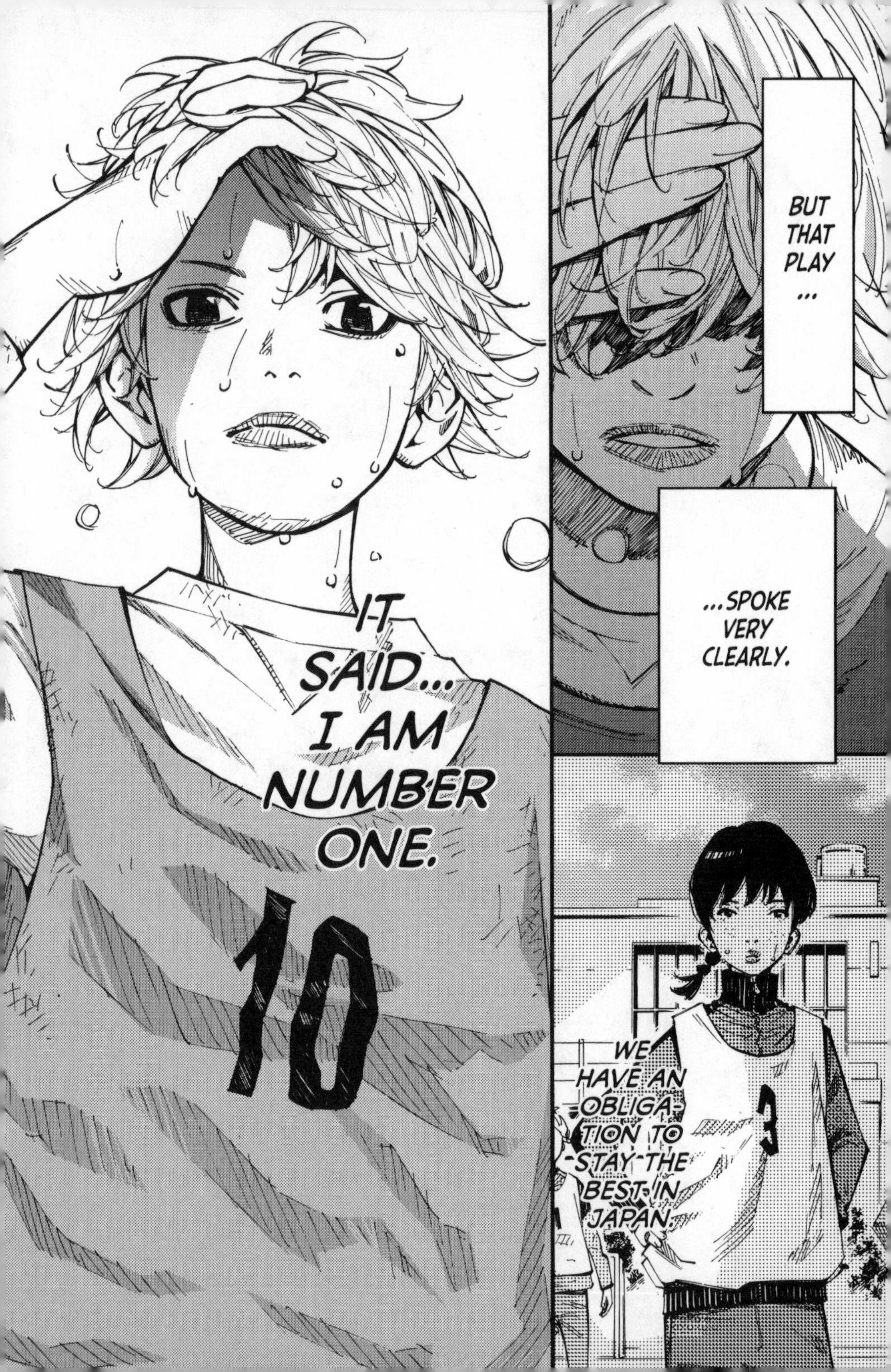
BUT THAT PLAY ...
...SPOKE VERY CLEARLY.
WE HAVE AN OBLIGATION TO STAY THE BEST IN JAPAN.
I-IT SAID... I AM NUMBER ONE.

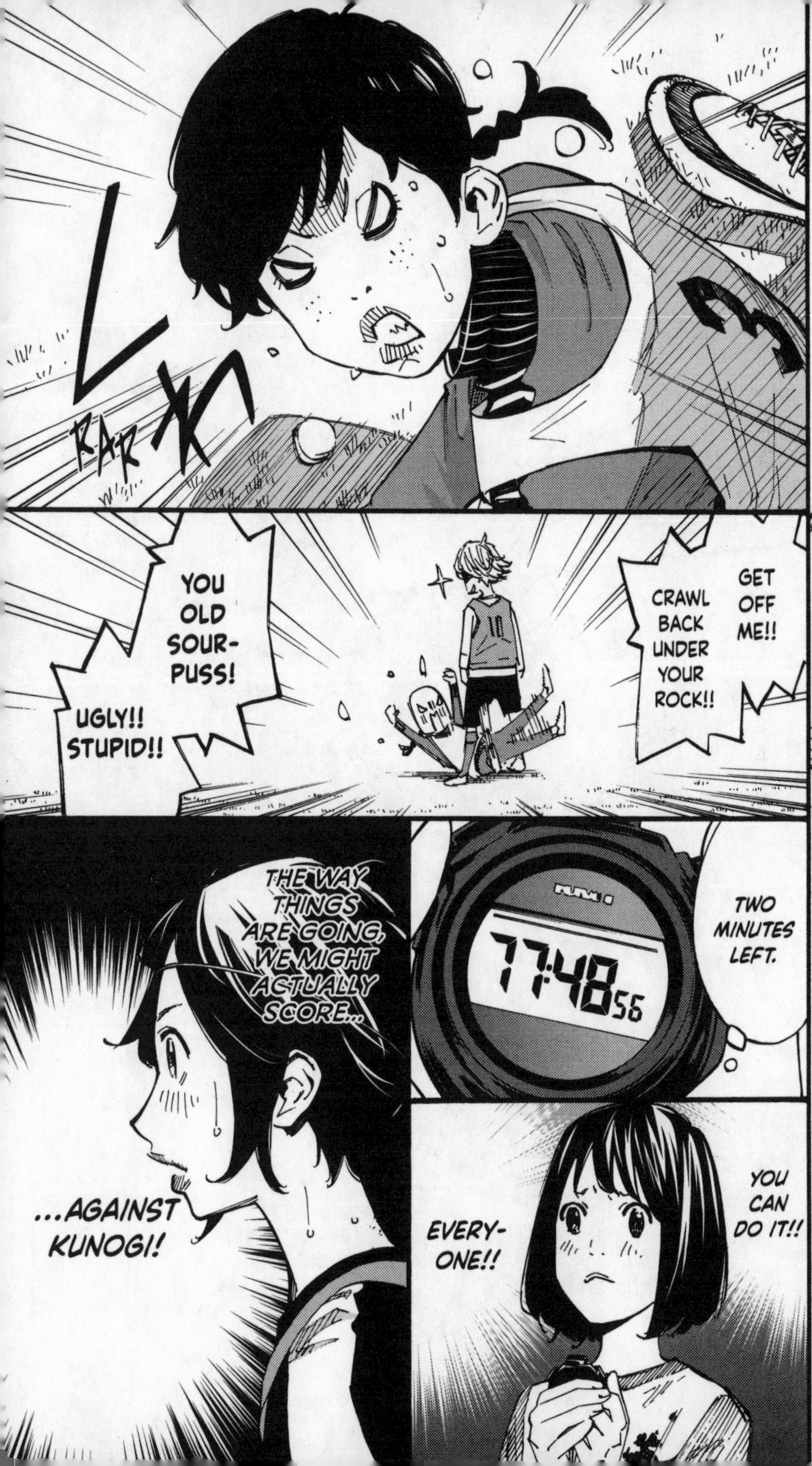
RAR
GET OFF ME!!
CRAWL BACK UNDER YOUR ROCK!!
YOU OLD SOUR-PUSS!
UGLY!! STUPID!!
77:48 56
TWO MINUTES LEFT.
YOU CAN DO IT!!
EVERY-ONE!!
THE WAY THINGS ARE GOING, WE MIGHT ACTUALLY SCORE...
...AGAINST KUNOGI!

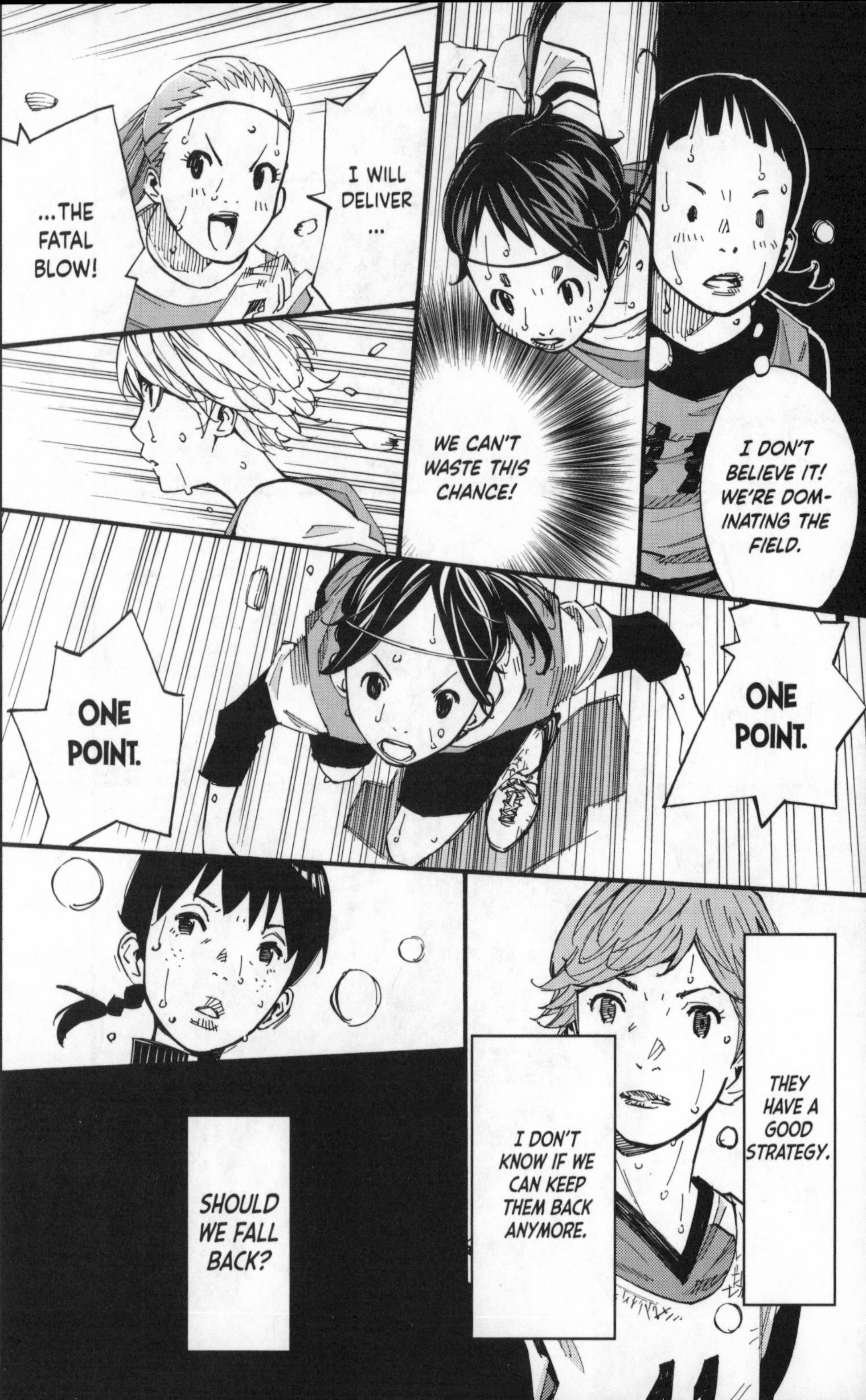
I DON'T BELIEVE IT! WE'RE DOMINATING THE FIELD.
WE CAN'T WASTE THIS CHANCE!
I WILL DELIVER ...
...THE FATAL BLOW!
ONE POINT.
ONE POINT.
THEY HAVE A GOOD STRATEGY.
I DON'T KNOW IF WE CAN KEEP THEM BACK ANYMORE.
SHOULD WE FALL BACK?

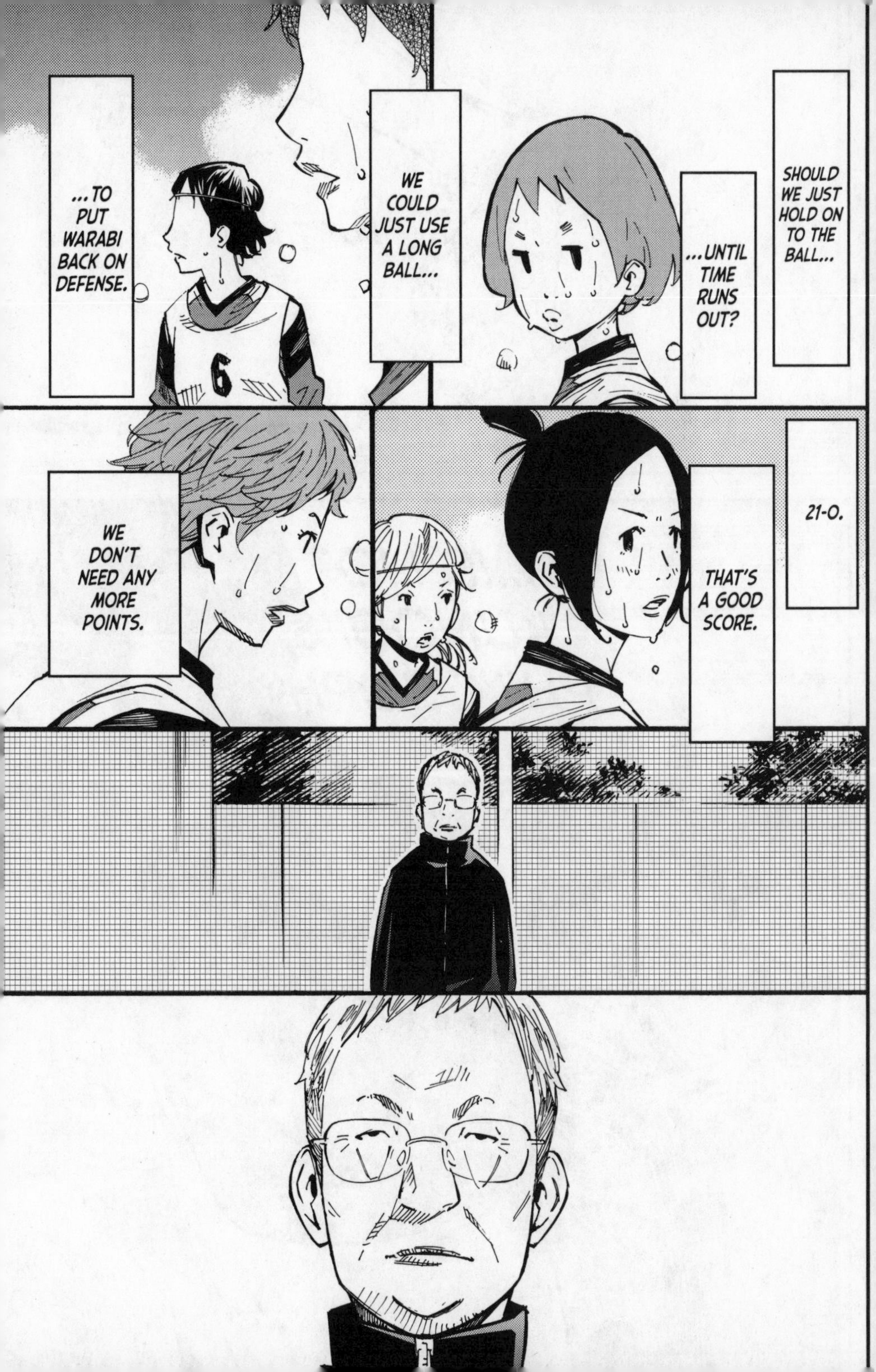
SHOULD WE JUST HOLD ON TO THE BALL...
...UNTIL TIME RUNS OUT?
WE COULD JUST USE A LONG BALL...
...TO PUT WARABI BACK ON DEFENSE.
21-0.
THAT'S A GOOD SCORE.
WE DON'T NEED ANY MORE POINTS.

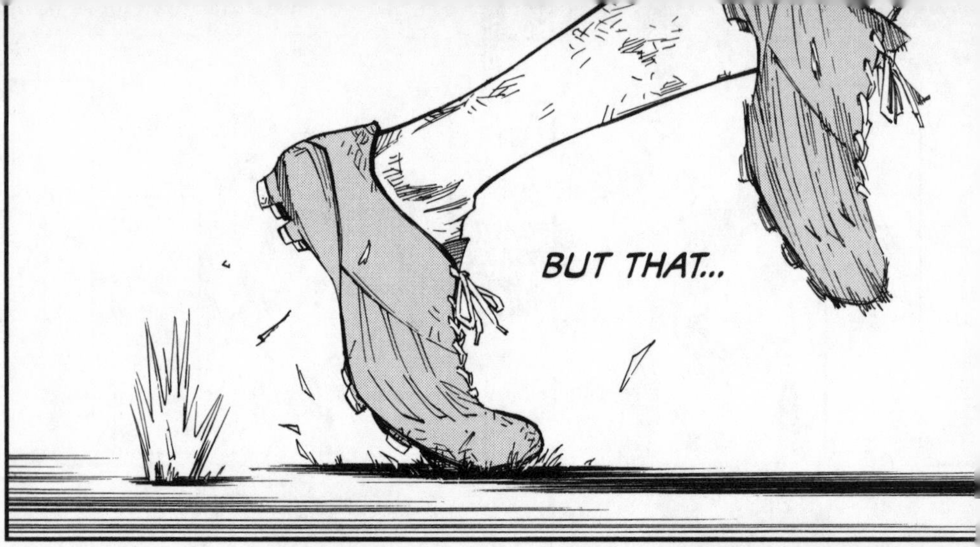
BUT THAT...
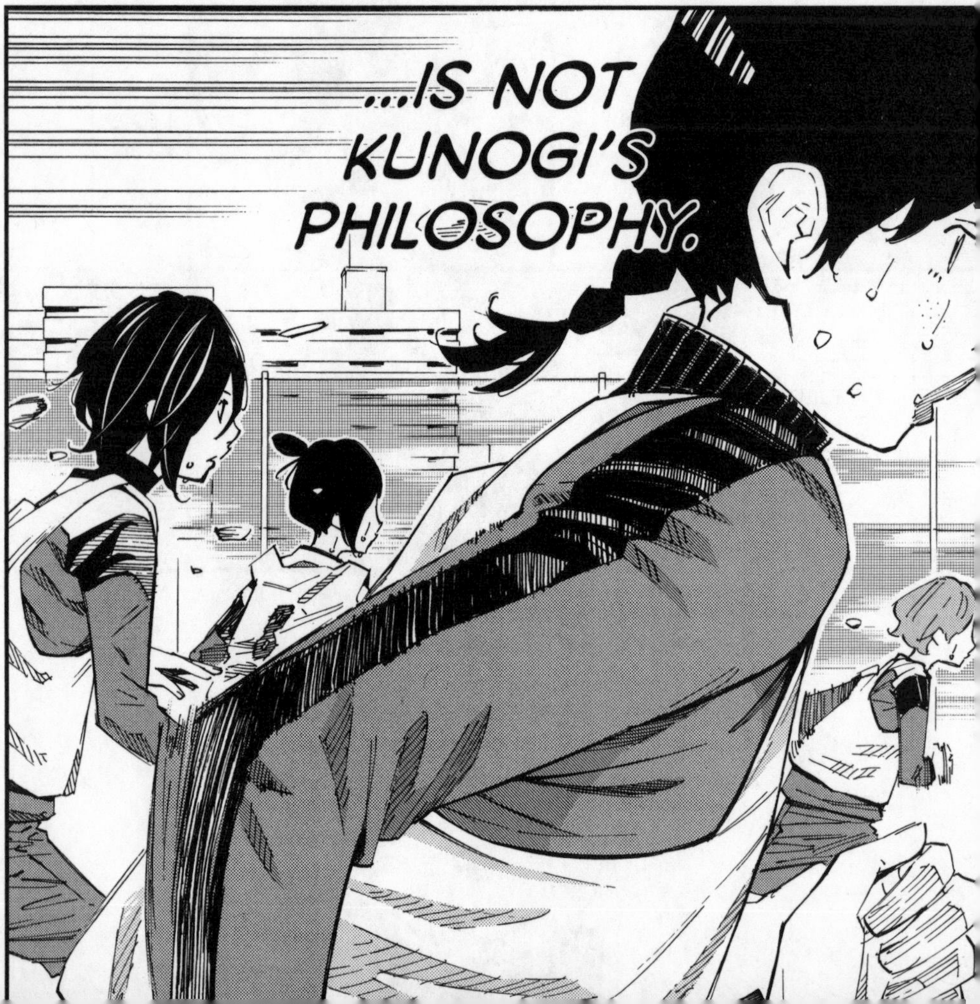
...IS NOT KUNOGI'S PHILOSOPHY.

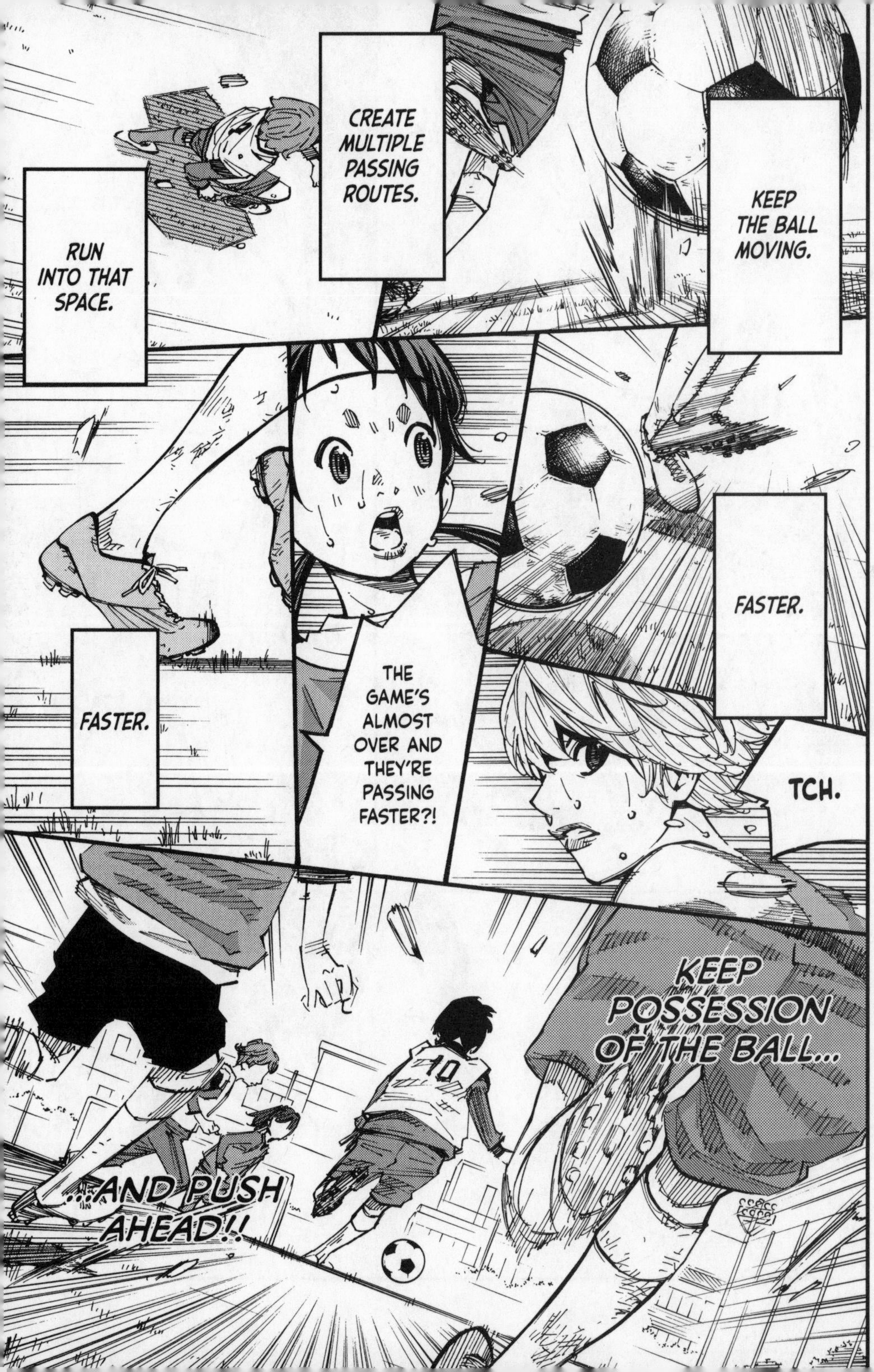
KEEP THE BALL MOVING.
CREATE MULTIPLE PASSING ROUTES.
RUN INTO THAT SPACE.
FASTER.
TCH.
THE GAME'S ALMOST OVER AND THEY'RE PASSING FASTER?!
FASTER.
KEEP POSSESSION OF THE BALL...
...AND PUSH AHEAD!!

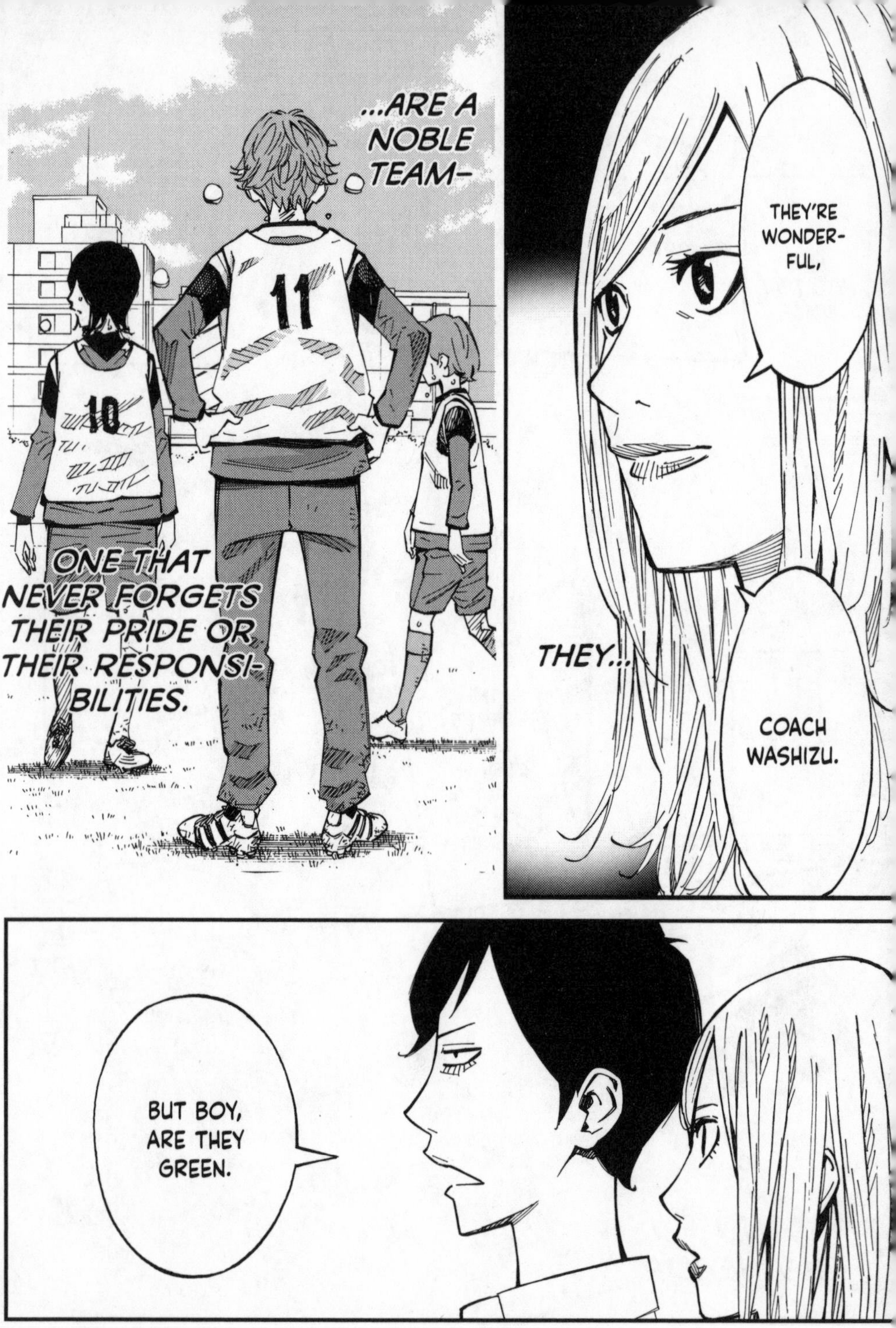
THEY'RE WONDER-FUL,
THEY...
COACH WASHIZU.
...ARE A NOBLE TEAM-
ONE THAT NEVER FORGETS THEIR PRIDE OR THEIR RESPONSI-BILITIES.
BUT BOY, ARE THEY GREEN.

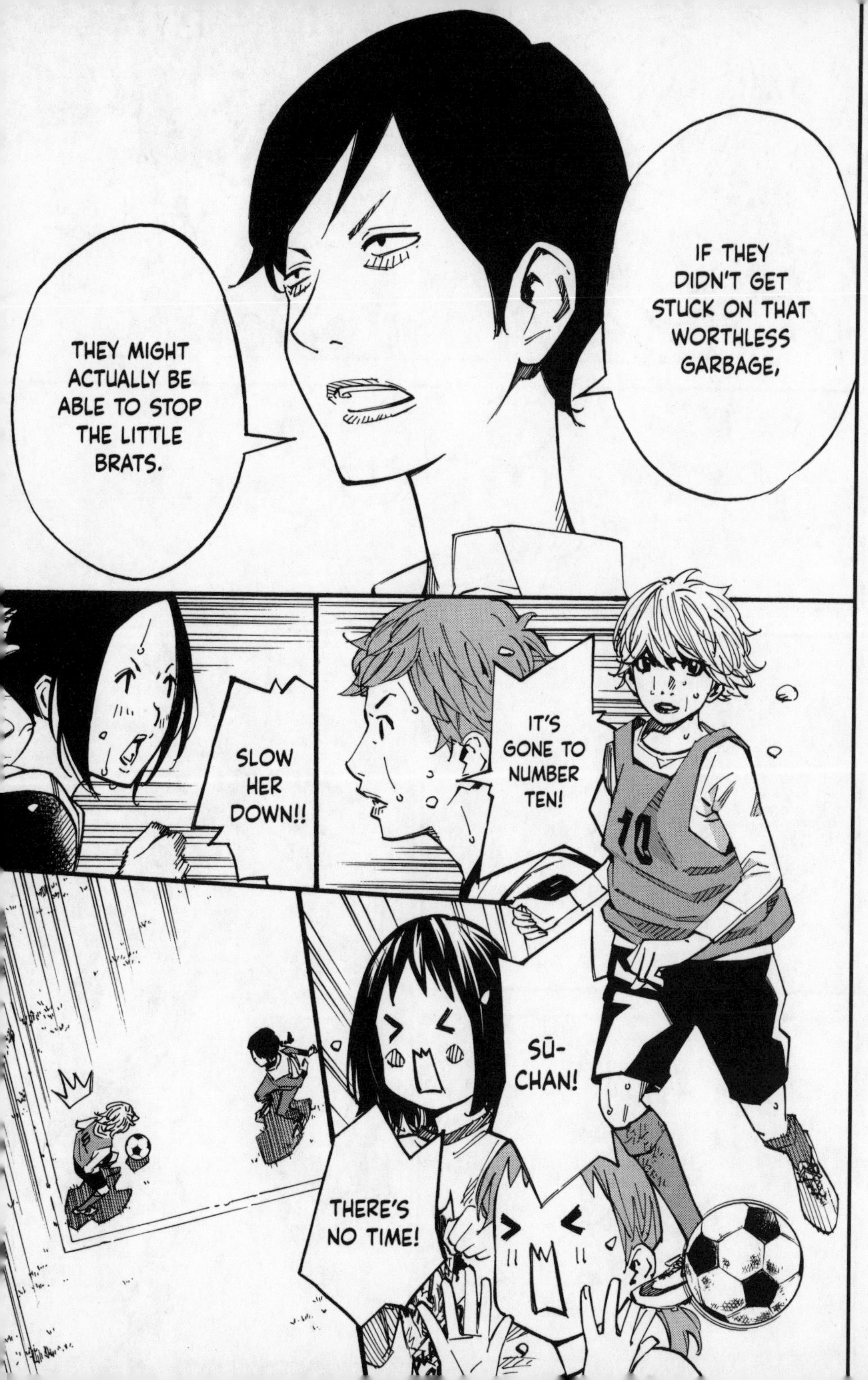
IF THEY DIDN'T GET STUCK ON THAT WORTHLESS GARBAGE,
THEY MIGHT ACTUALLY BE ABLE TO STOP THE LITTLE BRATS.
IT'S GONE TO NUMBER TEN!
SLOW HER DOWN!!
SŪ-CHAN!
THERE'S NO TIME!

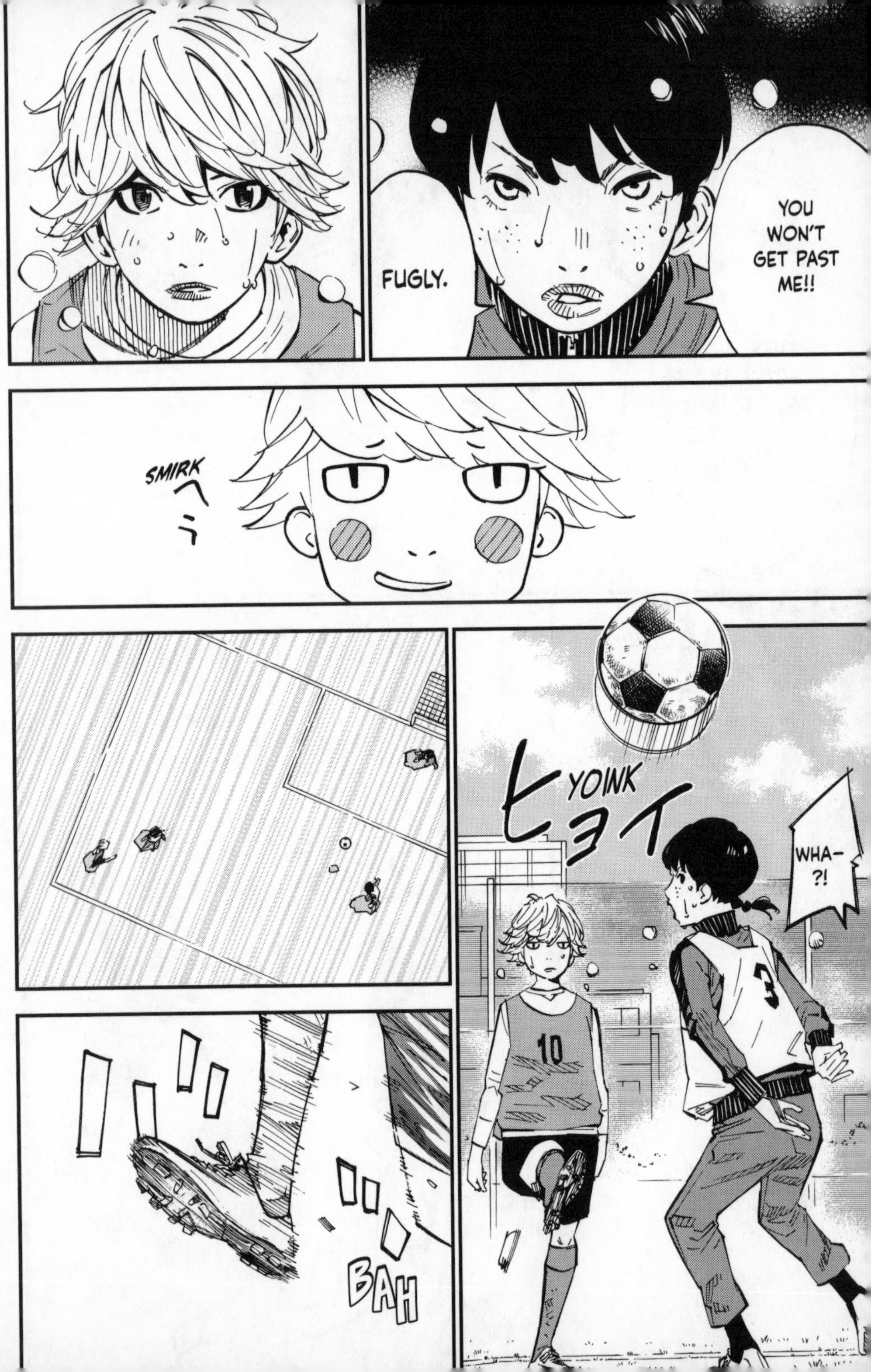

YOU WON'T GET PAST ME!!
FUGLY.
SMIRK
ヘラ
ヒョイ
YOINK
WHA-?!
BAH

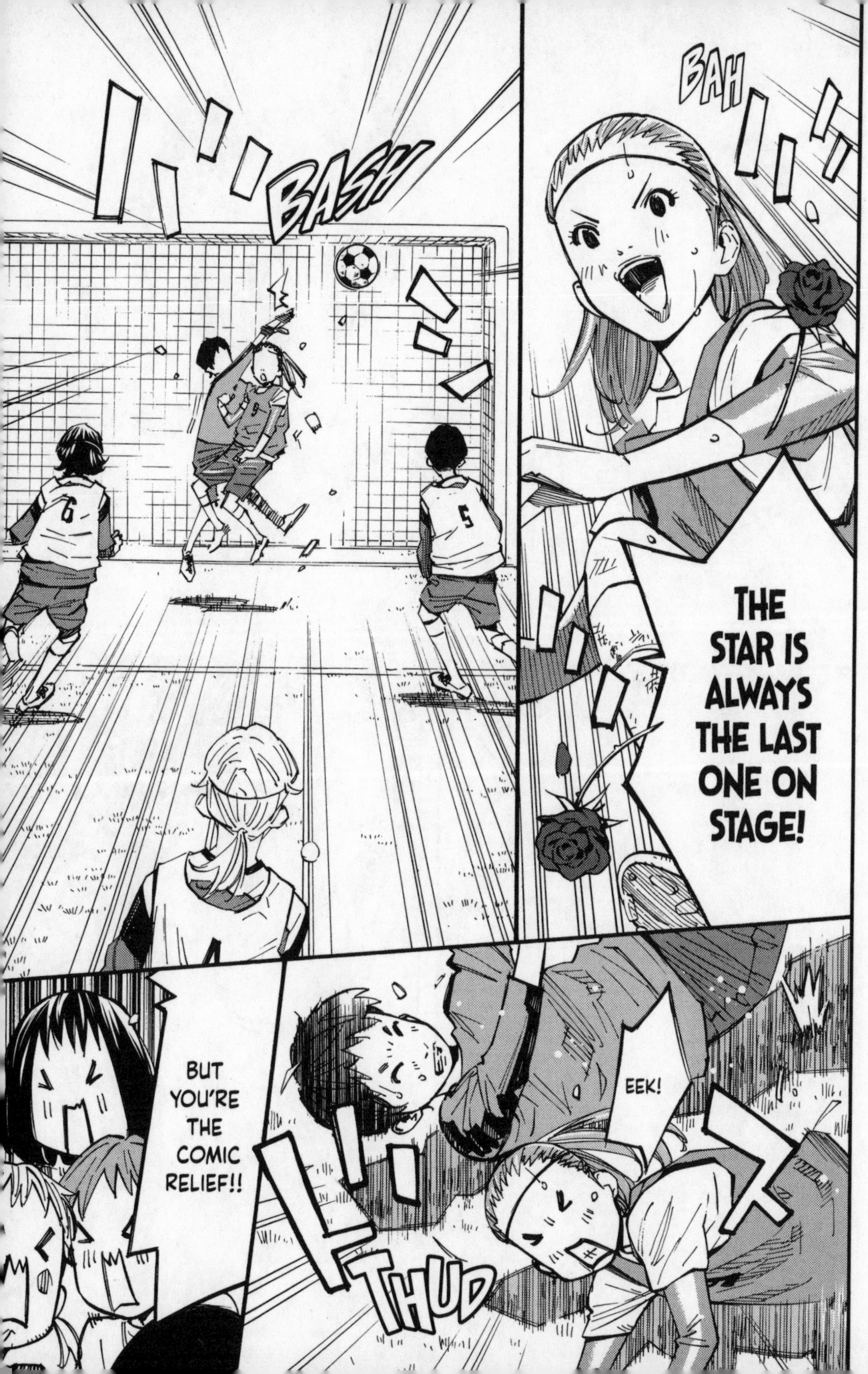
BAH
THE STAR IS ALWAYS THE LAST ONE ON STAGE!
BASH
EEK!
THUD
BUT YOU'RE THE COMIC RELIEF!!

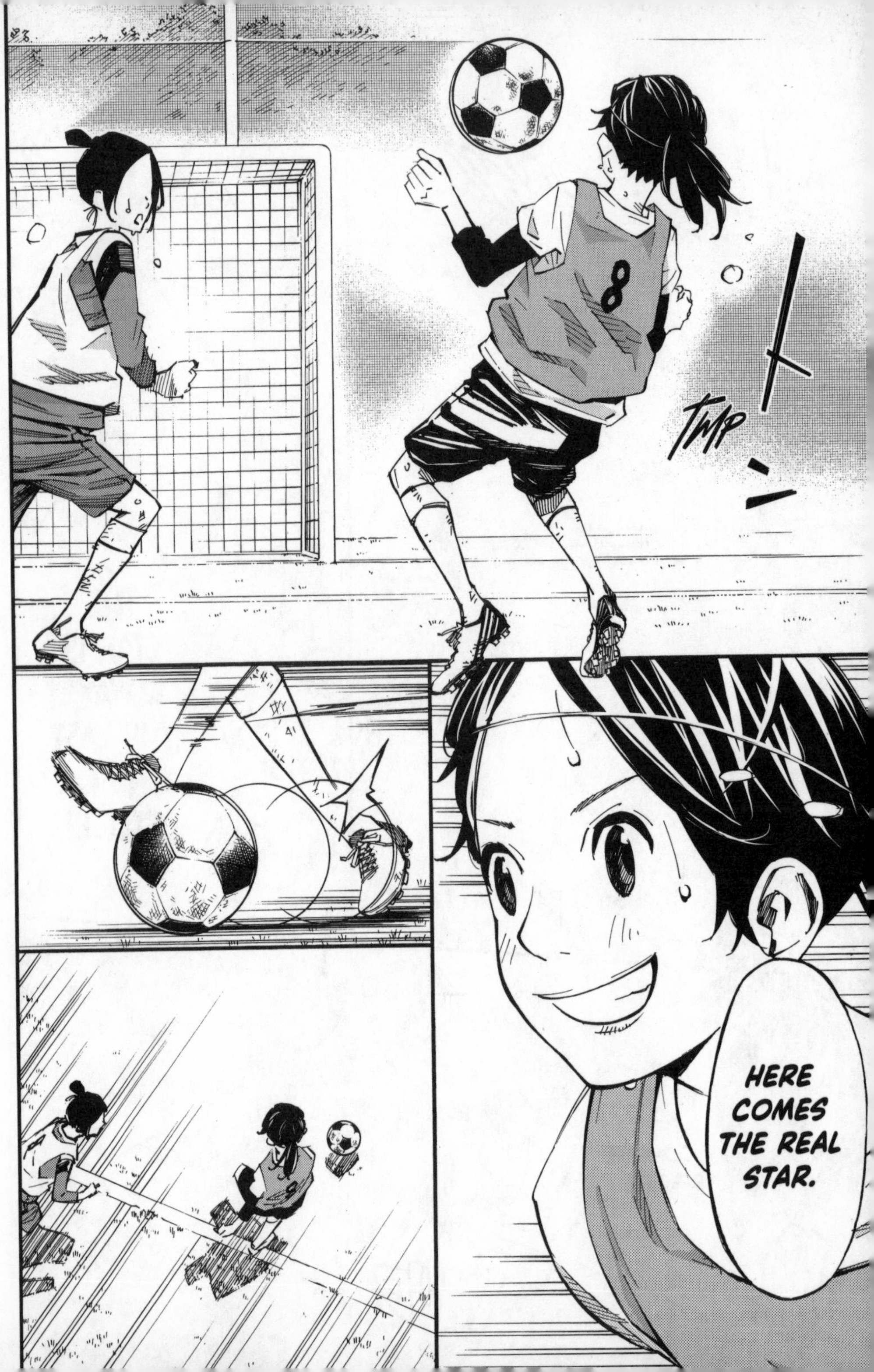
TMP
HERE COMES THE REAL STAR.

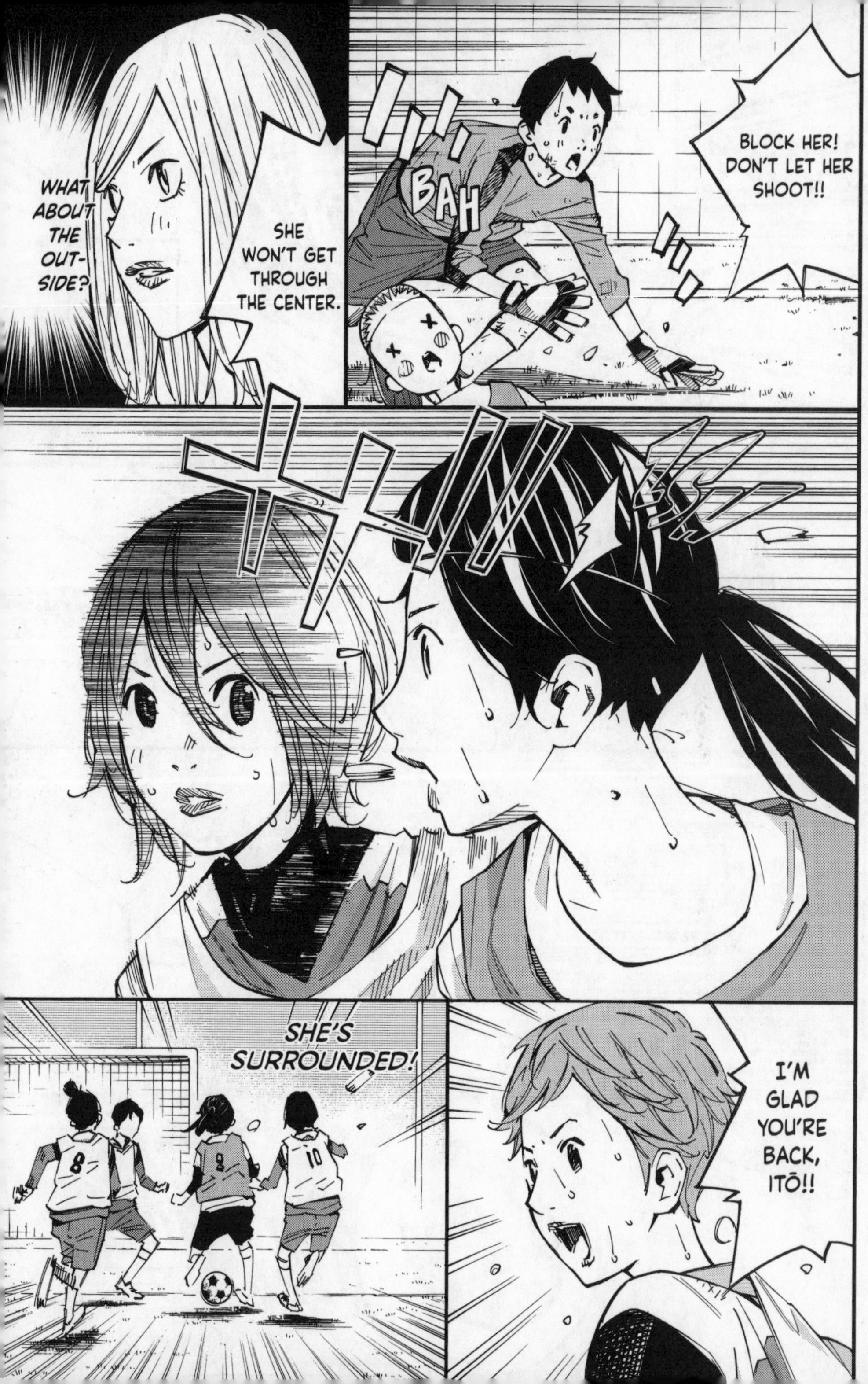
BLOCK HER! DON'T LET HER SHOOT!!
BAH
SHE WON'T GET THROUGH THE CENTER.
WHAT ABOUT THE OUT-SIDE?
I'M GLAD YOU'RE BACK, ITŌ!!
SHE'S SURROUNDED!

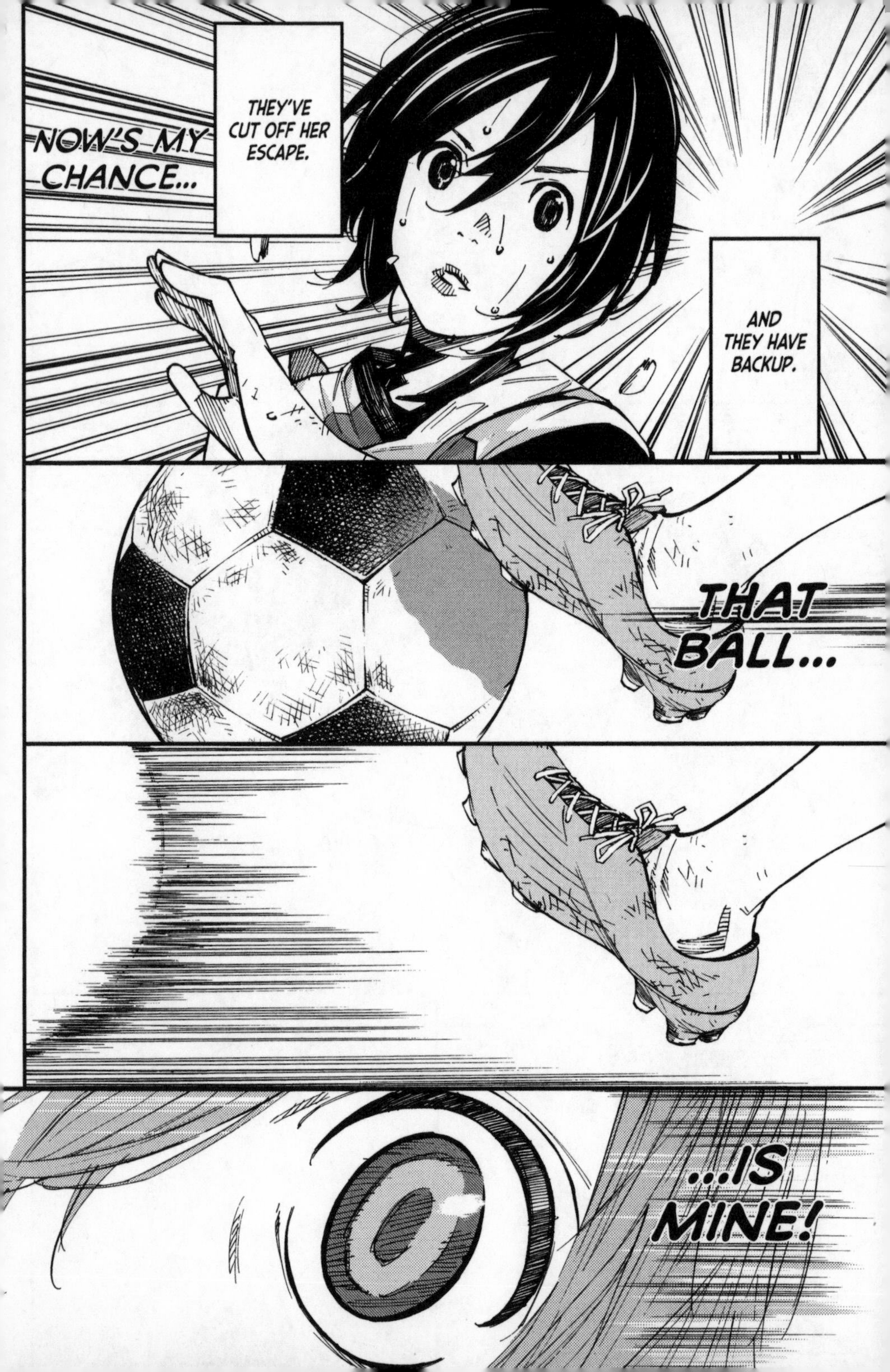
THEY'VE CUT OFF HER ESCAPE.
AND THEY HAVE BACKUP.
NOW'S MY CHANCE...
THAT BALL...
...IS MINE!

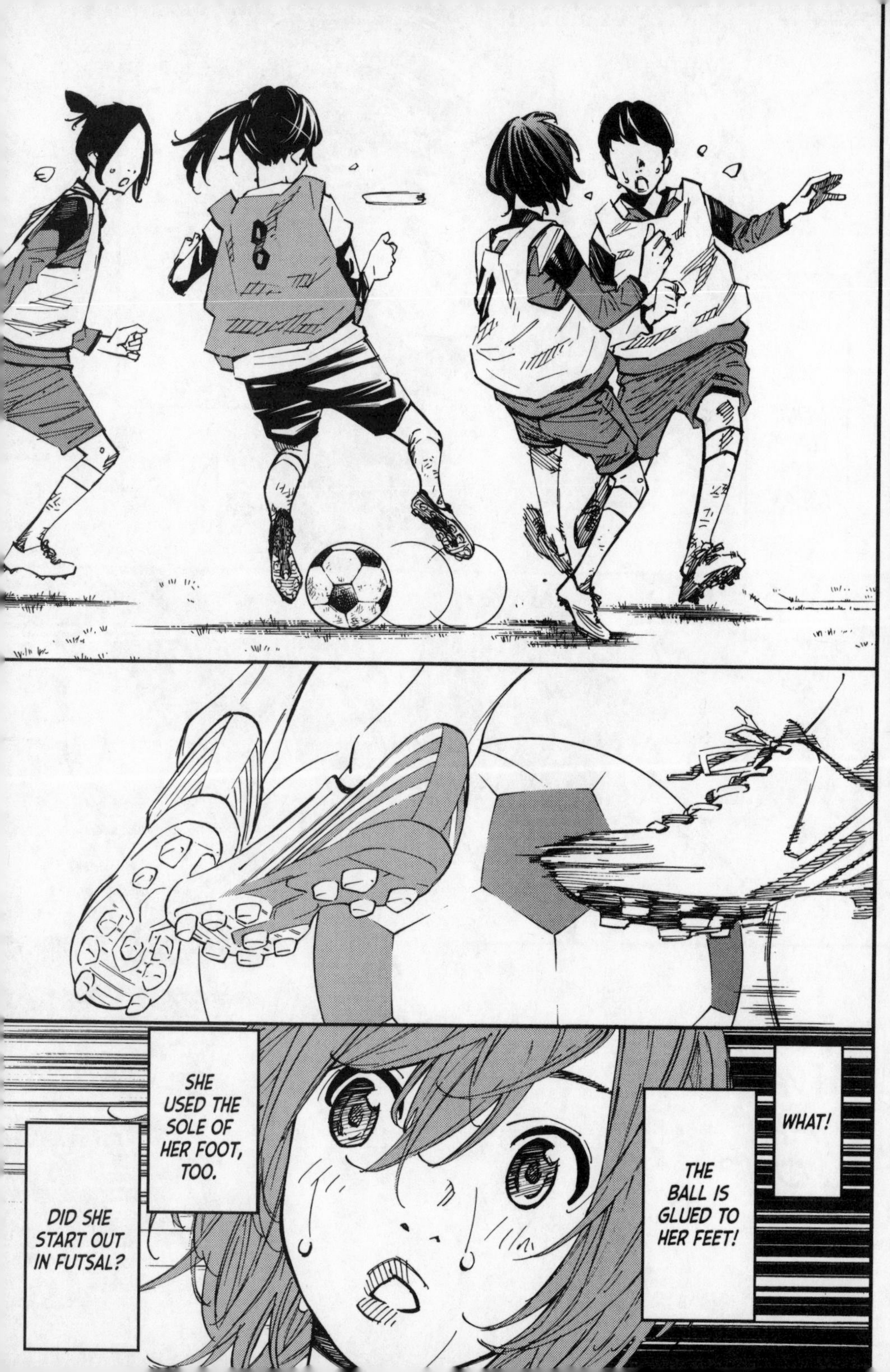
WHAT!
THE BALL IS GLUED TO HER FEET!
SHE USED THE SOLE OF HER FOOT, TOO.
DID SHE START OUT IN FUTSAL?

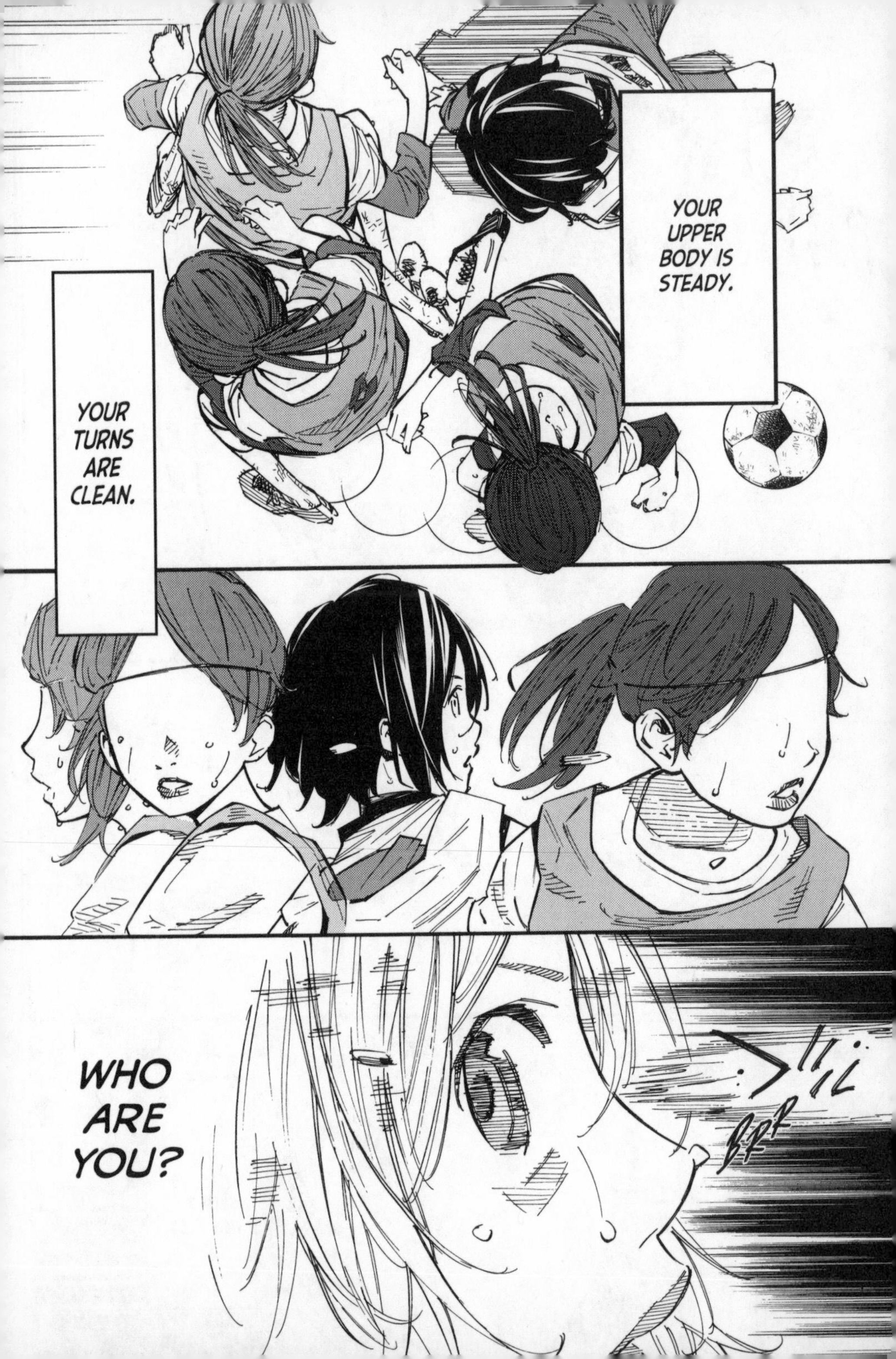
YOUR UPPER BODY IS STEADY.
YOUR TURNS ARE CLEAN.
BRR
WHO ARE YOU?

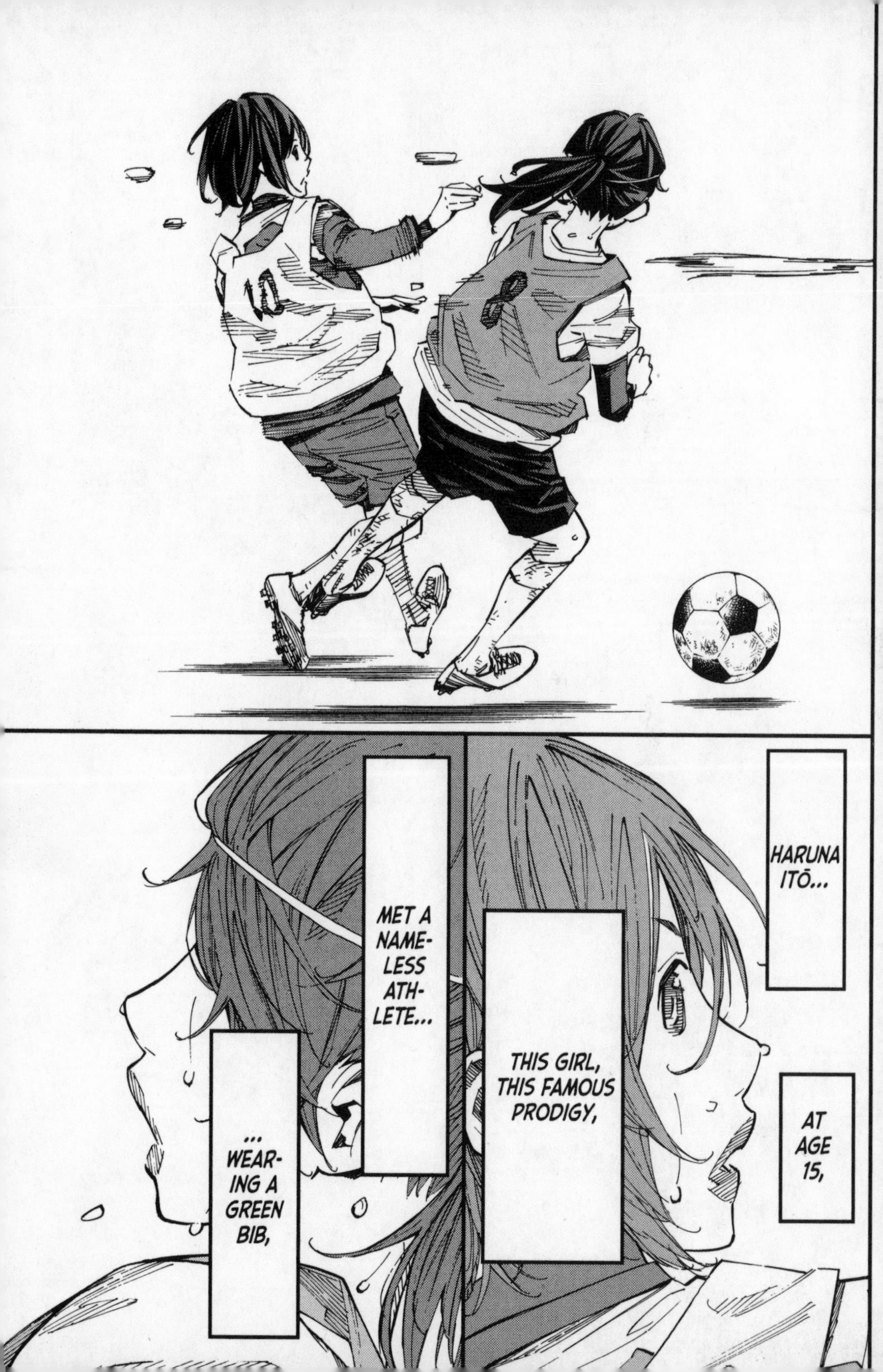
HARUNA ITŌ...
AT AGE 15,
THIS GIRL, THIS FAMOUS PRODIGY,
MET A NAME-LESS ATH-LETE...
... WEAR-ING A GREEN BIB,

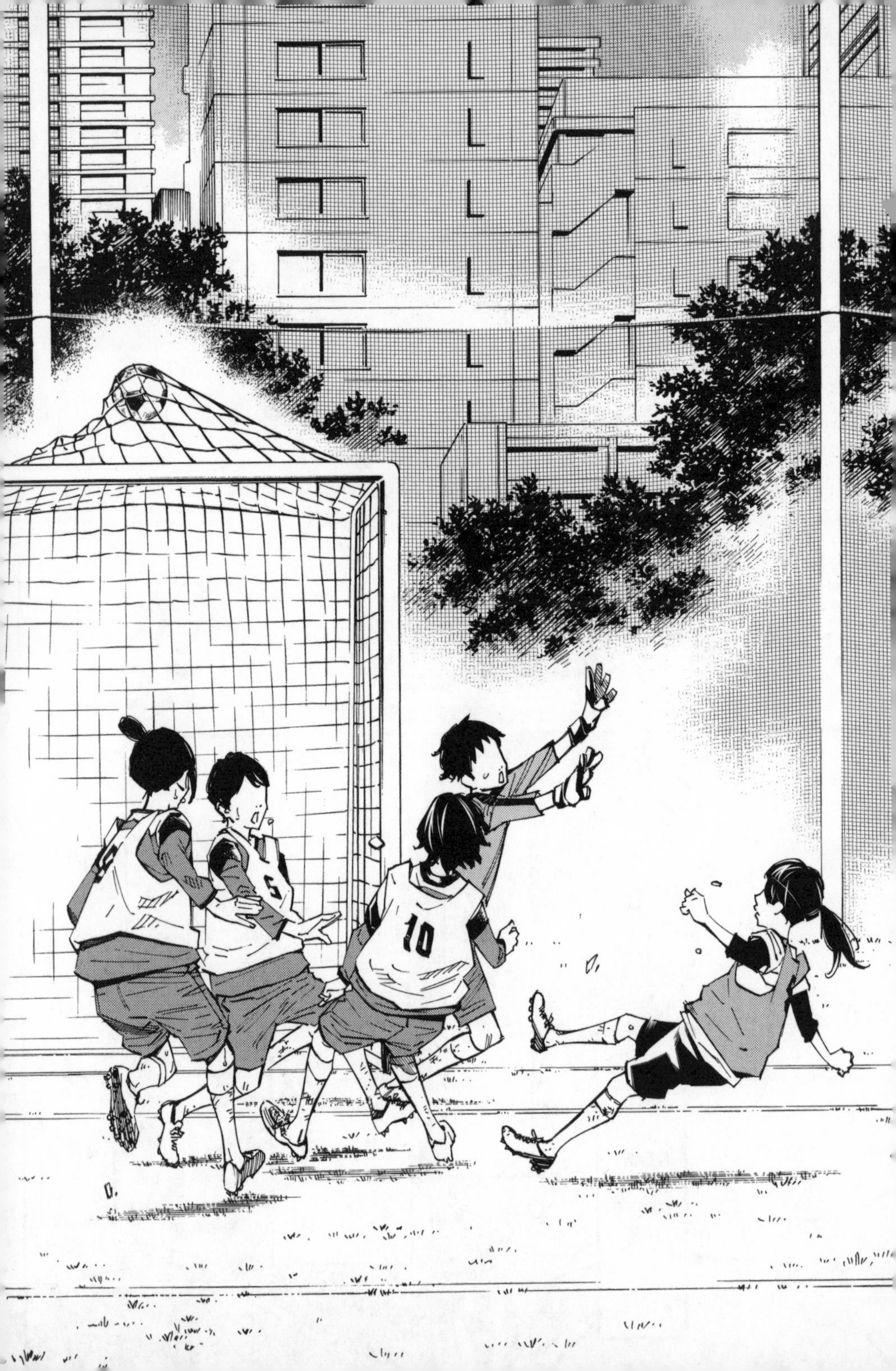
10
5

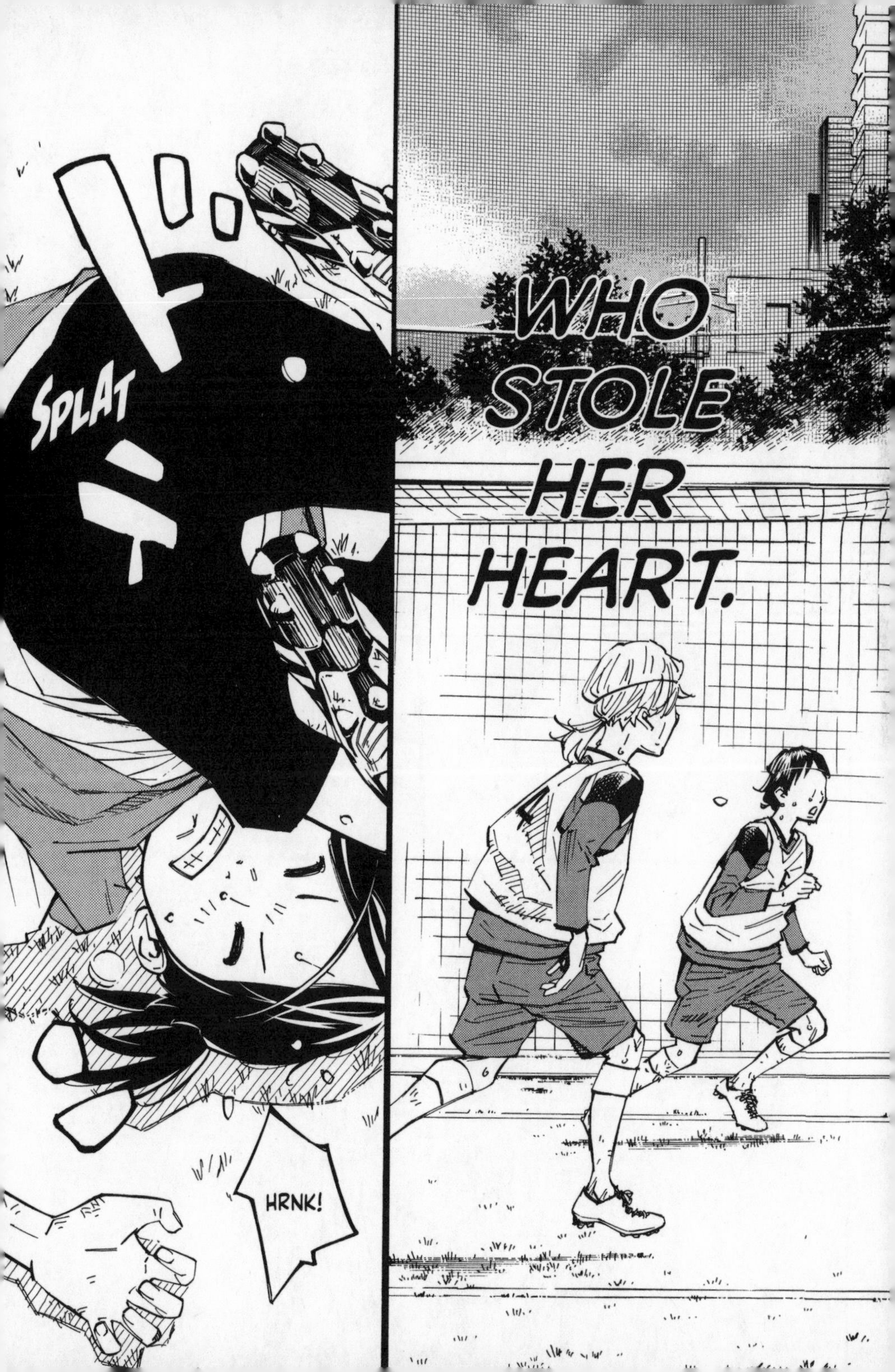
WHO STOLE HER HEART.
SPLAT
HRNK!

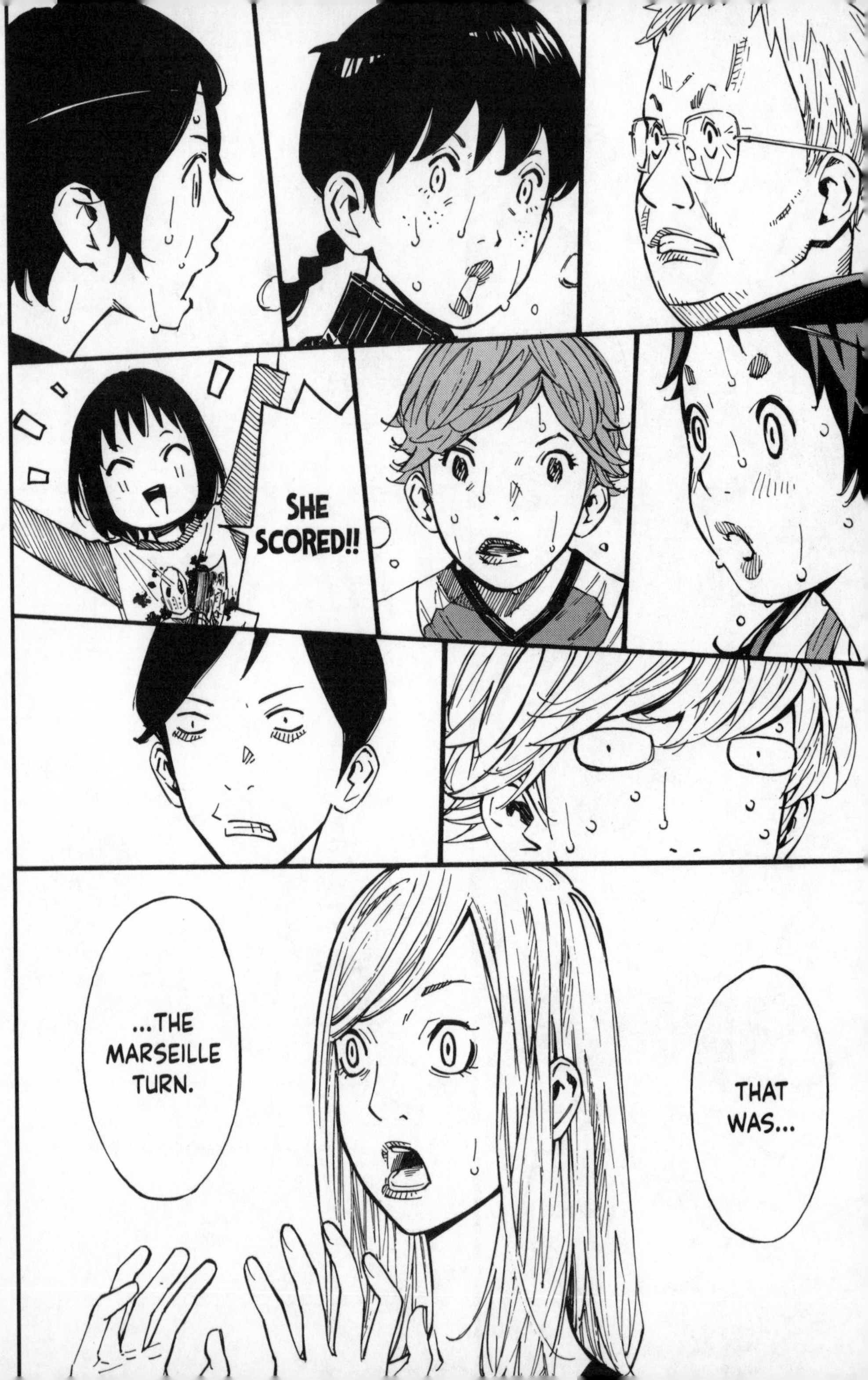
SHE SCORED!!
THAT WAS...
...THE MARSEILLE TURN.

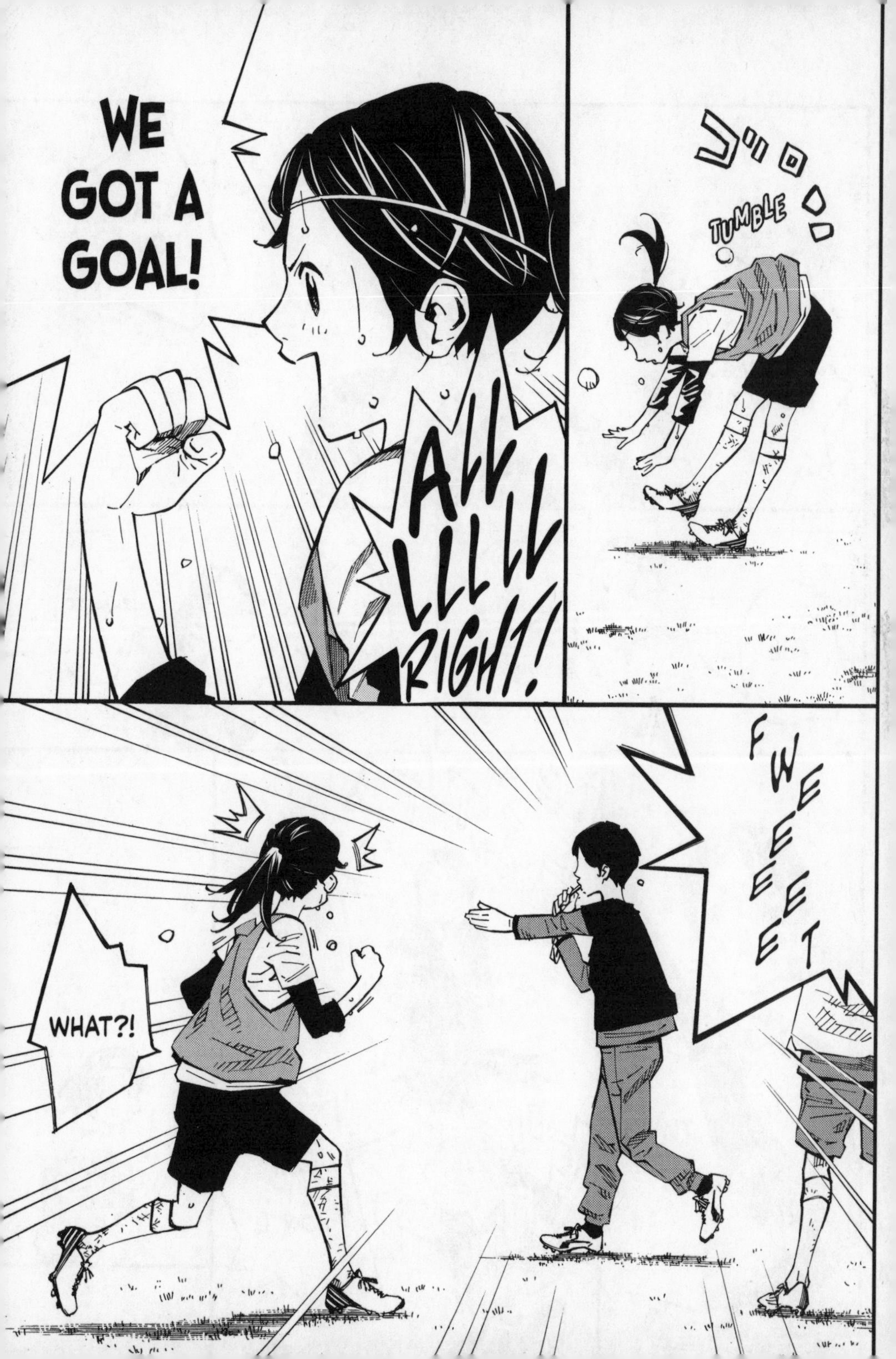
TUMBLE
WE GOT A GOAL!
ALLLLLL RIGHT!
FWEEEEET
WHAT?!

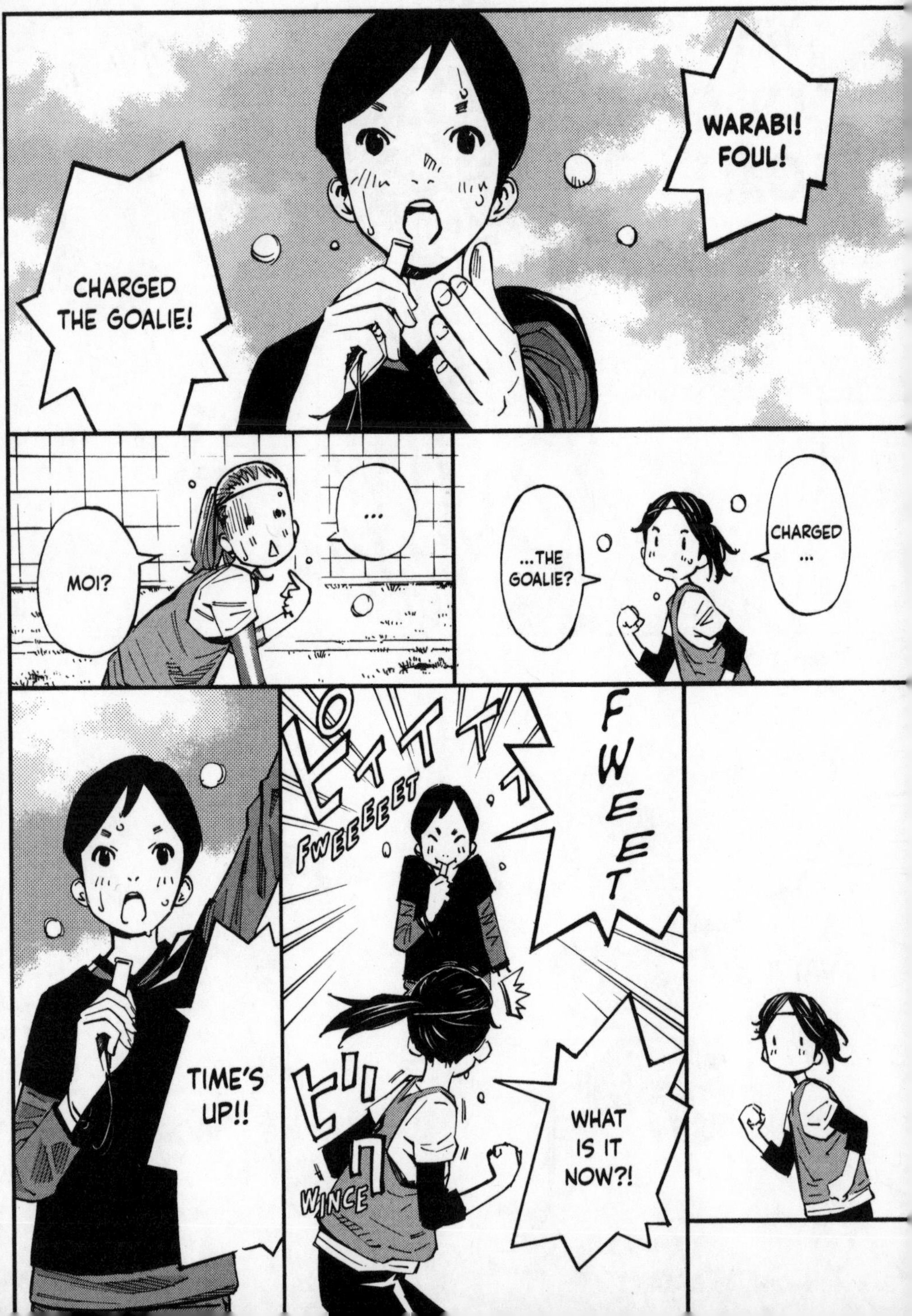
WARABI! FOUL!
CHARGED THE GOALIE!
CHARGED ...
...THE GOALIE?
...
MOI?
FWEET
FWEEEEET
WHAT IS IT NOW?!
WINCE
TIME'S UP!!

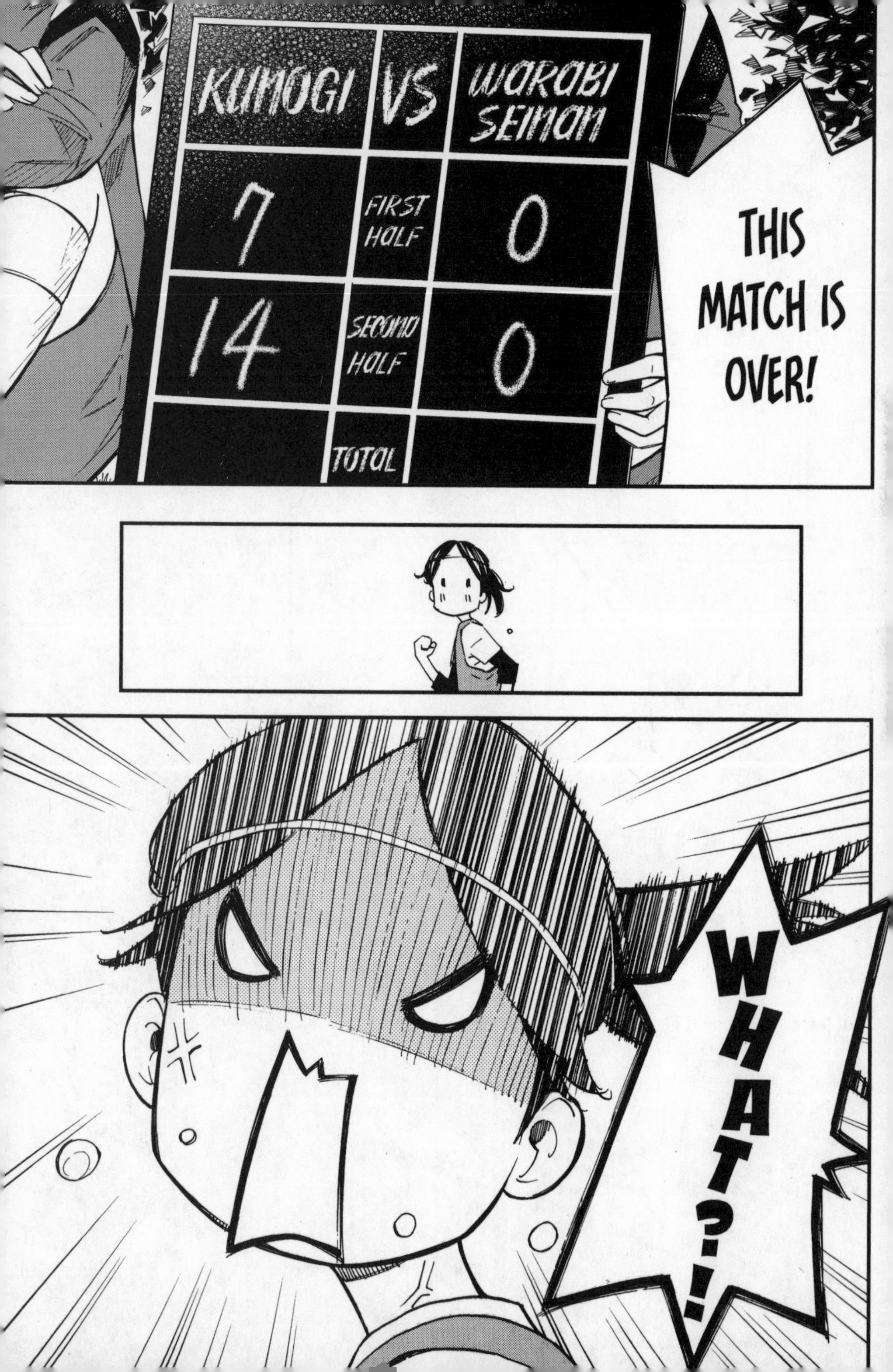
KUMOGI VS WARABI SEINAN
7 FIRST HALF 0
14 SECOND HALF 0
TOTAL
THIS MATCH IS OVER!
WHAT?!!

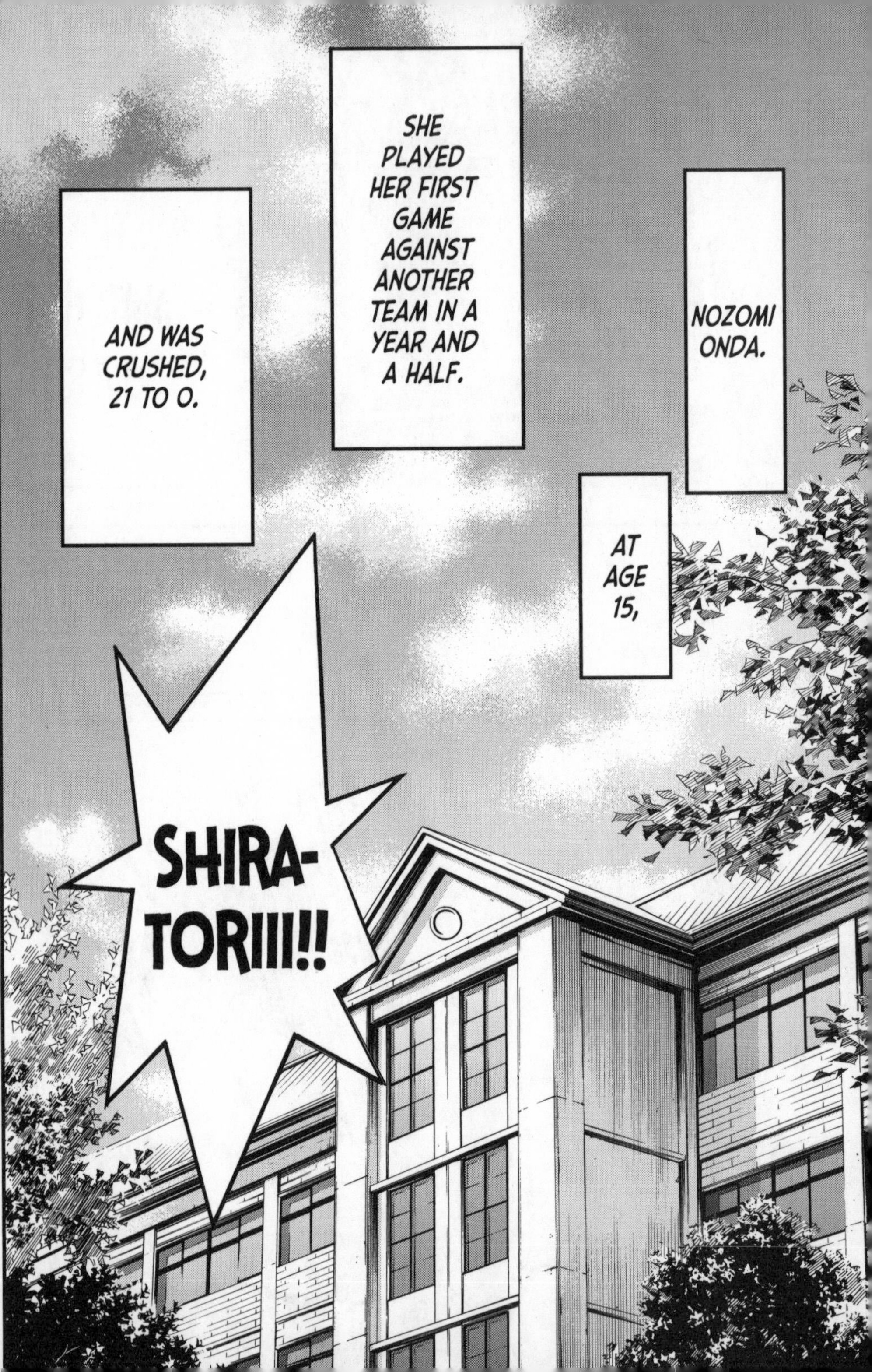
NOZOMI ONDA.
AT AGE 15,
SHE PLAYED HER FIRST GAME AGAINST ANOTHER TEAM IN A YEAR AND A HALF.
AND WAS CRUSHED, 21 TO 0.
SHIRA-TORIIII!!

Farewell, My Dear Cramer

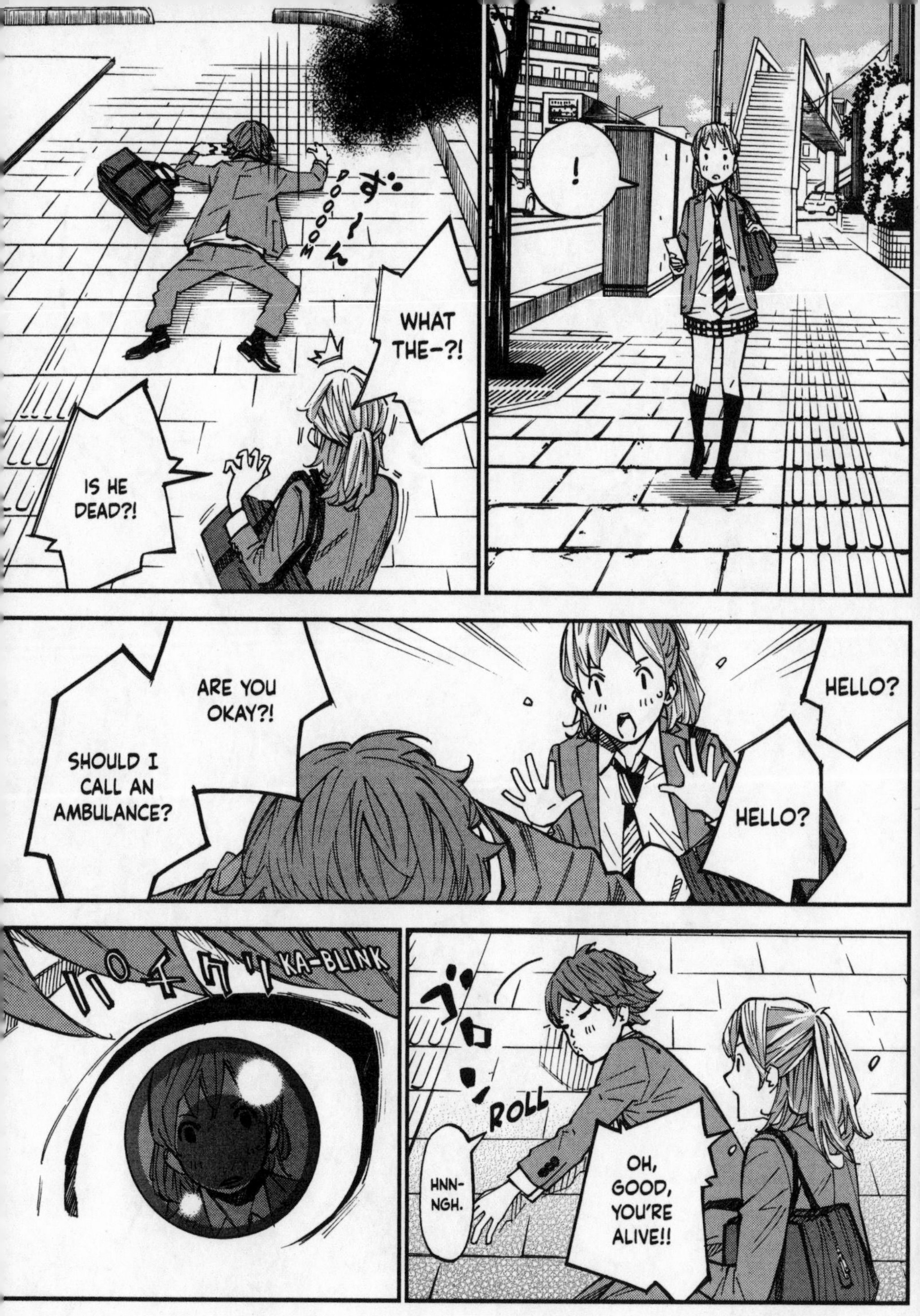
DOOOOOM
WHAT THE-?!
IS HE DEAD?!
!
ARE YOU OKAY?!
SHOULD I CALL AN AMBULANCE?
HELLO?
HELLO?
KA-BLINK
ROLL
HNN-NGH.
OH, GOOD, YOU'RE ALIVE!!

14. THE FRONTIER

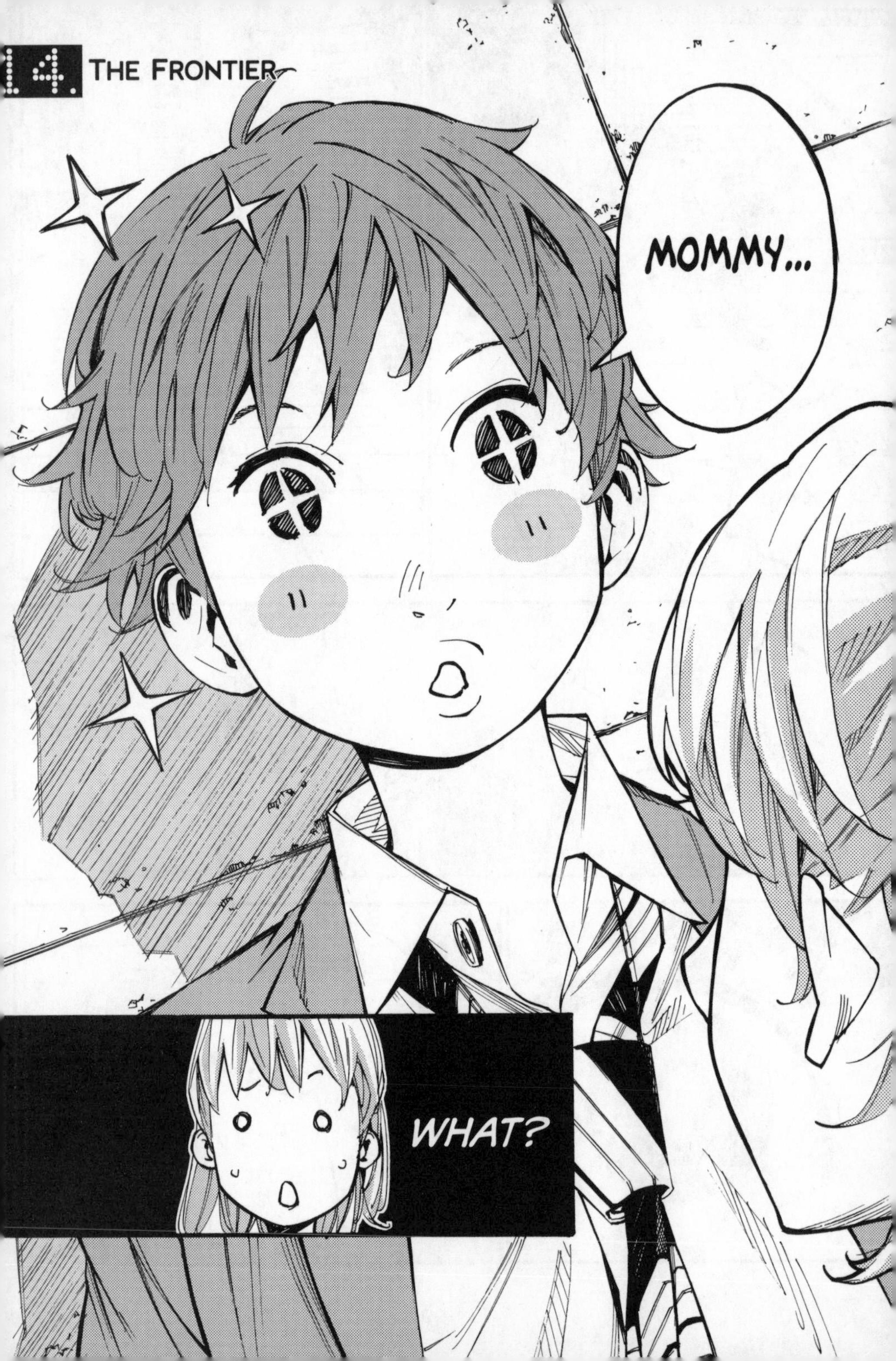
MOMMY...
WHAT?

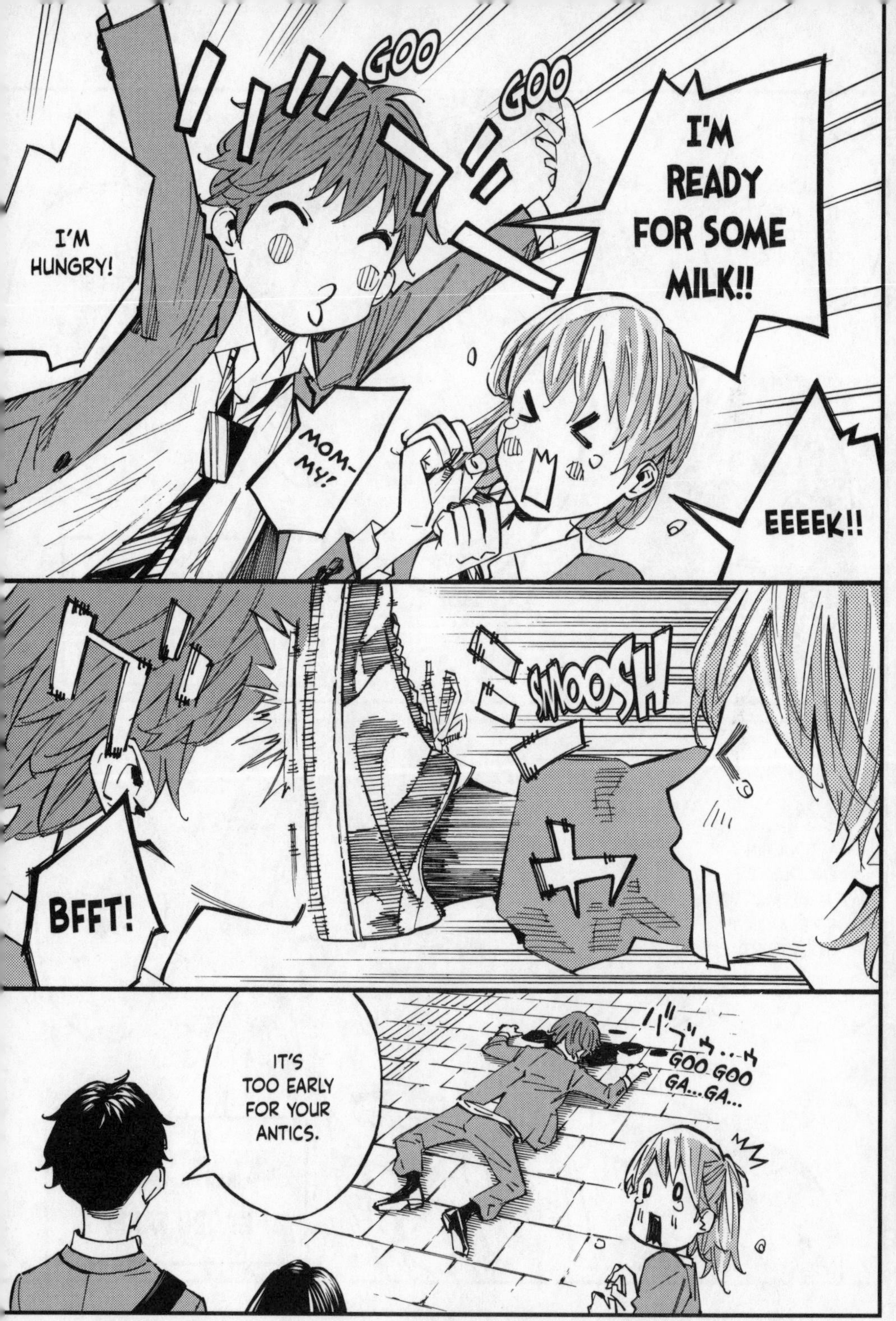
I'M READY FOR SOME MILK!!
GOO
GOO
I'M HUNGRY!
MOM-MY!
EEEEK!!
SMOOSH
BFFT!
GOO GOO GA...GA...
IT'S TOO EARLY FOR YOUR ANTICS.

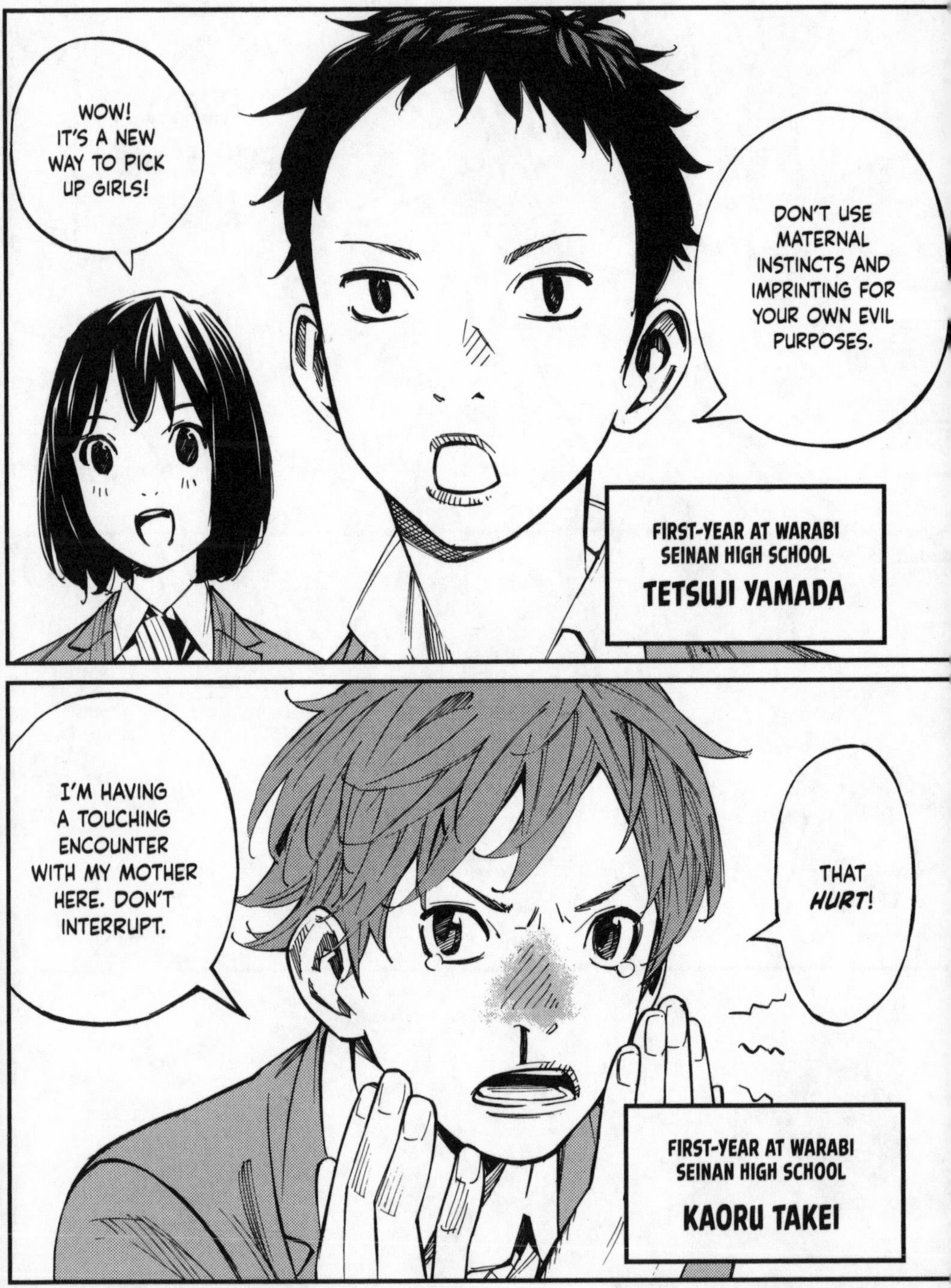
DON'T USE MATERNAL INSTINCTS AND IMPRINTING FOR YOUR OWN EVIL PURPOSES.
WOW! IT'S A NEW WAY TO PICK UP GIRLS!
FIRST-YEAR AT WARABI SEINAN HIGH SCHOOL
TETSUJI YAMADA
THAT *HURT*!
I'M HAVING A TOUCHING ENCOUNTER WITH MY MOTHER HERE. DON'T INTERRUPT.
FIRST-YEAR AT WARABI SEINAN HIGH SCHOOL
KAORU TAKEI

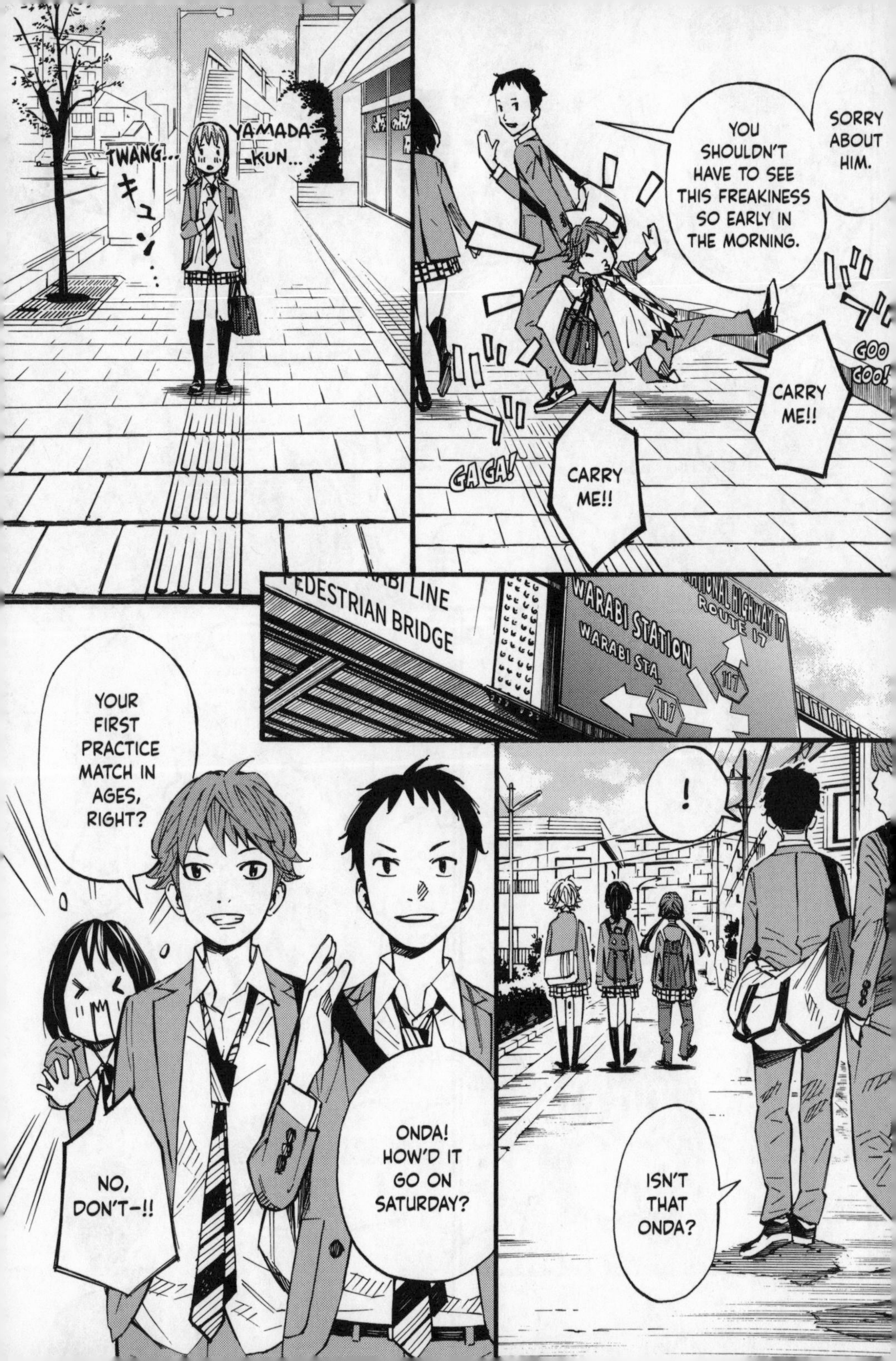
SORRY ABOUT HIM.
YOU SHOULDN'T HAVE TO SEE THIS FREAKINESS SO EARLY IN THE MORNING.
GOO GOO!
CARRY ME!!
CARRY ME!!
GAGA!
YAMADA-KUN...
TWANG...
キュン...
PEDESTRIAN BRIDGE
WARABI STATION
ROUTE 17
WARABI STA.
!
ISN'T THAT ONDA?
ONDA! HOW'D IT GO ON SATURDAY?
YOUR FIRST PRACTICE MATCH IN AGES, RIGHT?
NO, DON'T-!!

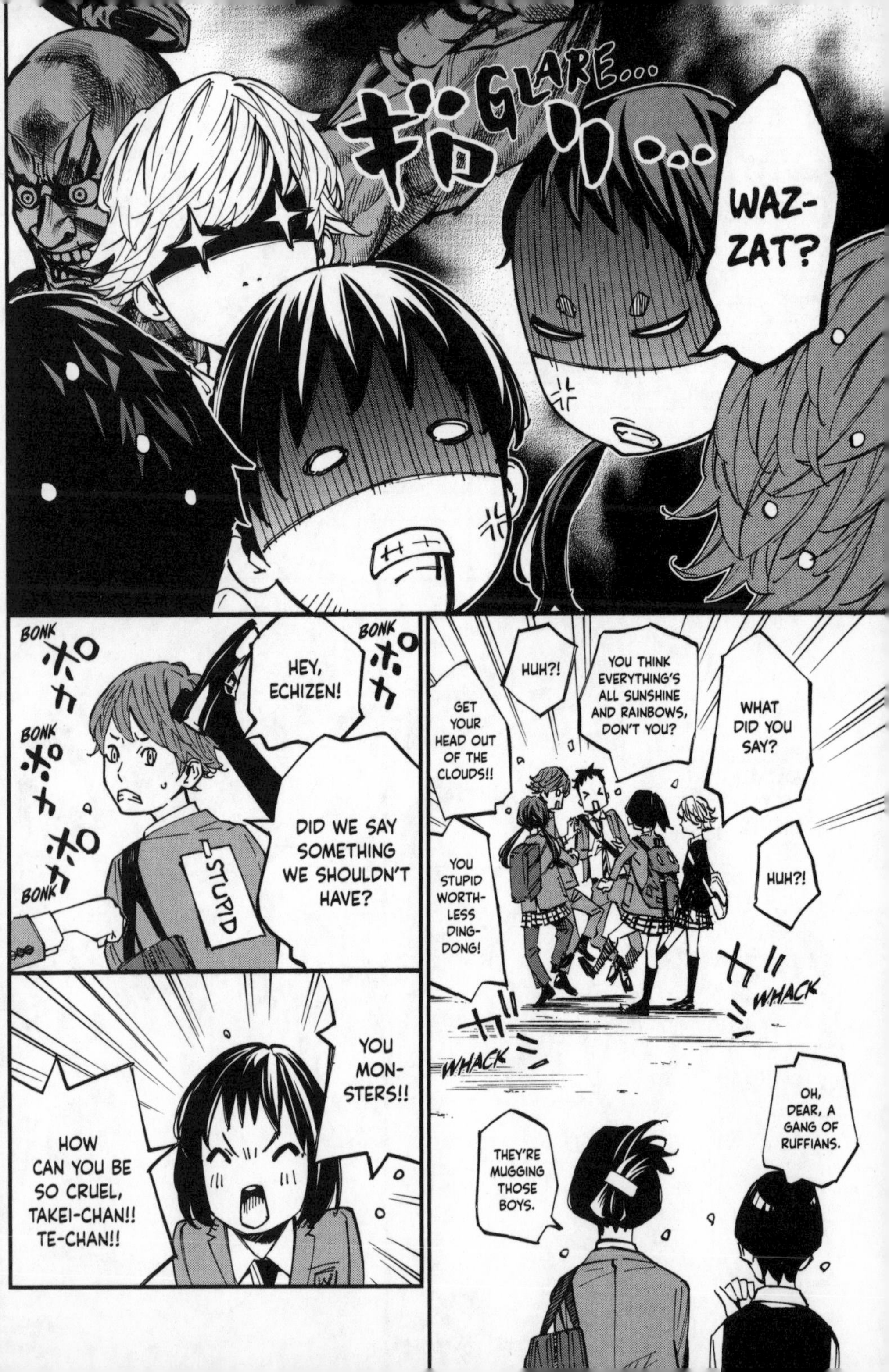
GLARE...
WAZ-ZAT?
WHAT DID YOU SAY?
YOU THINK EVERYTHING'S ALL SUNSHINE AND RAINBOWS, DON'T YOU?
HUH?!
GET YOUR HEAD OUT OF THE CLOUDS!!
HUH?!
YOU STUPID WORTHLESS DING-DONG!
WHACK
WHACK
OH, DEAR, A GANG OF RUFFIANS.
THEY'RE MUGGING THOSE BOYS.
BONK
HEY, ECHIZEN!
BONK
BONK
BONK
DID WE SAY SOMETHING WE SHOULDN'T HAVE?
STUPID
YOU MONSTERS!!
HOW CAN YOU BE SO CRUEL, TAKEI-CHAN!! TE-CHAN!!

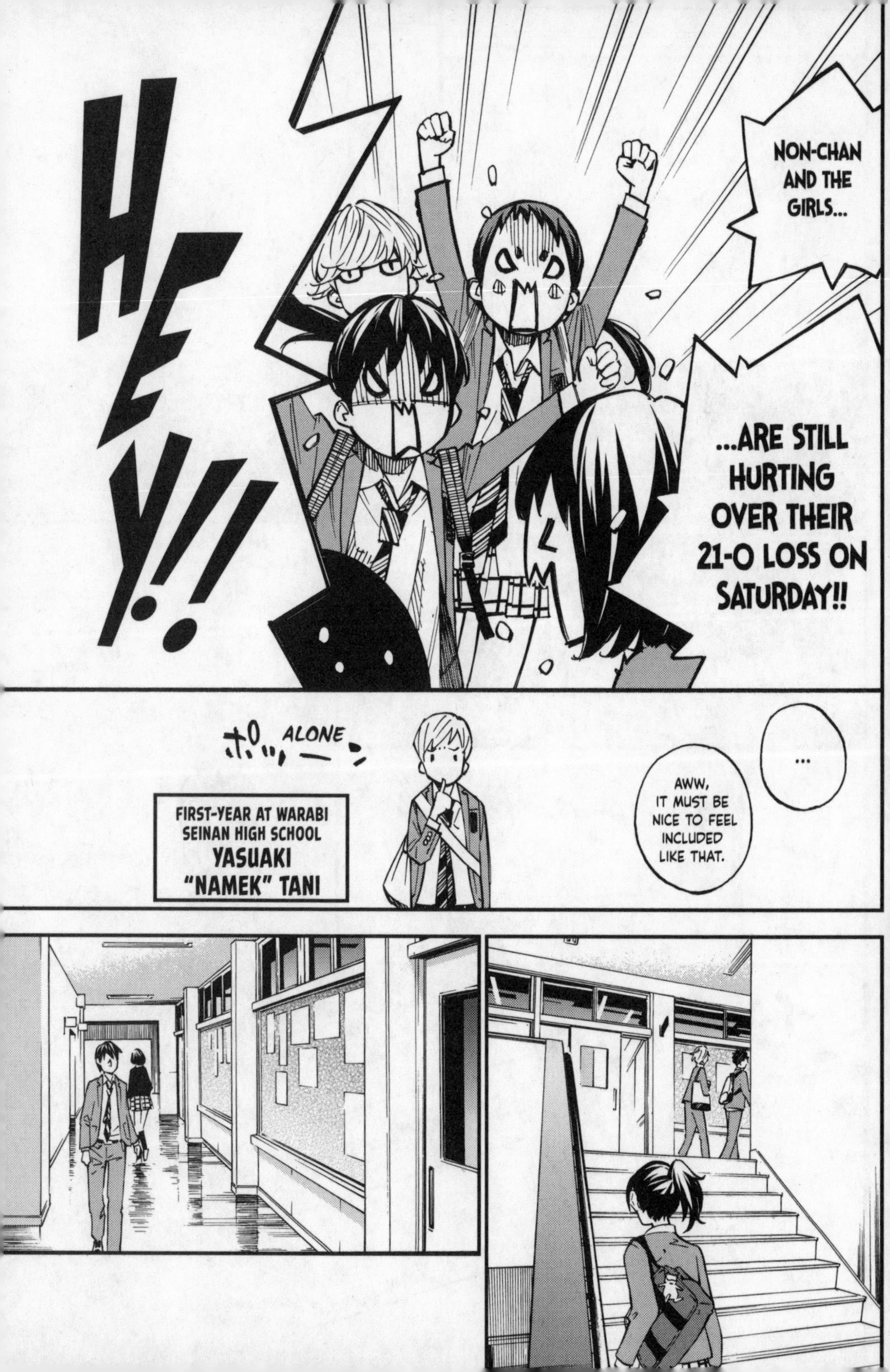
NON-CHAN AND THE GIRLS...
...ARE STILL HURTING OVER THEIR 21-0 LOSS ON SATURDAY!!
HEY!!
...
AWW, IT MUST BE NICE TO FEEL INCLUDED LIKE THAT.
FIRST-YEAR AT WARABI SEINAN HIGH SCHOOL
YASUAKI "NAMEK" TANI
ALONE

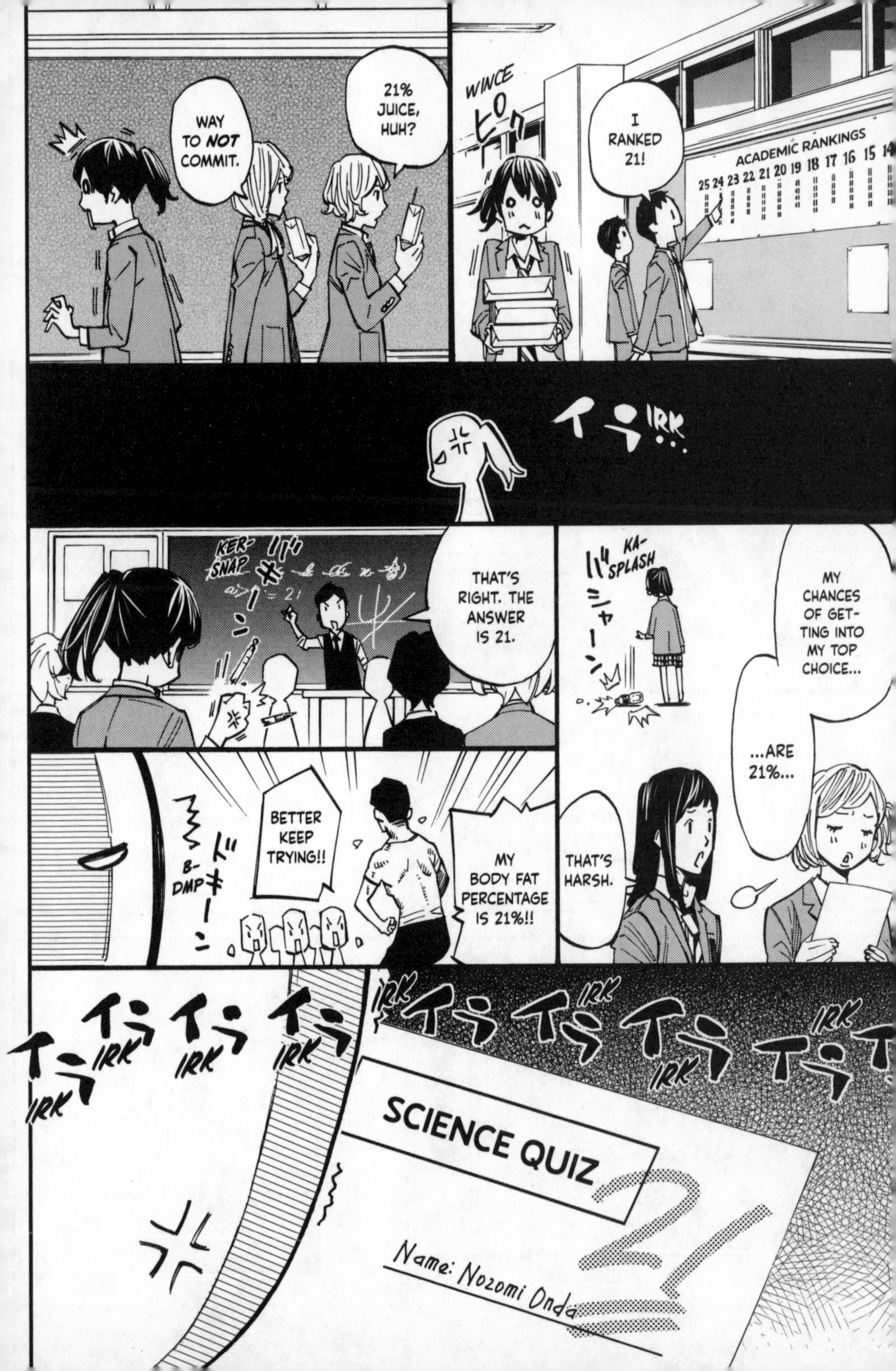
WINCE
ヒクッ
I RANKED 21!
ACADEMIC RANKINGS
25 24 23 22 21 20 19 18 17 16 15 14
21% JUICE, HUH?
WAY TO NOT COMMIT.
イラ IRK...
KA-SPLASH
バシャーン
MY CHANCES OF GETTING INTO MY TOP CHOICE...
...ARE 21%...
THAT'S HARSH.
KER-SNAP
バキ
THAT'S RIGHT. THE ANSWER IS 21.
MY BODY FAT PERCENTAGE IS 21%!!
BETTER KEEP TRYING!!
B-DMP
ドキーン
イラ IRK イラ IRK イラ IRK イラ IRK イラ IRK イラ IRK イラ IRK イラ
SCIENCE QUIZ
21
Name: Nozomi Onda

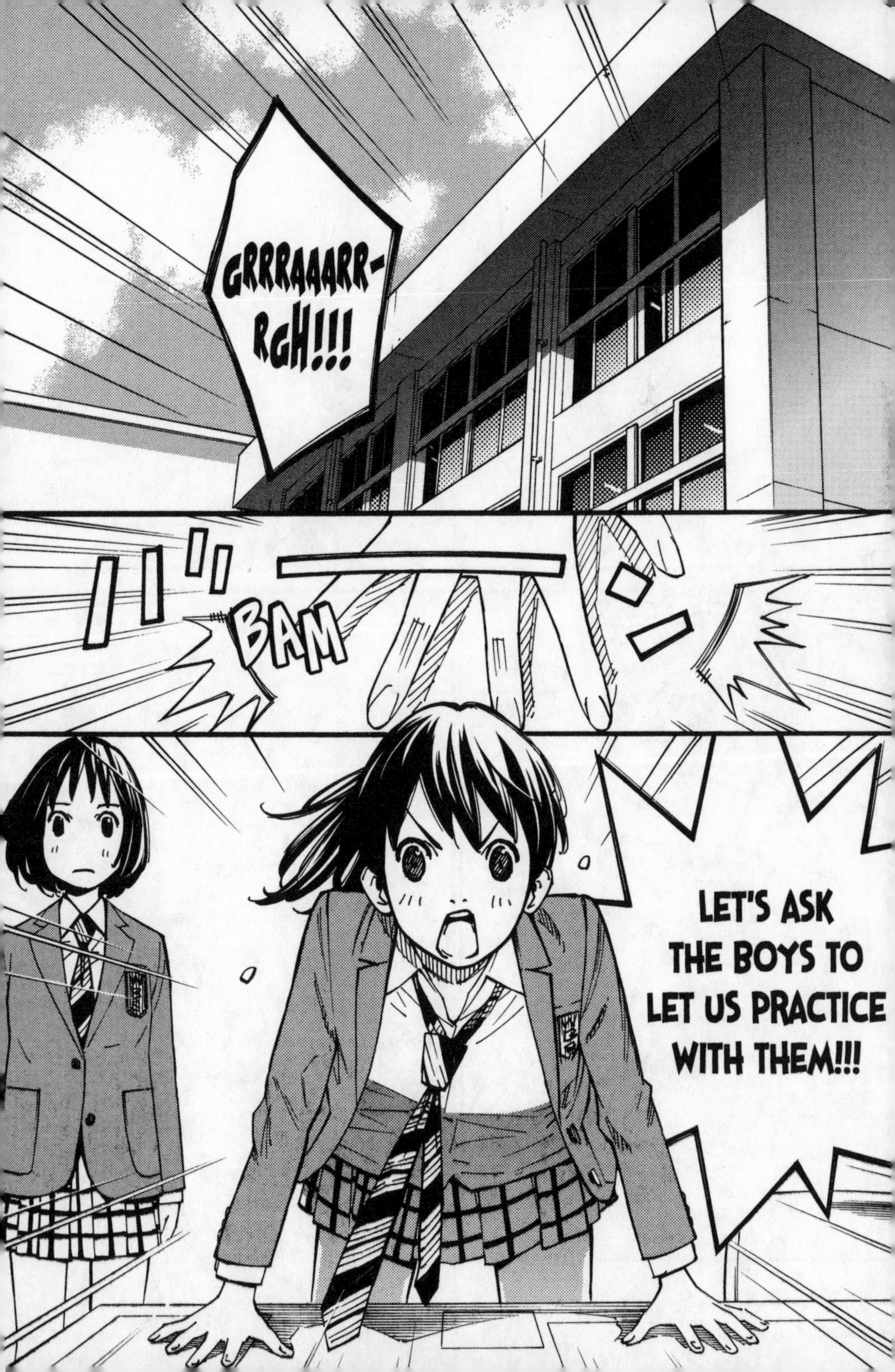
GRRRAAARR-RGH!!!
BAM
LET'S ASK THE BOYS TO LET US PRACTICE WITH THEM!!!

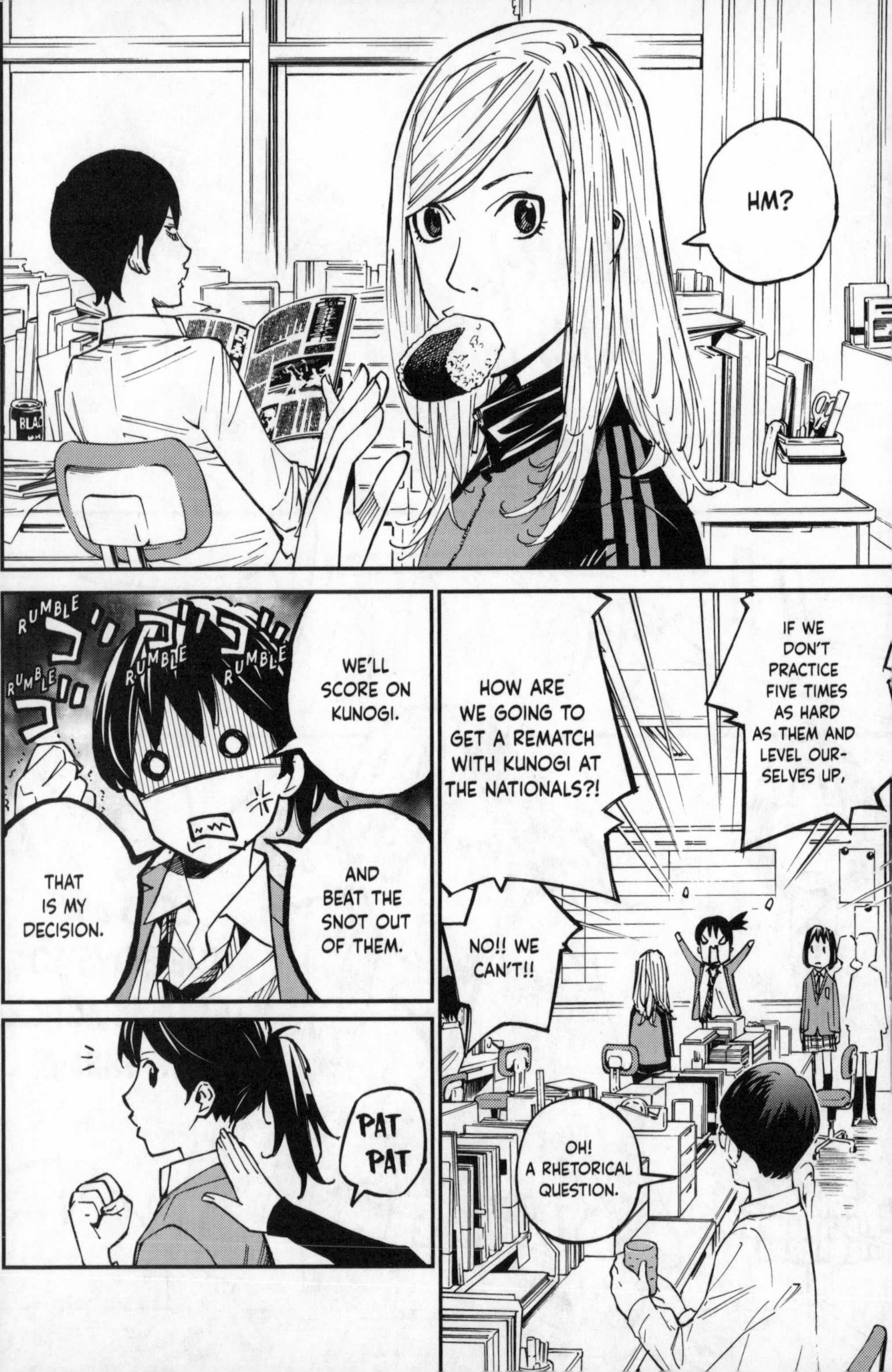
HM?
IF WE DON'T PRACTICE FIVE TIMES AS HARD AS THEM AND LEVEL OUR-SELVES UP,
HOW ARE WE GOING TO GET A REMATCH WITH KUNOGI AT THE NATIONALS?!
NO!! WE CAN'T!!
OH! A RHETORICAL QUESTION.
RUMBLE RUMBLE RUMBLE RUMBLE
WE'LL SCORE ON KUNOGI.
AND BEAT THE SNOT OUT OF THEM.
THAT IS MY DECISION.
PAT PAT

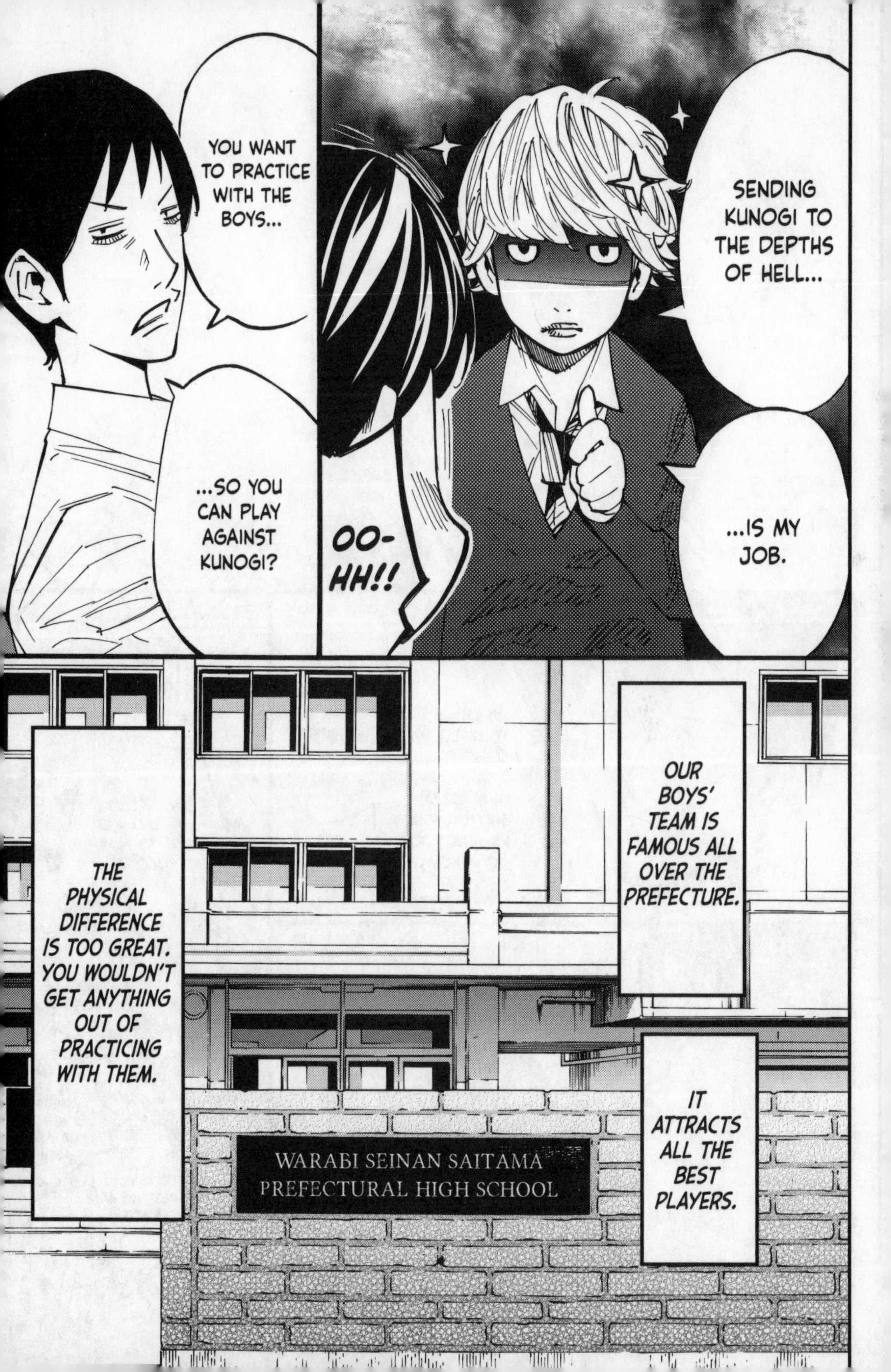

SENDING KUNOGI TO THE DEPTHS OF HELL...
...IS MY JOB.
OO-HH!!
YOU WANT TO PRACTICE WITH THE BOYS...
...SO YOU CAN PLAY AGAINST KUNOGI?
OUR BOYS' TEAM IS FAMOUS ALL OVER THE PREFECTURE.
IT ATTRACTS ALL THE BEST PLAYERS.
WARABI SEINAN SAITAMA PREFECTURAL HIGH SCHOOL
THE PHYSICAL DIFFERENCE IS TOO GREAT. YOU WOULDN'T GET ANYTHING OUT OF PRACTICING WITH THEM.

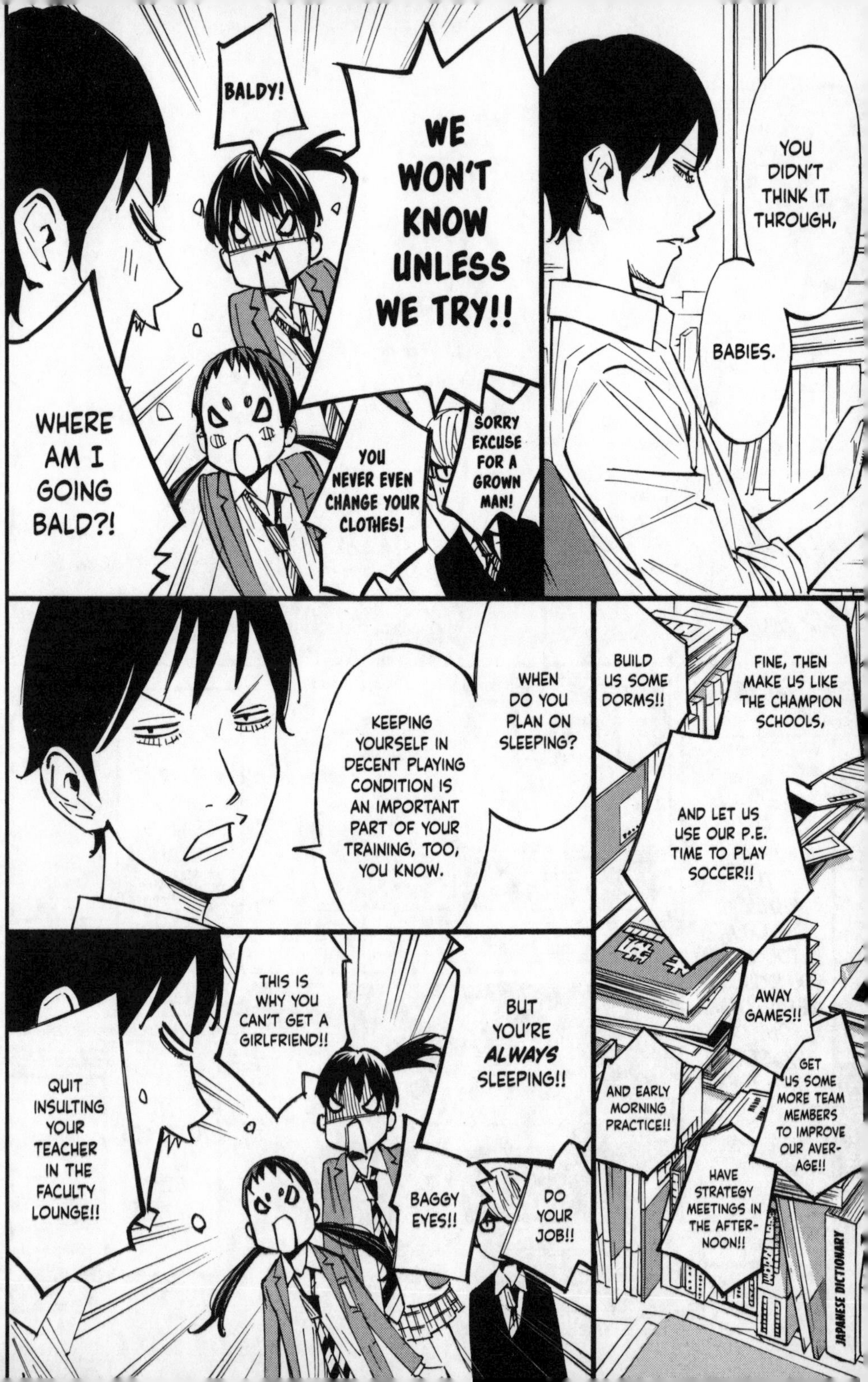
YOU DIDN'T THINK IT THROUGH,
BABIES.
BALDY!
WE WON'T KNOW UNLESS WE TRY!!
SORRY EXCUSE FOR A GROWN MAN!
YOU NEVER EVEN CHANGE YOUR CLOTHES!
WHERE AM I GOING BALD?!
FINE, THEN MAKE US LIKE THE CHAMPION SCHOOLS,
BUILD US SOME DORMS!!
AND LET US USE OUR P.E. TIME TO PLAY SOCCER!!
AWAY GAMES!!
GET US SOME MORE TEAM MEMBERS TO IMPROVE OUR AVER-AGE!!
AND EARLY MORNING PRACTICE!!
HAVE STRATEGY MEETINGS IN THE AFTER-NOON!!
JAPANESE DICTIONARY
WHEN DO YOU PLAN ON SLEEPING?
KEEPING YOURSELF IN DECENT PLAYING CONDITION IS AN IMPORTANT PART OF YOUR TRAINING, TOO, YOU KNOW.
BUT YOU'RE *ALWAYS* SLEEPING!!
THIS IS WHY YOU CAN'T GET A GIRLFRIEND!!
DO YOUR JOB!!
BAGGY EYES!!
QUIT INSULTING YOUR TEACHER IN THE FACULTY LOUNGE!!

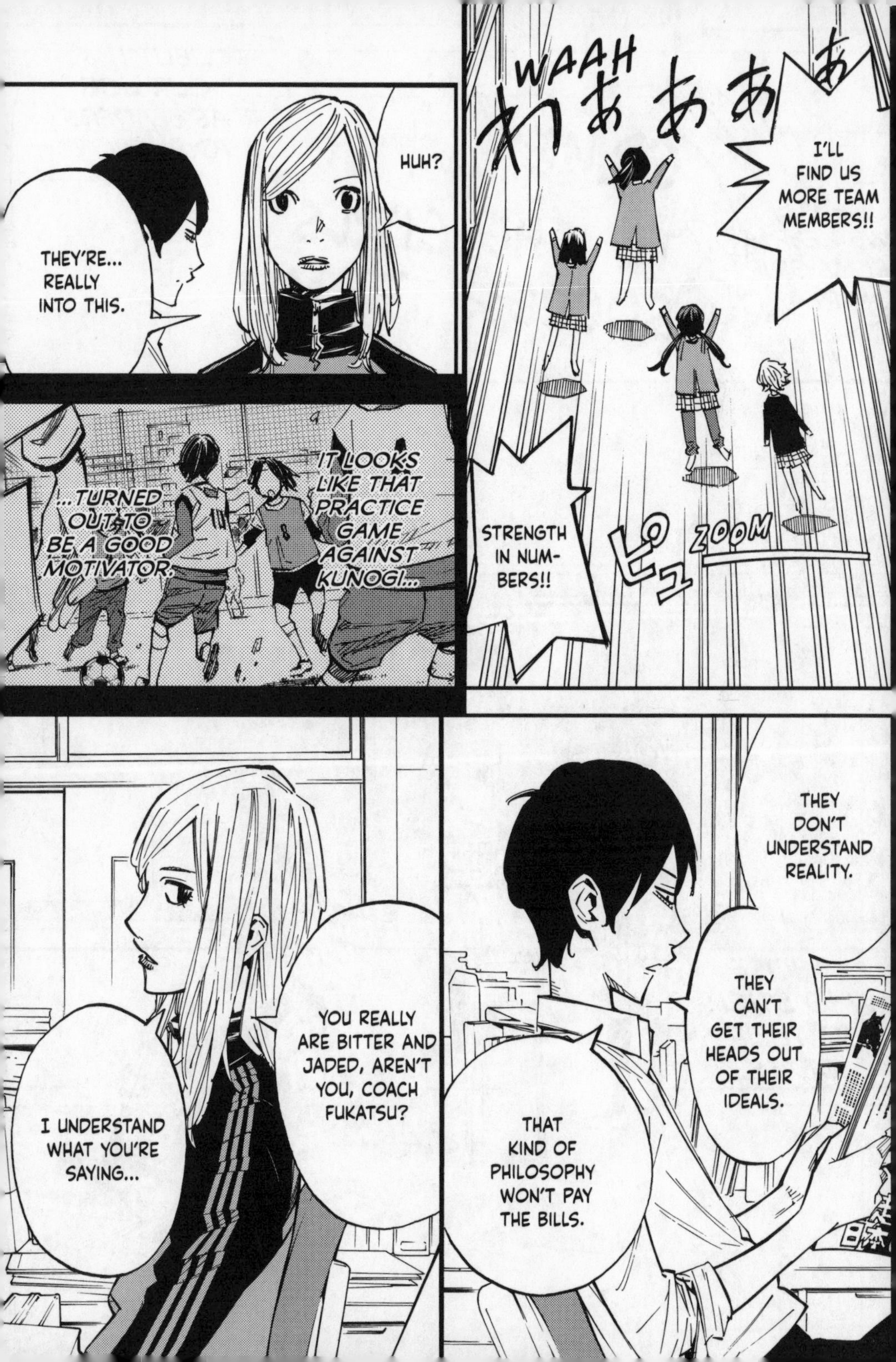
WAAH
わあああ
I'LL FIND US MORE TEAM MEMBERS!!
STRENGTH IN NUM-BERS!!
ZOOM
ピュ
HUH?
THEY'RE... REALLY INTO THIS.
IT LOOKS LIKE THAT PRACTICE GAME AGAINST KUNOGI...
...TURNED OUT TO BE A GOOD MOTIVATOR.
THEY DON'T UNDERSTAND REALITY.
THEY CAN'T GET THEIR HEADS OUT OF THEIR IDEALS.
THAT KIND OF PHILOSOPHY WON'T PAY THE BILLS.
YOU REALLY ARE BITTER AND JADED, AREN'T YOU, COACH FUKATSU?
I UNDERSTAND WHAT YOU'RE SAYING...

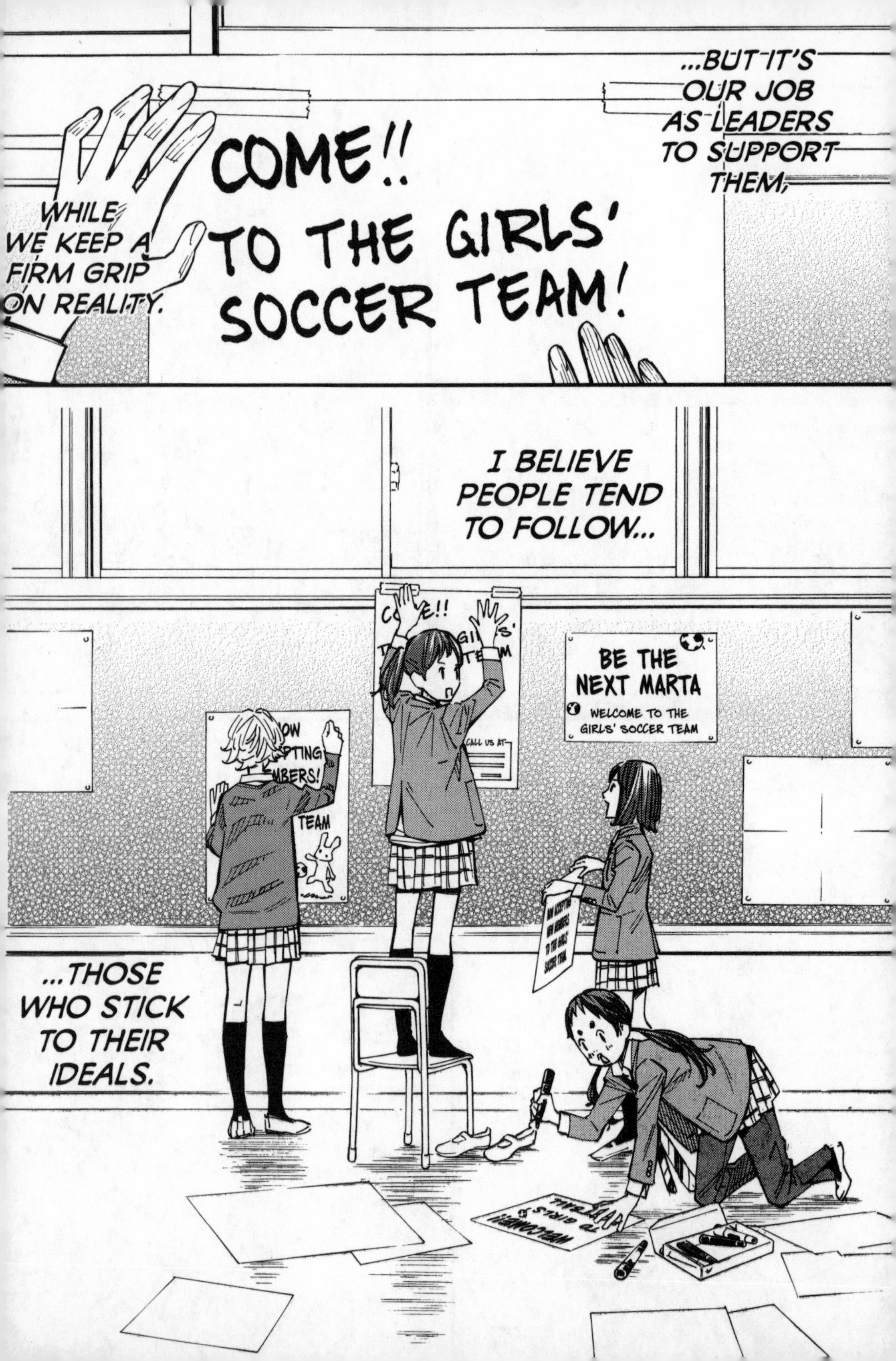
...BUT IT'S OUR JOB AS LEADERS TO SUPPORT THEM,
COME!! TO THE GIRLS' SOCCER TEAM!
WHILE WE KEEP A FIRM GRIP ON REALITY.
I BELIEVE PEOPLE TEND TO FOLLOW...
BE THE NEXT MARTA
WELCOME TO THE GIRLS' SOCCER TEAM
CALL US AT
...THOSE WHO STICK TO THEIR IDEALS.

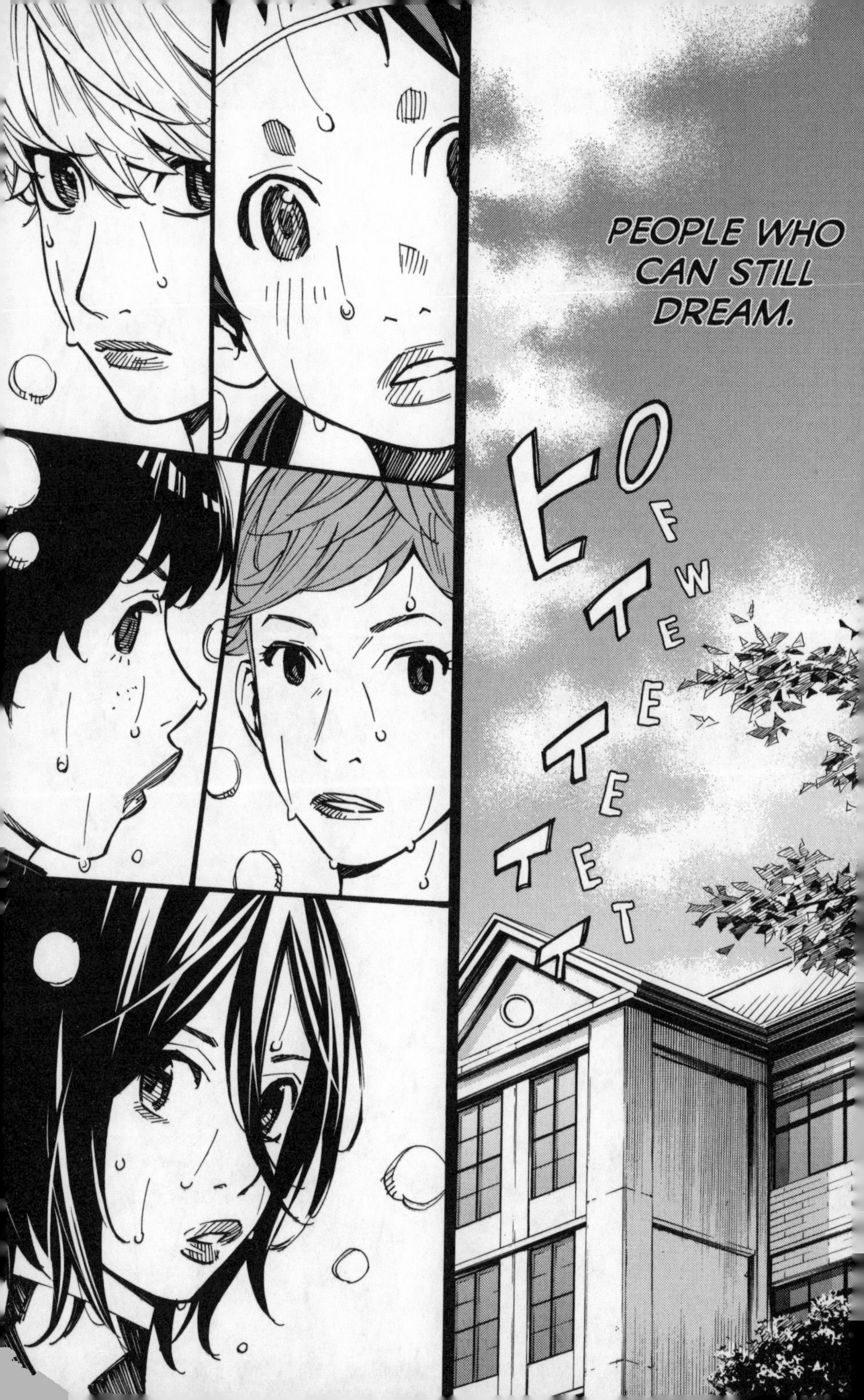
PEOPLE WHO CAN STILL DREAM.
ピテテテ
FWEEEET

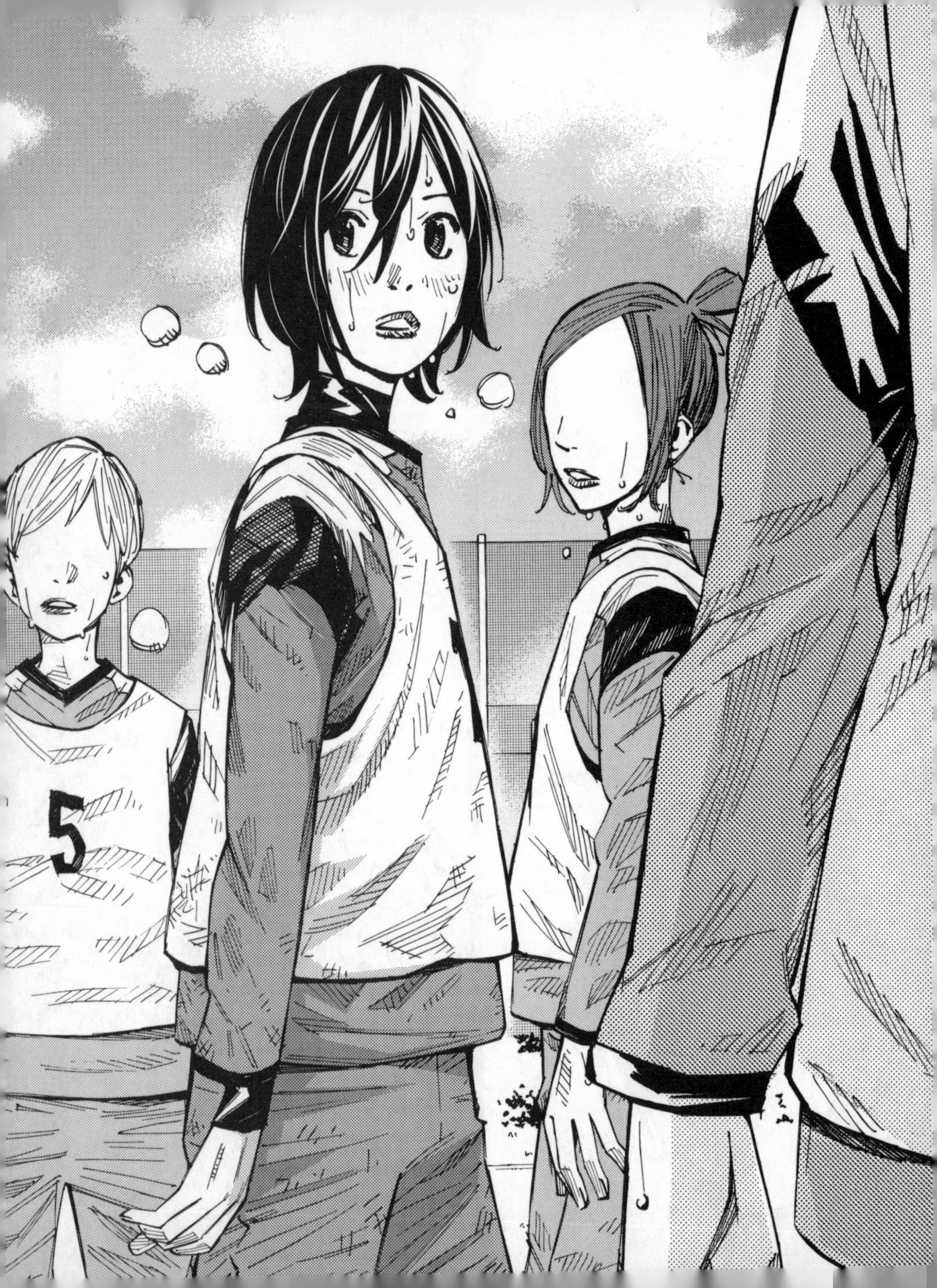
5

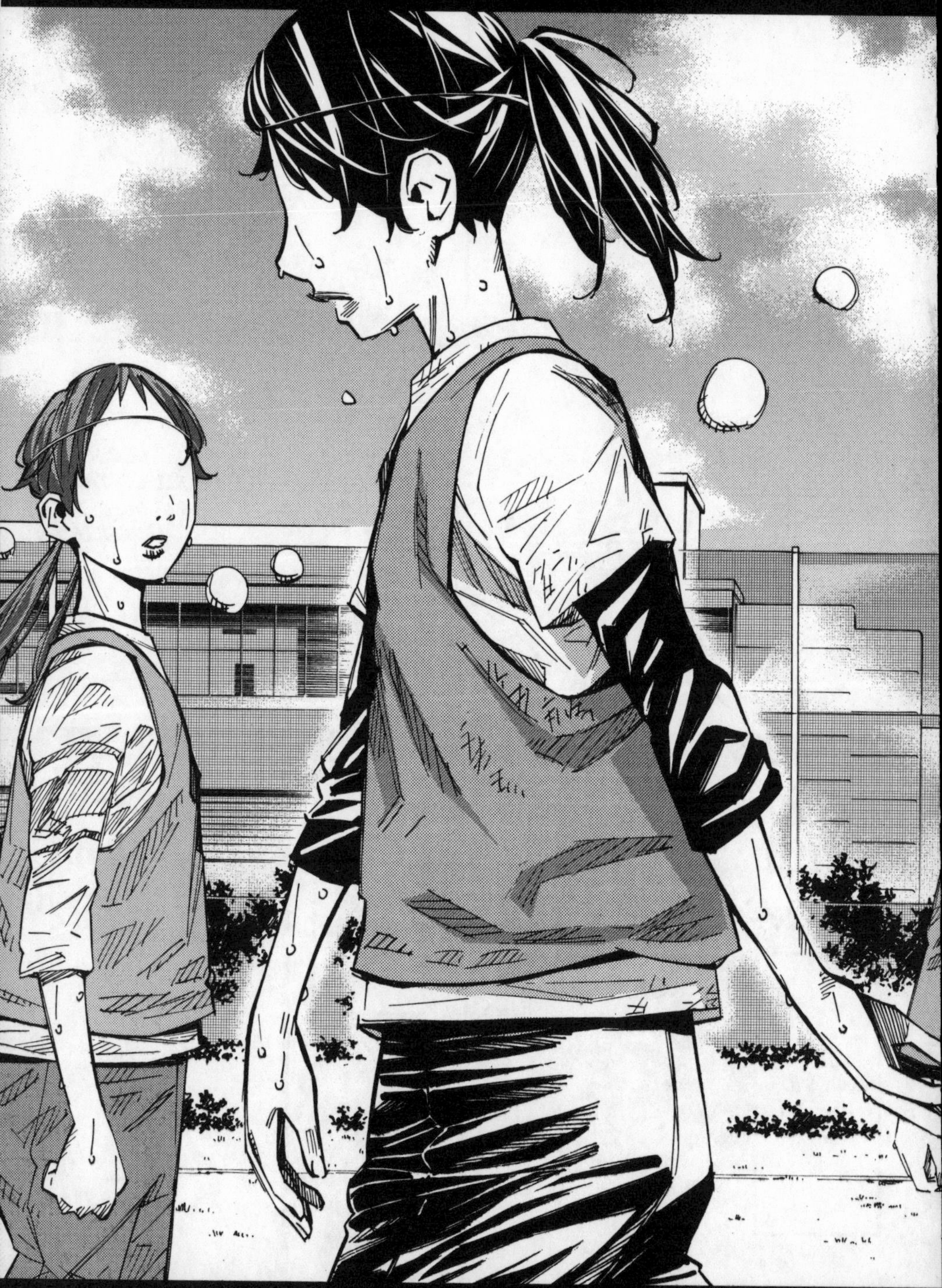

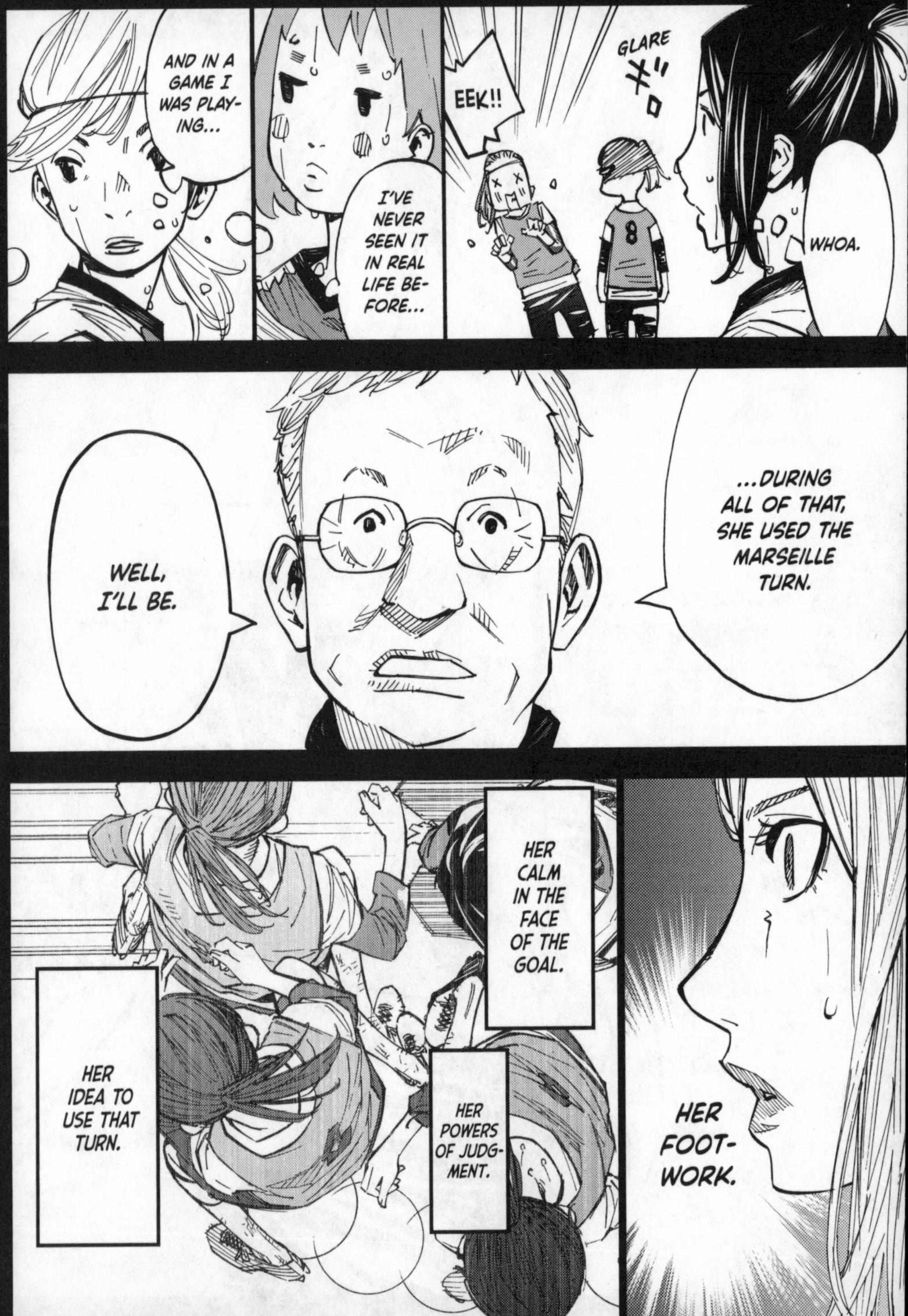
WHOA.
GLARE
EEK!!
I'VE NEVER SEEN IT IN REAL LIFE BEFORE...
AND IN A GAME I WAS PLAYING...
...DURING ALL OF THAT, SHE USED THE MARSEILLE TURN.
WELL, I'LL BE.
HER FOOTWORK.
HER CALM IN THE FACE OF THE GOAL.
HER POWERS OF JUDGMENT.
HER IDEA TO USE THAT TURN.

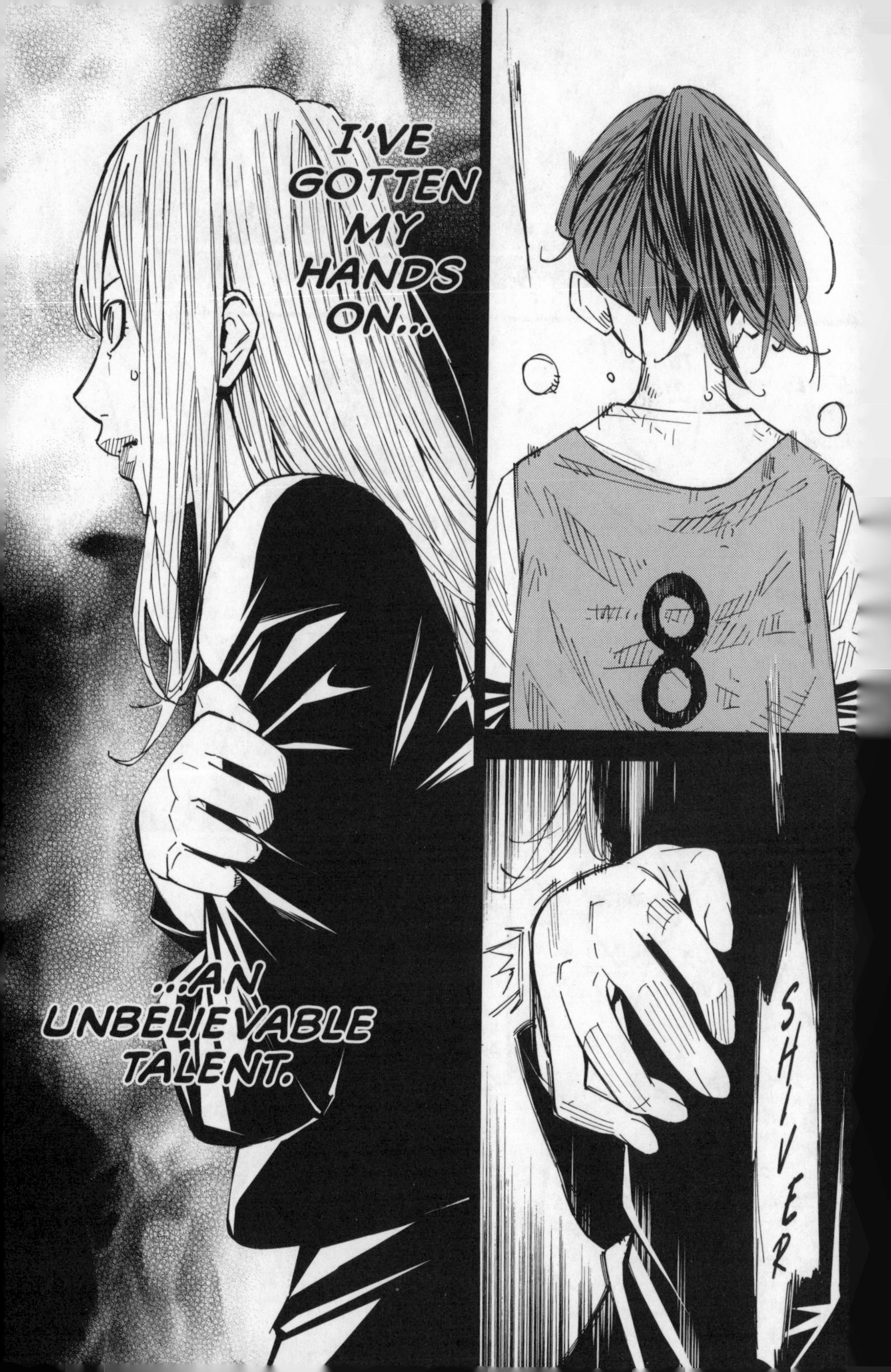
SHIVER
I'VE GOTTEN MY HANDS ON...
...AN UNBELIEVABLE TALENT.

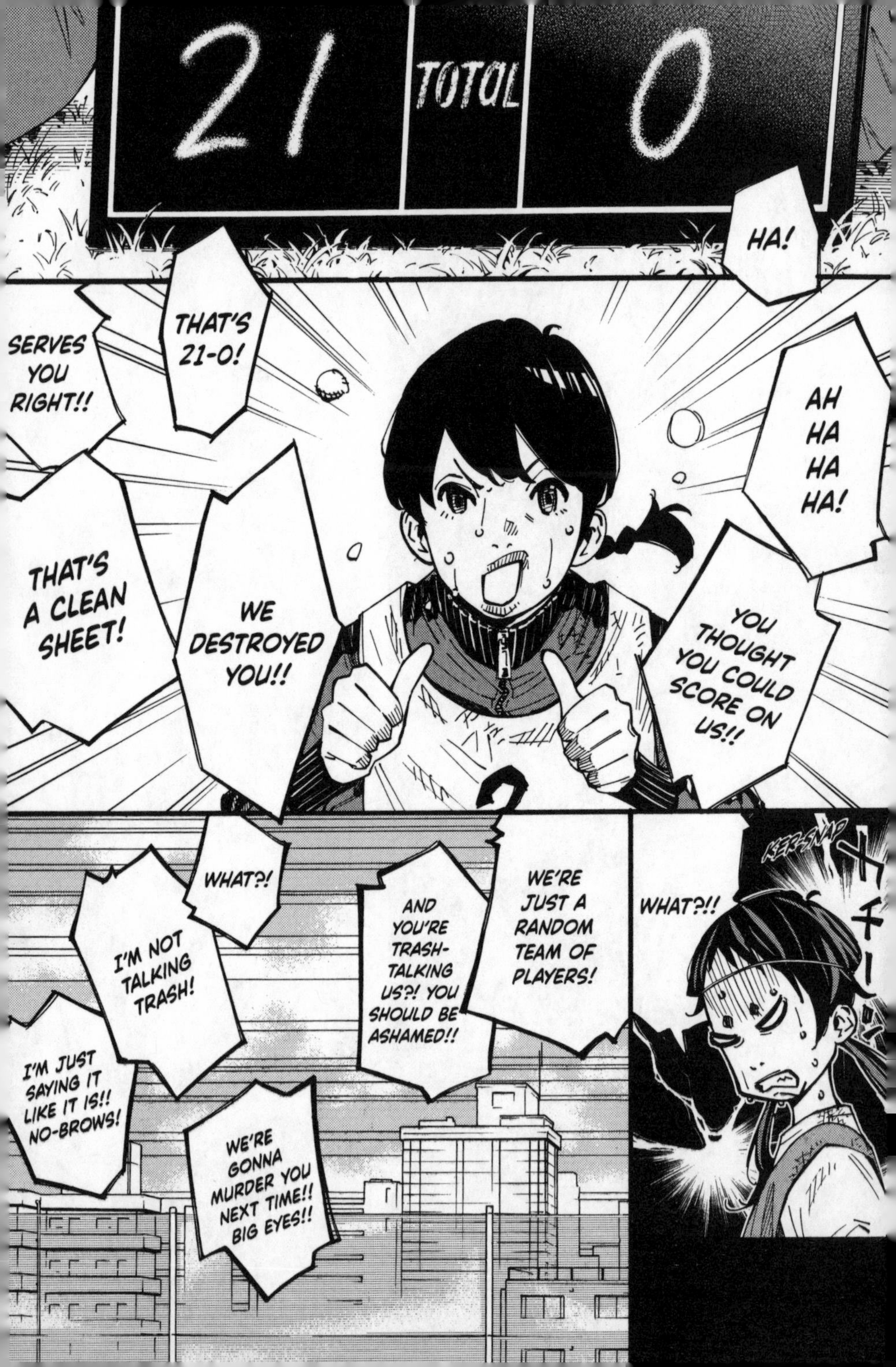
21
TOTAL
0
HA!
AH HA HA HA!
YOU THOUGHT YOU COULD SCORE ON US!!
THAT'S 21-0!
SERVES YOU RIGHT!!
WE DESTROYED YOU!!
THAT'S A CLEAN SHEET!
KER-SNAP
WHAT?!!
WE'RE JUST A RANDOM TEAM OF PLAYERS!
AND YOU'RE TRASH-TALKING US?! YOU SHOULD BE ASHAMED!!
WHAT?!
I'M NOT TALKING TRASH!
I'M JUST SAYING IT LIKE IT IS!! NO-BROWS!
WE'RE GONNA MURDER YOU NEXT TIME!! BIG EYES!!

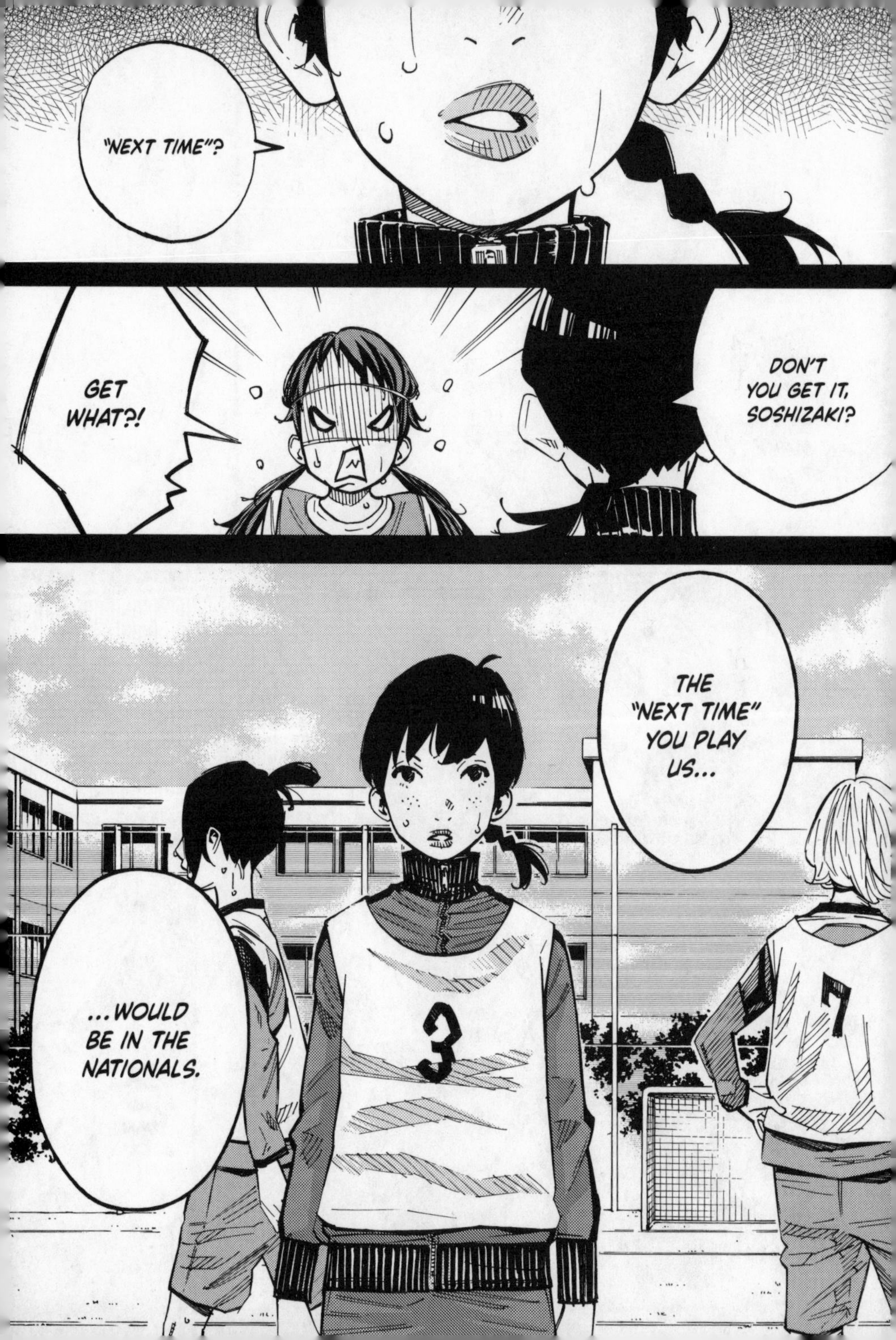
"NEXT TIME"?
DON'T YOU GET IT, SOSHIZAKI?
GET WHAT?!
THE "NEXT TIME" YOU PLAY US...
...WOULD BE IN THE NATIONALS.

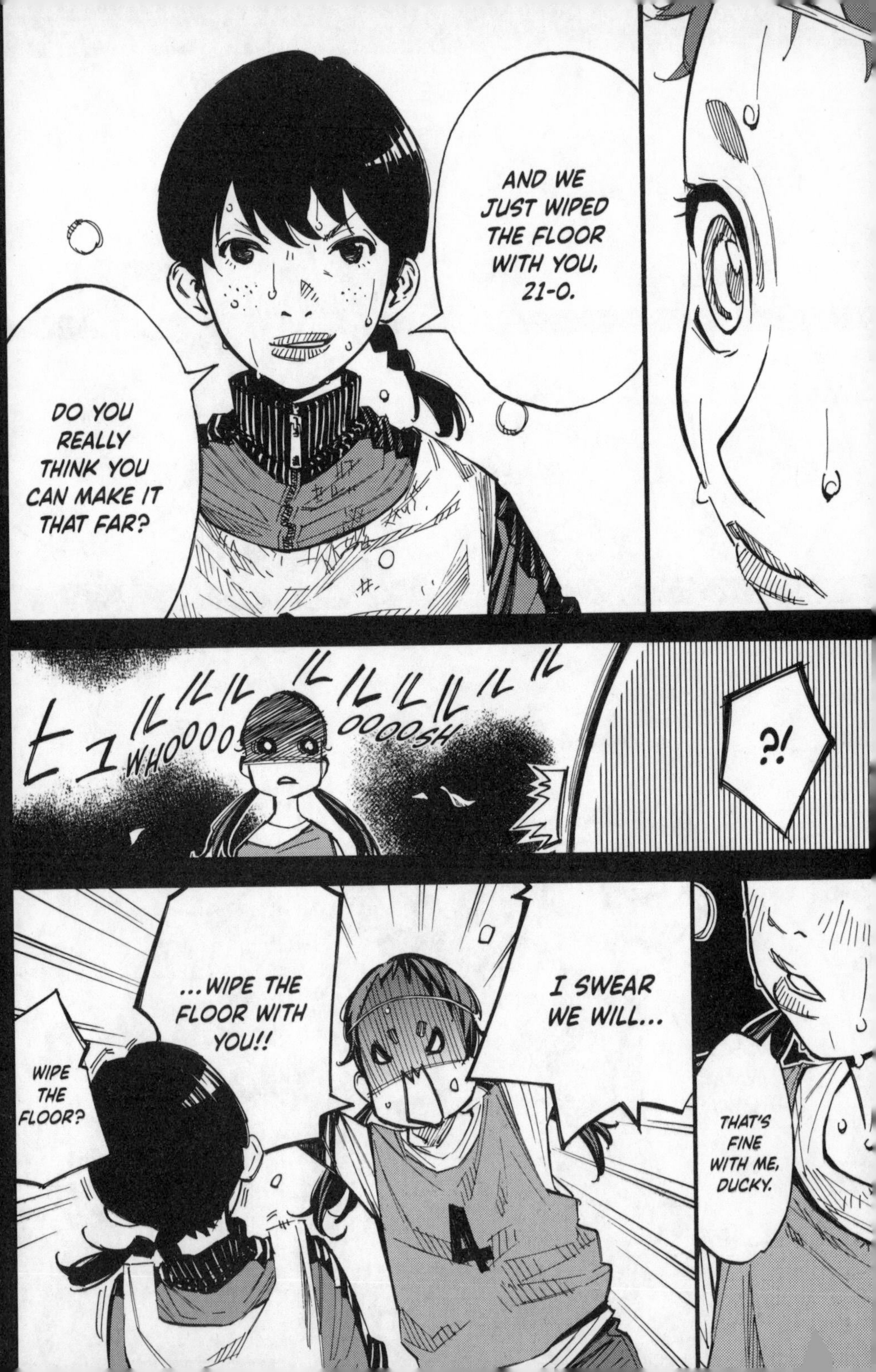
AND WE JUST WIPED THE FLOOR WITH YOU, 21-0.
DO YOU REALLY THINK YOU CAN MAKE IT THAT FAR?
?!
ヒュルルルルルルルルル
WHOOOOOOOOOSH
THAT'S FINE WITH ME, DUCKY.
I SWEAR WE WILL...
...WIPE THE FLOOR WITH YOU!!
WIPE THE FLOOR?

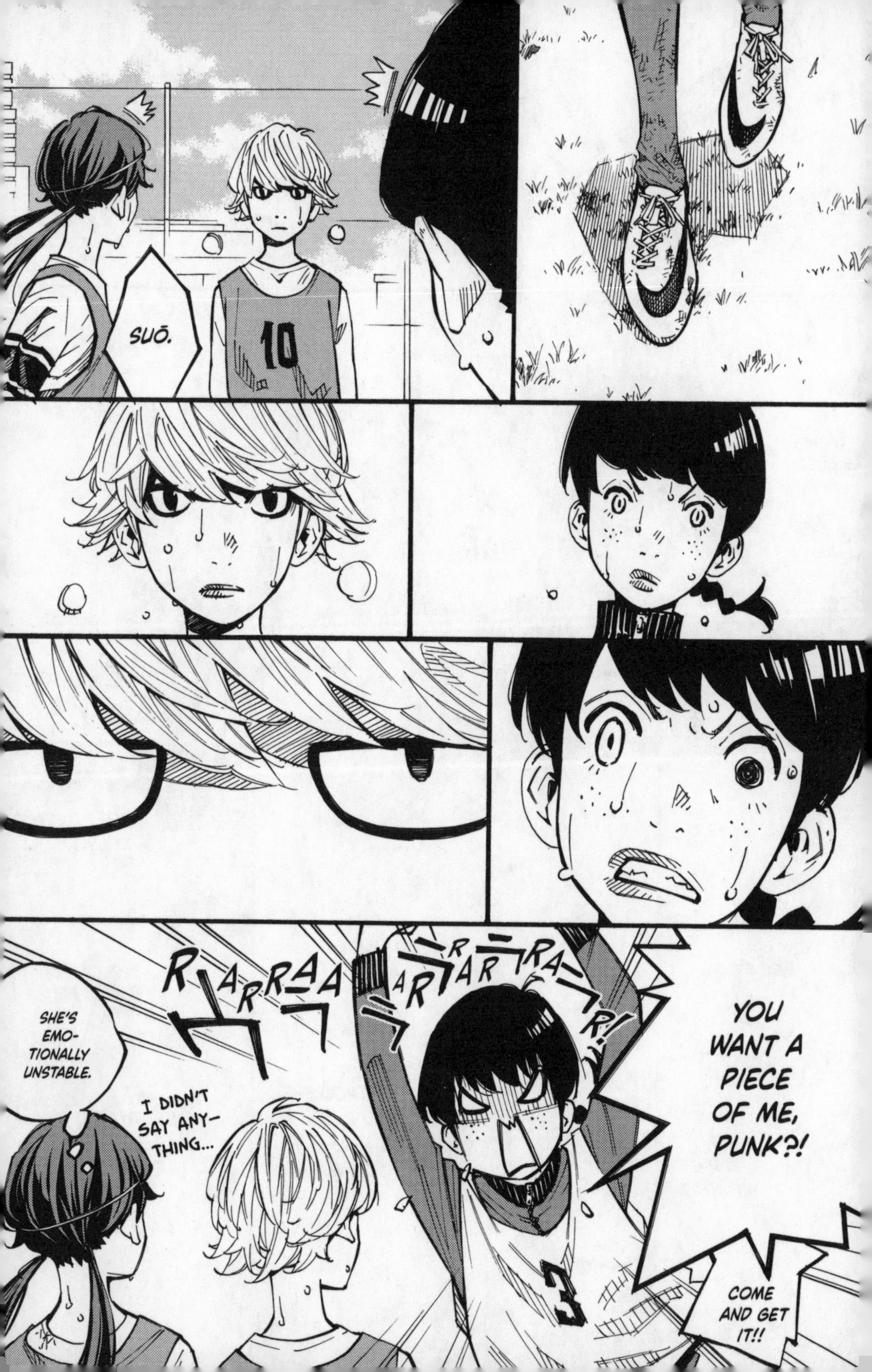
SUŌ.
YOU WANT A PIECE OF ME, PUNK?!
COME AND GET IT!!
I DIDN'T SAY ANY-THING...
SHE'S EMO-TIONALLY UNSTABLE.

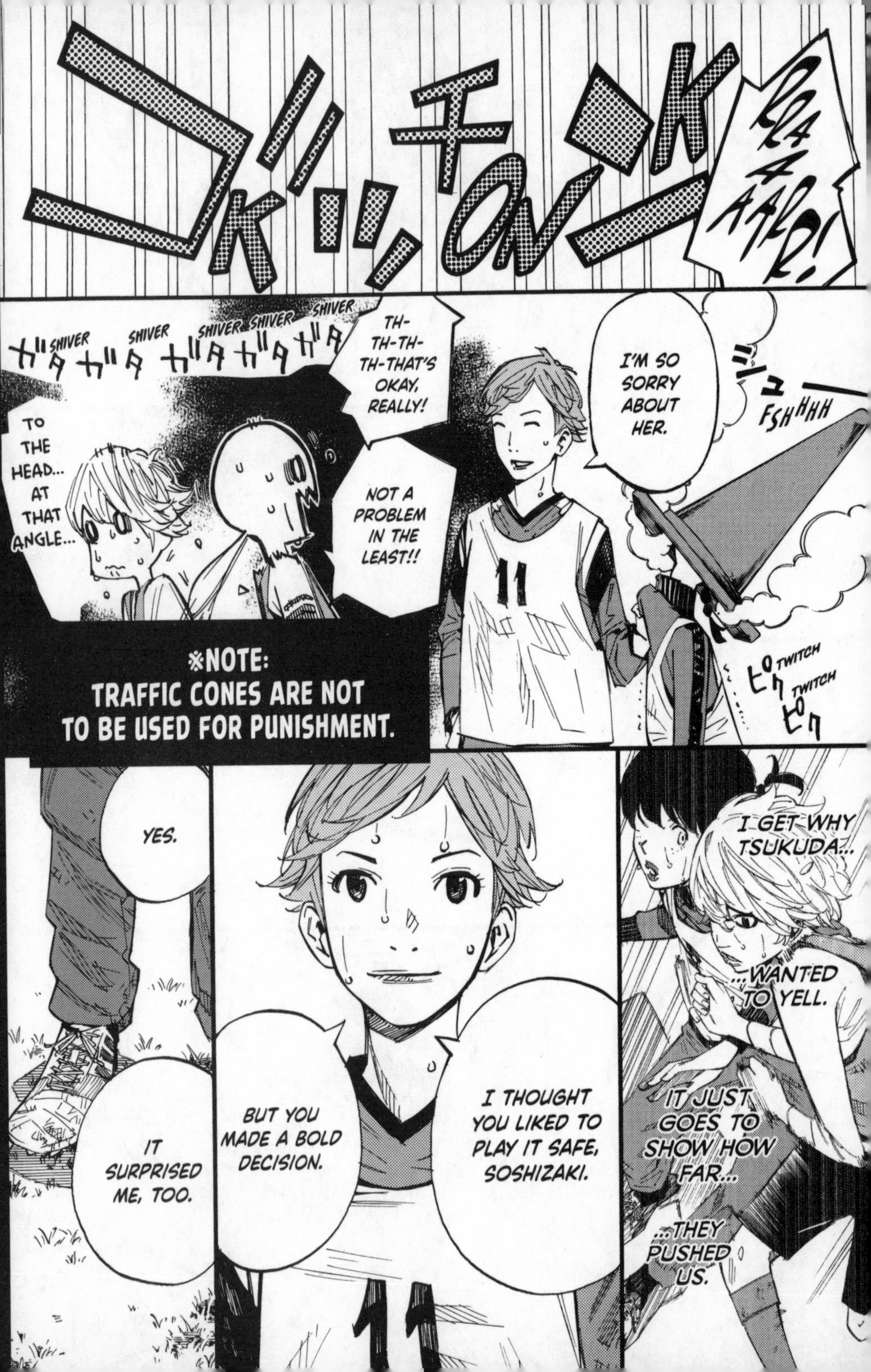
RAAAAAAR!
KONK
I'M SO SORRY ABOUT HER.
FSHHHH
TWITCH TWITCH
TH-TH-TH-TH-THAT'S OKAY, REALLY!
NOT A PROBLEM IN THE LEAST!!
SHIVER SHIVER SHIVER SHIVER SHIVER
TO THE HEAD... AT THAT ANGLE...
※NOTE: TRAFFIC CONES ARE NOT TO BE USED FOR PUNISHMENT.
I GET WHY TSUKUDA...
...WANTED TO YELL.
IT JUST GOES TO SHOW HOW FAR...
...THEY PUSHED US.
I THOUGHT YOU LIKED TO PLAY IT SAFE, SOSHIZAKI.
BUT YOU MADE A BOLD DECISION.
YES.
IT SURPRISED ME, TOO.

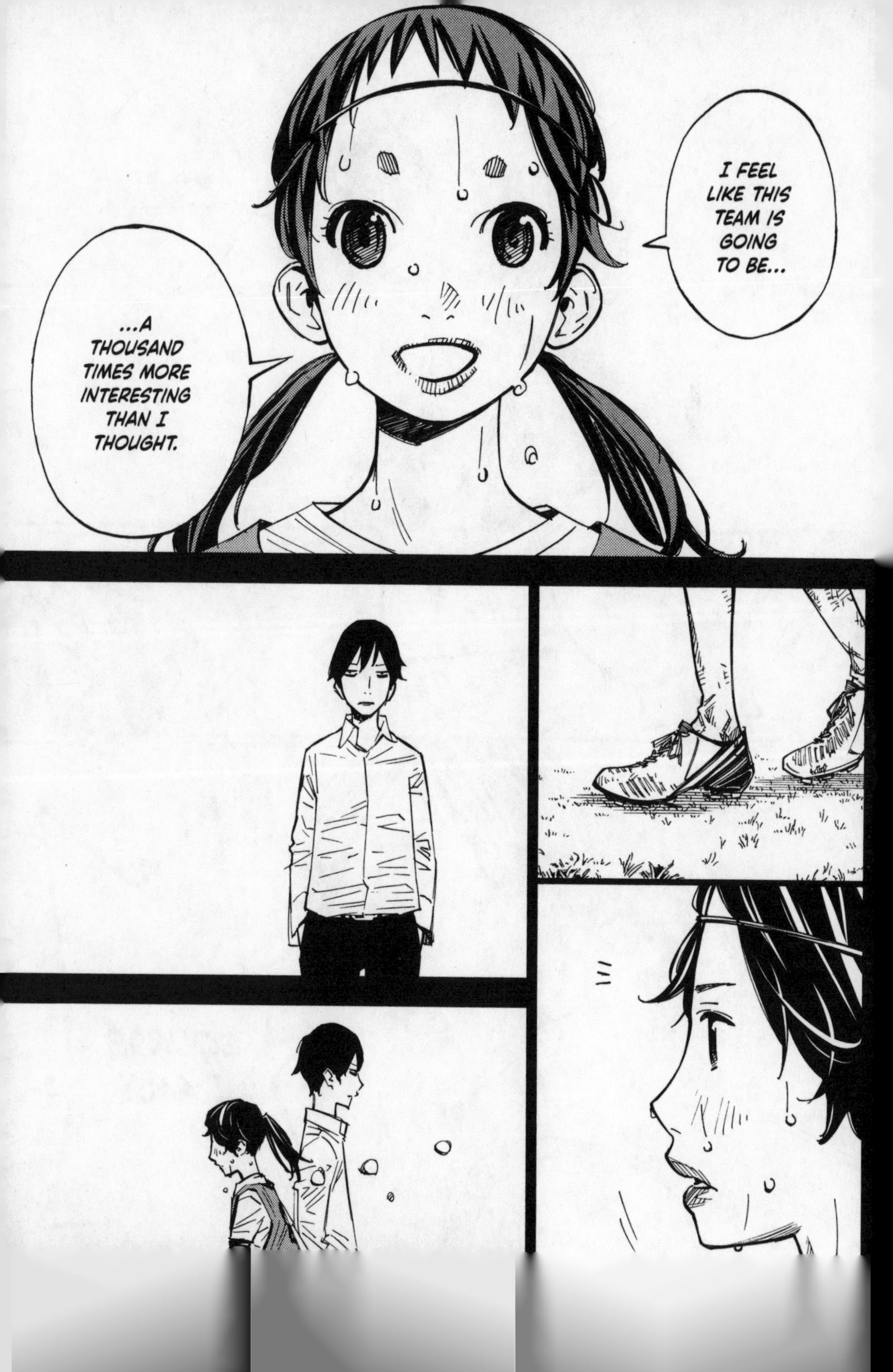
I FEEL LIKE THIS TEAM IS GOING TO BE...
...A THOUSAND TIMES MORE INTERESTING THAN I THOUGHT.

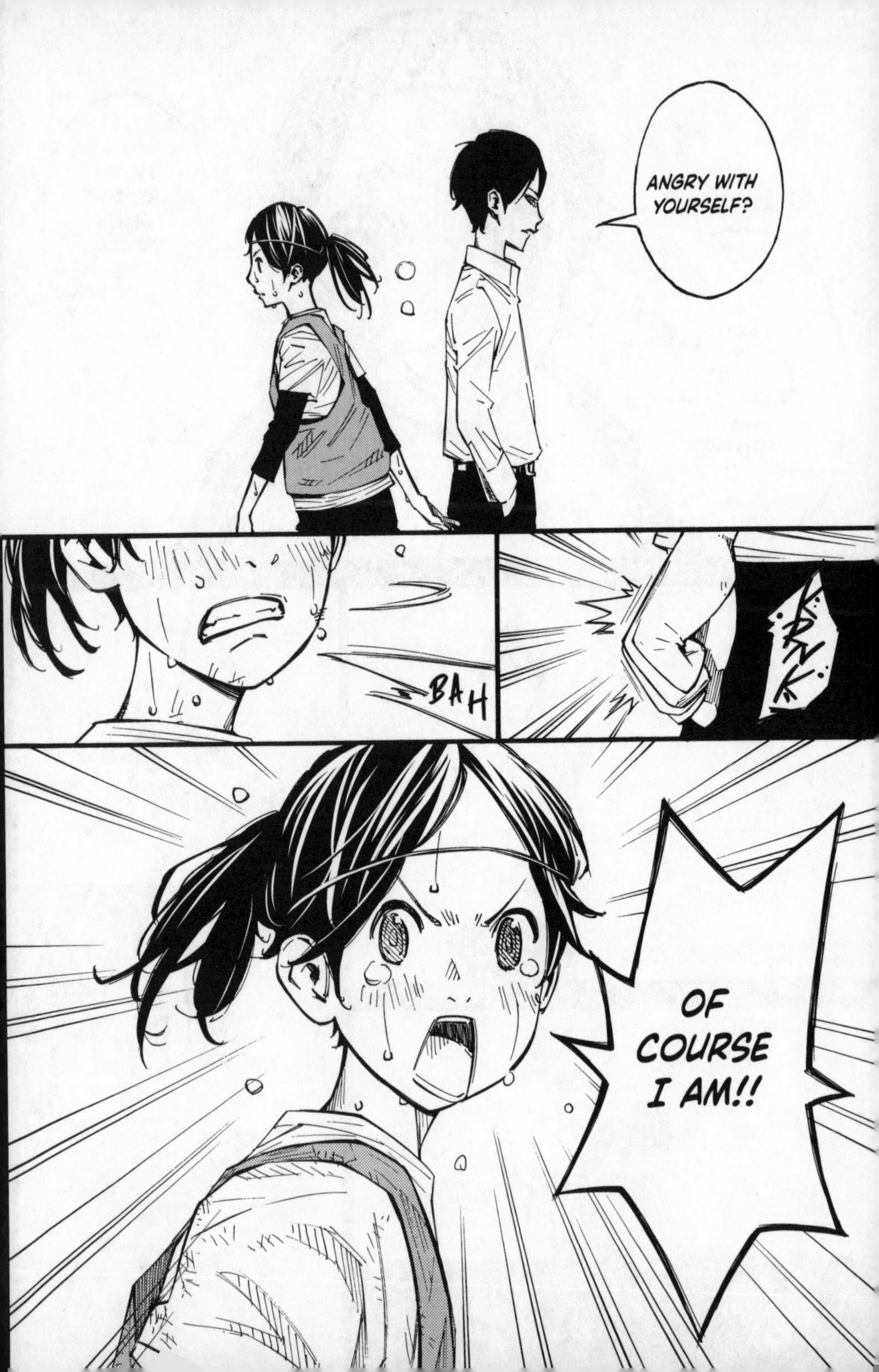
ANGRY WITH YOURSELF?
KRNK
BAH
OF COURSE I AM!!

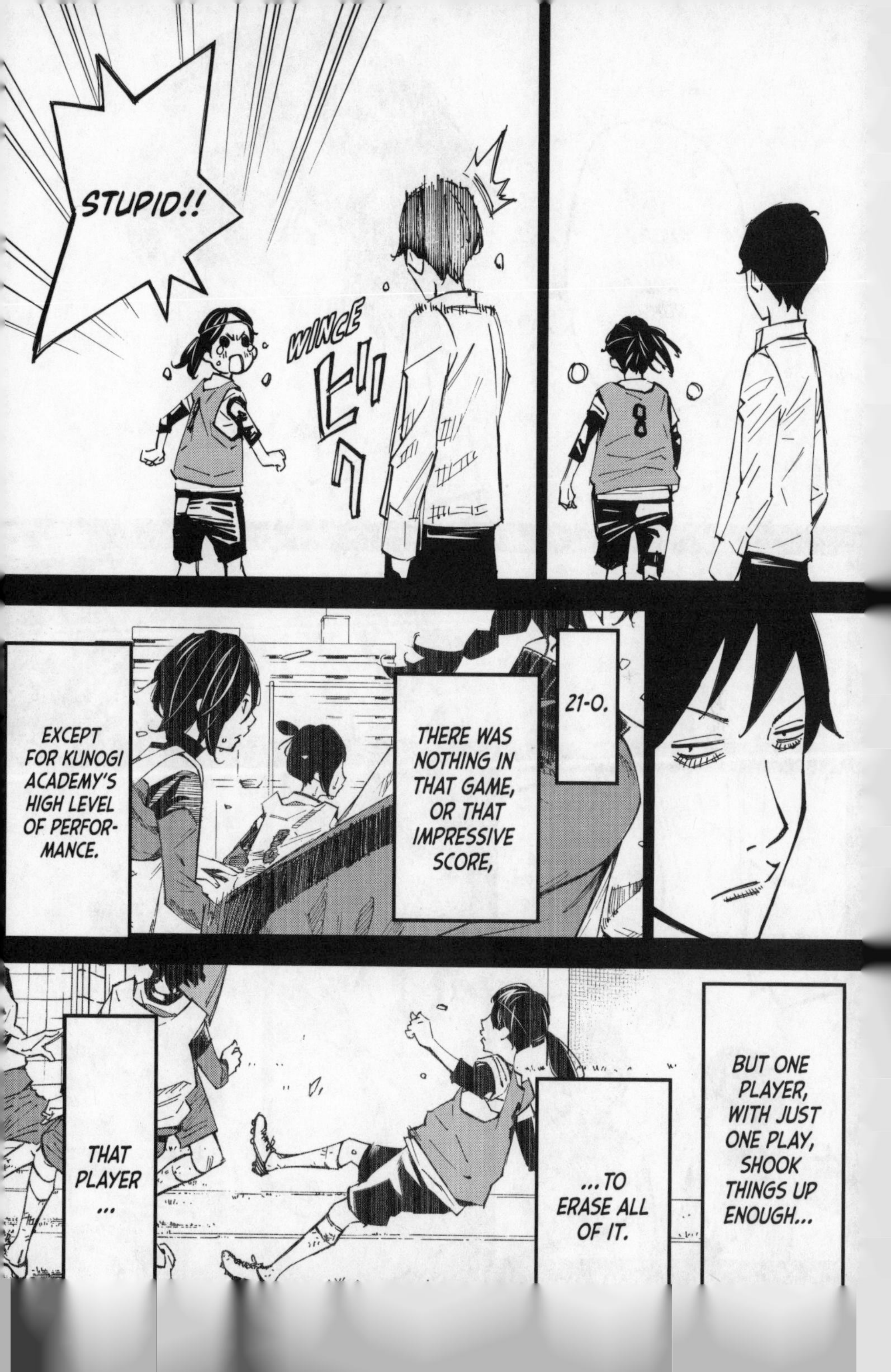
STUPID!!
WINCE
21-0.
THERE WAS NOTHING IN THAT GAME, OR THAT IMPRESSIVE SCORE,
EXCEPT FOR KUNOGI ACADEMY'S HIGH LEVEL OF PERFORMANCE.
BUT ONE PLAYER, WITH JUST ONE PLAY, SHOOK THINGS UP ENOUGH...
...TO ERASE ALL OF IT.
THAT PLAYER ...

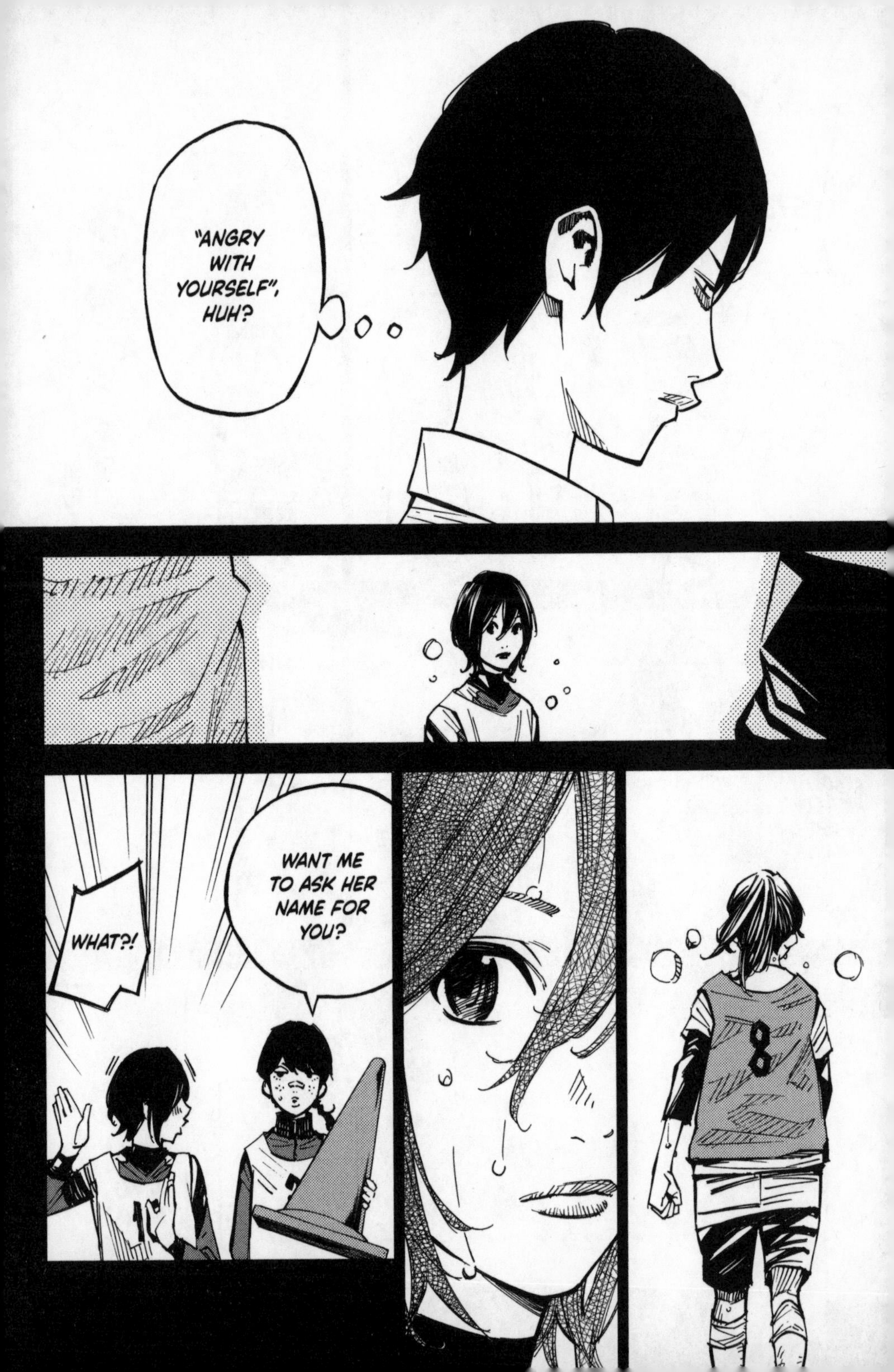
"ANGRY WITH YOURSELF", HUH?
WANT ME TO ASK HER NAME FOR YOU?
WHAT?!

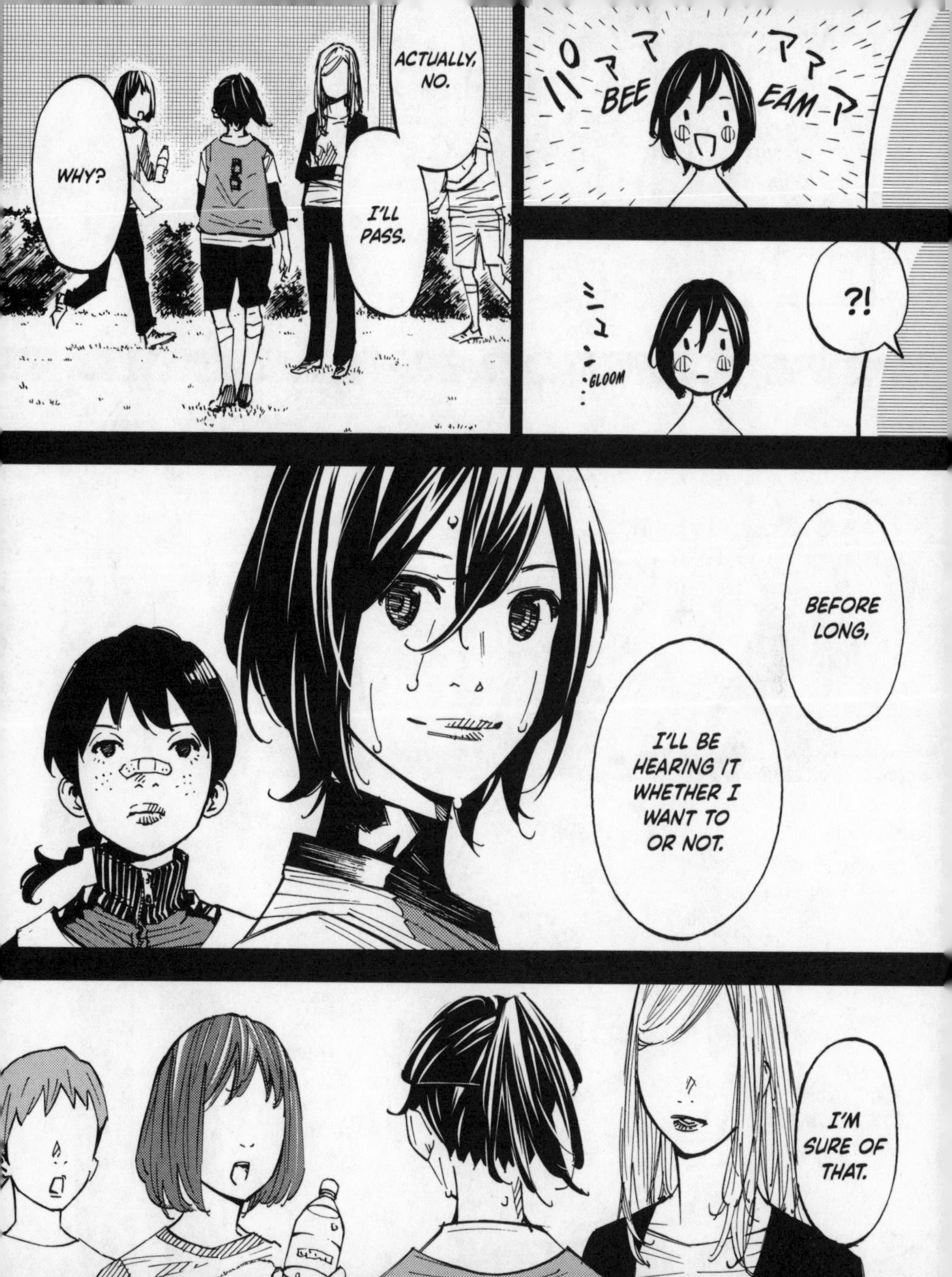
BEE
EAM
?!
GLOOM
ACTUALLY, NO.
I'LL PASS.
WHY?
BEFORE LONG,
I'LL BE HEARING IT WHETHER I WANT TO OR NOT.
I'M SURE OF THAT.

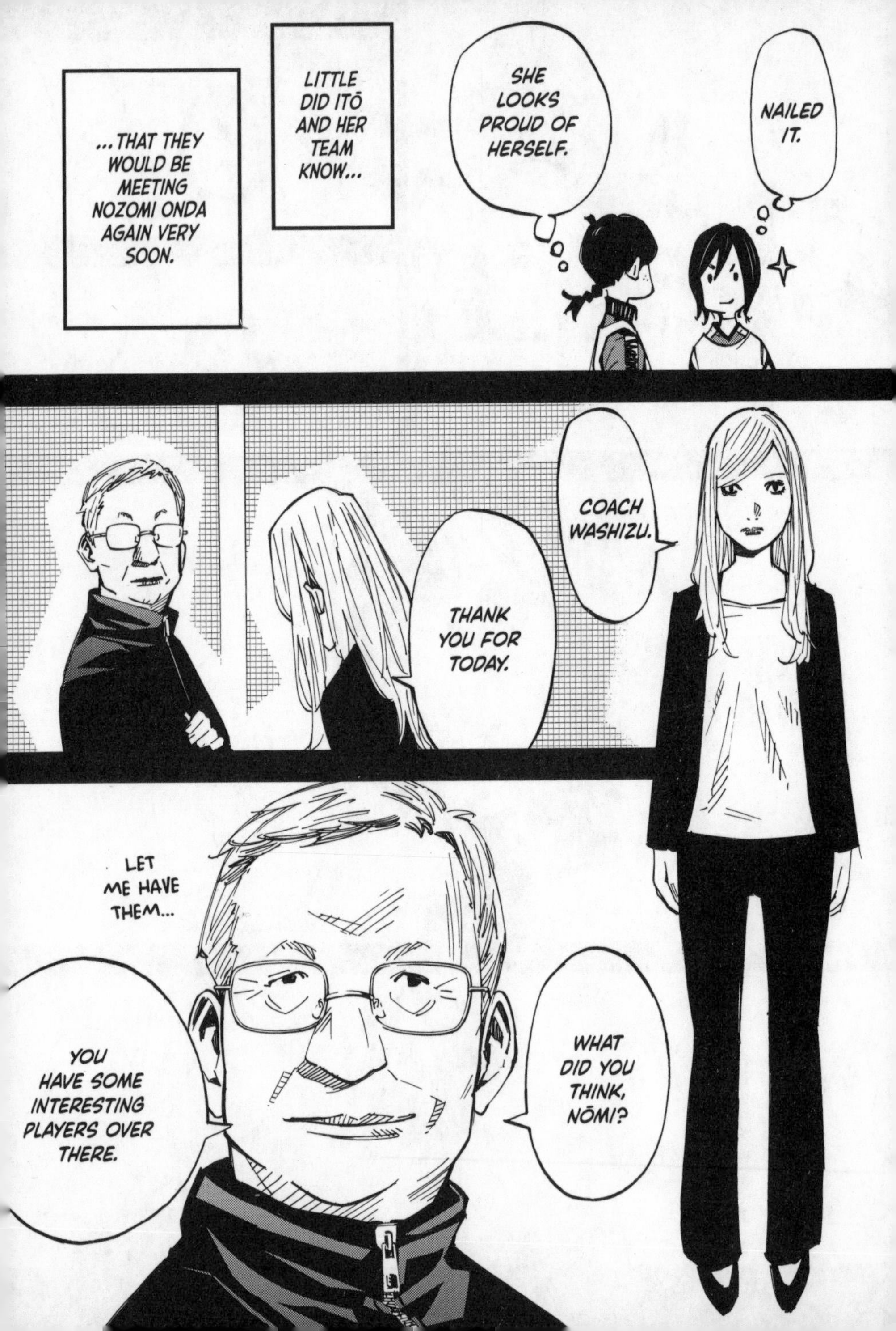
NAILED IT.
SHE LOOKS PROUD OF HERSELF.
LITTLE DID ITŌ AND HER TEAM KNOW...
...THAT THEY WOULD BE MEETING NOZOMI ONDA AGAIN VERY SOON.
COACH WASHIZU.
THANK YOU FOR TODAY.
WHAT DID YOU THINK, NŌMI?
YOU HAVE SOME INTERESTING PLAYERS OVER THERE.
LET ME HAVE THEM...

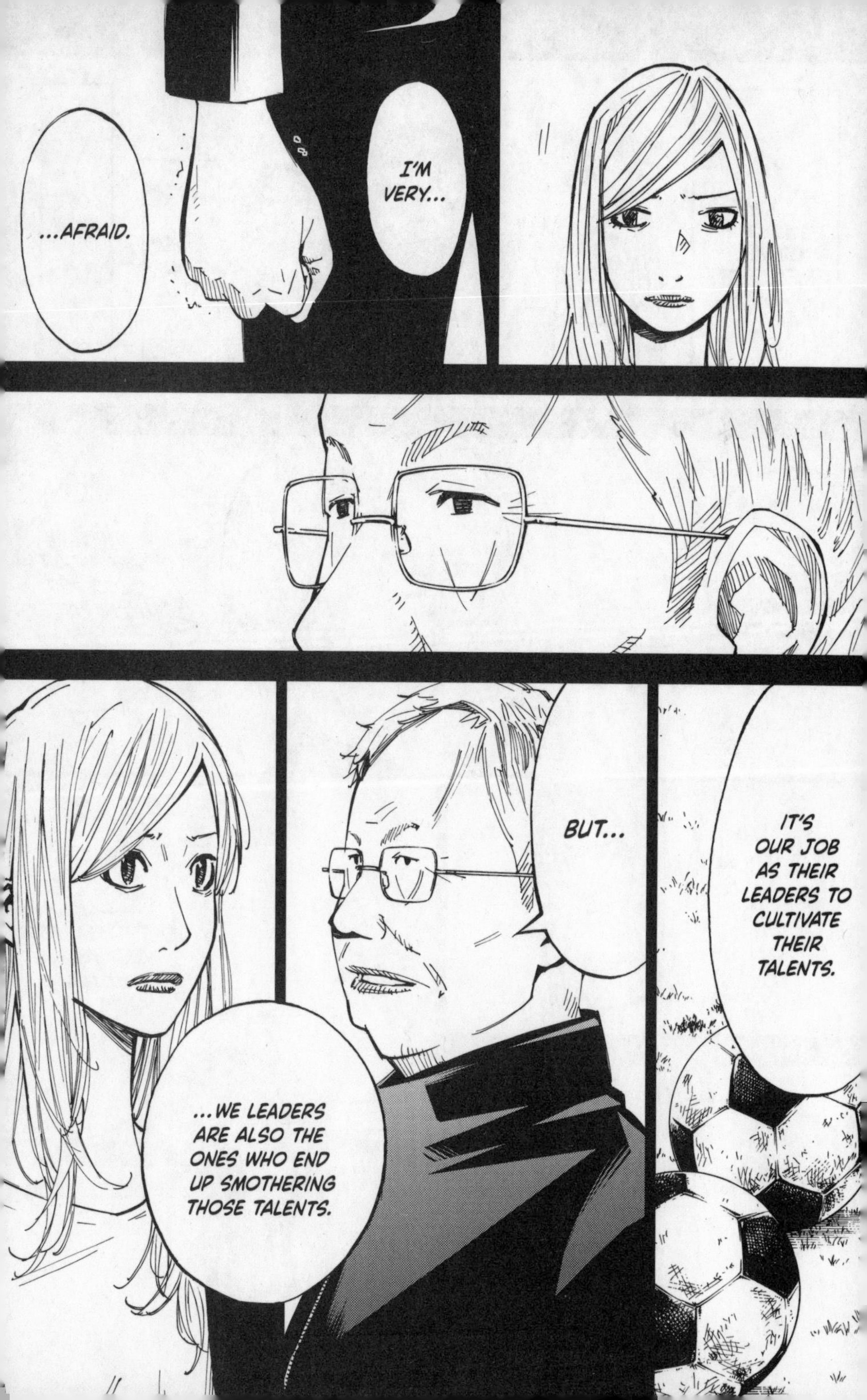
I'M VERY...
...AFRAID.
IT'S OUR JOB AS THEIR LEADERS TO CULTIVATE THEIR TALENTS.
BUT...
...WE LEADERS ARE ALSO THE ONES WHO END UP SMOTHERING THOSE TALENTS.

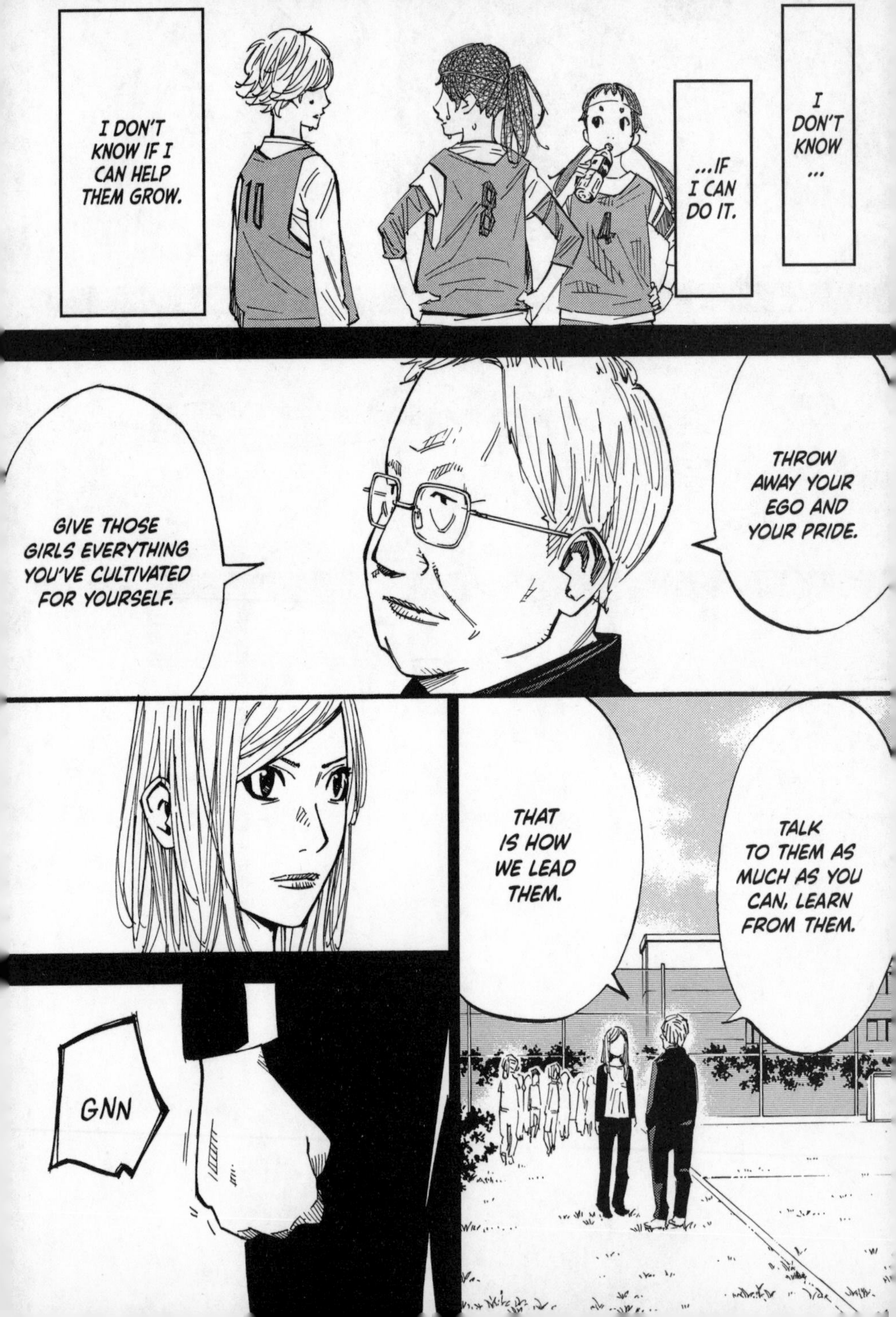
I DON'T KNOW ...
...IF I CAN DO IT.
I DON'T KNOW IF I CAN HELP THEM GROW.
THROW AWAY YOUR EGO AND YOUR PRIDE.
GIVE THOSE GIRLS EVERYTHING YOU'VE CULTIVATED FOR YOURSELF.
TALK TO THEM AS MUCH AS YOU CAN, LEARN FROM THEM.
THAT IS HOW WE LEAD THEM.
GNN

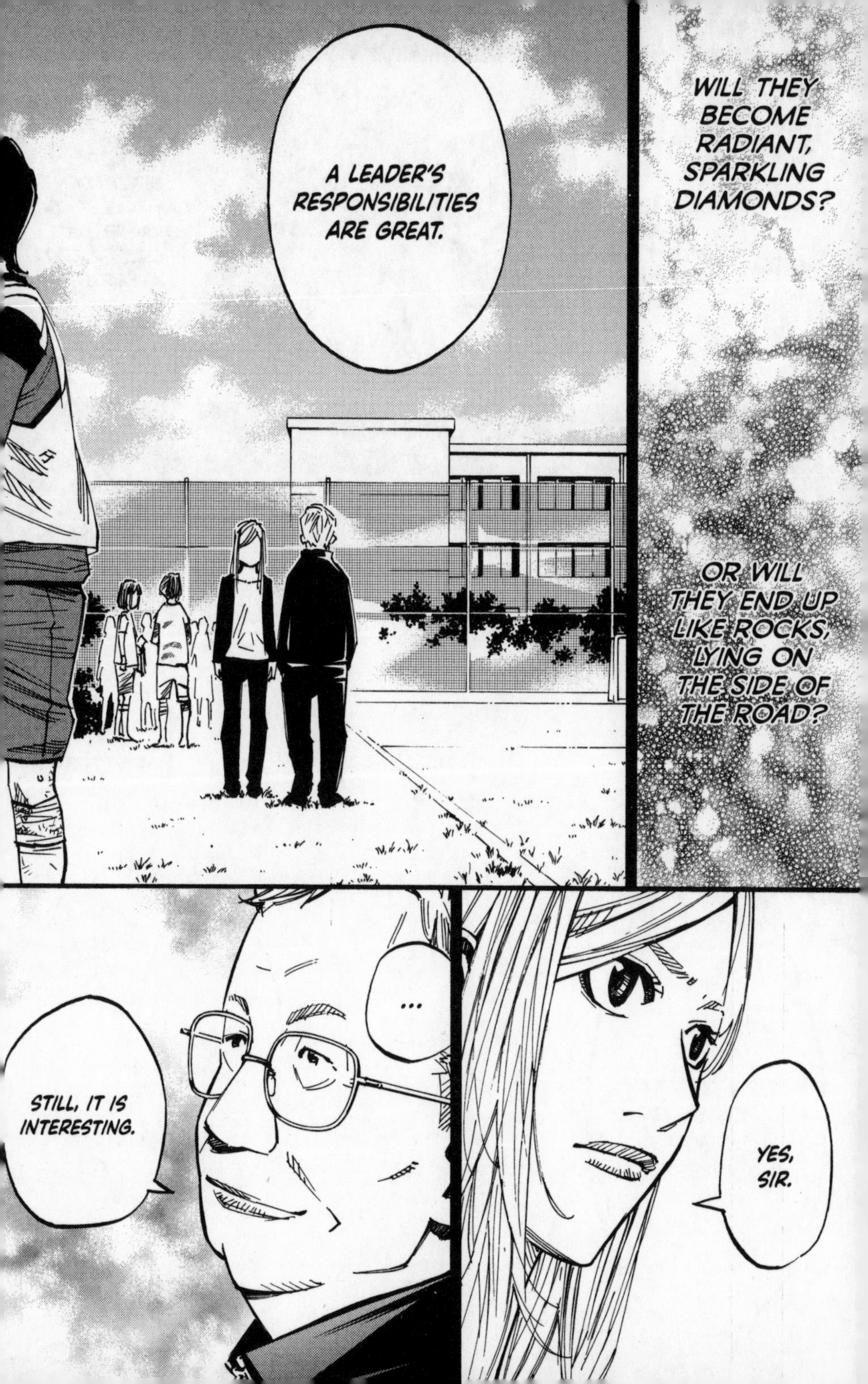
WILL THEY BECOME RADIANT, SPARKLING DIAMONDS?
OR WILL THEY END UP LIKE ROCKS, LYING ON THE SIDE OF THE ROAD?
A LEADER'S RESPONSIBILITIES ARE GREAT.
YES, SIR.
...
STILL, IT IS INTERESTING.

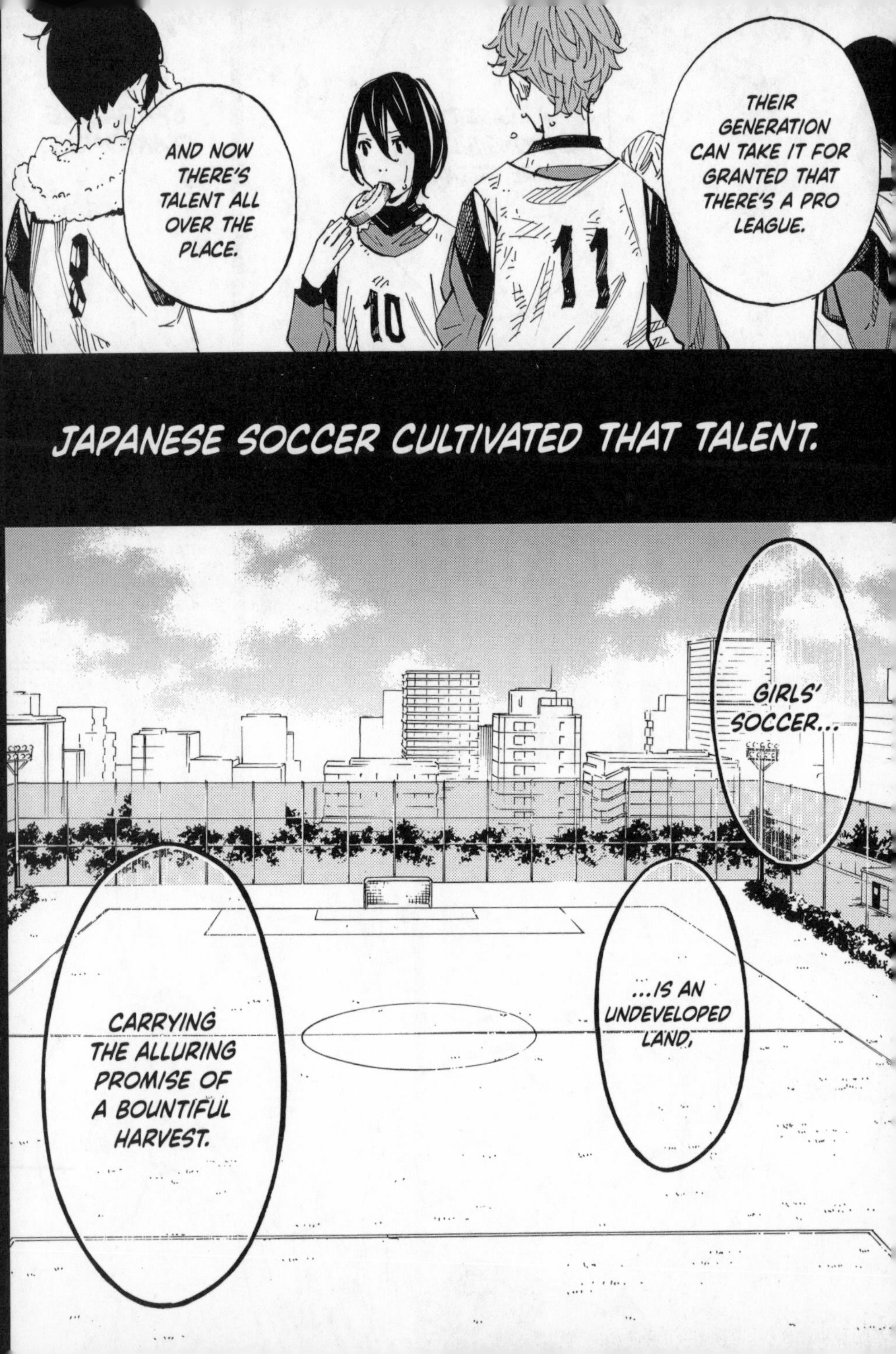
THEIR GENERATION CAN TAKE IT FOR GRANTED THAT THERE'S A PRO LEAGUE.
AND NOW THERE'S TALENT ALL OVER THE PLACE.
JAPANESE SOCCER CULTIVATED THAT TALENT.
GIRLS' SOCCER...
...IS AN UNDEVELOPED LAND,
CARRYING THE ALLURING PROMISE OF A BOUNTIFUL HARVEST.

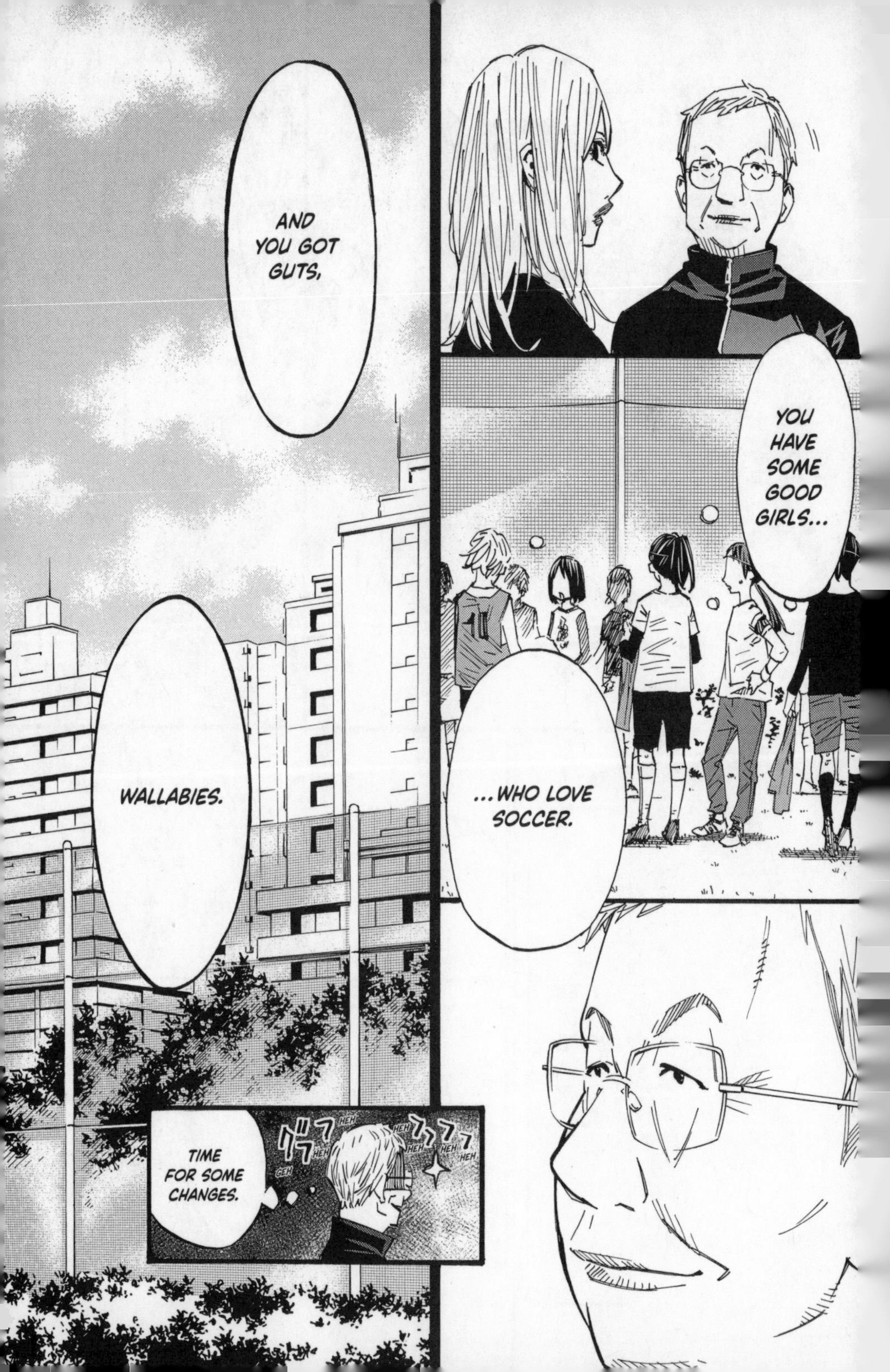
YOU HAVE SOME GOOD GIRLS...
...WHO LOVE SOCCER.
AND YOU GOT GUTS,
WALLABIES.
HEH
HEH
HEH
HEH
GEH
TIME FOR SOME CHANGES.

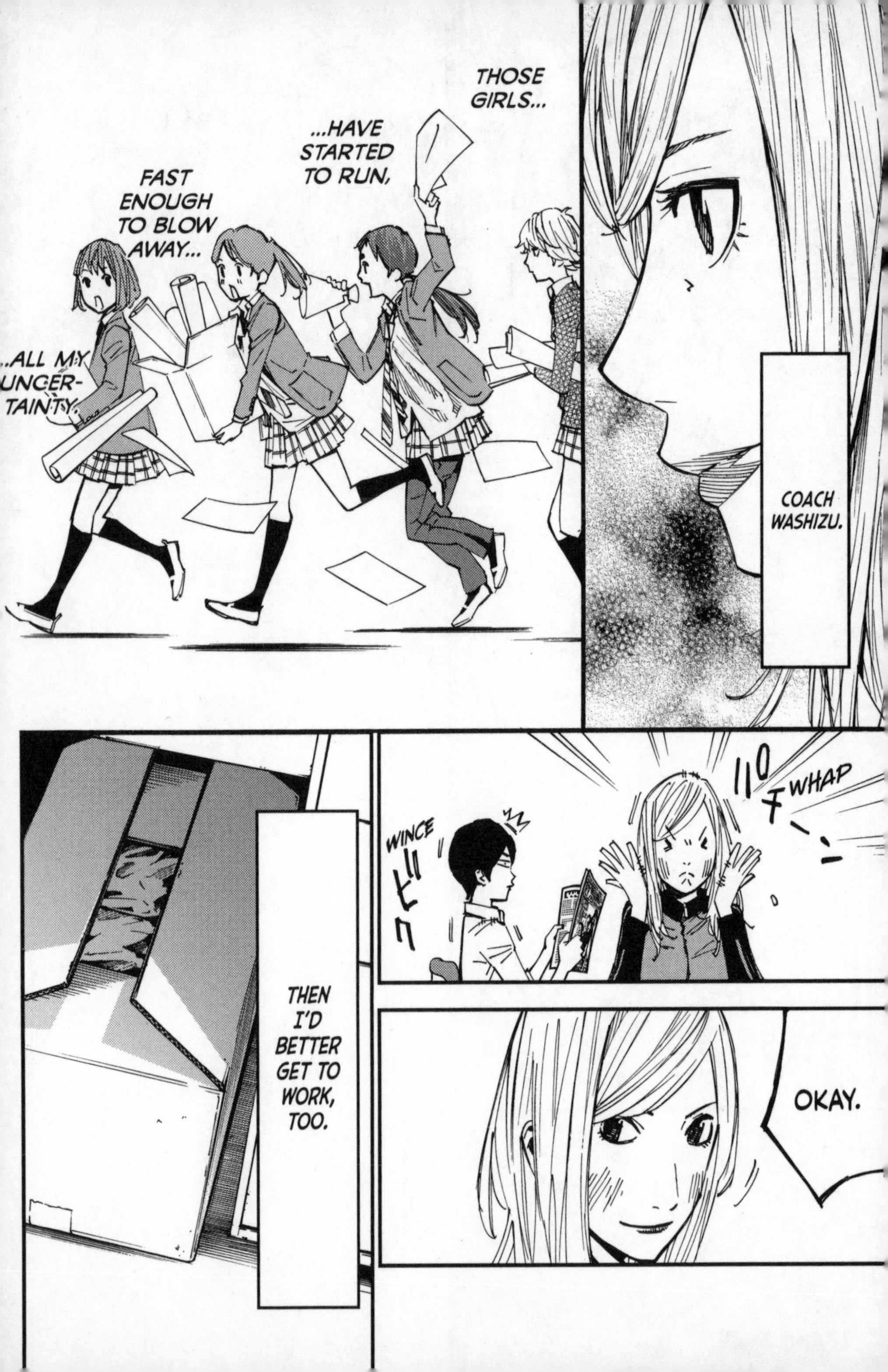
COACH WASHIZU.
THOSE GIRLS...
...HAVE STARTED TO RUN,
FAST ENOUGH TO BLOW AWAY...
...ALL MY UNCERTAINTY.
WHAP
WINCE
OKAY.
THEN I'D BETTER GET TO WORK, TOO.

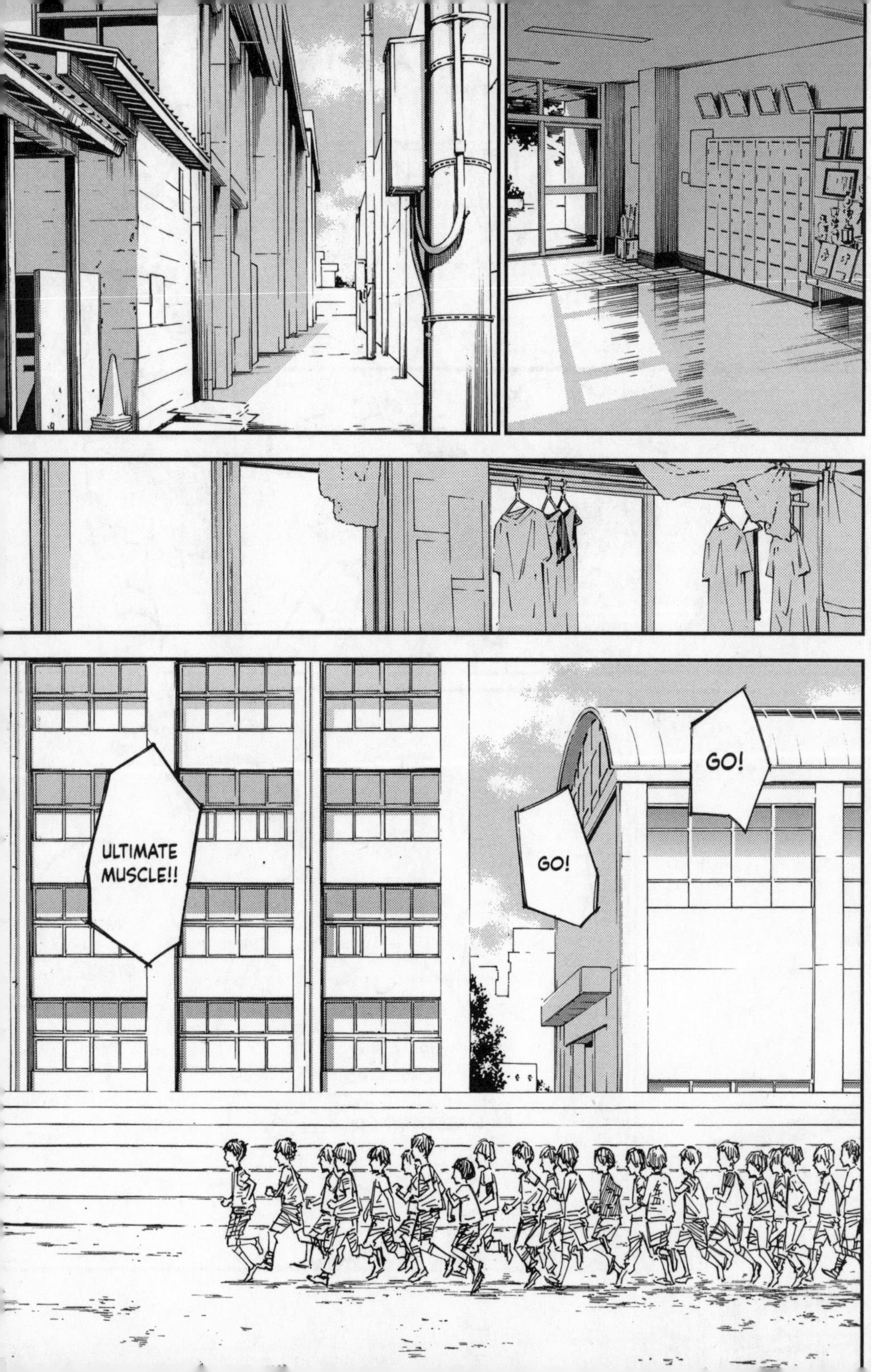
GO!
GO!
ULTIMATE MUSCLE!!

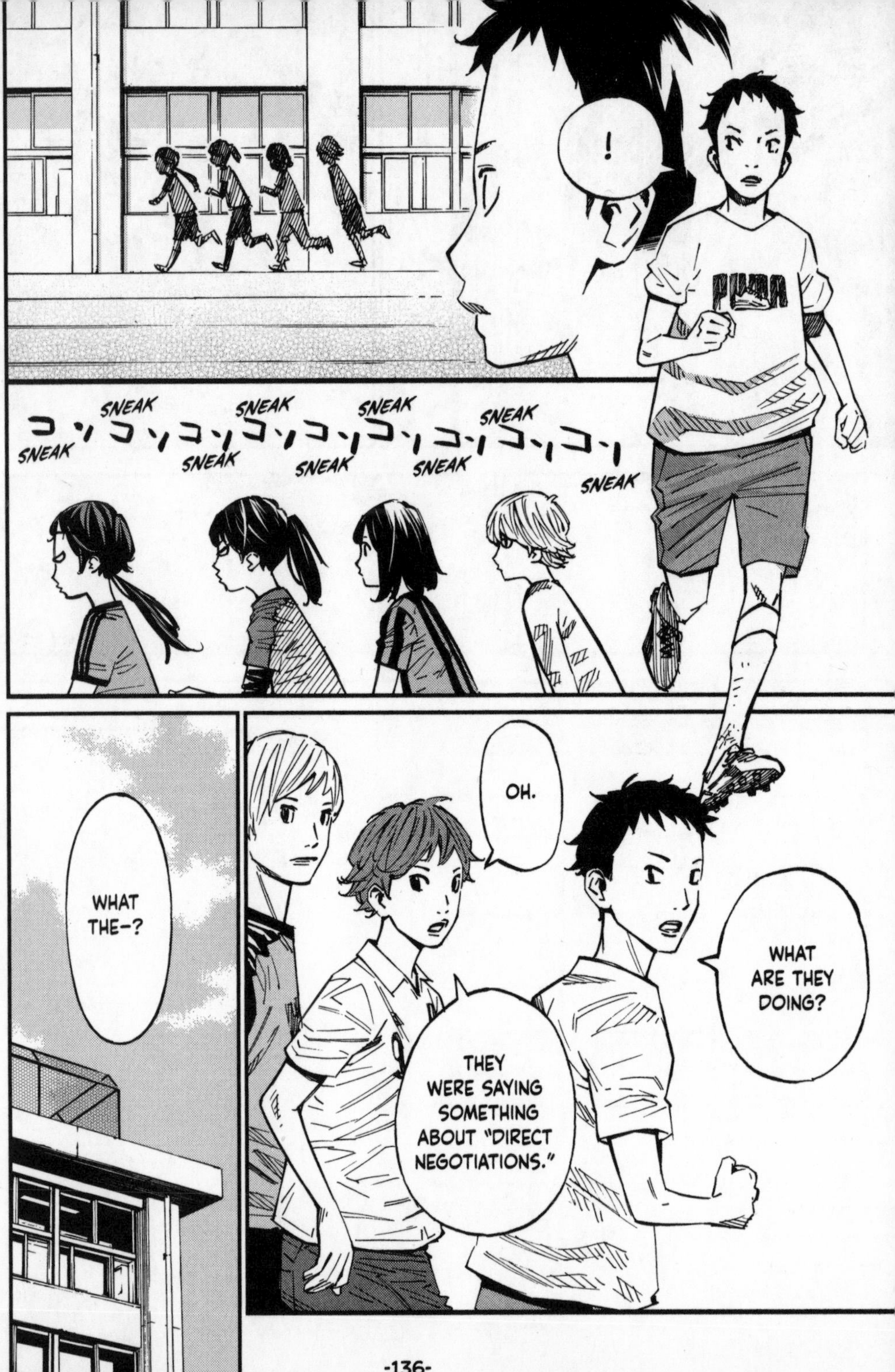
!
コソコソコソコソコソコソコソコソコソ
SNEAK SNEAK SNEAK SNEAK SNEAK SNEAK SNEAK SNEAK SNEAK
OH.
WHAT ARE THEY DOING?
THEY WERE SAYING SOMETHING ABOUT "DIRECT NEGOTIATIONS."
WHAT THE–?

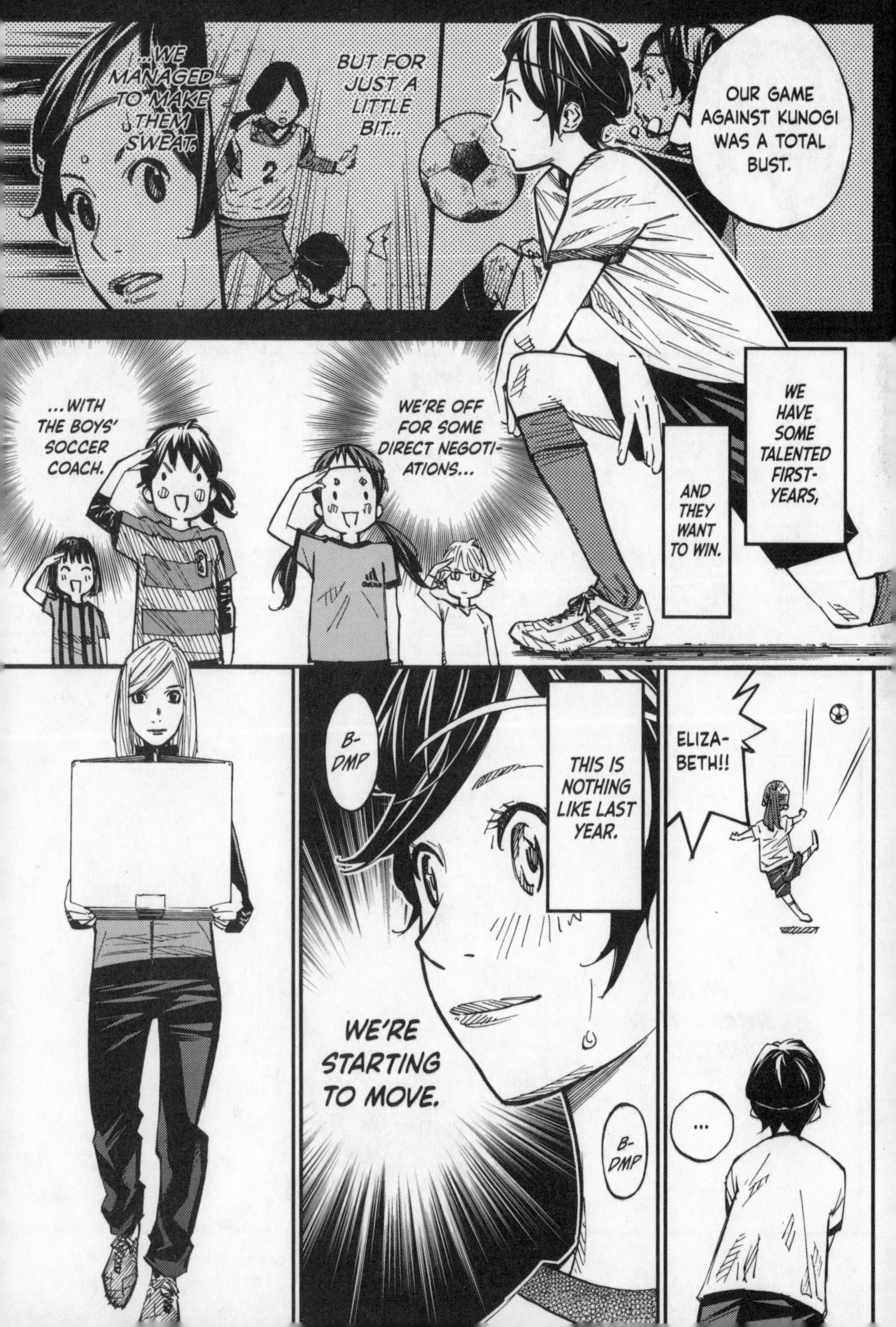
OUR GAME AGAINST KUNOGI WAS A TOTAL BUST.
BUT FOR JUST A LITTLE BIT...
...WE MANAGED TO MAKE THEM SWEAT.
WE HAVE SOME TALENTED FIRST-YEARS,
AND THEY WANT TO WIN.
WE'RE OFF FOR SOME DIRECT NEGOTI-ATIONS...
...WITH THE BOYS' SOCCER COACH.
ELIZA-BETH!!
...
THIS IS NOTHING LIKE LAST YEAR.
B-DMP
WE'RE STARTING TO MOVE.
B-DMP

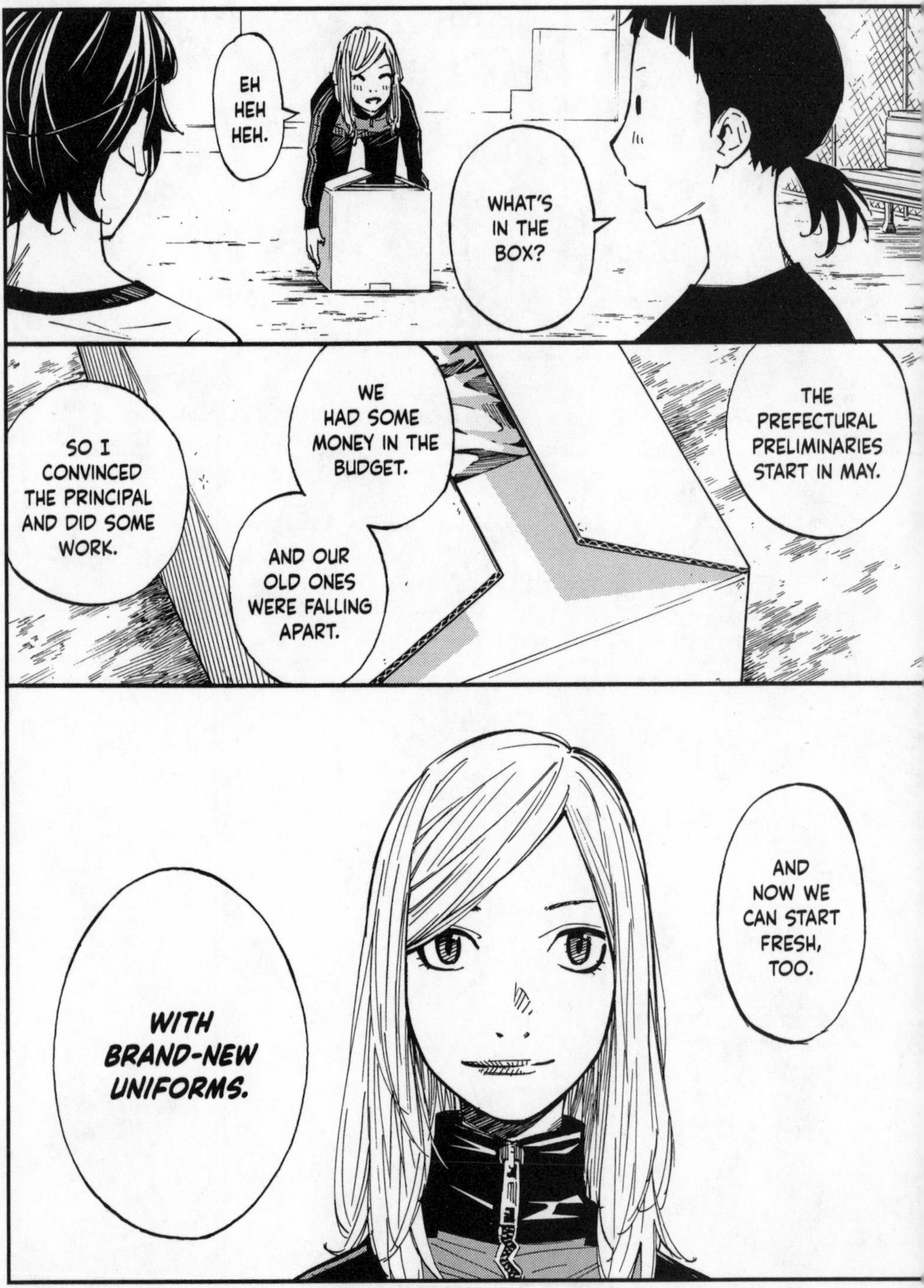
WHAT'S IN THE BOX?
EH HEH HEH.
THE PREFECTURAL PRELIMINARIES START IN MAY.
WE HAD SOME MONEY IN THE BUDGET.
AND OUR OLD ONES WERE FALLING APART.
SO I CONVINCED THE PRINCIPAL AND DID SOME WORK.
AND NOW WE CAN START FRESH, TOO.
WITH BRAND-NEW UNIFORMS.

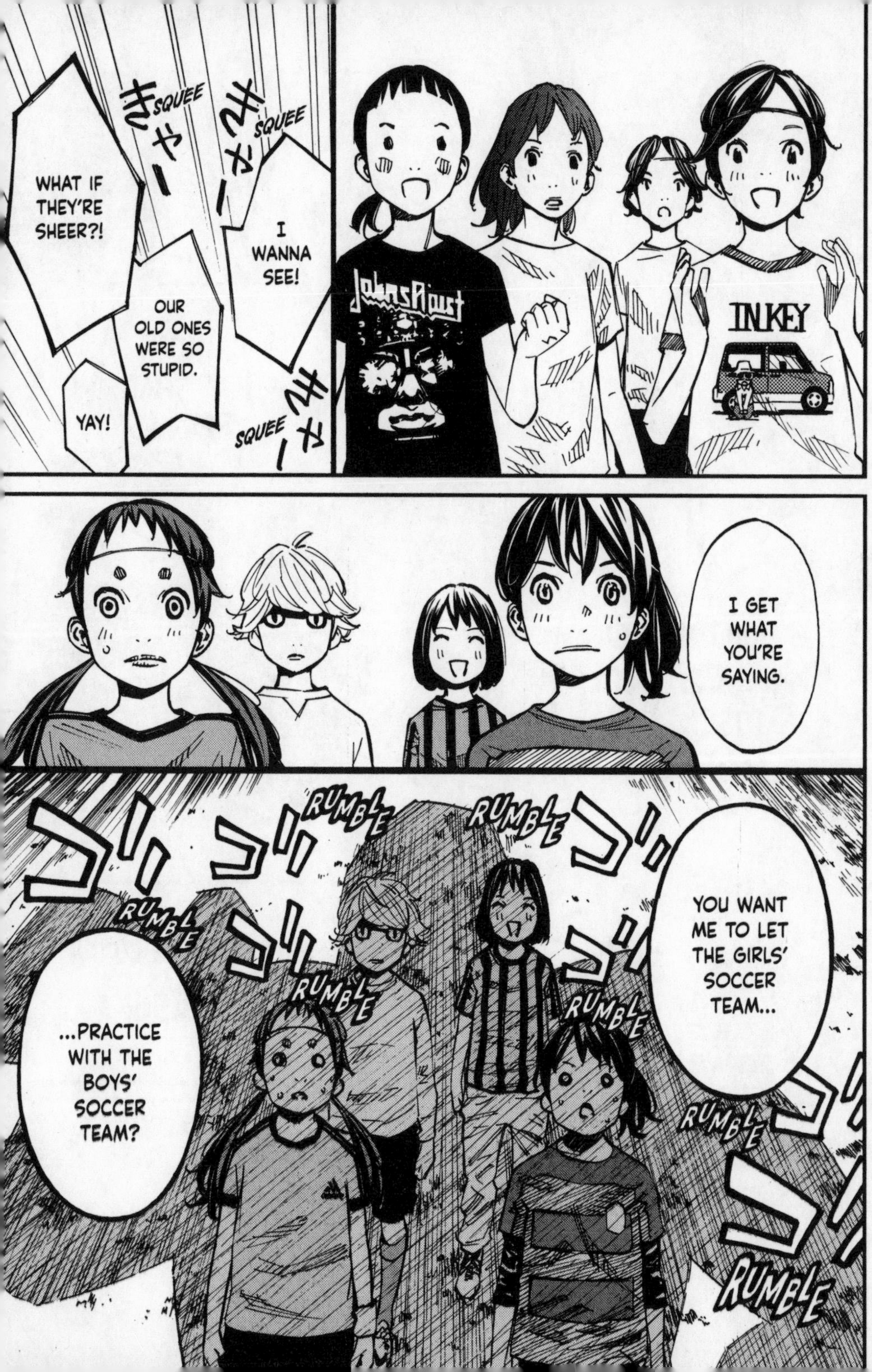

きゃー SQUEE
I WANNA SEE!
きゃー SQUEE
WHAT IF THEY'RE SHEER?!
OUR OLD ONES WERE SO STUPID.
きゃー SQUEE
YAY!
I GET WHAT YOU'RE SAYING.
RUMBLE
RUMBLE
YOU WANT ME TO LET THE GIRLS' SOCCER TEAM...
RUMBLE
RUMBLE
RUMBLE
...PRACTICE WITH THE BOYS' SOCCER TEAM?
RUMBLE
RUMBLE

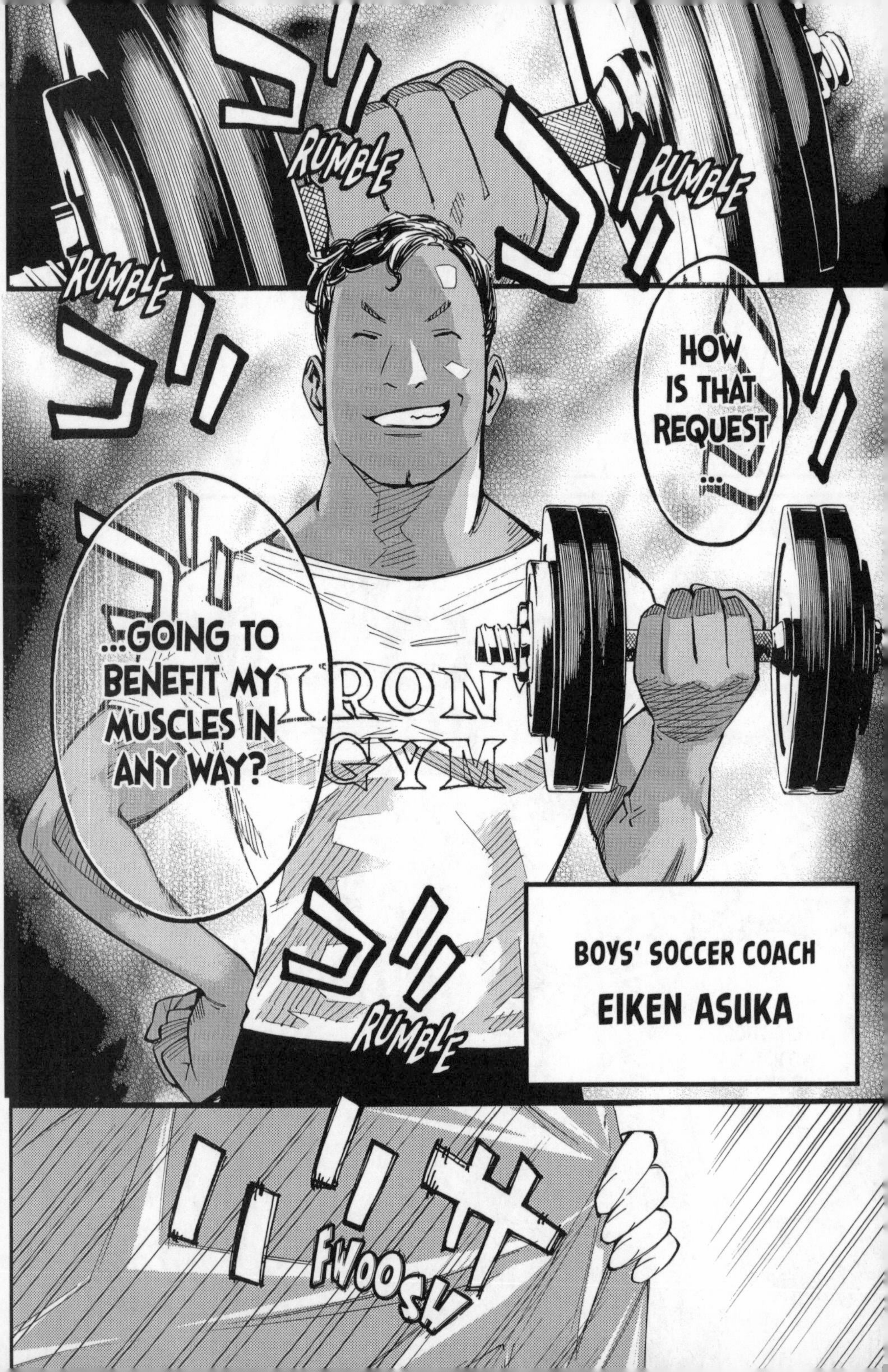
RUMBLE
RUMBLE
RUMBLE
HOW IS THAT REQUEST...
...GOING TO BENEFIT MY MUSCLES IN ANY WAY?
IRON GYM
BOYS' SOCCER COACH
EIKEN ASUKA
RUMBLE
FWOOSH

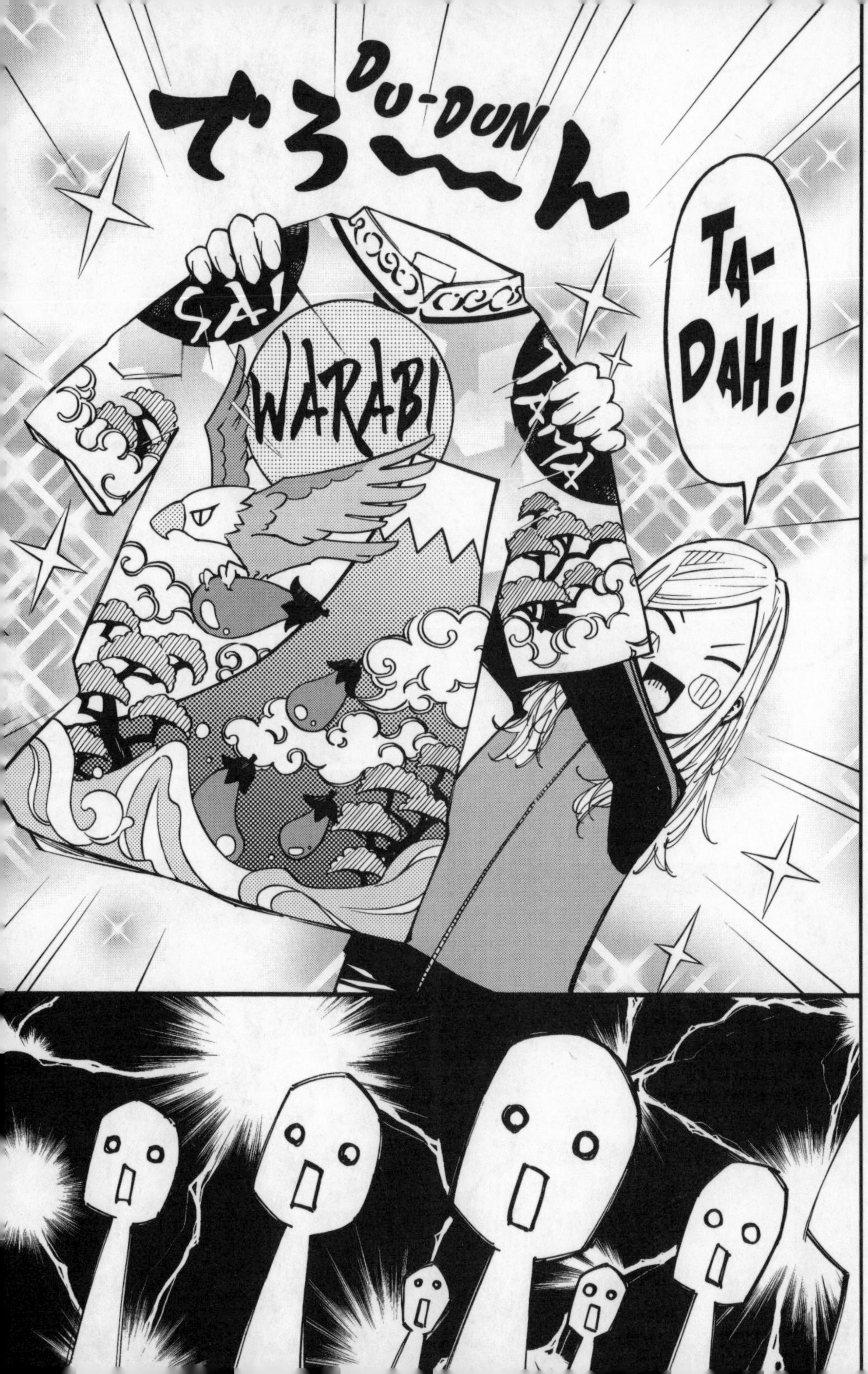
TA-DAH!
でろ〜〜ん
DU-DUN
WARABI

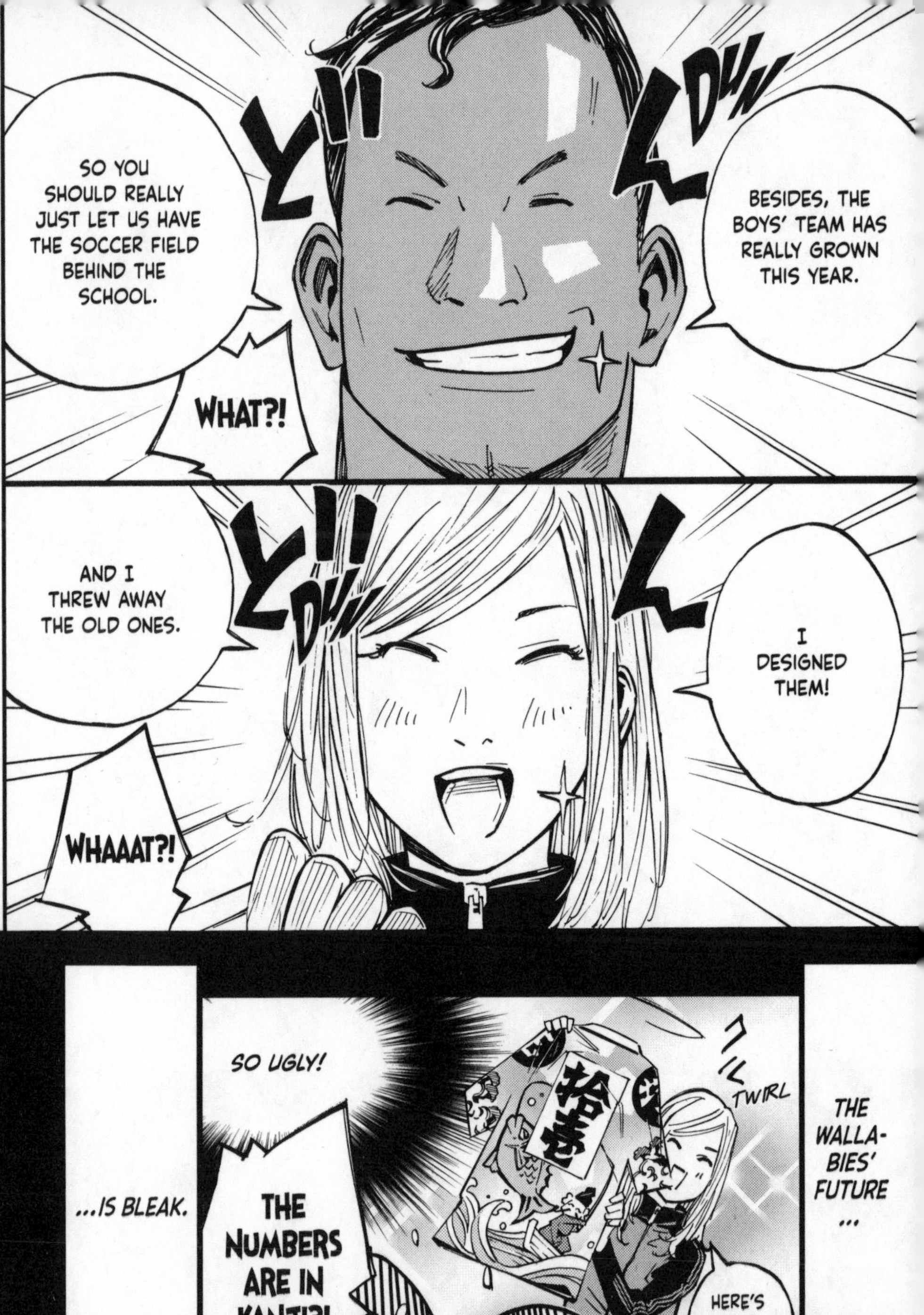
BESIDES, THE BOYS' TEAM HAS REALLY GROWN THIS YEAR.
DUN
SO YOU SHOULD REALLY JUST LET US HAVE THE SOCCER FIELD BEHIND THE SCHOOL.
WHAT?!
I DESIGNED THEM!
DUN
AND I THREW AWAY THE OLD ONES.
WHAAAT?!
THE WALLABIES' FUTURE ...
HERE'S THE BACK!
TWIRL
拾壱
THE NUMBERS ARE IN KANJI?!
SO UGLY!
...IS BLEAK.

Farewell, My Dear Cramer

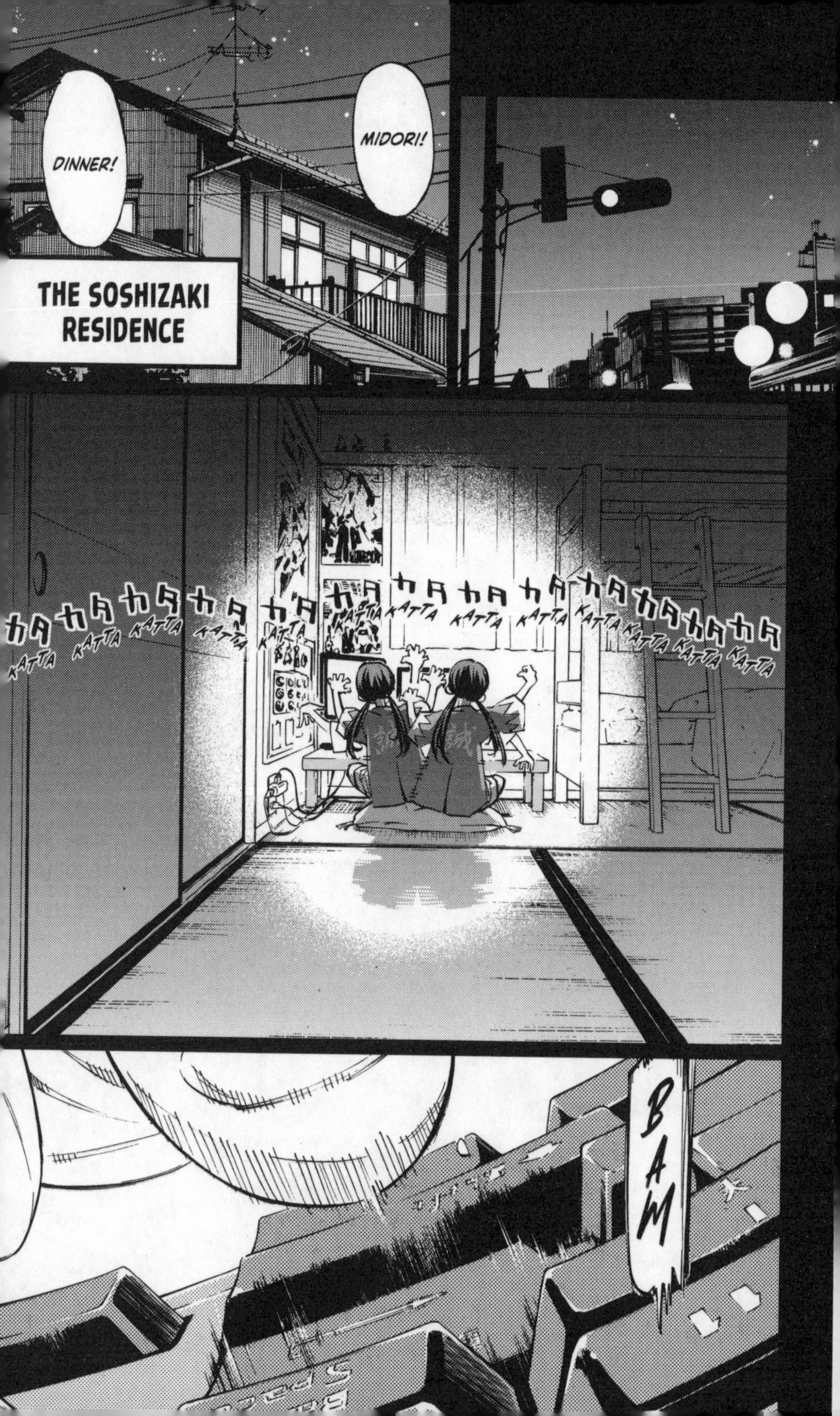
MIDORI!
DINNER!
THE SOSHIZAKI RESIDENCE
カタカタカタカタカタカタカタカタカタカタカタカタカタカタ
KATTA KATTA KATTA KATTA KATTA KATTA KATTA KATTA KATTA KATTA KATTA KATTA KATTA
BAM

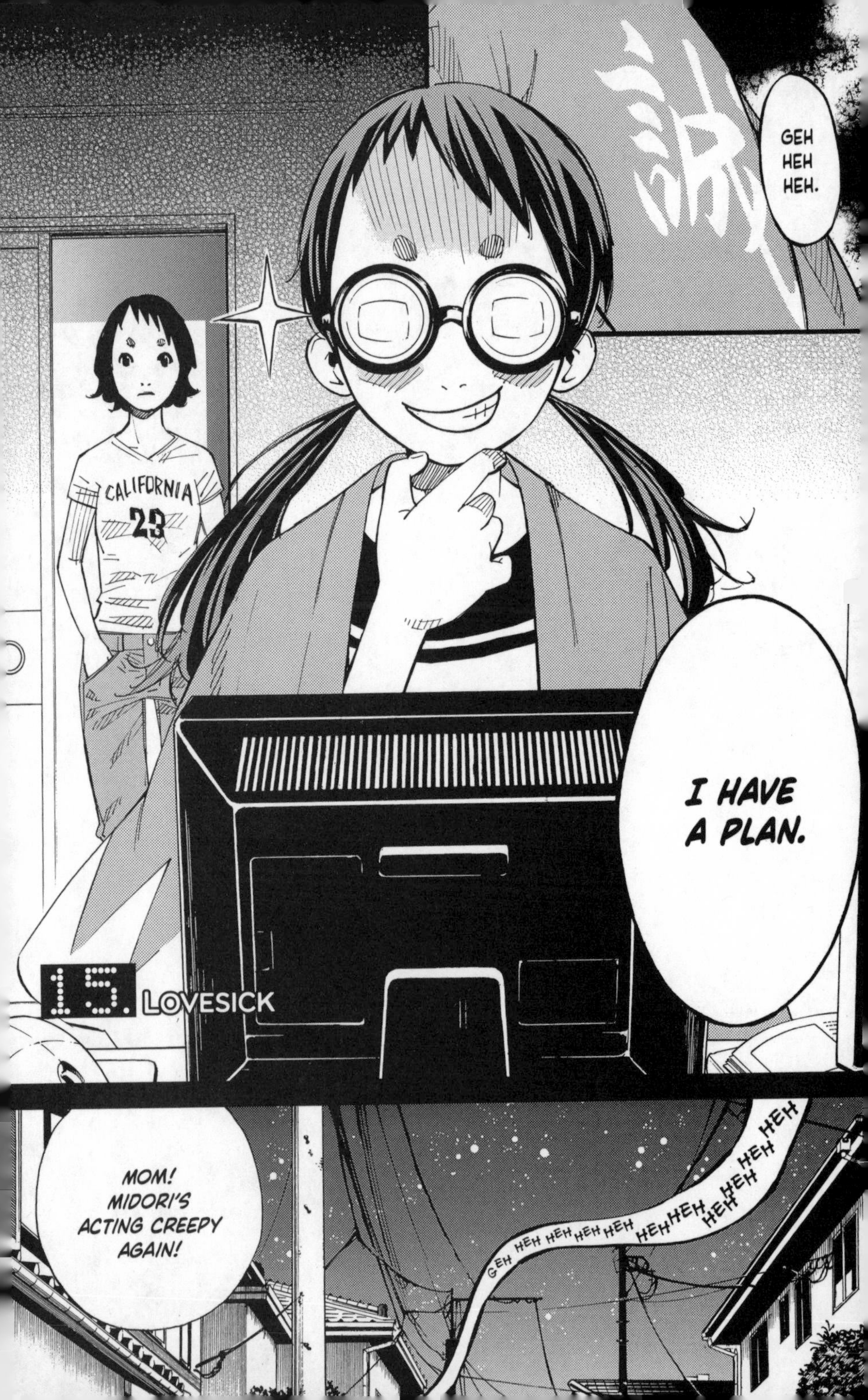
GEH HEH HEH.
I HAVE A PLAN.
15. LOVESICK
CALIFORNIA 23
GEH HEH HEH HEH HEH HEH HEH HEH HEH HEH HEH HEH HEH
MOM! MIDORI'S ACTING CREEPY AGAIN!

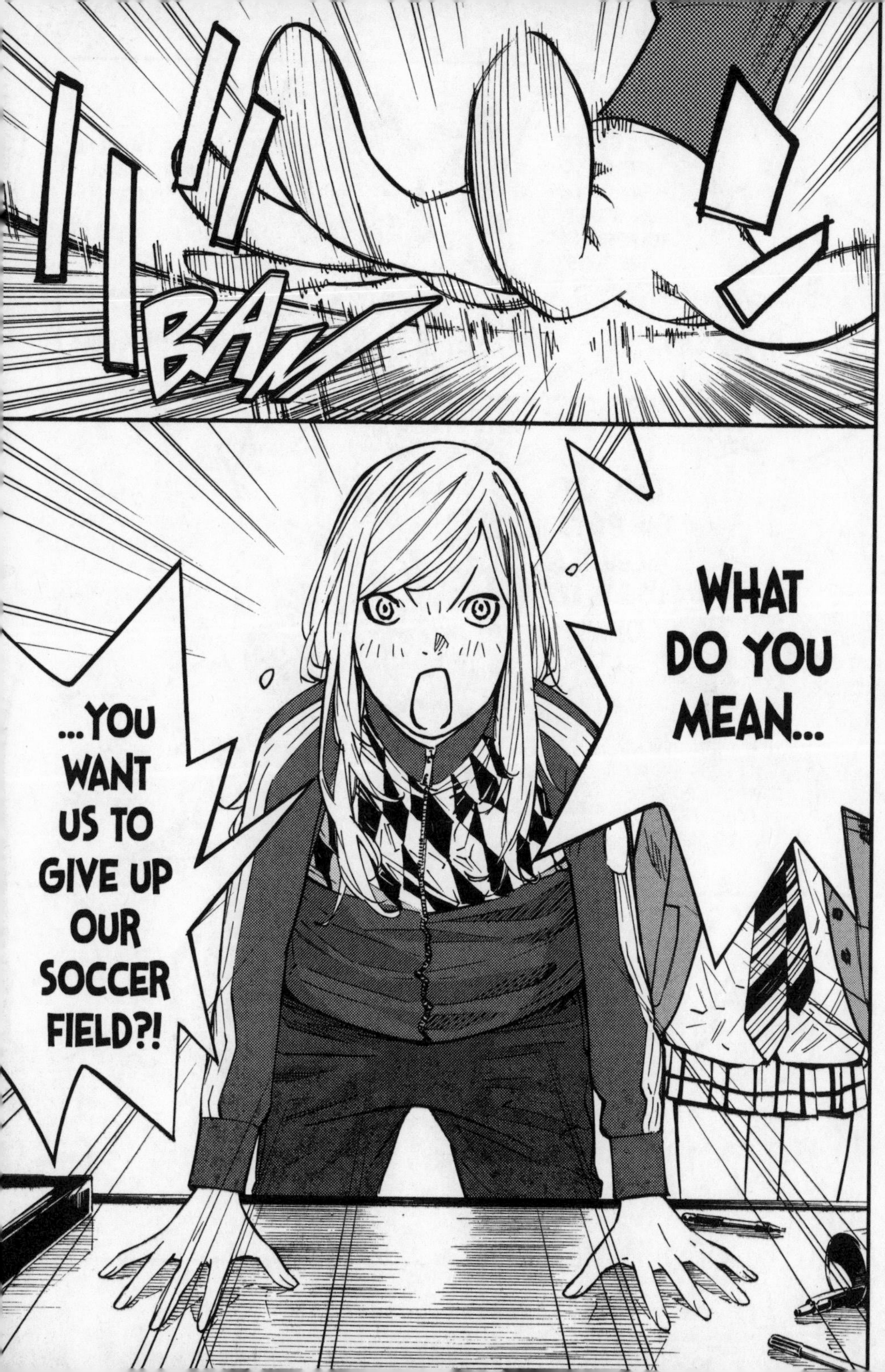
BAM
WHAT DO YOU MEAN...
...YOU WANT US TO GIVE UP OUR SOCCER FIELD?!

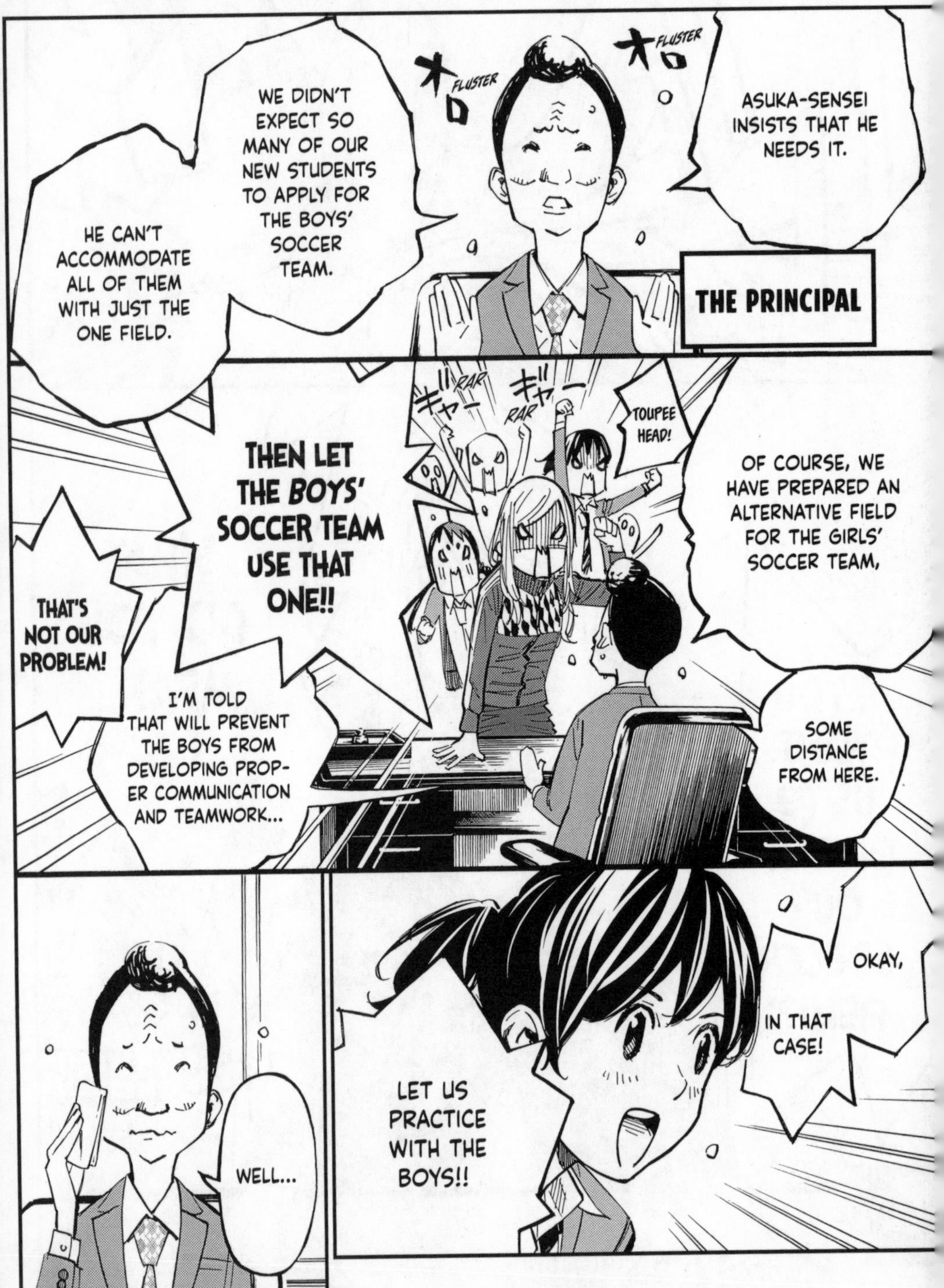
ASUKA-SENSEI INSISTS THAT HE NEEDS IT.
FLUSTER
FLUSTER
WE DIDN'T EXPECT SO MANY OF OUR NEW STUDENTS TO APPLY FOR THE BOYS' SOCCER TEAM.
HE CAN'T ACCOMMODATE ALL OF THEM WITH JUST THE ONE FIELD.
THE PRINCIPAL
OF COURSE, WE HAVE PREPARED AN ALTERNATIVE FIELD FOR THE GIRLS' SOCCER TEAM,
SOME DISTANCE FROM HERE.
TOUPEE HEAD!
RAR
RAR
THEN LET THE *BOYS'* SOCCER TEAM USE THAT ONE!!
I'M TOLD THAT WILL PREVENT THE BOYS FROM DEVELOPING PROPER COMMUNICATION AND TEAMWORK...
THAT'S NOT OUR PROBLEM!
OKAY,
IN THAT CASE!
LET US PRACTICE WITH THE BOYS!!
WELL...

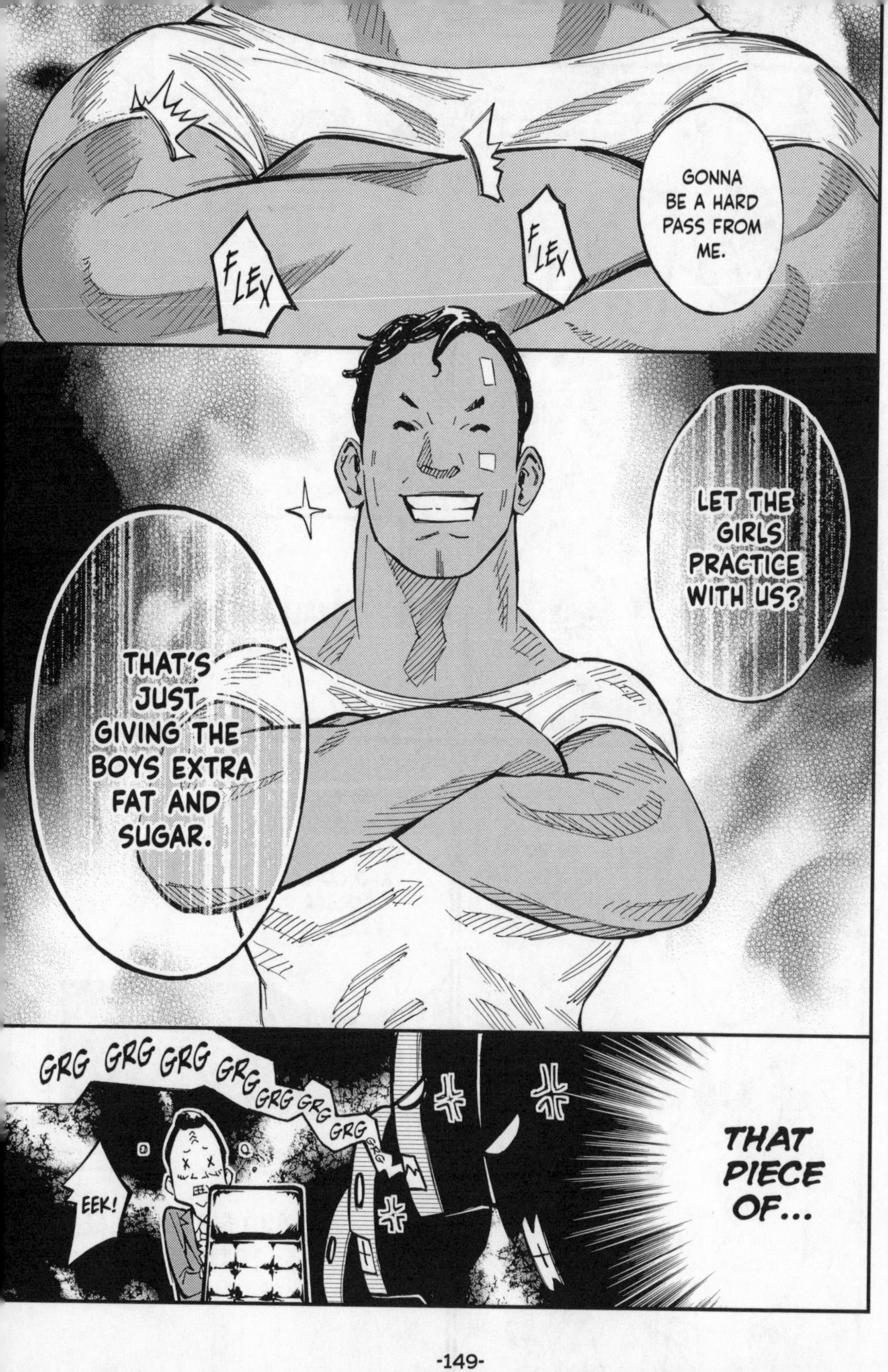
GONNA BE A HARD PASS FROM ME.
FLEX
FLEX
LET THE GIRLS PRACTICE WITH US?
THAT'S JUST GIVING THE BOYS EXTRA FAT AND SUGAR.
THAT PIECE OF...
GRG GRG GRG GRG GRG GRG GRG
EEK!

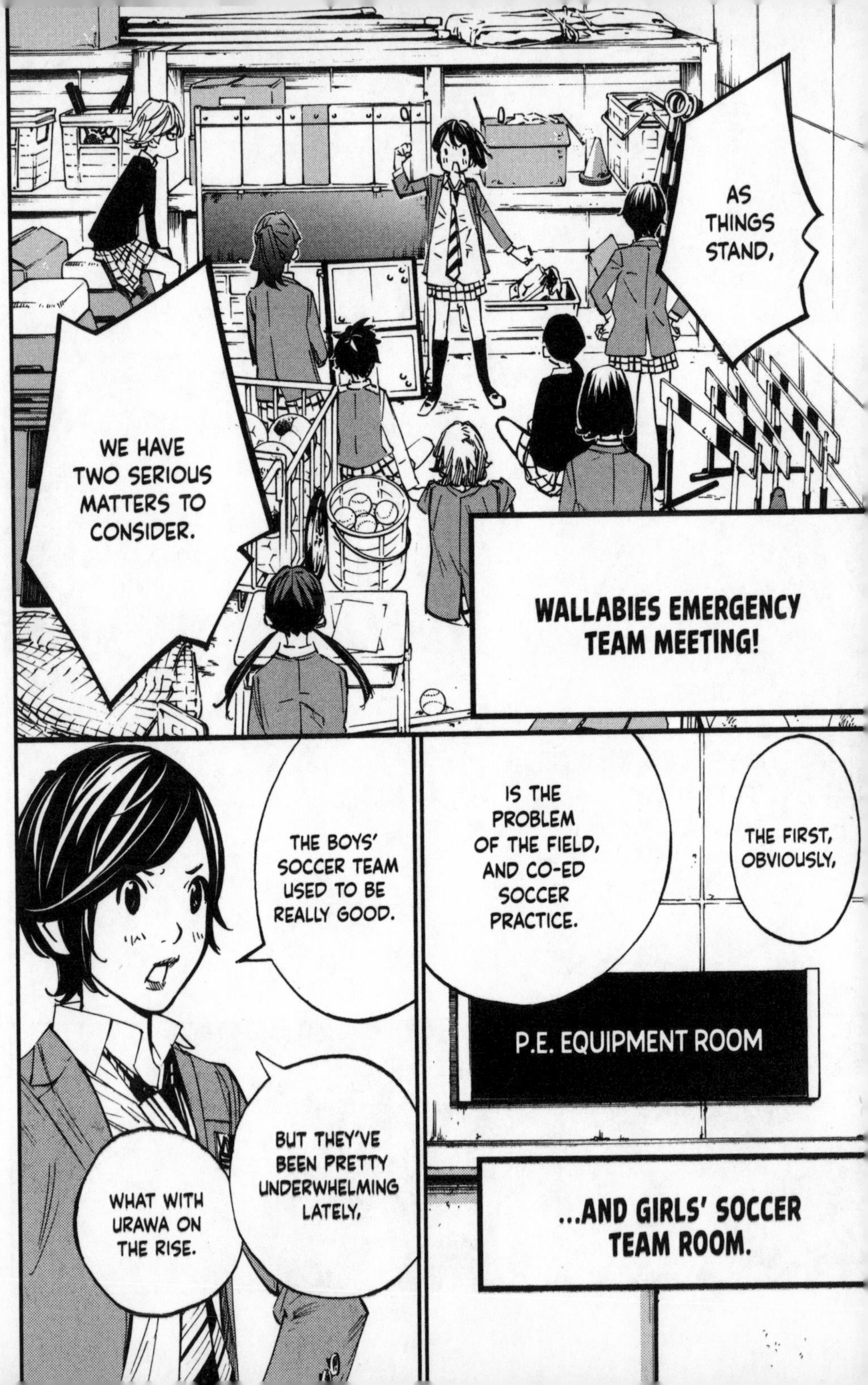
AS THINGS STAND,
WE HAVE TWO SERIOUS MATTERS TO CONSIDER.
WALLABIES EMERGENCY TEAM MEETING!
THE FIRST, OBVIOUSLY,
IS THE PROBLEM OF THE FIELD, AND CO-ED SOCCER PRACTICE.
P.E. EQUIPMENT ROOM
...AND GIRLS' SOCCER TEAM ROOM.
THE BOYS' SOCCER TEAM USED TO BE REALLY GOOD.
BUT THEY'VE BEEN PRETTY UNDERWHELMING LATELY,
WHAT WITH URAWA ON THE RISE.

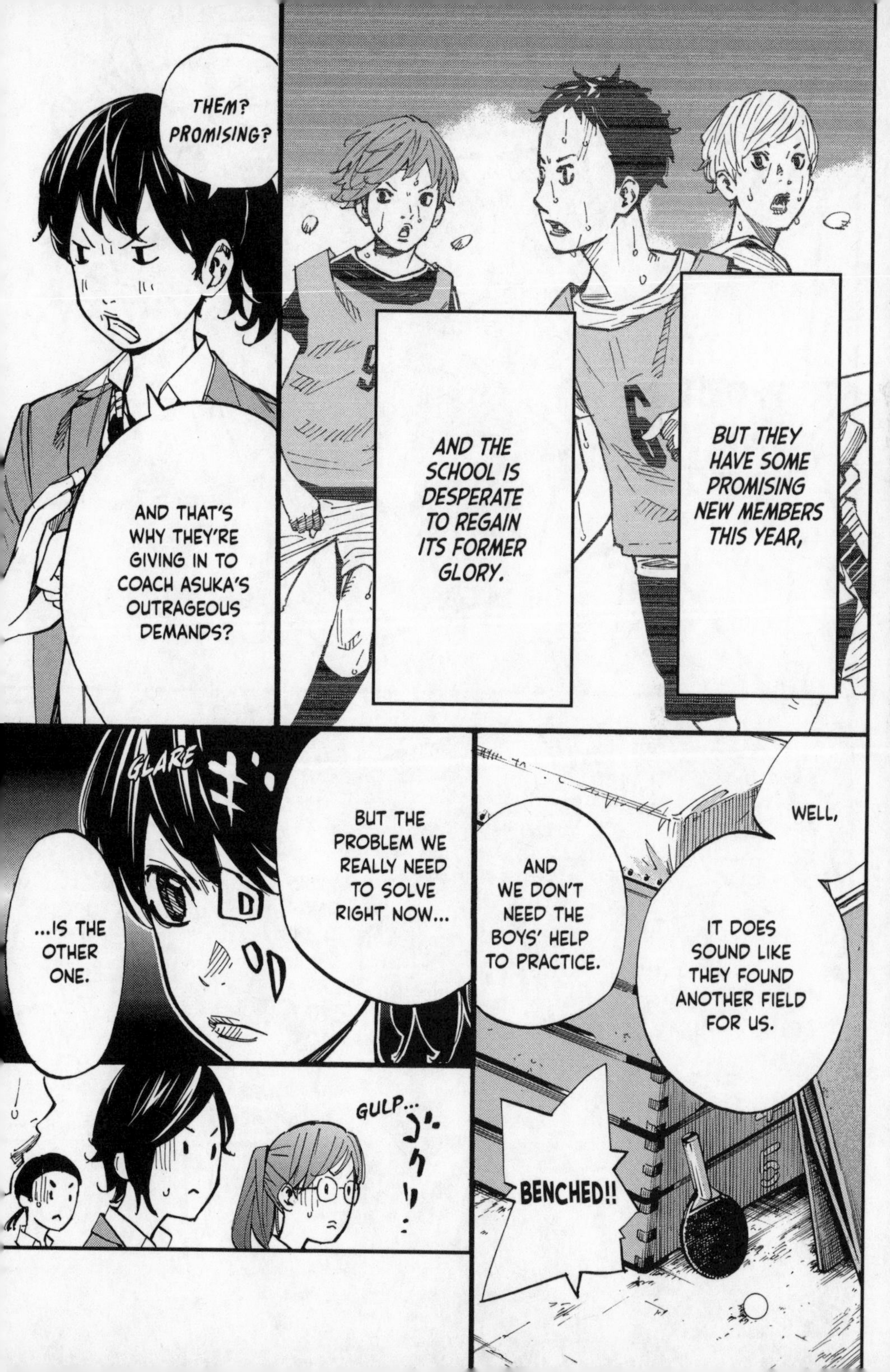
BUT THEY HAVE SOME PROMISING NEW MEMBERS THIS YEAR,
AND THE SCHOOL IS DESPERATE TO REGAIN ITS FORMER GLORY.
THEM? PROMISING?
AND THAT'S WHY THEY'RE GIVING IN TO COACH ASUKA'S OUTRAGEOUS DEMANDS?
WELL,
IT DOES SOUND LIKE THEY FOUND ANOTHER FIELD FOR US.
AND WE DON'T NEED THE BOYS' HELP TO PRACTICE.
BENCHED!!
GLARE
BUT THE PROBLEM WE REALLY NEED TO SOLVE RIGHT NOW...
...IS THE OTHER ONE.
GULP...

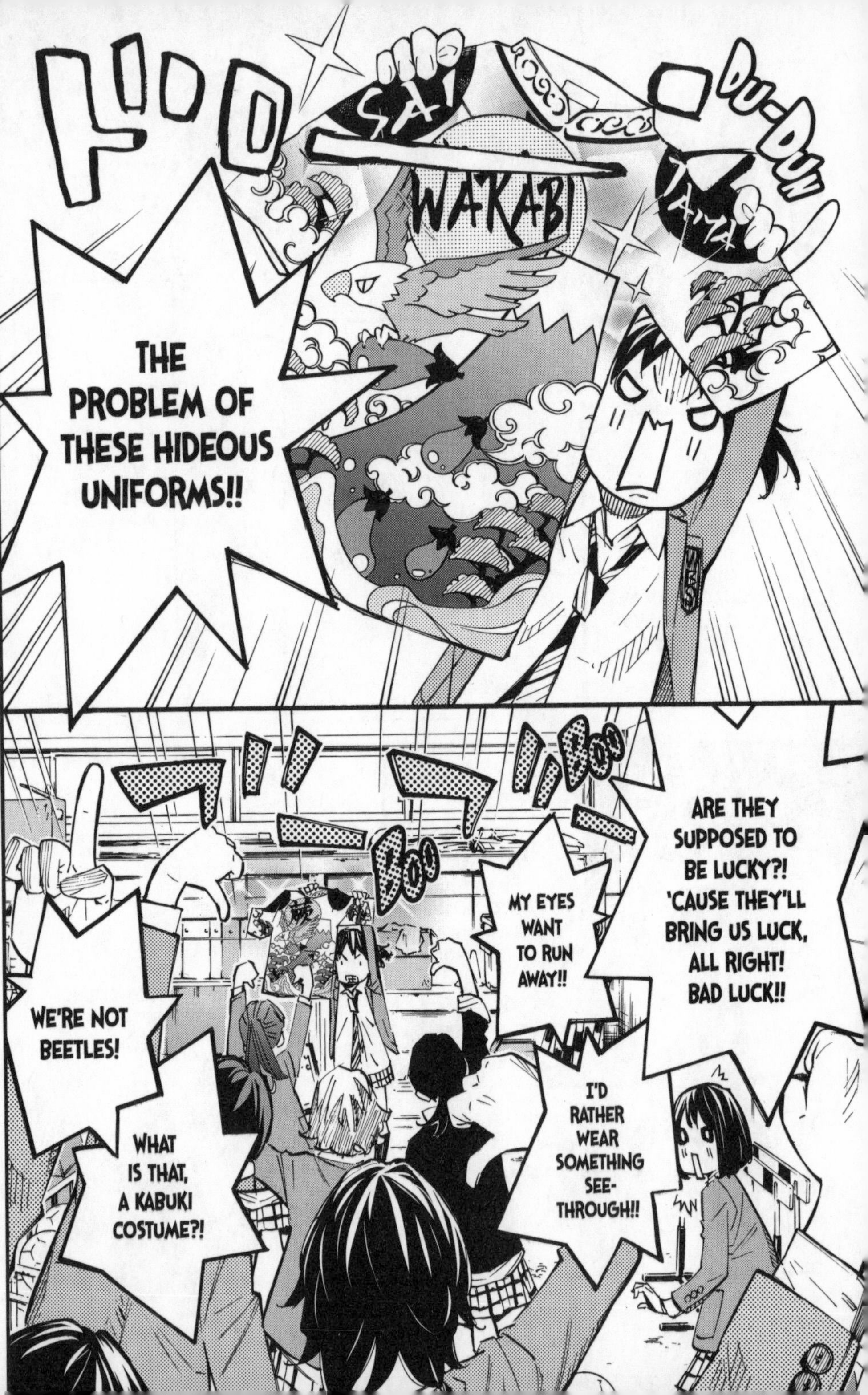
DU-DUN
SAI
WAKABI
TAIYA
THE PROBLEM OF THESE HIDEOUS UNIFORMS!!
BOO
ARE THEY SUPPOSED TO BE LUCKY?! 'CAUSE THEY'LL BRING US LUCK, ALL RIGHT! BAD LUCK!!
MY EYES WANT TO RUN AWAY!!
BOO
WE'RE NOT BEETLES!
I'D RATHER WEAR SOMETHING SEE-THROUGH!!
WHAT IS THAT, A KABUKI COSTUME?!

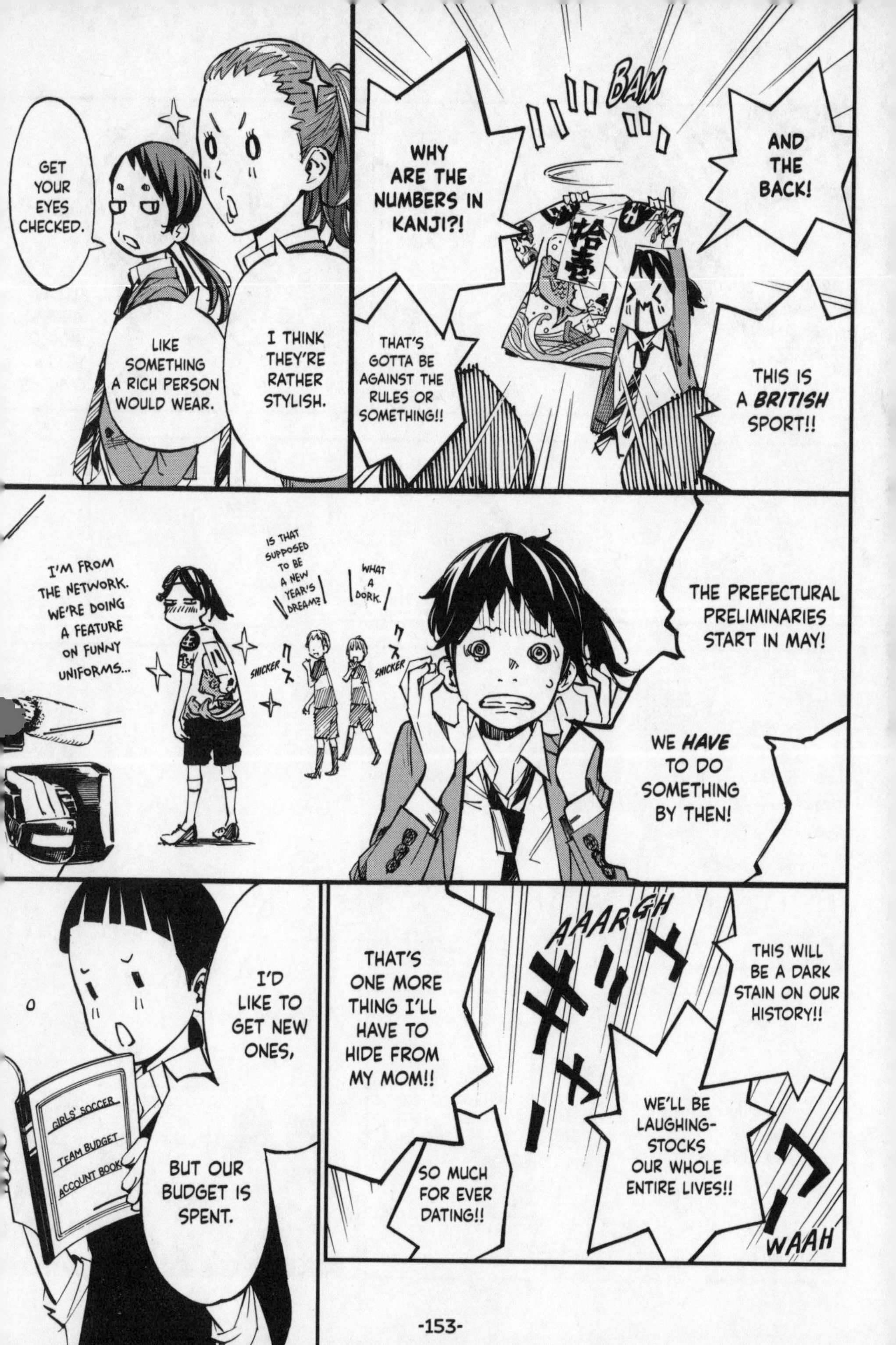
BAM
AND THE BACK!
WHY ARE THE NUMBERS IN KANJI?!
THIS IS A BRITISH SPORT!!
THAT'S GOTTA BE AGAINST THE RULES OR SOMETHING!!
I THINK THEY'RE RATHER STYLISH.
GET YOUR EYES CHECKED.
LIKE SOMETHING A RICH PERSON WOULD WEAR.
THE PREFECTURAL PRELIMINARIES START IN MAY!
WE HAVE TO DO SOMETHING BY THEN!
WHAT A DORK.
SNICKER
IS THAT SUPPOSED TO BE A NEW YEAR'S DREAM?
SNICKER
I'M FROM THE NETWORK. WE'RE DOING A FEATURE ON FUNNY UNIFORMS...
THIS WILL BE A DARK STAIN ON OUR HISTORY!!
AAARGH
THAT'S ONE MORE THING I'LL HAVE TO HIDE FROM MY MOM!!
WE'LL BE LAUGHING-STOCKS OUR WHOLE ENTIRE LIVES!!
WAAH
SO MUCH FOR EVER DATING!!
I'D LIKE TO GET NEW ONES,
GIRLS' SOCCER TEAM BUDGET ACCOUNT BOOK
BUT OUR BUDGET IS SPENT.

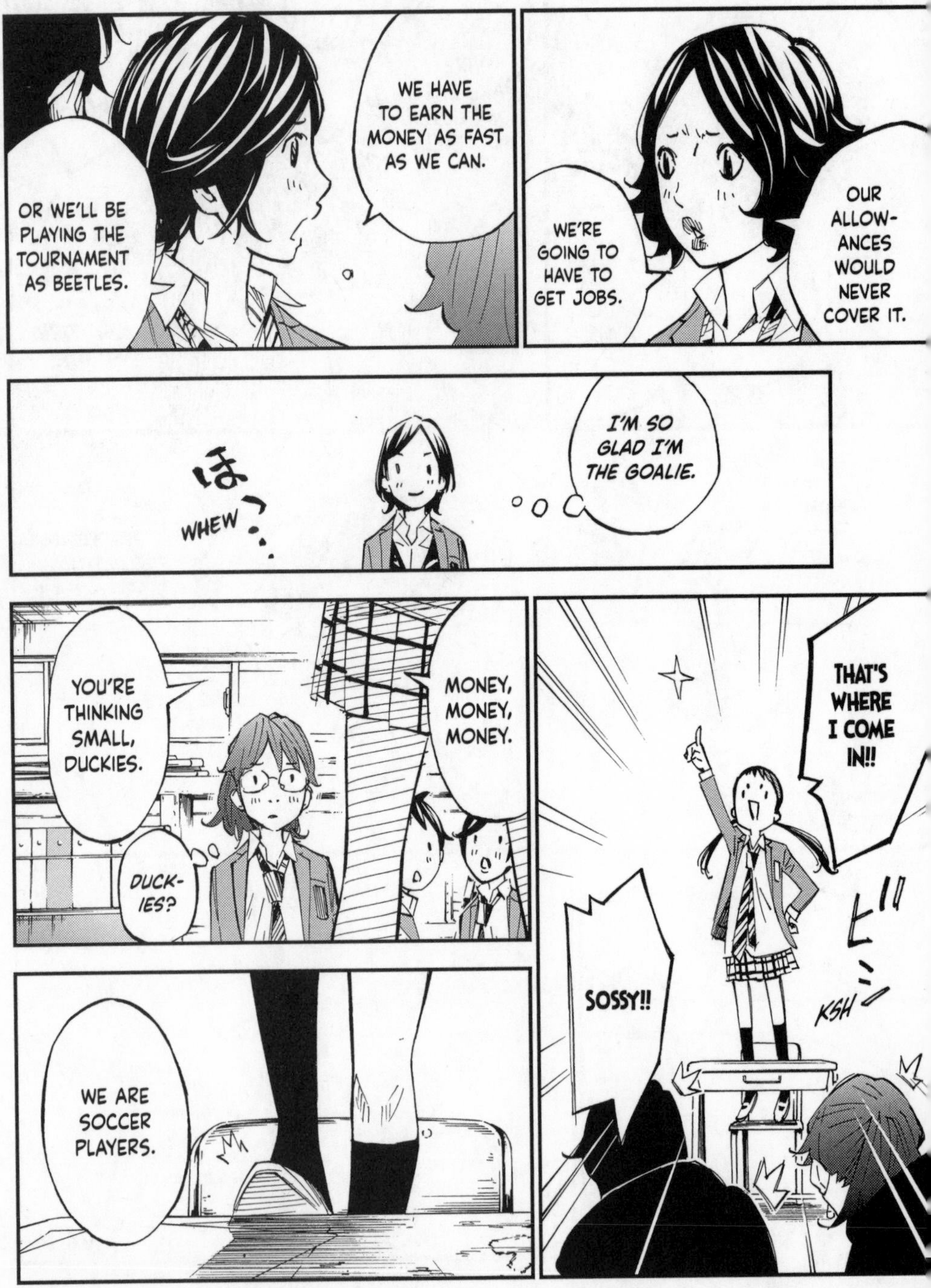
OUR ALLOWANCES WOULD NEVER COVER IT.
WE'RE GOING TO HAVE TO GET JOBS.
WE HAVE TO EARN THE MONEY AS FAST AS WE CAN.
OR WE'LL BE PLAYING THE TOURNAMENT AS BEETLES.
I'M SO GLAD I'M THE GOALIE.
ほっ
WHEW...
THAT'S WHERE I COME IN!!
ビッ
KSH
SOSSY!!
MONEY, MONEY, MONEY.
YOU'RE THINKING SMALL, DUCKIES.
DUCKIES?
WE ARE SOCCER PLAYERS.

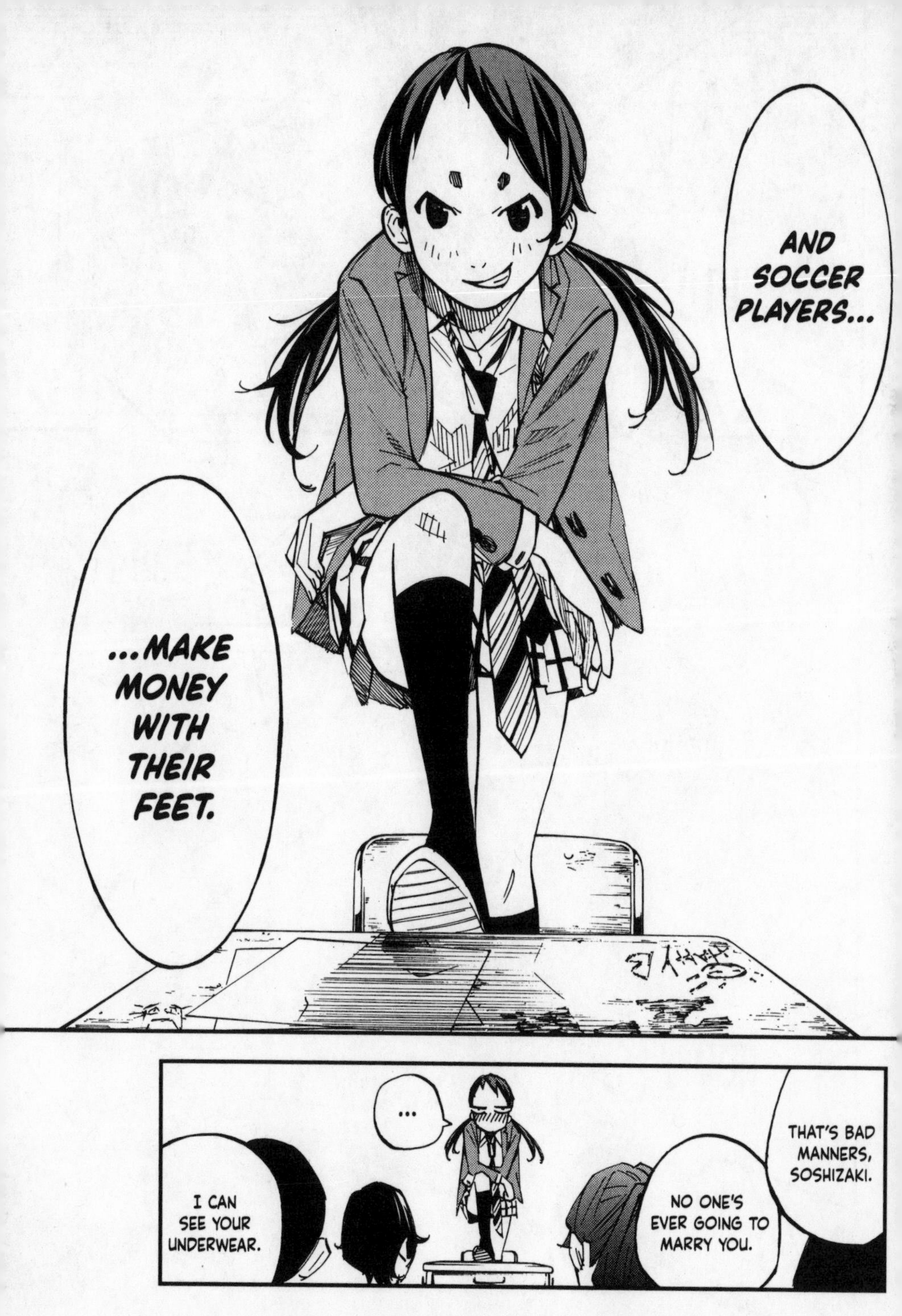
AND SOCCER PLAYERS...
...MAKE MONEY WITH THEIR FEET.
THAT'S BAD MANNERS, SOSHIZAKI.
NO ONE'S EVER GOING TO MARRY YOU.
...
I CAN SEE YOUR UNDERWEAR.

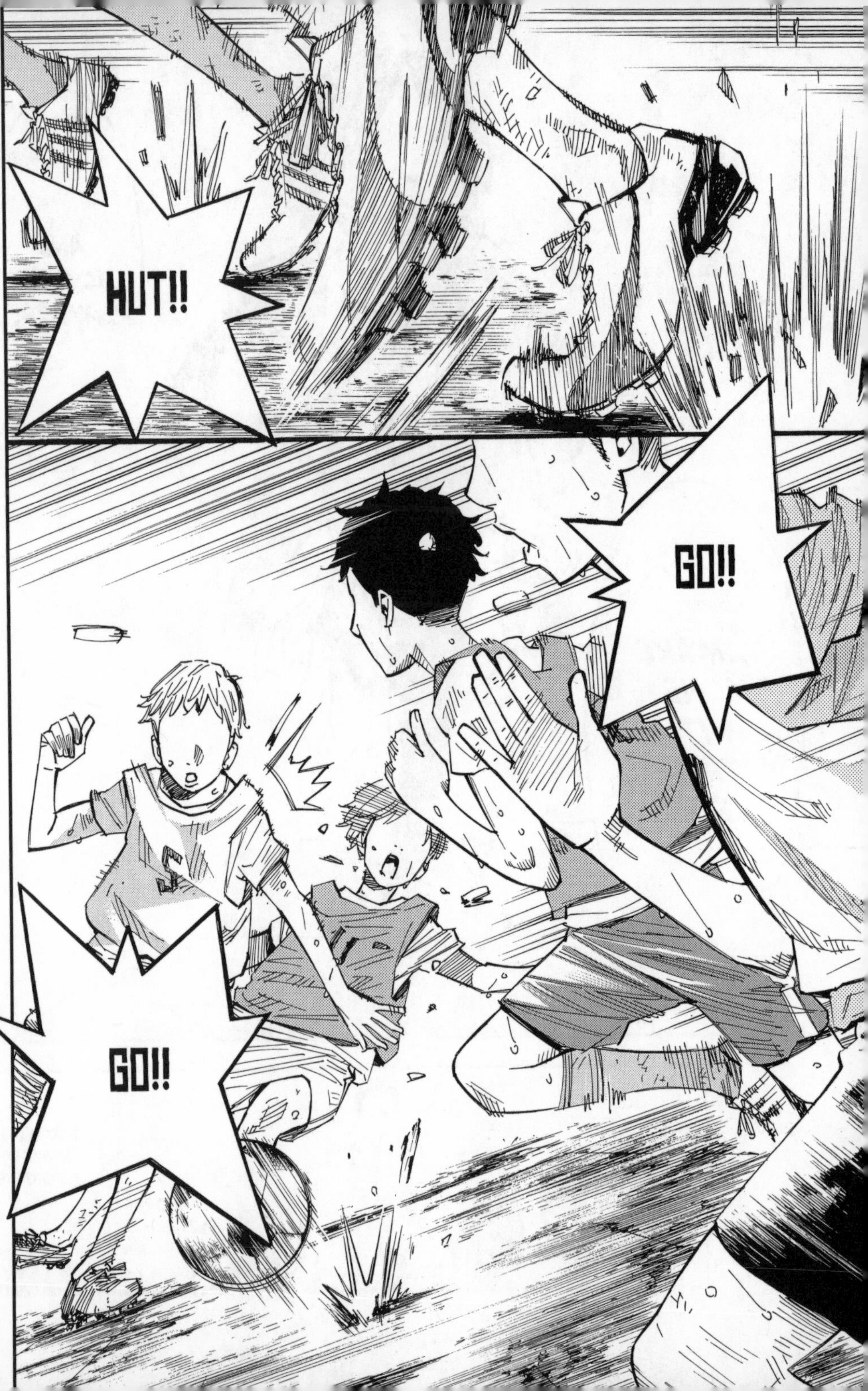
HUT!!
GO!!
GO!!

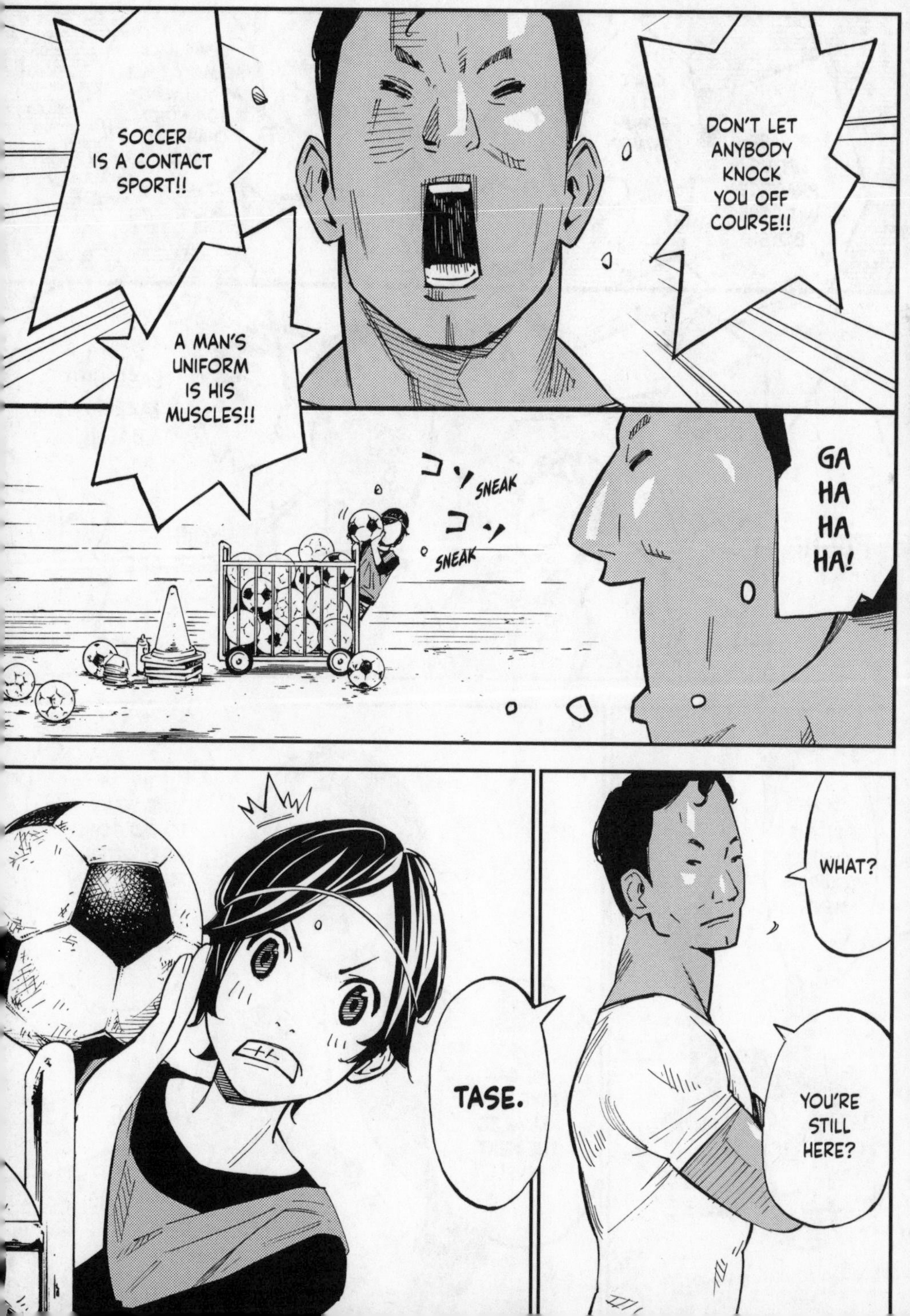

DON'T LET ANYBODY KNOCK YOU OFF COURSE!!
SOCCER IS A CONTACT SPORT!!
A MAN'S UNIFORM IS HIS MUSCLES!!
GA HA HA HA!
コソ SNEAK
コソ SNEAK
WHAT?
YOU'RE STILL HERE?
TASE.

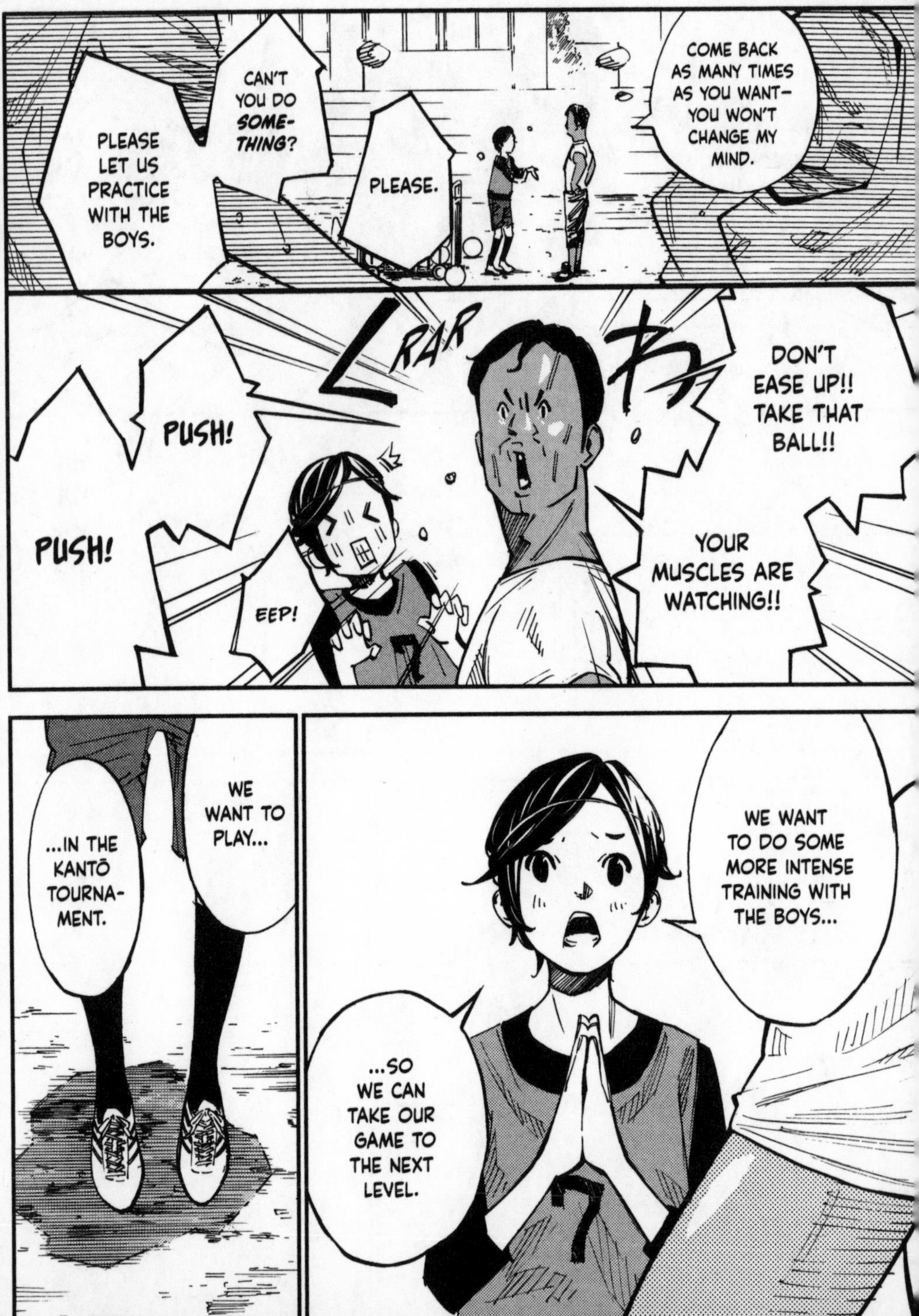
COME BACK AS MANY TIMES AS YOU WANT— YOU WON'T CHANGE MY MIND.
PLEASE.
CAN'T YOU DO SOMETHING?
PLEASE LET US PRACTICE WITH THE BOYS.
DON'T EASE UP!! TAKE THAT BALL!!
RAR
YOUR MUSCLES ARE WATCHING!!
PUSH!
EEP!
PUSH!
WE WANT TO DO SOME MORE INTENSE TRAINING WITH THE BOYS...
...SO WE CAN TAKE OUR GAME TO THE NEXT LEVEL.
WE WANT TO PLAY...
...IN THE KANTŌ TOURNAMENT.

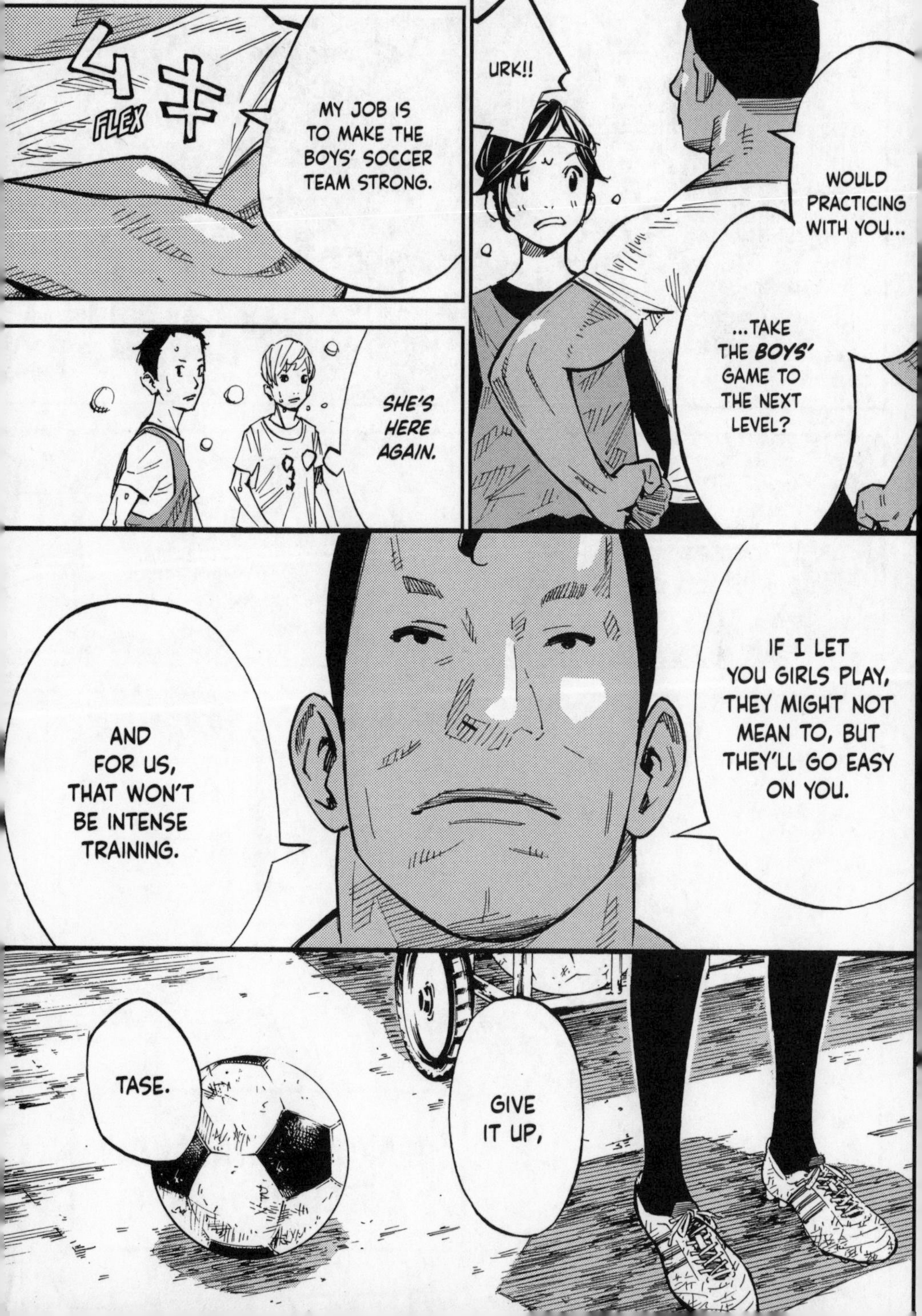
WOULD PRACTICING WITH YOU...
...TAKE THE *BOYS'* GAME TO THE NEXT LEVEL?
URK!!
FLEX
MY JOB IS TO MAKE THE BOYS' SOCCER TEAM STRONG.
SHE'S HERE AGAIN.
IF I LET YOU GIRLS PLAY, THEY MIGHT NOT MEAN TO, BUT THEY'LL GO EASY ON YOU.
AND FOR US, THAT WON'T BE INTENSE TRAINING.
GIVE IT UP,
TASE.

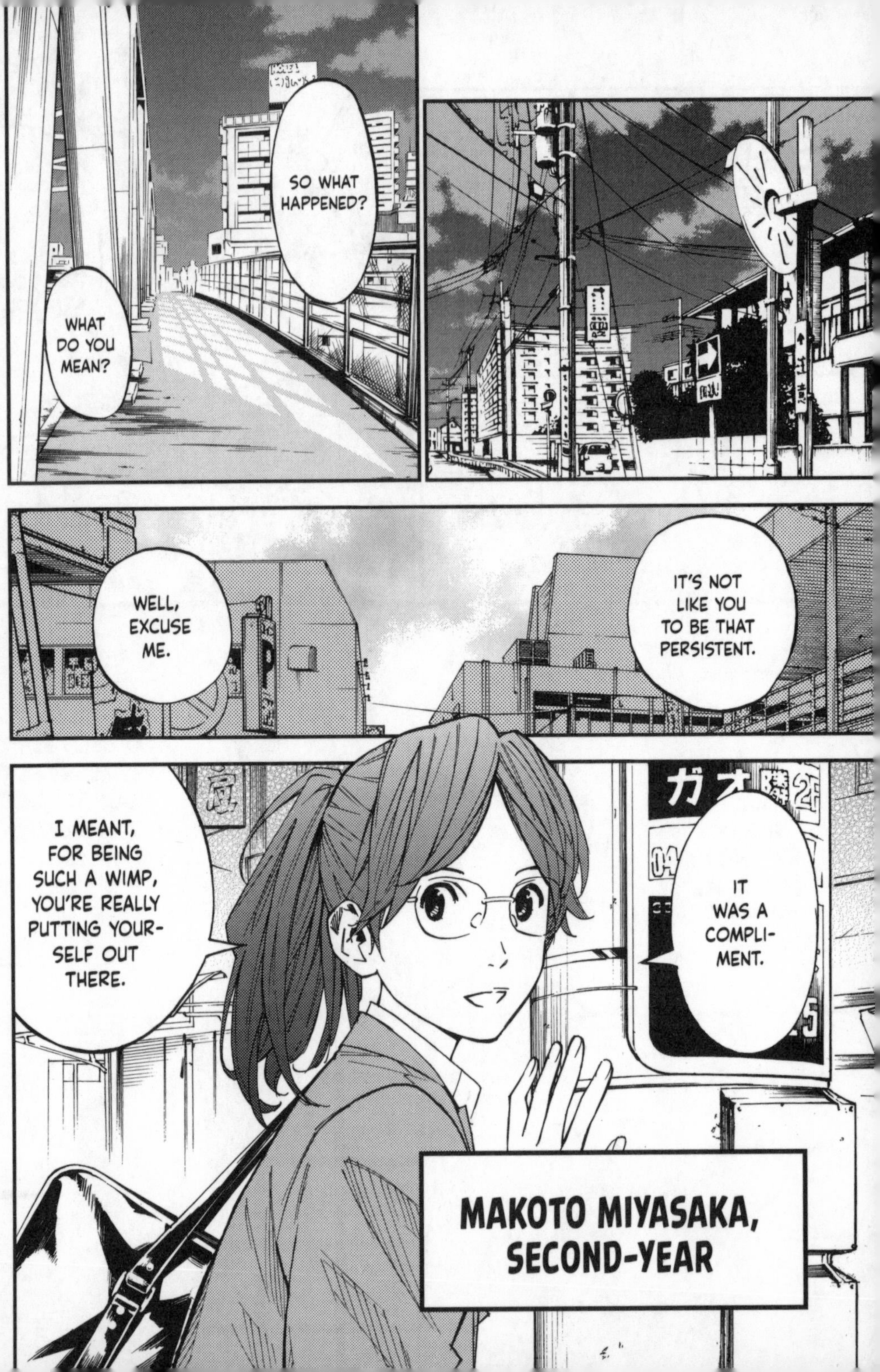
SO WHAT HAPPENED?
WHAT DO YOU MEAN?
IT'S NOT LIKE YOU TO BE THAT PERSISTENT.
WELL, EXCUSE ME.
I MEANT, FOR BEING SUCH A WIMP, YOU'RE REALLY PUTTING YOUR-SELF OUT THERE.
IT WAS A COMPLI-MENT.
MAKOTO MIYASAKA, SECOND-YEAR

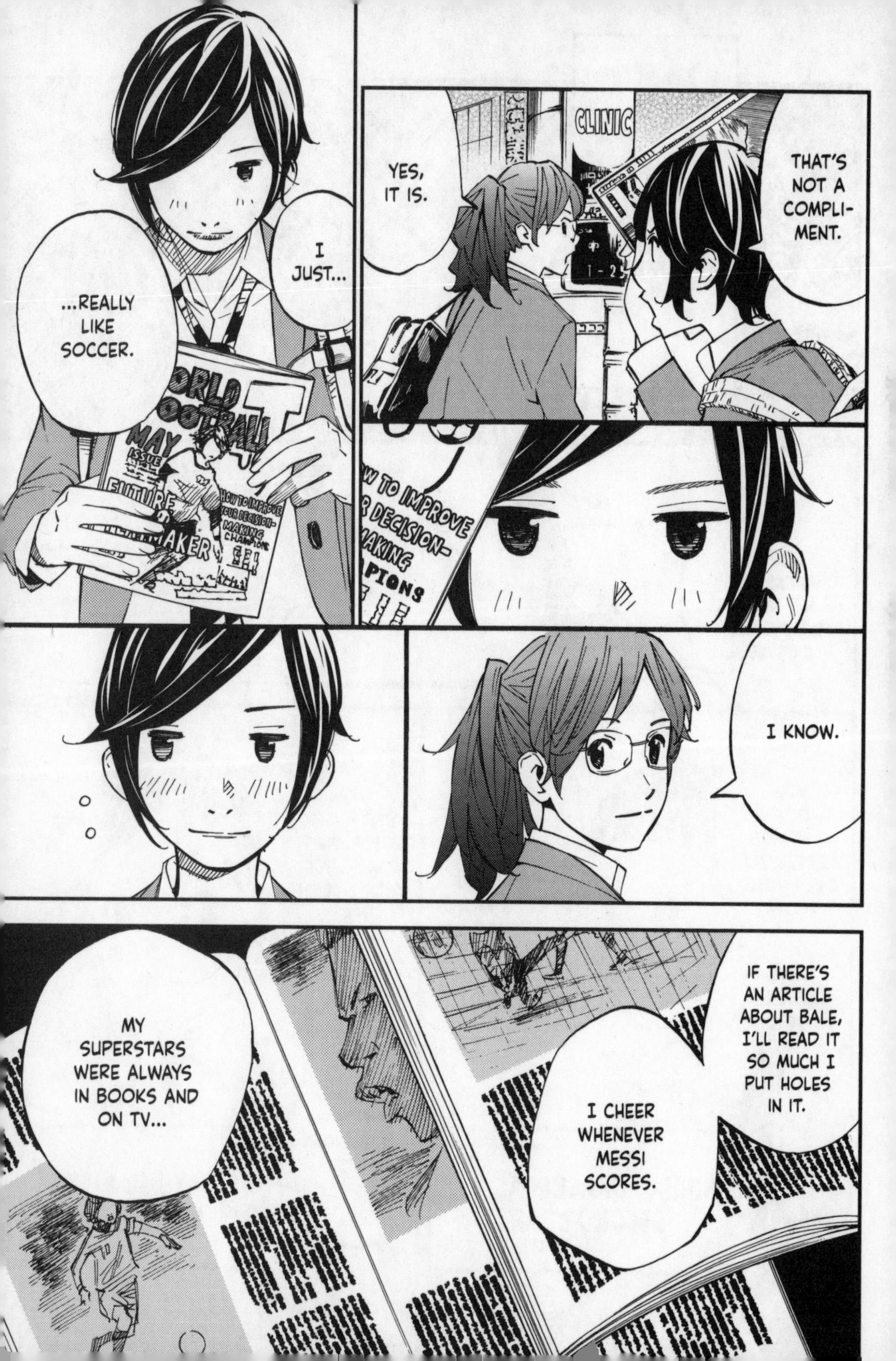
CLINIC
THAT'S NOT A COMPLIMENT.
YES, IT IS.
I JUST...
...REALLY LIKE SOCCER.
MAY ISSUE
HOW TO IMPROVE YOUR DECISION-MAKING CHAMPIONS
I KNOW.
IF THERE'S AN ARTICLE ABOUT BALE, I'LL READ IT SO MUCH I PUT HOLES IN IT.
I CHEER WHENEVER MESSI SCORES.
MY SUPERSTARS WERE ALWAYS IN BOOKS AND ON TV...

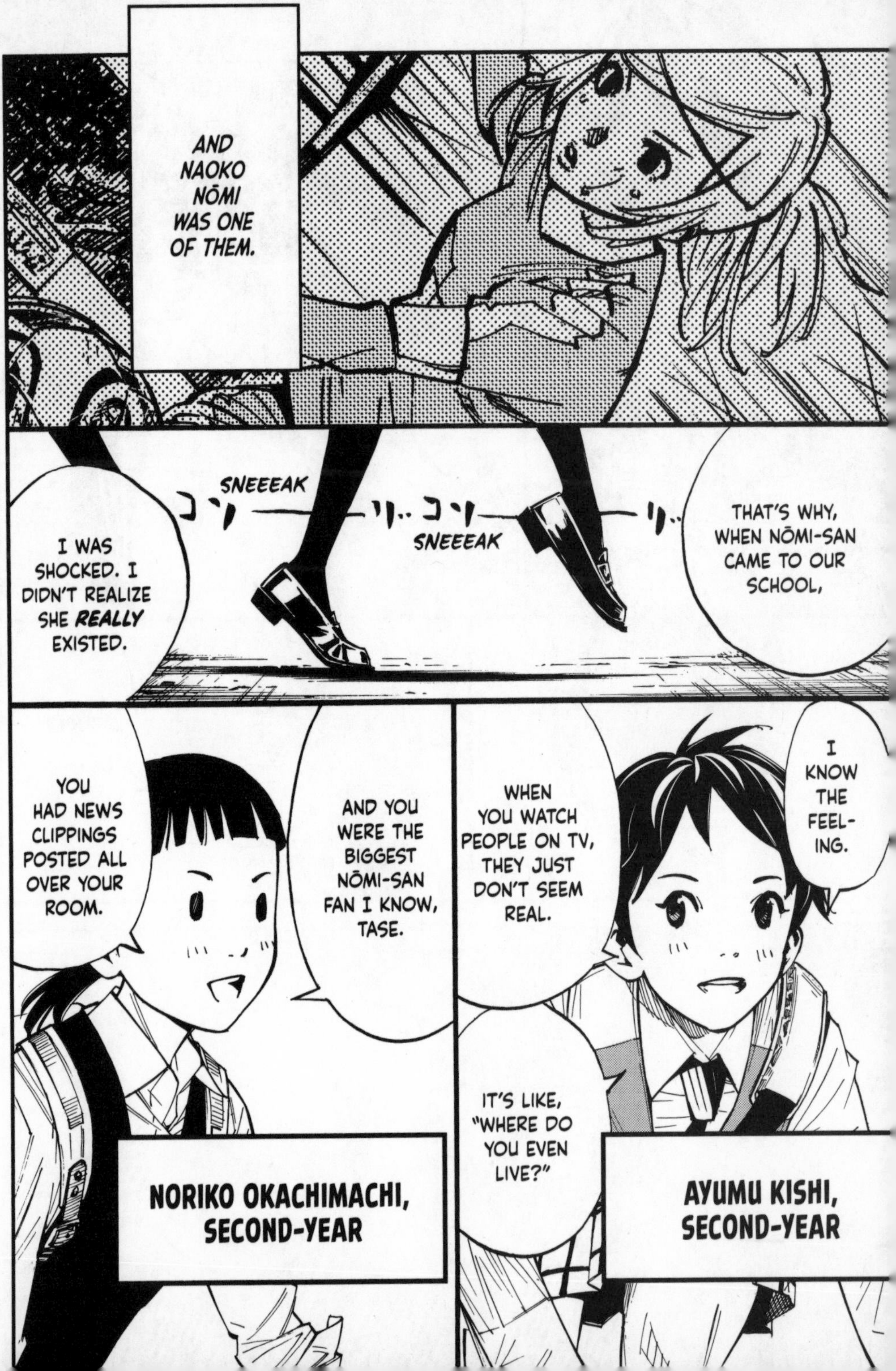
AND NAOKO NŌMI WAS ONE OF THEM.
THAT'S WHY, WHEN NŌMI-SAN CAME TO OUR SCHOOL,
SNEEEAK
SNEEEAK
I WAS SHOCKED. I DIDN'T REALIZE SHE *REALLY* EXISTED.
I KNOW THE FEEL-ING.
WHEN YOU WATCH PEOPLE ON TV, THEY JUST DON'T SEEM REAL.
IT'S LIKE, "WHERE DO YOU EVEN LIVE?"
AYUMU KISHI, SECOND-YEAR
AND YOU WERE THE BIGGEST NŌMI-SAN FAN I KNOW, TASE.
YOU HAD NEWS CLIPPINGS POSTED ALL OVER YOUR ROOM.
NORIKO OKACHIMACHI, SECOND-YEAR

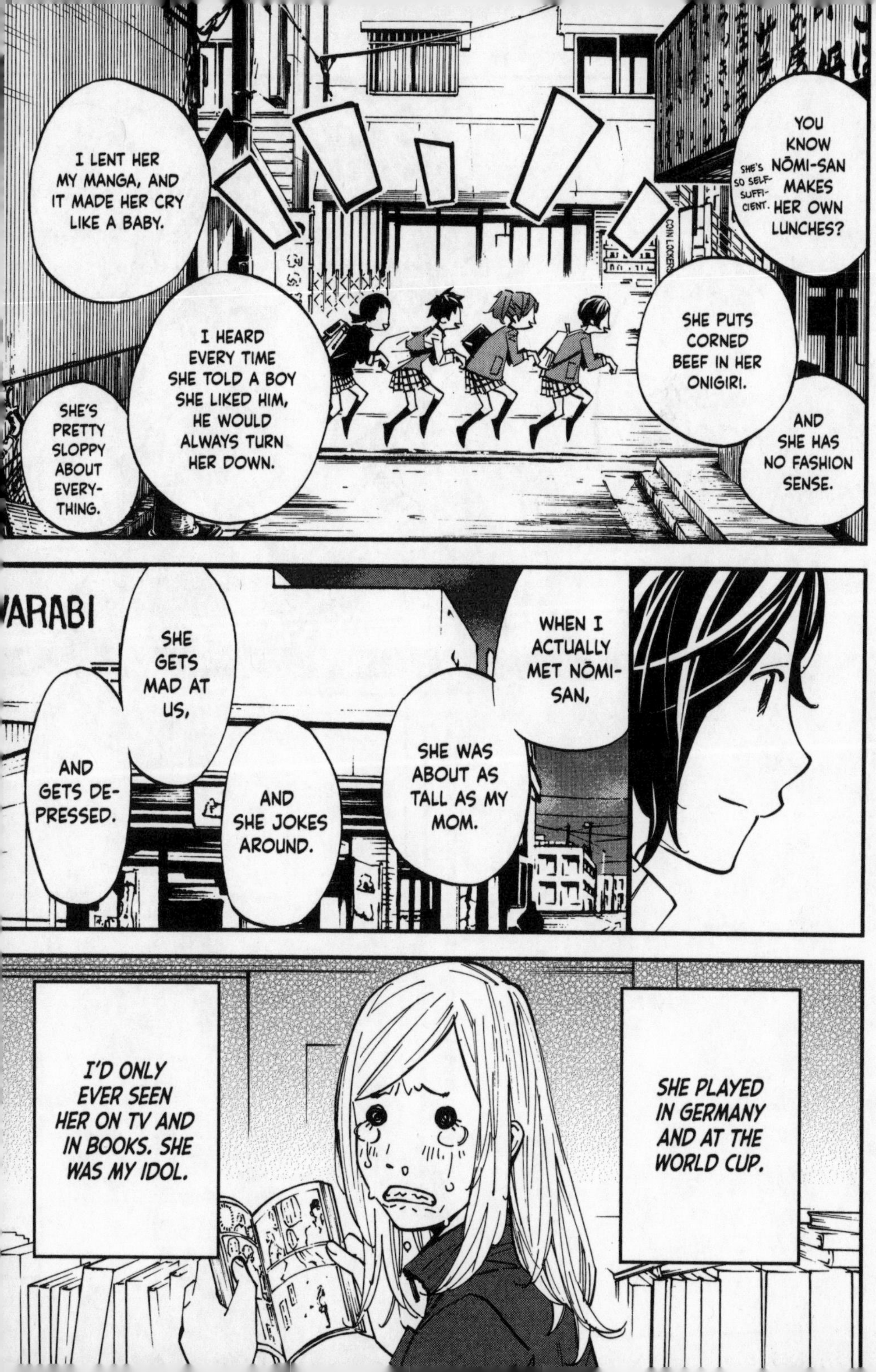
YOU KNOW NŌMI-SAN MAKES HER OWN LUNCHES?
SHE'S SO SELF-SUFFICIENT.
COIN LOCKERS
SHE PUTS CORNED BEEF IN HER ONIGIRI.
AND SHE HAS NO FASHION SENSE.
I LENT HER MY MANGA, AND IT MADE HER CRY LIKE A BABY.
I HEARD EVERY TIME SHE TOLD A BOY SHE LIKED HIM, HE WOULD ALWAYS TURN HER DOWN.
SHE'S PRETTY SLOPPY ABOUT EVERYTHING.
WHEN I ACTUALLY MET NŌMI-SAN,
SHE WAS ABOUT AS TALL AS MY MOM.
SHE GETS MAD AT US,
AND SHE JOKES AROUND.
AND GETS DEPRESSED.
ARABI
SHE PLAYED IN GERMANY AND AT THE WORLD CUP.
I'D ONLY EVER SEEN HER ON TV AND IN BOOKS. SHE WAS MY IDOL.

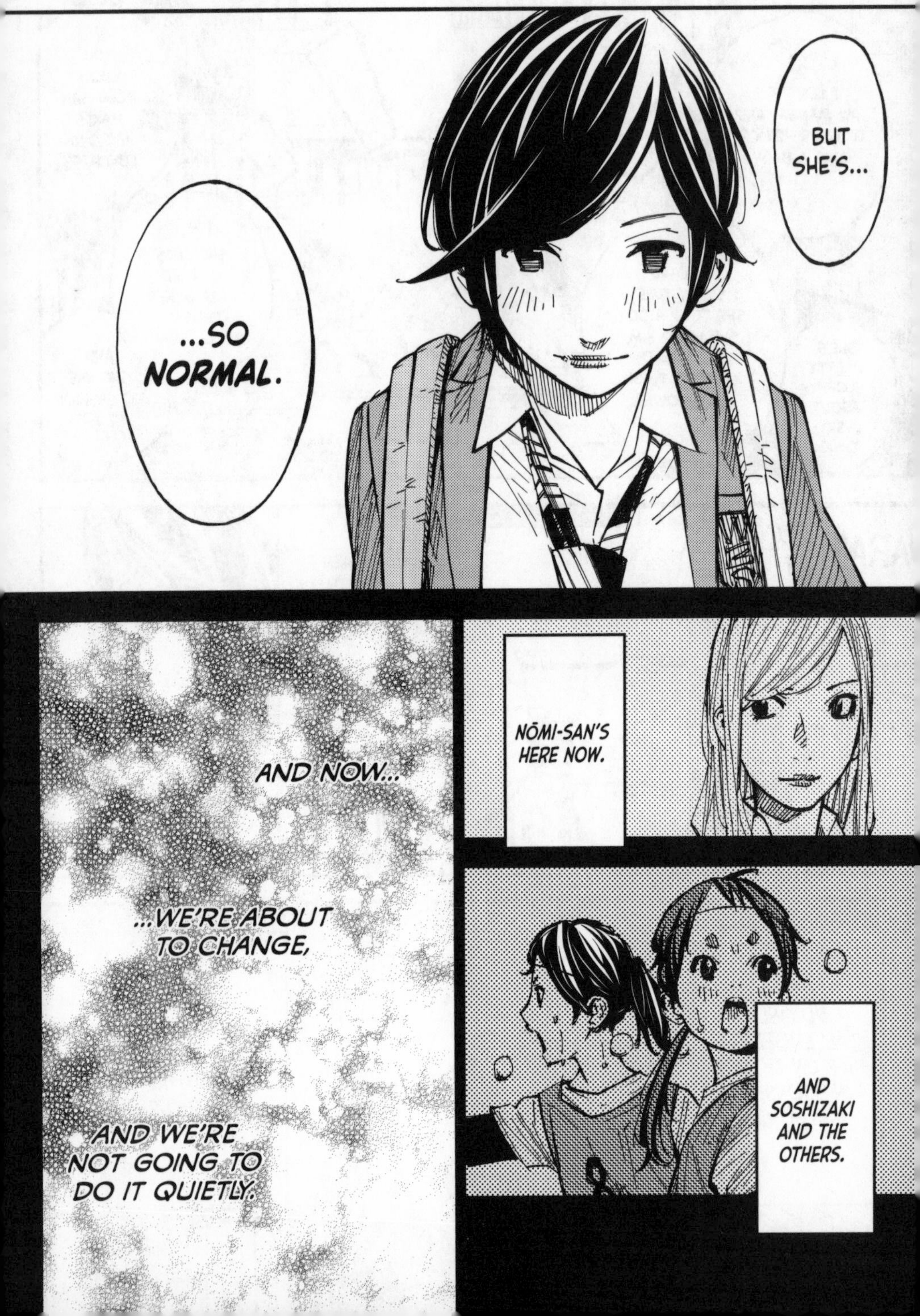
BUT SHE'S...
...SO NORMAL.
NŌMI-SAN'S HERE NOW.
AND SOSHIZAKI AND THE OTHERS.
AND NOW...
...WE'RE ABOUT TO CHANGE,
AND WE'RE NOT GOING TO DO IT QUIETLY.

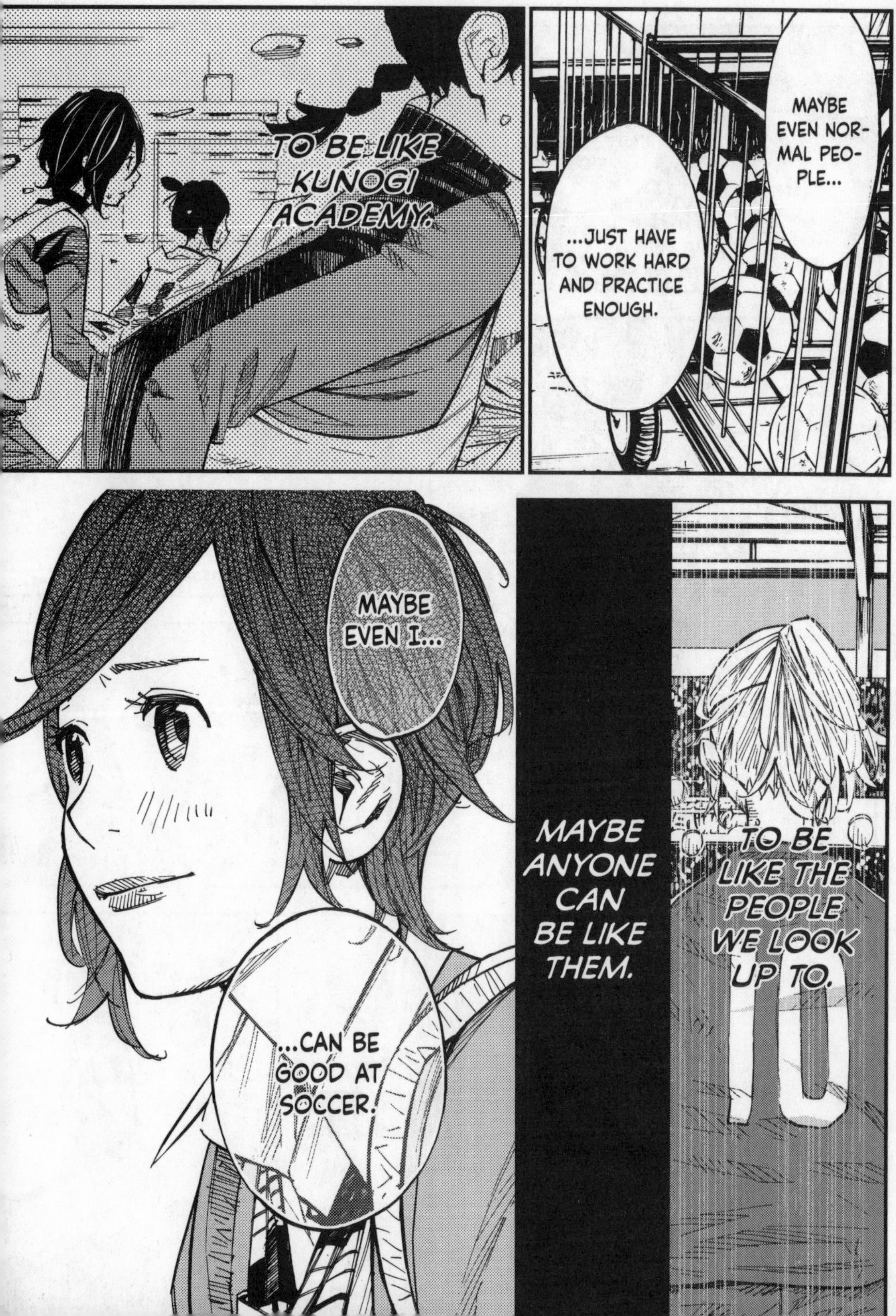
MAYBE EVEN NORMAL PEOPLE...
...JUST HAVE TO WORK HARD AND PRACTICE ENOUGH.
TO BE LIKE KUNOGI ACADEMY.
TO BE LIKE THE PEOPLE WE LOOK UP TO.
MAYBE ANYONE CAN BE LIKE THEM.
MAYBE EVEN I...
...CAN BE GOOD AT SOCCER.

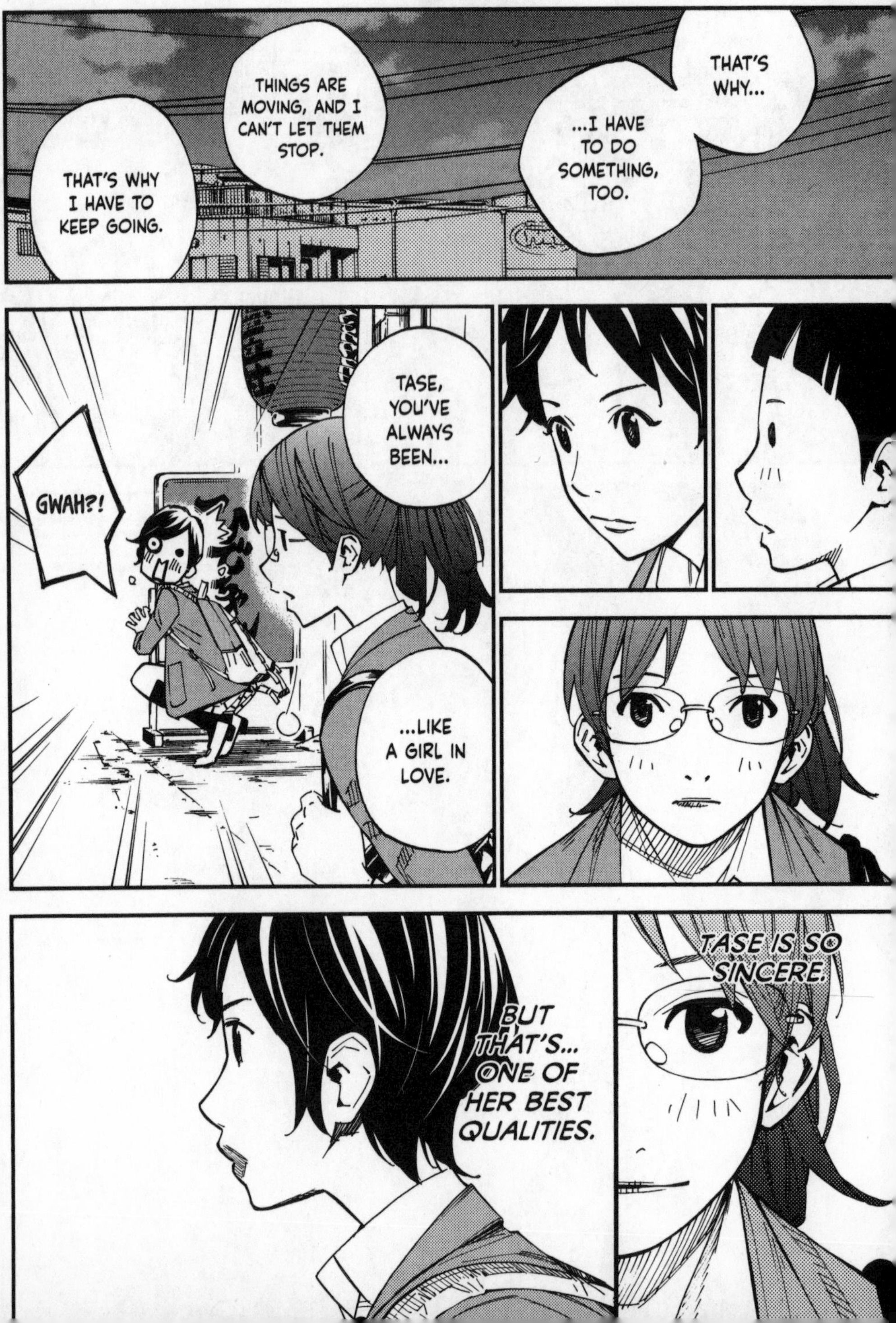
THAT'S WHY...
...I HAVE TO DO SOMETHING, TOO.
THINGS ARE MOVING, AND I CAN'T LET THEM STOP.
THAT'S WHY I HAVE TO KEEP GOING.
TASE, YOU'VE ALWAYS BEEN...
...LIKE A GIRL IN LOVE.
GWAH?!
TASE IS SO SINCERE.
BUT THAT'S... ONE OF HER BEST QUALITIES.

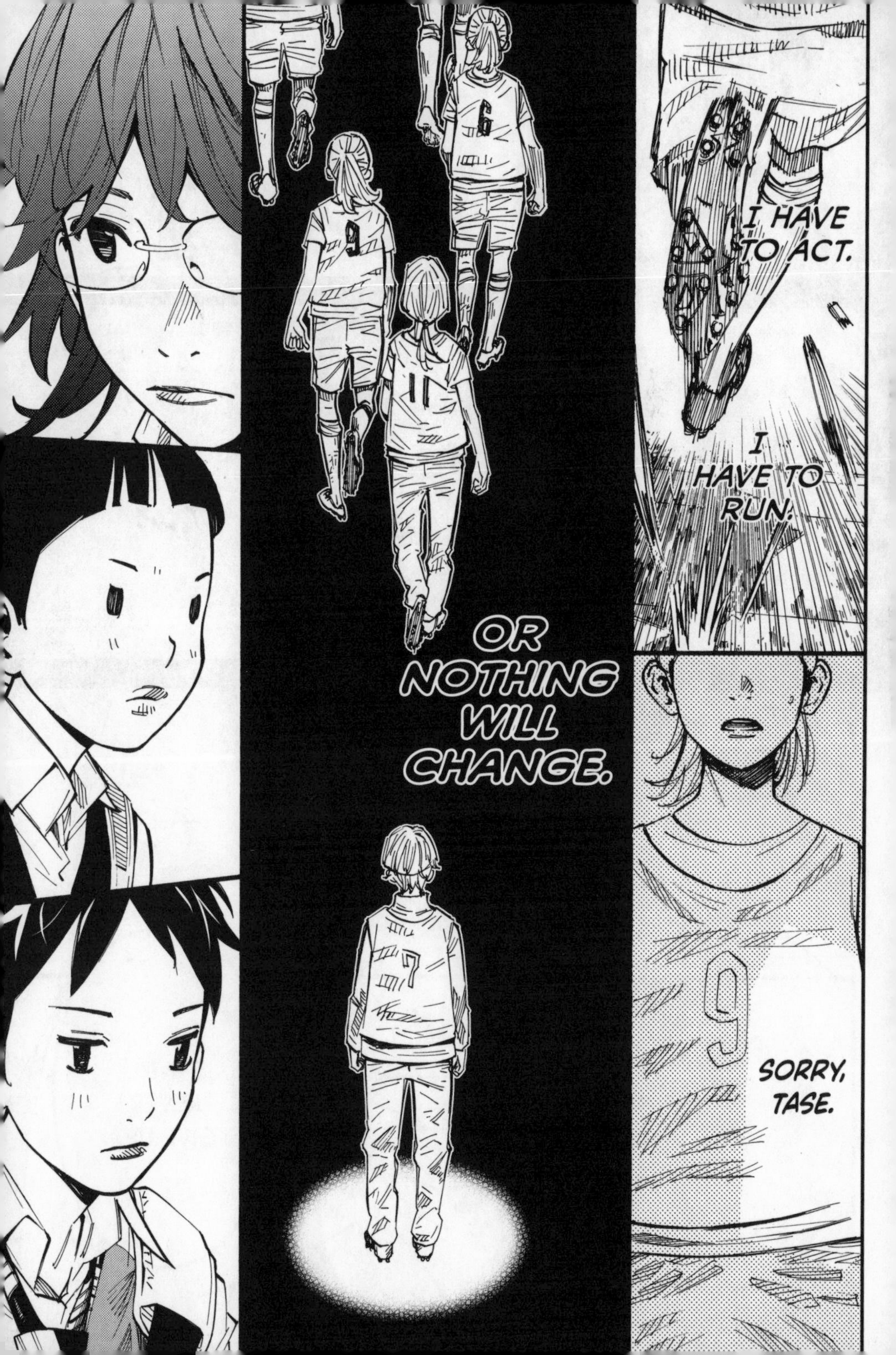
I HAVE TO ACT.
I HAVE TO RUN.
SORRY, TASE.
OR NOTHING WILL CHANGE.

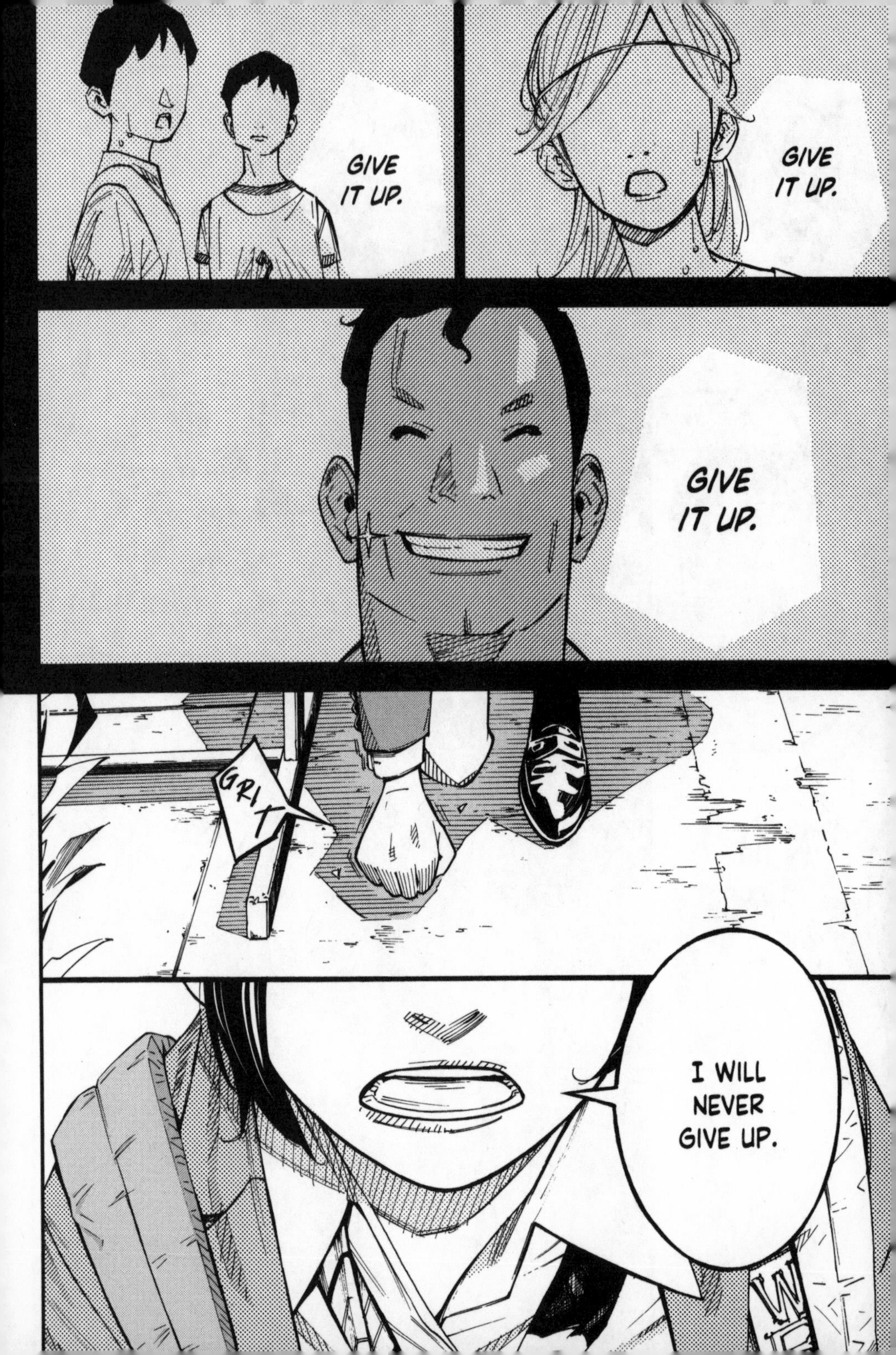
GIVE IT UP.
GIVE IT UP.
GIVE IT UP.
GRIT
I WILL NEVER GIVE UP.

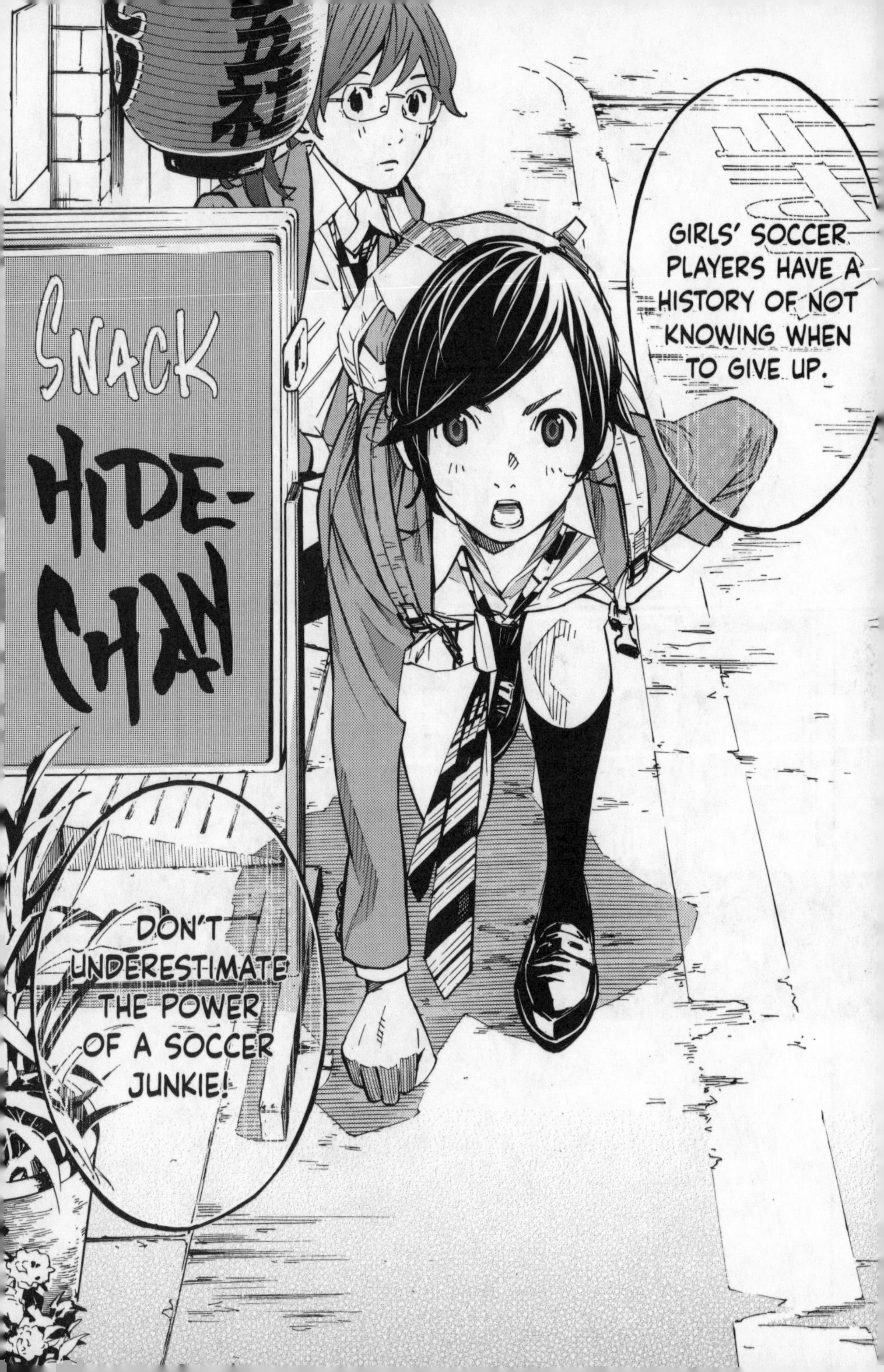
GIRLS' SOCCER PLAYERS HAVE A HISTORY OF NOT KNOWING WHEN TO GIVE UP.
SNACK HIDE-CHAN
DON'T UNDERESTIMATE THE POWER OF A SOCCER JUNKIE!

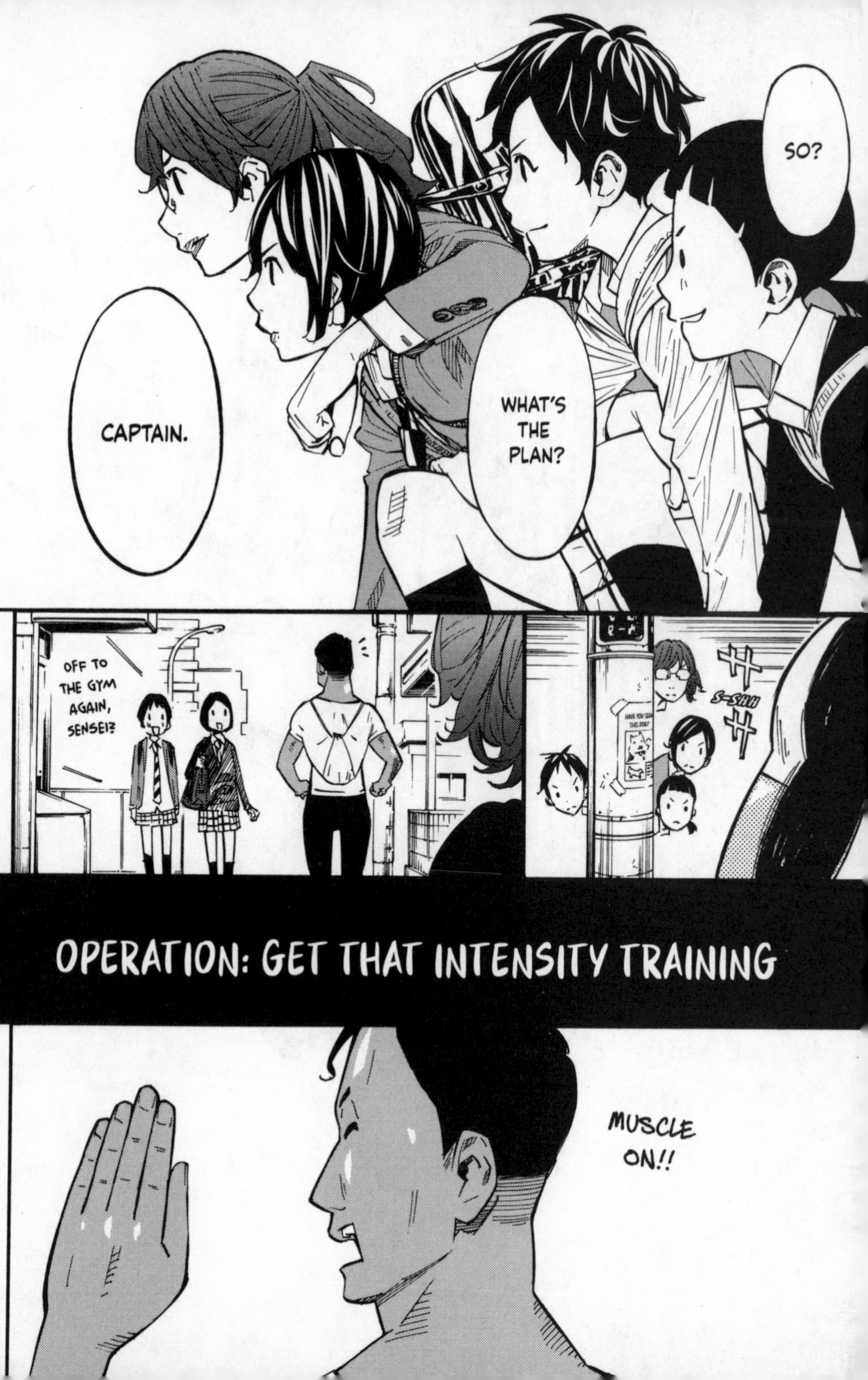
SO?
WHAT'S THE PLAN?
CAPTAIN.
S-SHH
OFF TO THE GYM AGAIN, SENSEI?
OPERATION: GET THAT INTENSITY TRAINING
MUSCLE ON!!

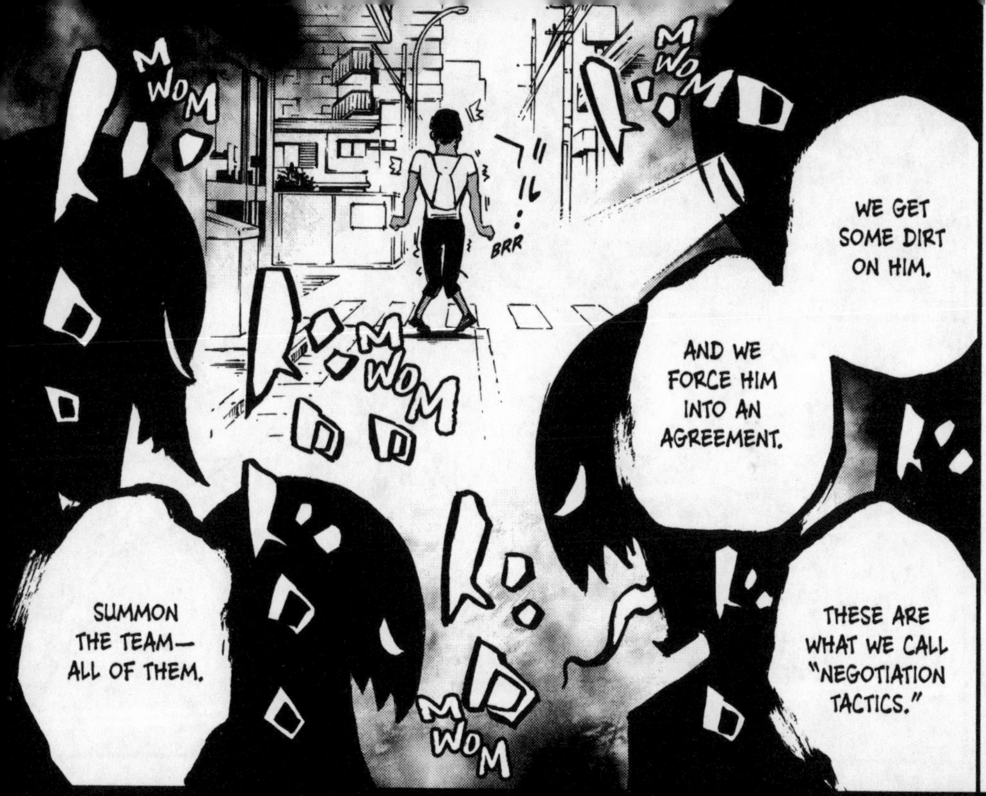
MWOM
MWOM
ブル…
BRR
WE GET SOME DIRT ON HIM.
AND WE FORCE HIM INTO AN AGREEMENT.
THESE ARE WHAT WE CALL "NEGOTIATION TACTICS."
MWOM
MWOM
SUMMON THE TEAM—ALL OF THEM.

PART 1: SURVEILLANCE

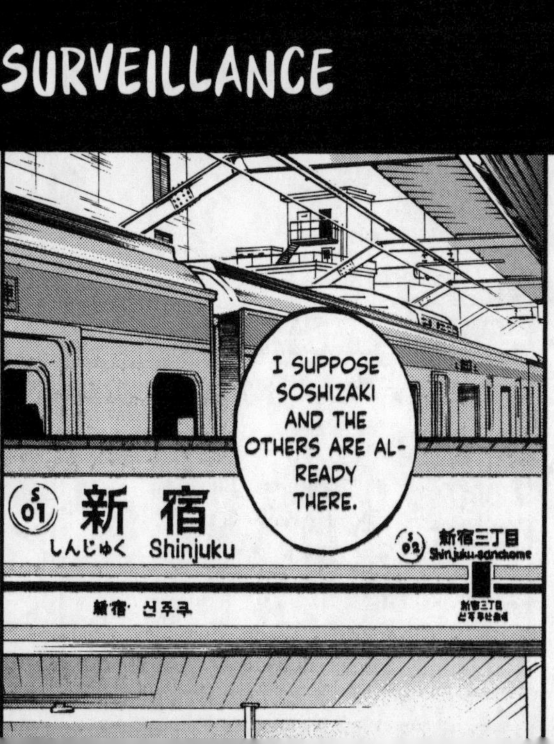
I SUPPOSE SOSHIZAKI AND THE OTHERS ARE AL-READY THERE.
S 01 新宿
しんじゅく Shinjuku
S 02 新宿三丁目
Shinjuku-sanchome
新宿· 신주쿠

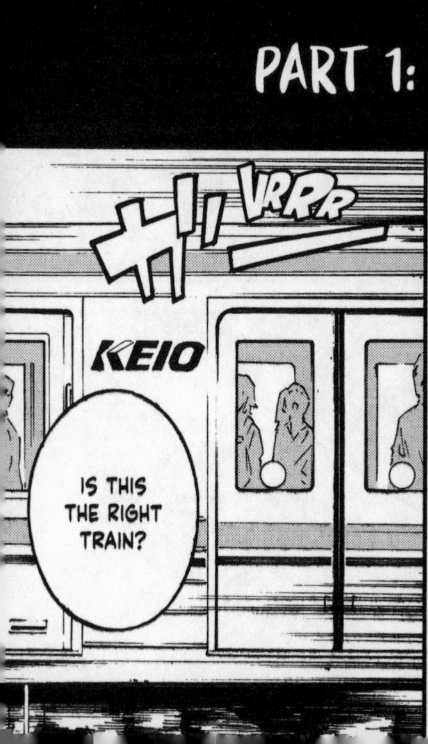
ガー
VRRR
KEIO
IS THIS THE RIGHT TRAIN?

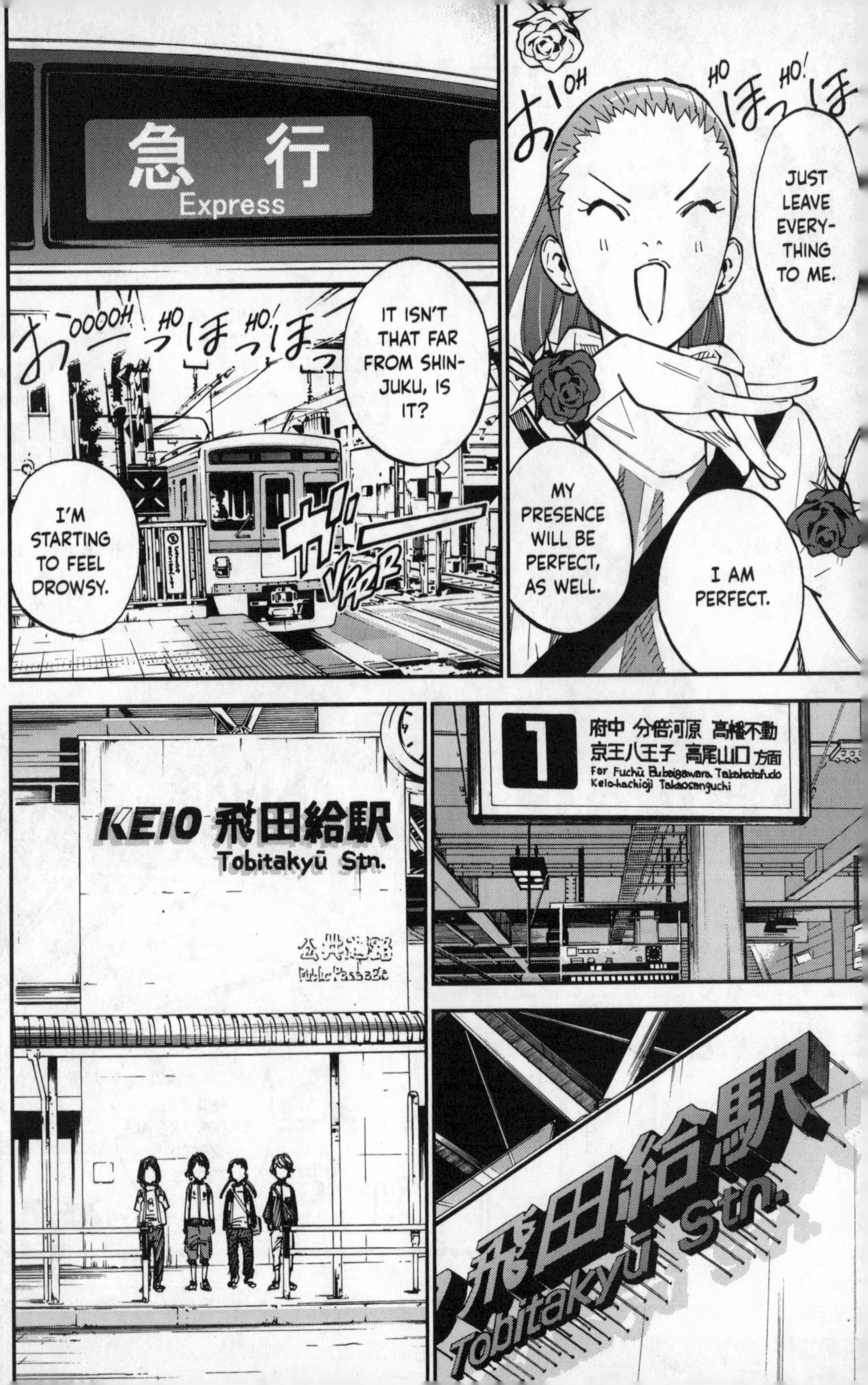

おっほっほっ
OH HO HO!
JUST LEAVE EVERYTHING TO ME.
I AM PERFECT.
MY PRESENCE WILL BE PERFECT, AS WELL.
急行
Express
おーっほっほっ
OOOOH HO HO!
IT ISN'T THAT FAR FROM SHINJUKU, IS IT?
ザー
VRRR
I'M STARTING TO FEEL DROWSY.
1
府中 分倍河原 高幡不動
京王八王子 高尾山口 方面
For Fuchū Bubaigawara Takahatafudo
Keio-hachioji Takaosanguchi
飛田給駅
Tobitakyū Stn.
KEIO 飛田給駅
Tobitakyū Stn.
Public Passage

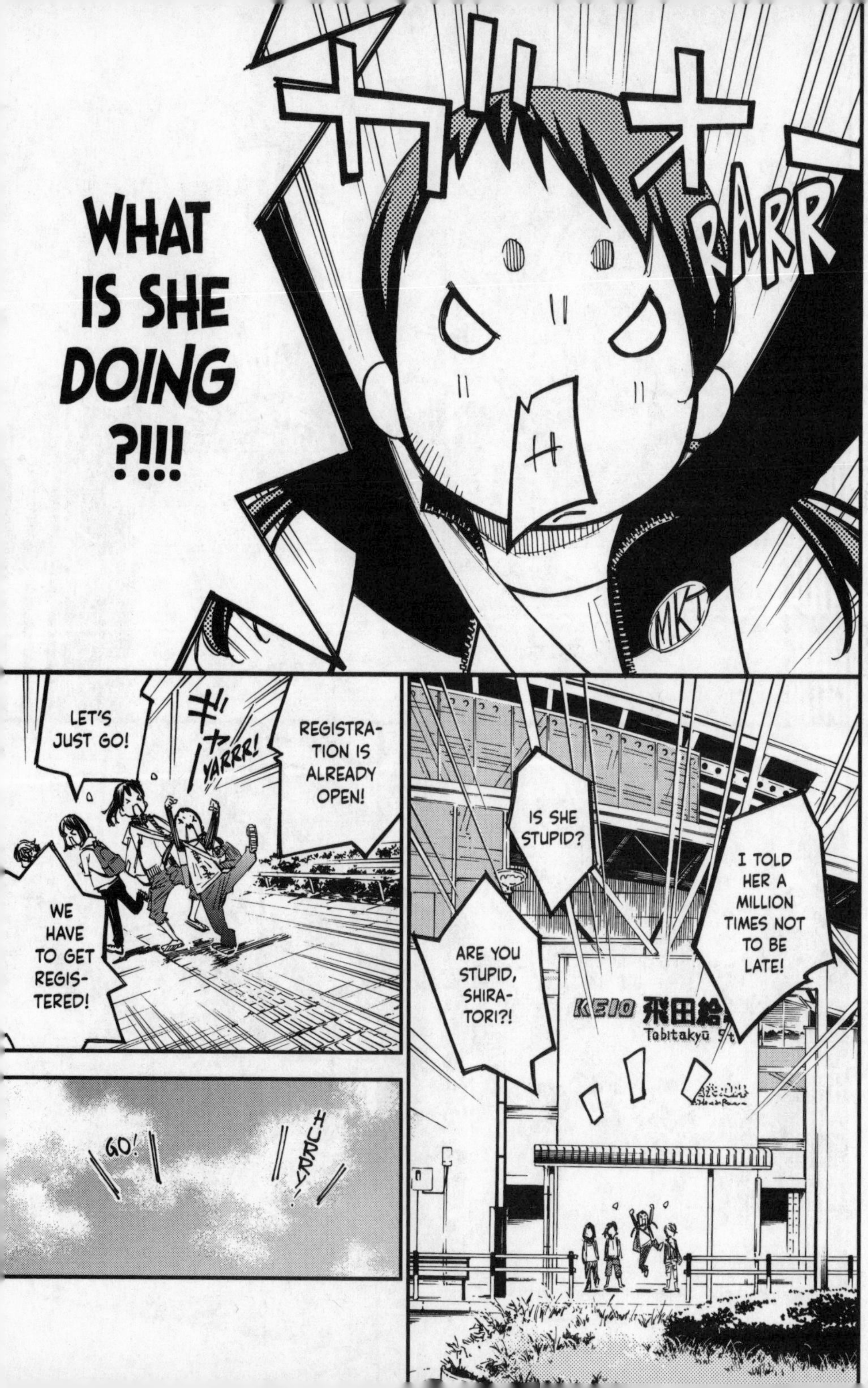
ギャオー
RARR
WHAT IS SHE DOING?!!!
IS SHE STUPID?
I TOLD HER A MILLION TIMES NOT TO BE LATE!
ARE YOU STUPID, SHIRATORI?!
KEIO 飛田給
Tobitakyū St
REGISTRATION IS ALREADY OPEN!
ギャ YARRR!
LET'S JUST GO!
WE HAVE TO GET REGISTERED!
HURRY!
GO!

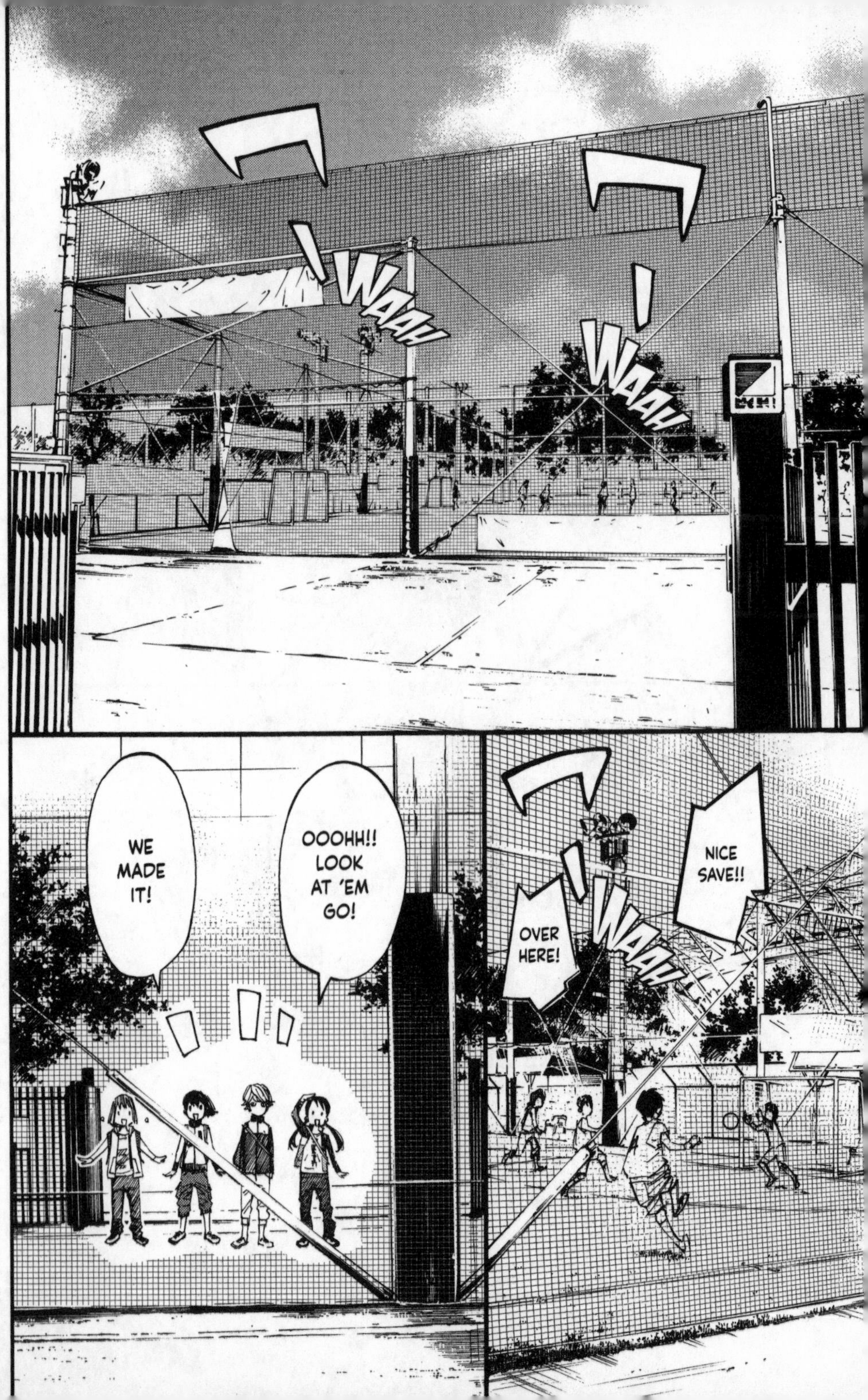
WAAH
WAAH
NICE SAVE!!
WAAH
OVER HERE!
OOOHH!! LOOK AT 'EM GO!
WE MADE IT!

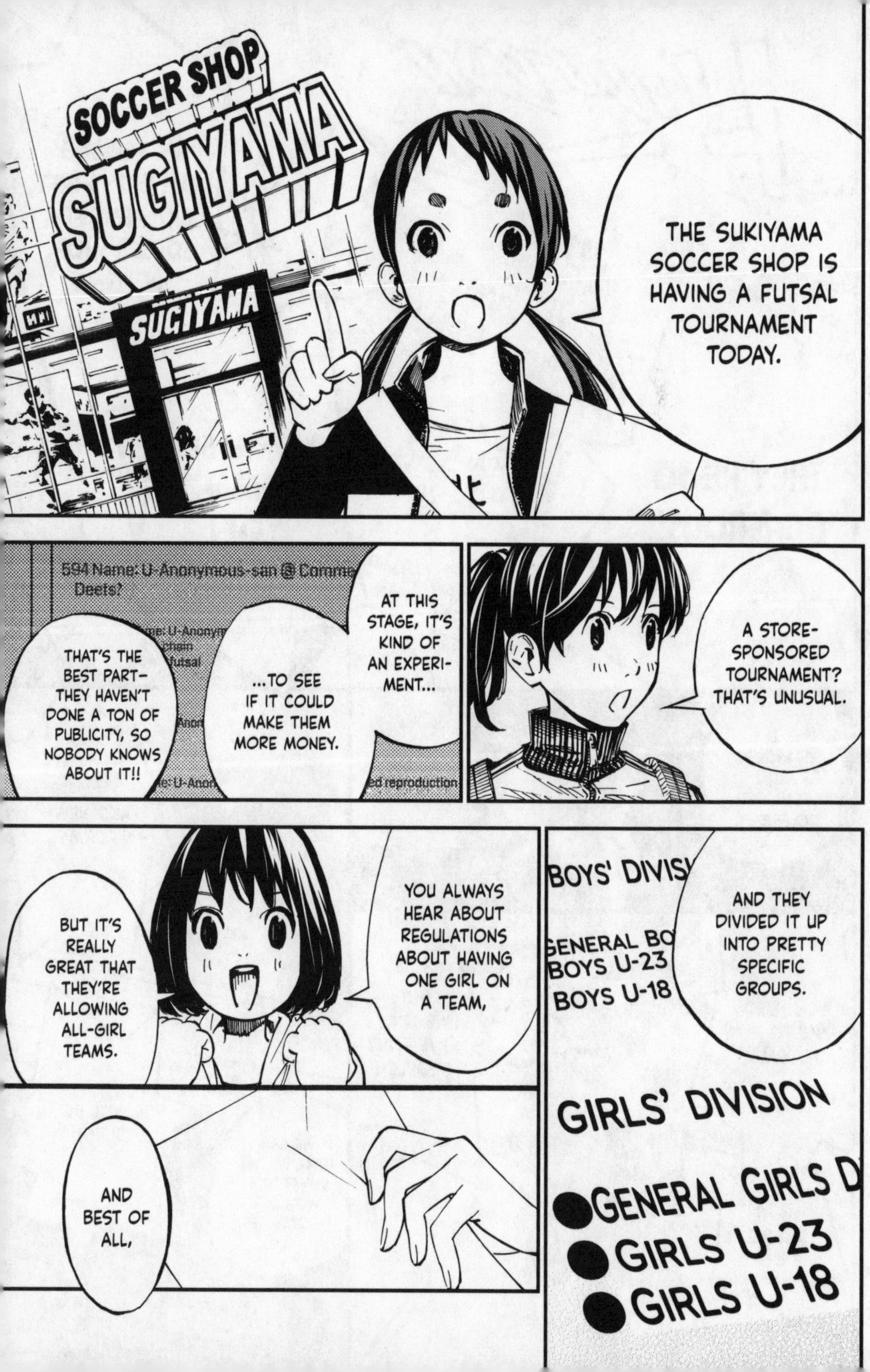
SOCCER SHOP SUGIYAMA
SUGIYAMA
THE SUKIYAMA SOCCER SHOP IS HAVING A FUTSAL TOURNAMENT TODAY.
A STORE-SPONSORED TOURNAMENT? THAT'S UNUSUAL.
594 Name: U-Anonymous-san @ Comme
Deets?
AT THIS STAGE, IT'S KIND OF AN EXPERIMENT...
...TO SEE IF IT COULD MAKE THEM MORE MONEY.
THAT'S THE BEST PART—THEY HAVEN'T DONE A TON OF PUBLICITY, SO NOBODY KNOWS ABOUT IT!!
BOYS' DIVIS
GENERAL BO
BOYS U-23
BOYS U-18
AND THEY DIVIDED IT UP INTO PRETTY SPECIFIC GROUPS.
GIRLS' DIVISION
●GENERAL GIRLS D
●GIRLS U-23
●GIRLS U-18
YOU ALWAYS HEAR ABOUT REGULATIONS ABOUT HAVING ONE GIRL ON A TEAM,
BUT IT'S REALLY GREAT THAT THEY'RE ALLOWING ALL-GIRL TEAMS.
AND BEST OF ALL,

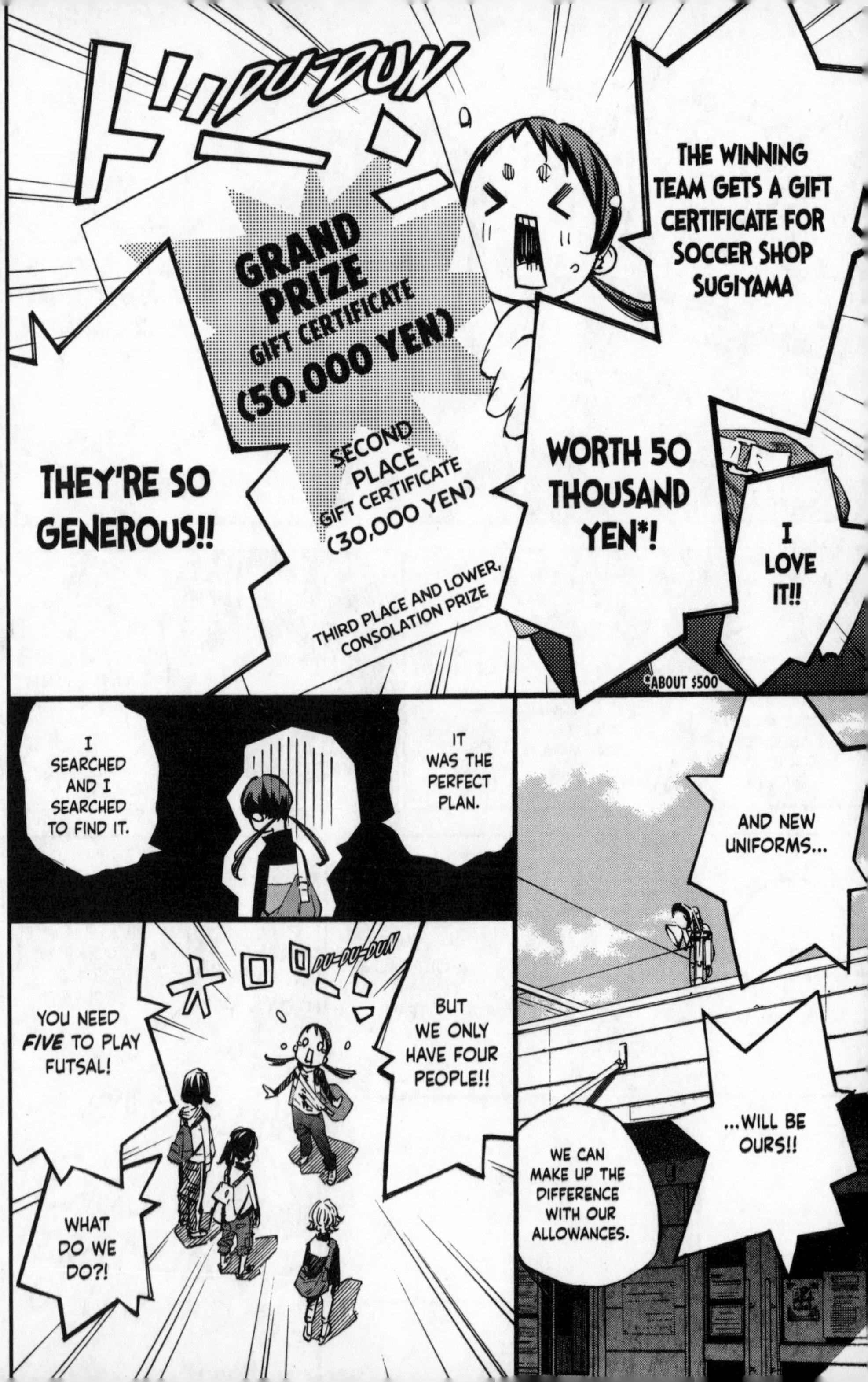
THE WINNING TEAM GETS A GIFT CERTIFICATE FOR SOCCER SHOP SUGIYAMA
DU-DUN
WORTH 50 THOUSAND YEN*!
I LOVE IT!!
GRAND PRIZE GIFT CERTIFICATE (50,000 YEN)
SECOND PLACE GIFT CERTIFICATE (30,000 YEN)
THIRD PLACE AND LOWER, CONSOLATION PRIZE
THEY'RE SO GENEROUS!!
*ABOUT $500
AND NEW UNIFORMS...
...WILL BE OURS!!
WE CAN MAKE UP THE DIFFERENCE WITH OUR ALLOWANCES.
IT WAS THE PERFECT PLAN.
I SEARCHED AND I SEARCHED TO FIND IT.
BUT WE ONLY HAVE FOUR PEOPLE!!
DU-DU-DUN
YOU NEED *FIVE* TO PLAY FUTSAL!
WHAT DO WE DO?!

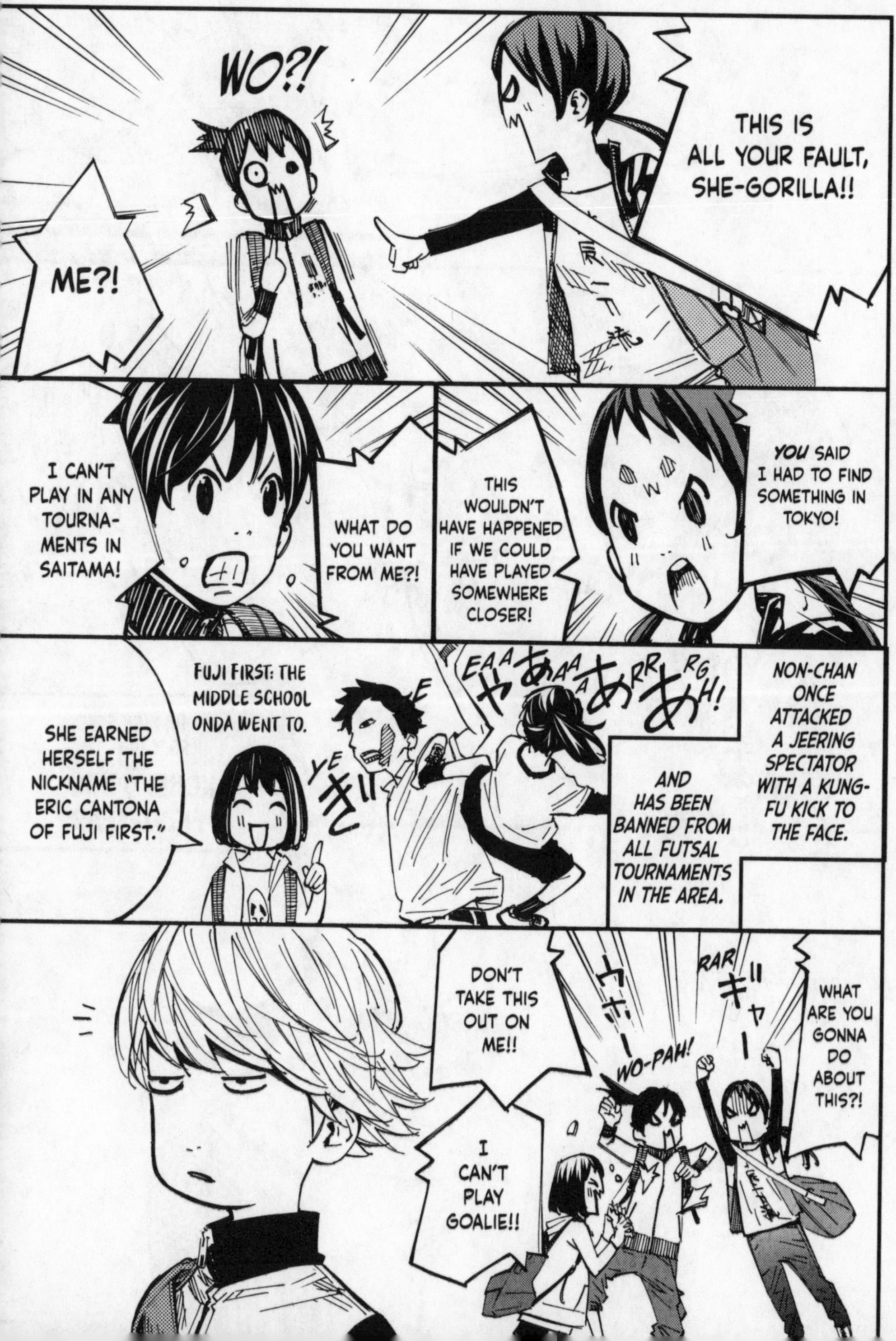

THIS IS ALL YOUR FAULT, SHE-GORILLA!!
WO?!
ME?!
YOU SAID I HAD TO FIND SOMETHING IN TOKYO!
THIS WOULDN'T HAVE HAPPENED IF WE COULD HAVE PLAYED SOMEWHERE CLOSER!
WHAT DO YOU WANT FROM ME?!
I CAN'T PLAY IN ANY TOURNA-MENTS IN SAITAMA!
NON-CHAN ONCE ATTACKED A JEERING SPECTATOR WITH A KUNG-FU KICK TO THE FACE.
AND HAS BEEN BANNED FROM ALL FUTSAL TOURNAMENTS IN THE AREA.
EAAAAARRRGH!
YE
FUJI FIRST: THE MIDDLE SCHOOL ONDA WENT TO.
SHE EARNED HERSELF THE NICKNAME "THE ERIC CANTONA OF FUJI FIRST."
WHAT ARE YOU GONNA DO ABOUT THIS?!
RAR
ギャー
WO-PAH!
ウホー
DON'T TAKE THIS OUT ON ME!!
I CAN'T PLAY GOALIE!!

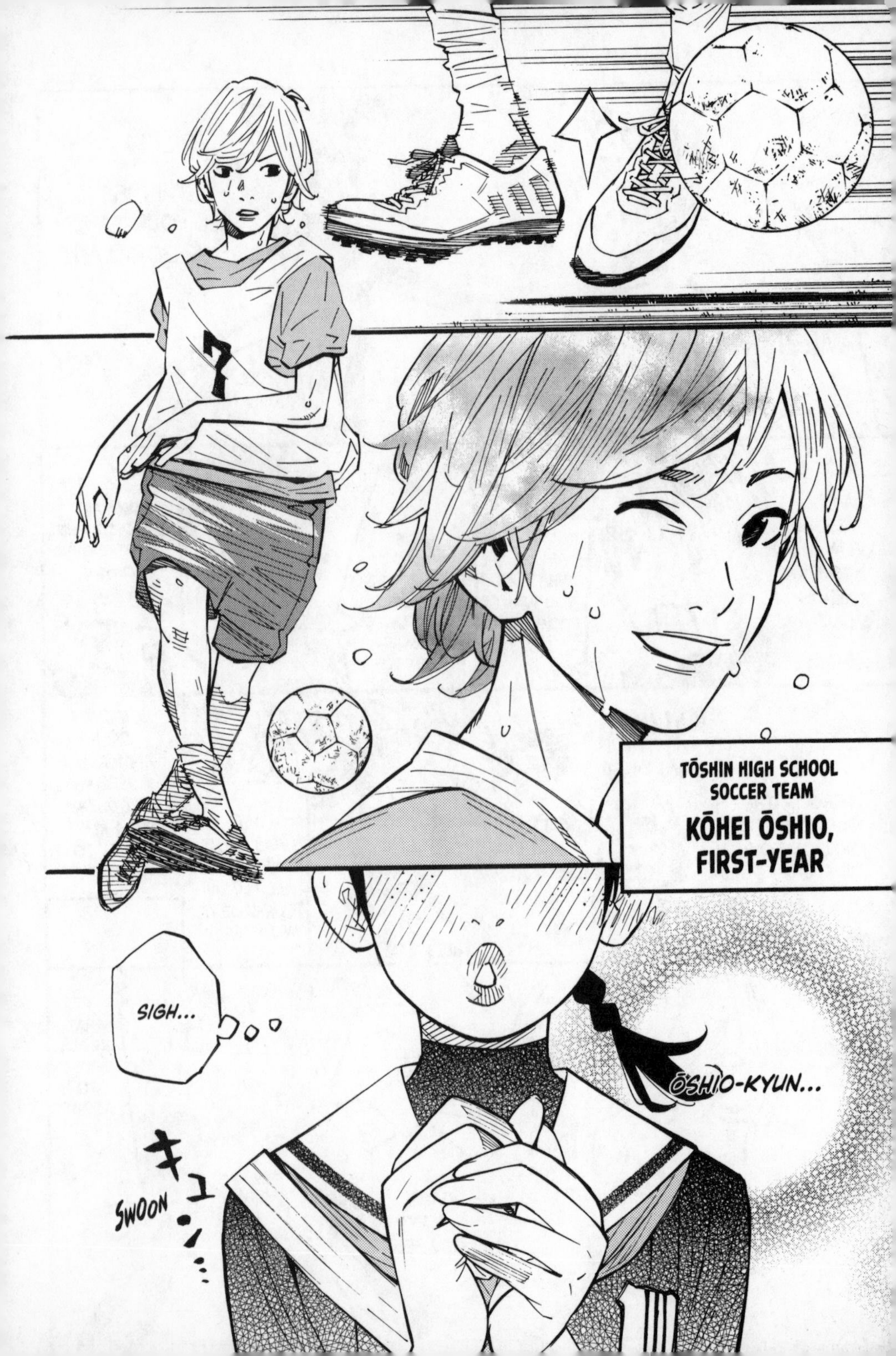
TŌSHIN HIGH SCHOOL SOCCER TEAM
KŌHEI ŌSHIO, FIRST-YEAR
SIGH...
ŌSHIO-KYUN...
キュン
SWOON

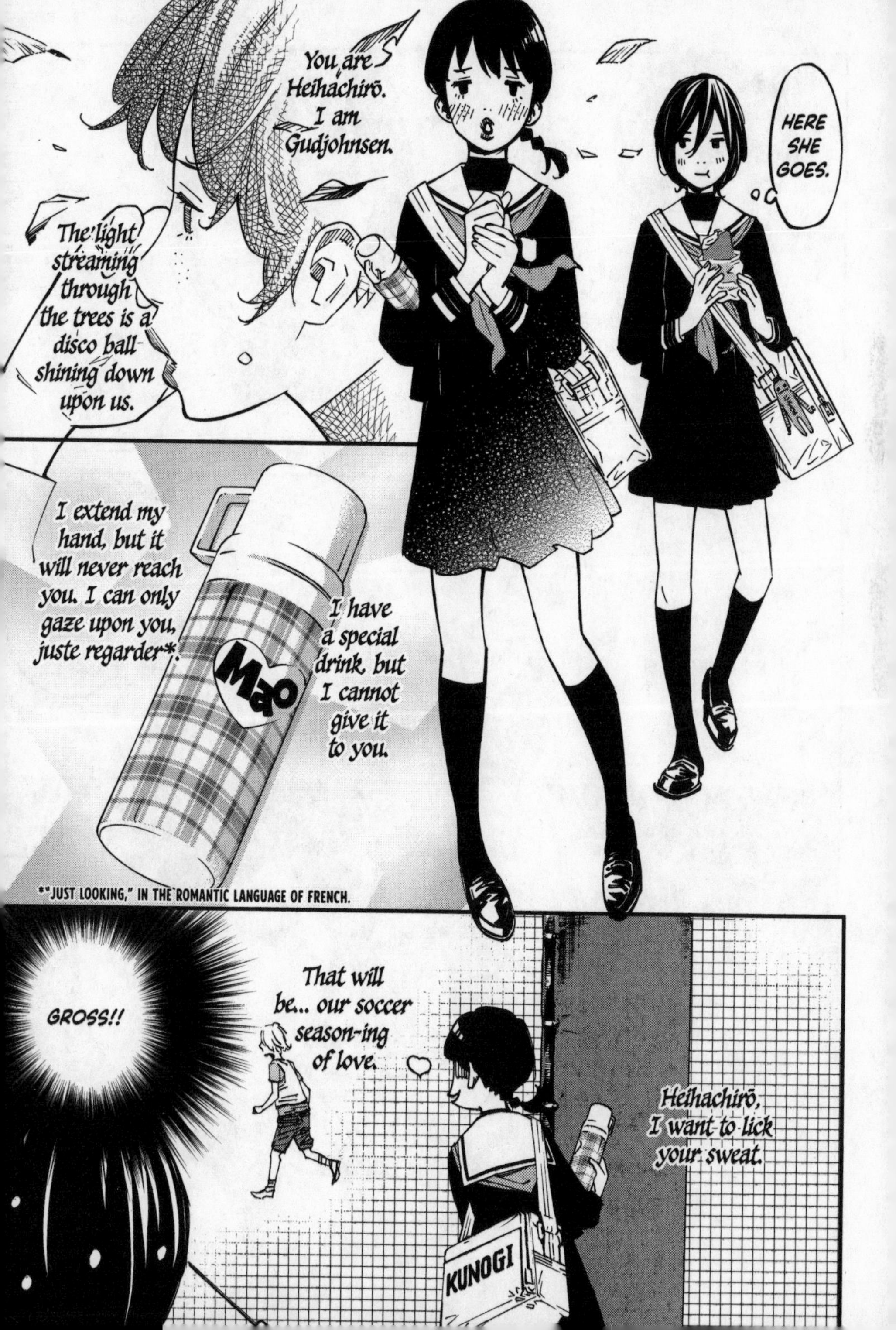

HERE SHE GOES.
You are Heihachirō. I am Gudjohnsen.
The light streaming through the trees is a disco ball shining down upon us.
I have a special drink, but I cannot give it to you.
I extend my hand, but it will never reach you. I can only gaze upon you, juste regarder*.
MaO
*"JUST LOOKING," IN THE ROMANTIC LANGUAGE OF FRENCH.
Heihachirō, I want to lick your sweat.
That will be... our soccer season-ing of love.
GROSS!!
KUNOGI

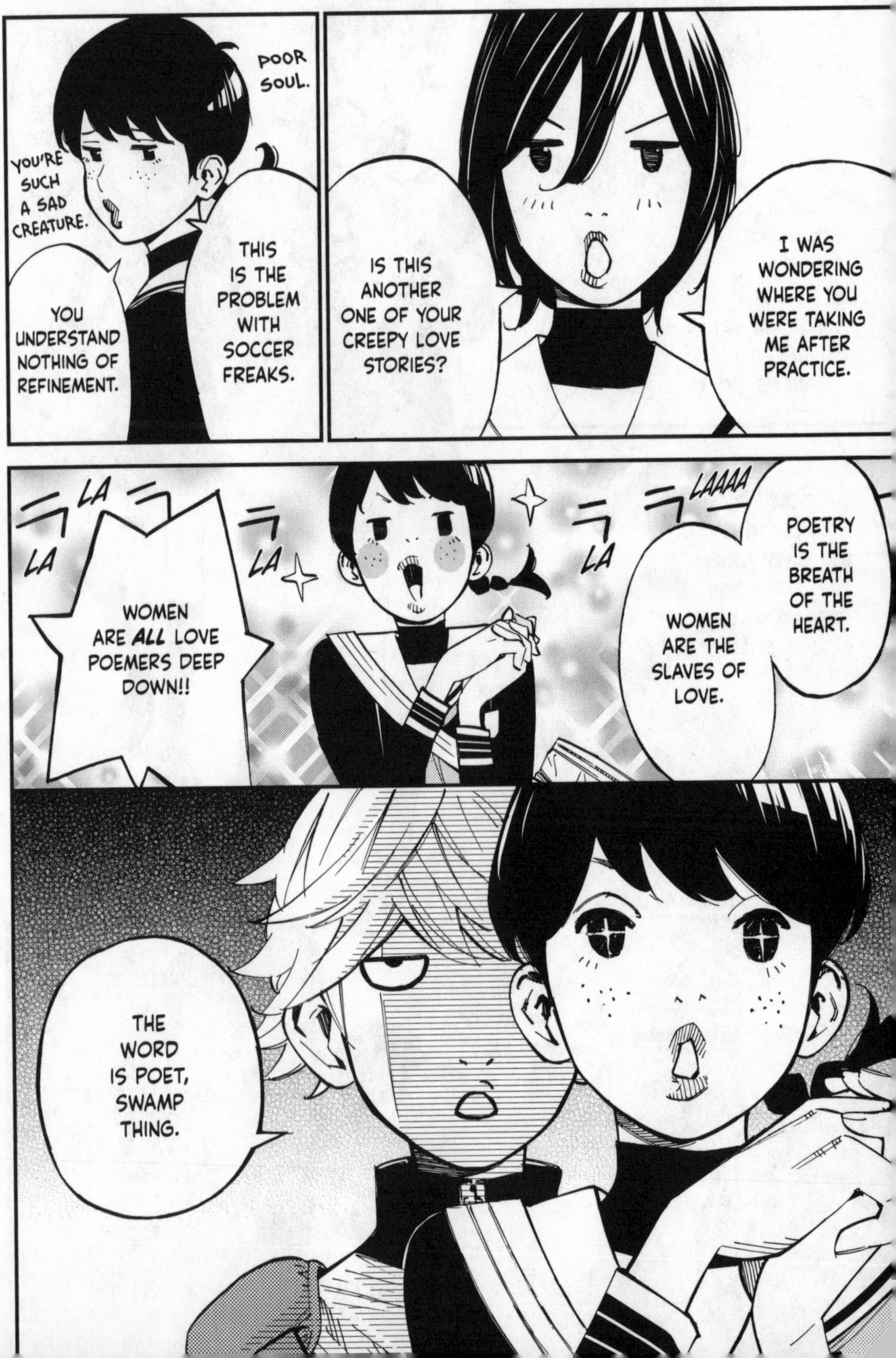
I WAS WONDERING WHERE YOU WERE TAKING ME AFTER PRACTICE.
IS THIS ANOTHER ONE OF YOUR CREEPY LOVE STORIES?
POOR SOUL.
THIS IS THE PROBLEM WITH SOCCER FREAKS.
YOU'RE SUCH A SAD CREATURE.
YOU UNDERSTAND NOTHING OF REFINEMENT.
LAAAA
POETRY IS THE BREATH OF THE HEART.
LA
WOMEN ARE THE SLAVES OF LOVE.
LA
LA
WOMEN ARE *ALL* LOVE POEMERS DEEP DOWN!!
LA
THE WORD IS POET, SWAMP THING.

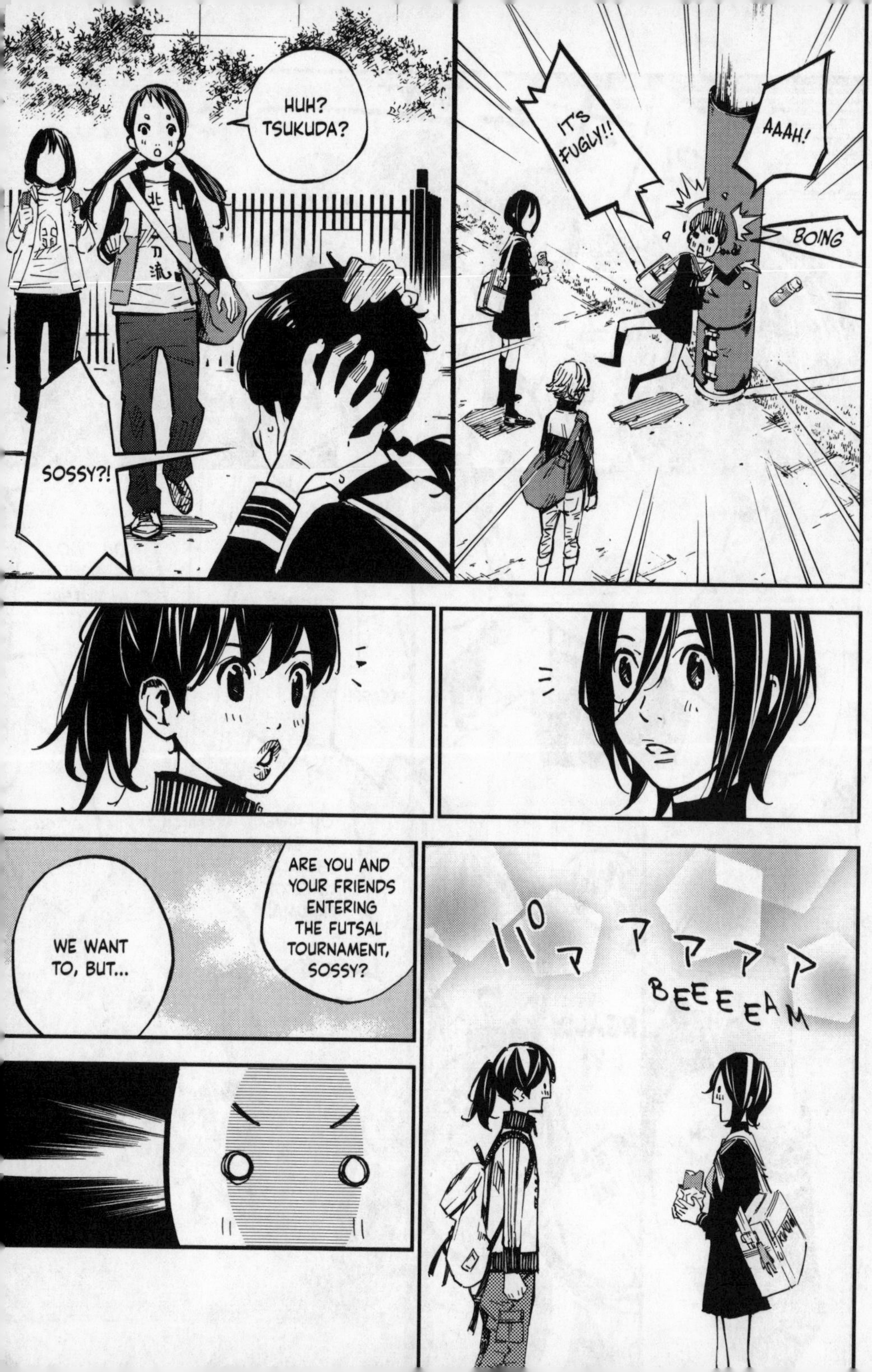
AAAH!
IT'S FUGLY!!
BOING
HUH? TSUKUDA?
SOSSY?!
パァアアア
BEEEEAM
ARE YOU AND YOUR FRIENDS ENTERING THE FUTSAL TOURNAMENT, SOSSY?
WE WANT TO, BUT...

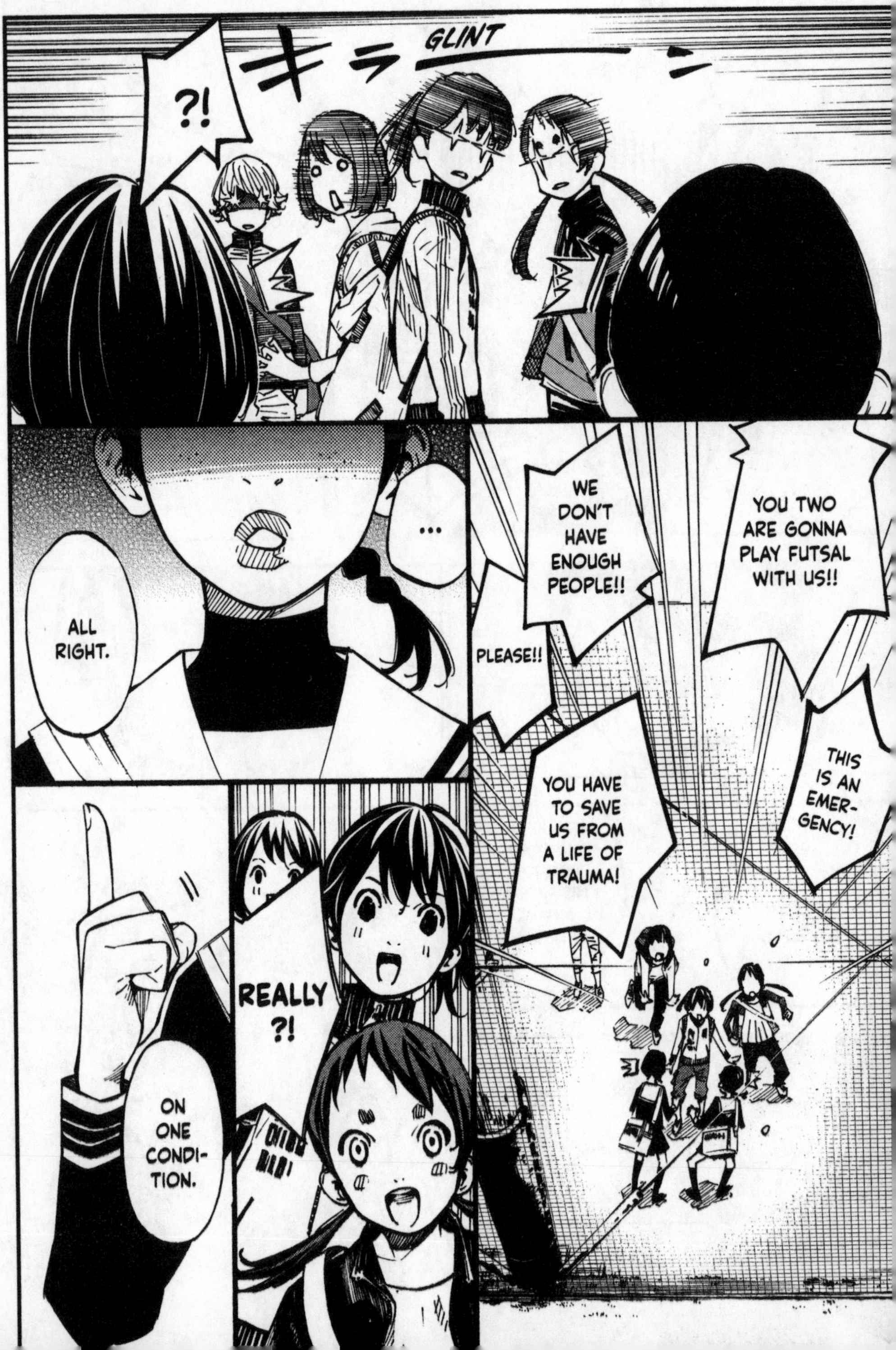
キラ GLINT
?!
YOU TWO ARE GONNA PLAY FUTSAL WITH US!!
WE DON'T HAVE ENOUGH PEOPLE!!
THIS IS AN EMER-GENCY!
PLEASE!!
YOU HAVE TO SAVE US FROM A LIFE OF TRAUMA!
...
ALL RIGHT.
REALLY?!
ON ONE CONDI-TION.

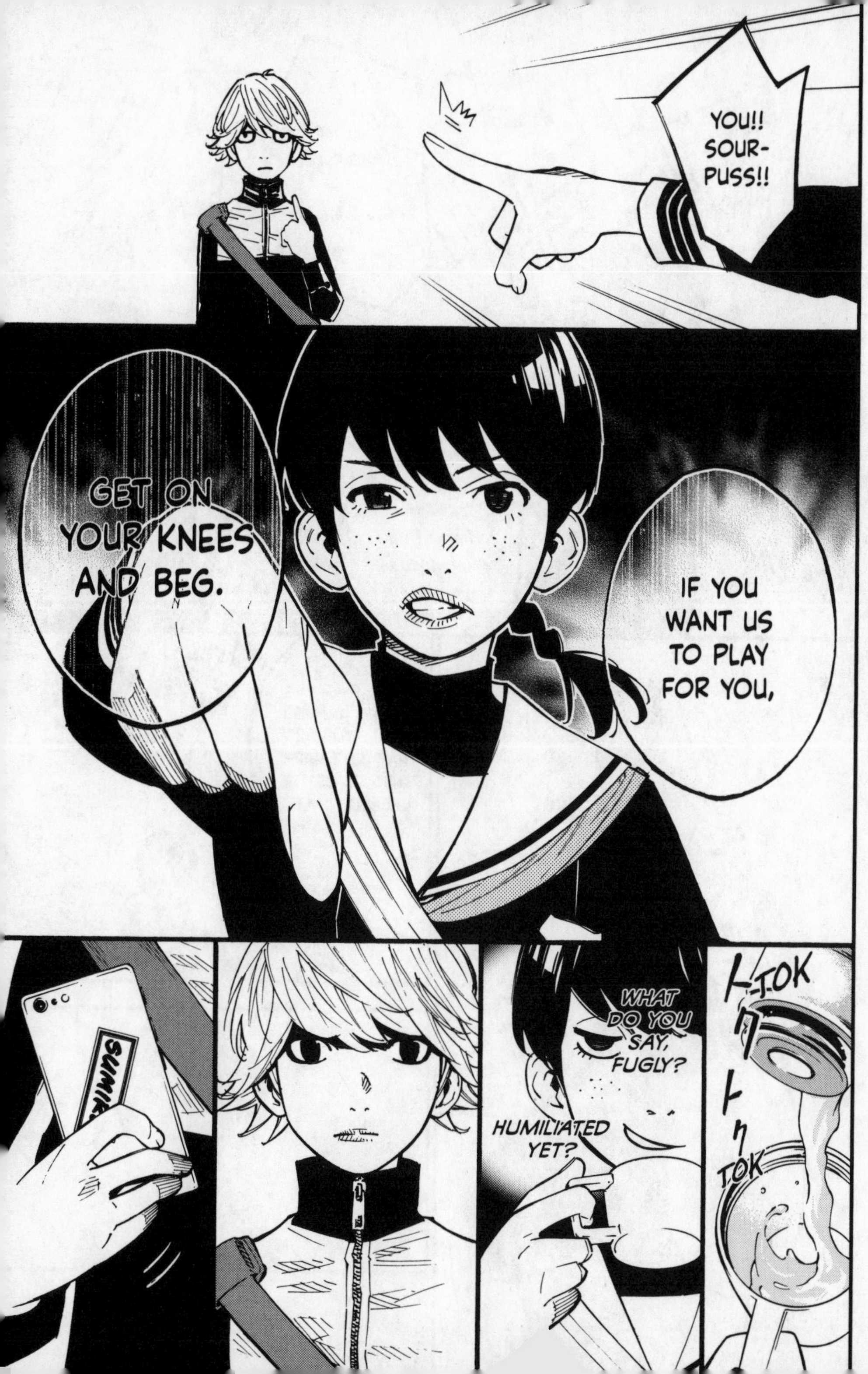
YOU!! SOUR-PUSS!!
IF YOU WANT US TO PLAY FOR YOU,
GET ON YOUR KNEES AND BEG.
TOK
TOK
WHAT DO YOU SAY, FUGLY?
HUMILIATED YET?

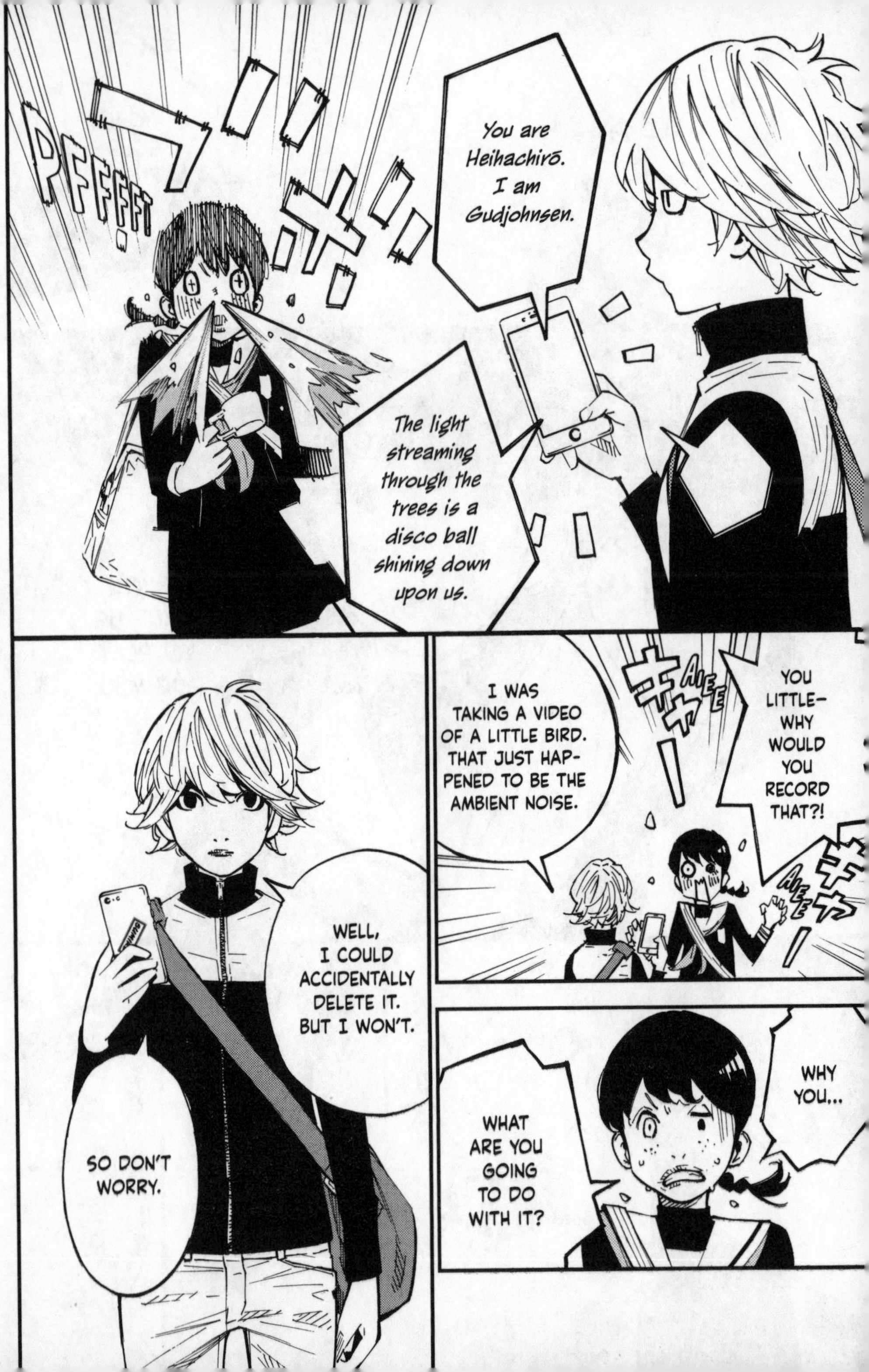
You are Heihachirō. I am Gudjohnsen.
The light streaming through the trees is a disco ball shining down upon us.
PFFFFT!
YOU LITTLE— WHY WOULD YOU RECORD THAT?!
AIEE
AIEE
I WAS TAKING A VIDEO OF A LITTLE BIRD. THAT JUST HAPPENED TO BE THE AMBIENT NOISE.
WHY YOU...
WHAT ARE YOU GOING TO DO WITH IT?
WELL, I COULD ACCIDENTALLY DELETE IT. BUT I WON'T.
SO DON'T WORRY.

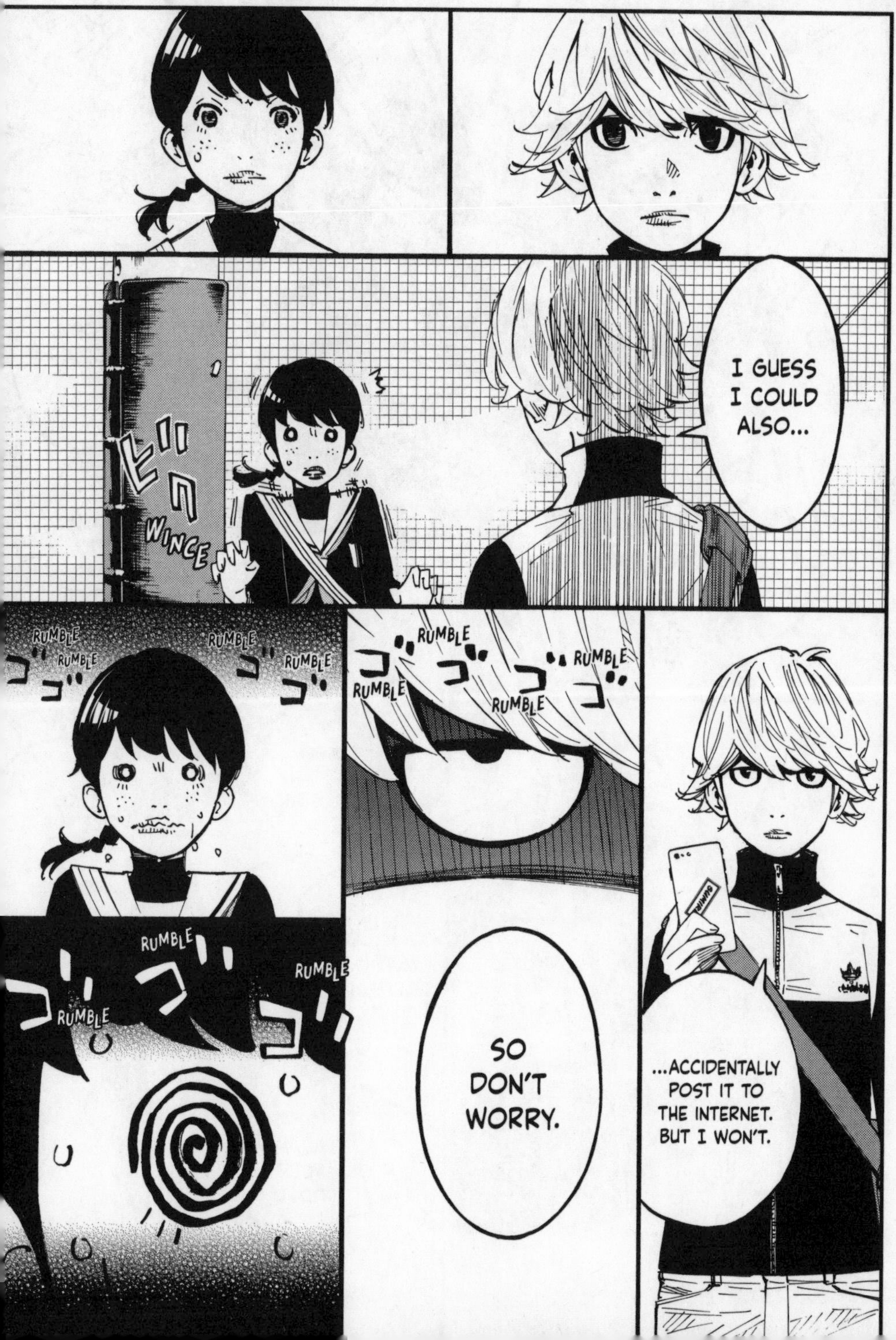
I GUESS I COULD ALSO...
WINCE
...ACCIDENTALLY POST IT TO THE INTERNET. BUT I WON'T.
RUMBLE RUMBLE RUMBLE RUMBLE
SO DON'T WORRY.
RUMBLE RUMBLE RUMBLE RUMBLE
RUMBLE RUMBLE RUMBLE

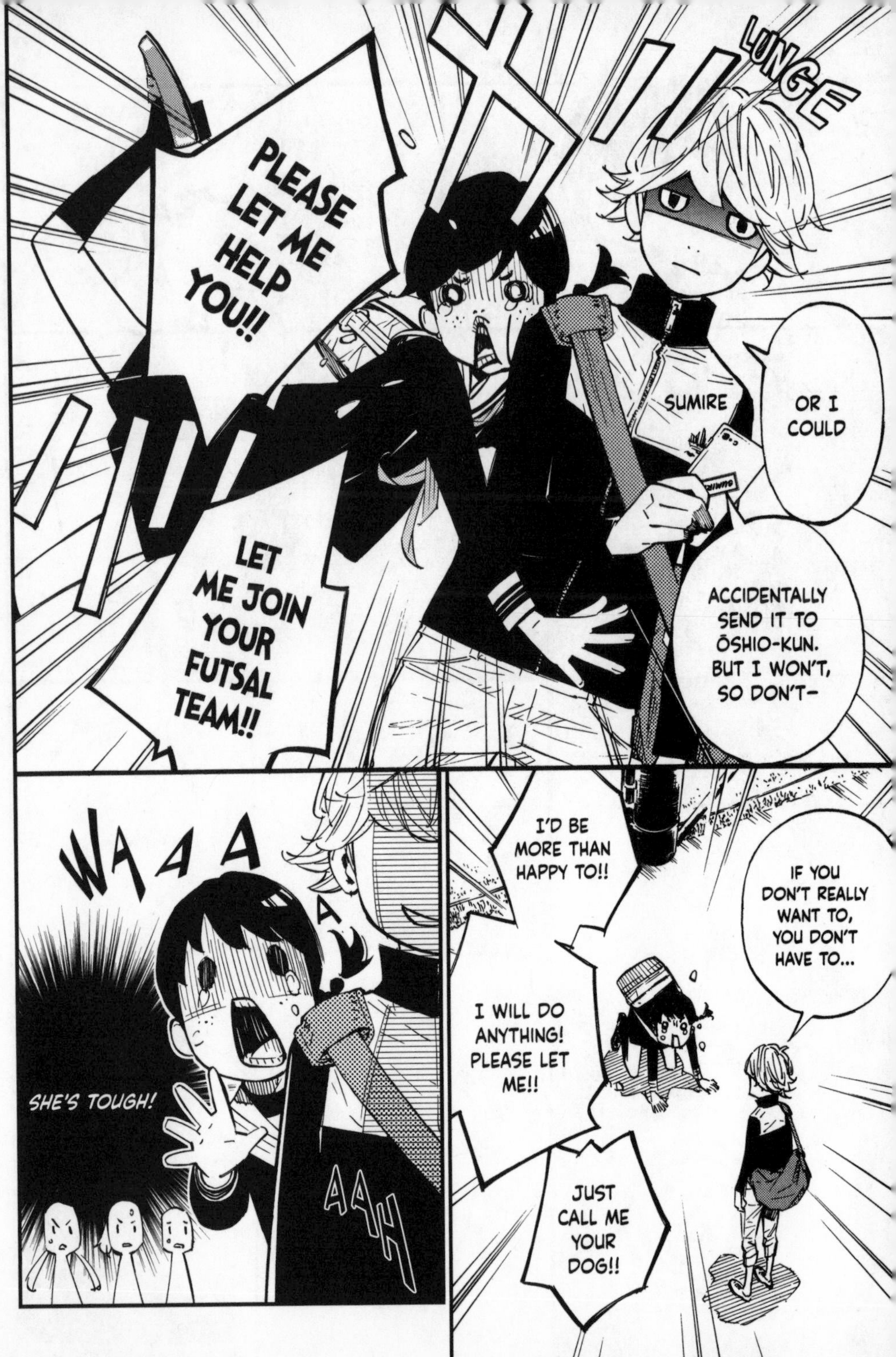
LUNGE
OR I COULD
SUMIRE
ACCIDENTALLY SEND IT TO ŌSHIO-KUN. BUT I WON'T, SO DON'T-
PLEASE LET ME HELP YOU!!
LET ME JOIN YOUR FUTSAL TEAM!!
IF YOU DON'T REALLY WANT TO, YOU DON'T HAVE TO...
I'D BE MORE THAN HAPPY TO!!
I WILL DO ANYTHING! PLEASE LET ME!!
JUST CALL ME YOUR DOG!!
WAAAA
AAH
SHE'S TOUGH!

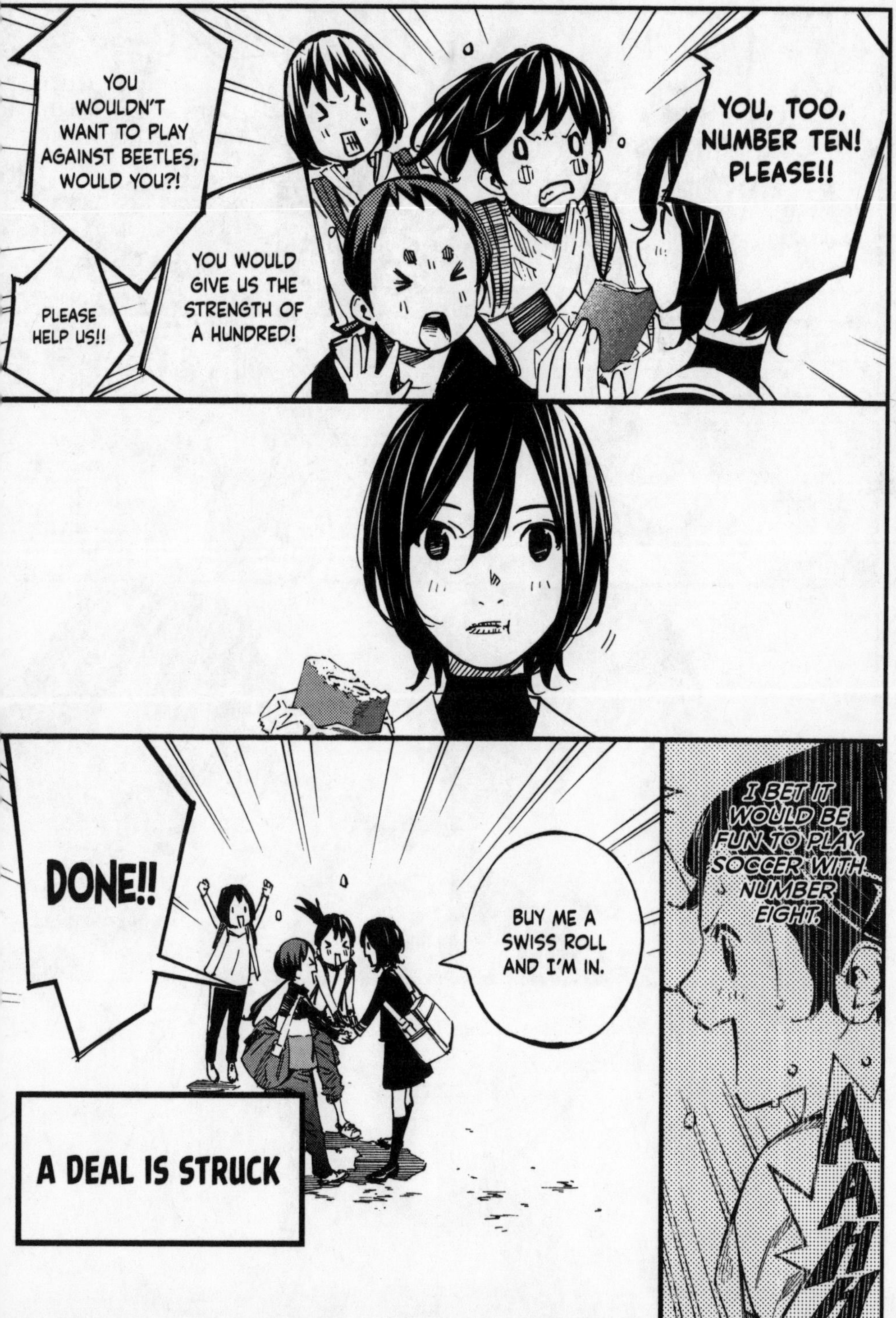
YOU, TOO, NUMBER TEN! PLEASE!!
YOU WOULDN'T WANT TO PLAY AGAINST BEETLES, WOULD YOU?!
YOU WOULD GIVE US THE STRENGTH OF A HUNDRED!
PLEASE HELP US!!
I BET IT WOULD BE FUN TO PLAY SOCCER WITH NUMBER EIGHT.
AAHH
BUY ME A SWISS ROLL AND I'M IN.
DONE!!
A DEAL IS STRUCK

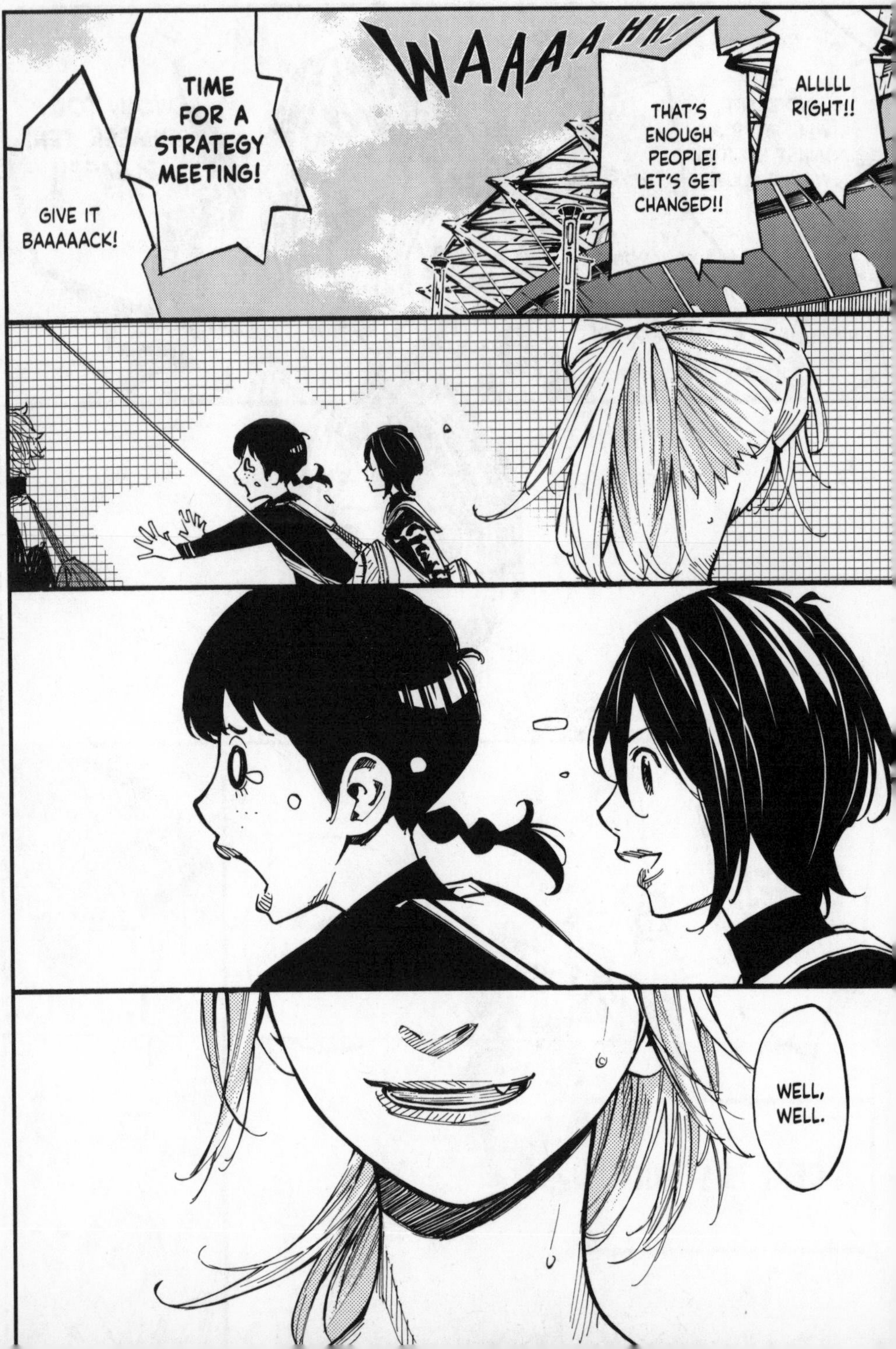
ALLLLL RIGHT!!
THAT'S ENOUGH PEOPLE! LET'S GET CHANGED!!
WAAAAHH!
TIME FOR A STRATEGY MEETING!
GIVE IT BAAAAACK!
WELL, WELL.

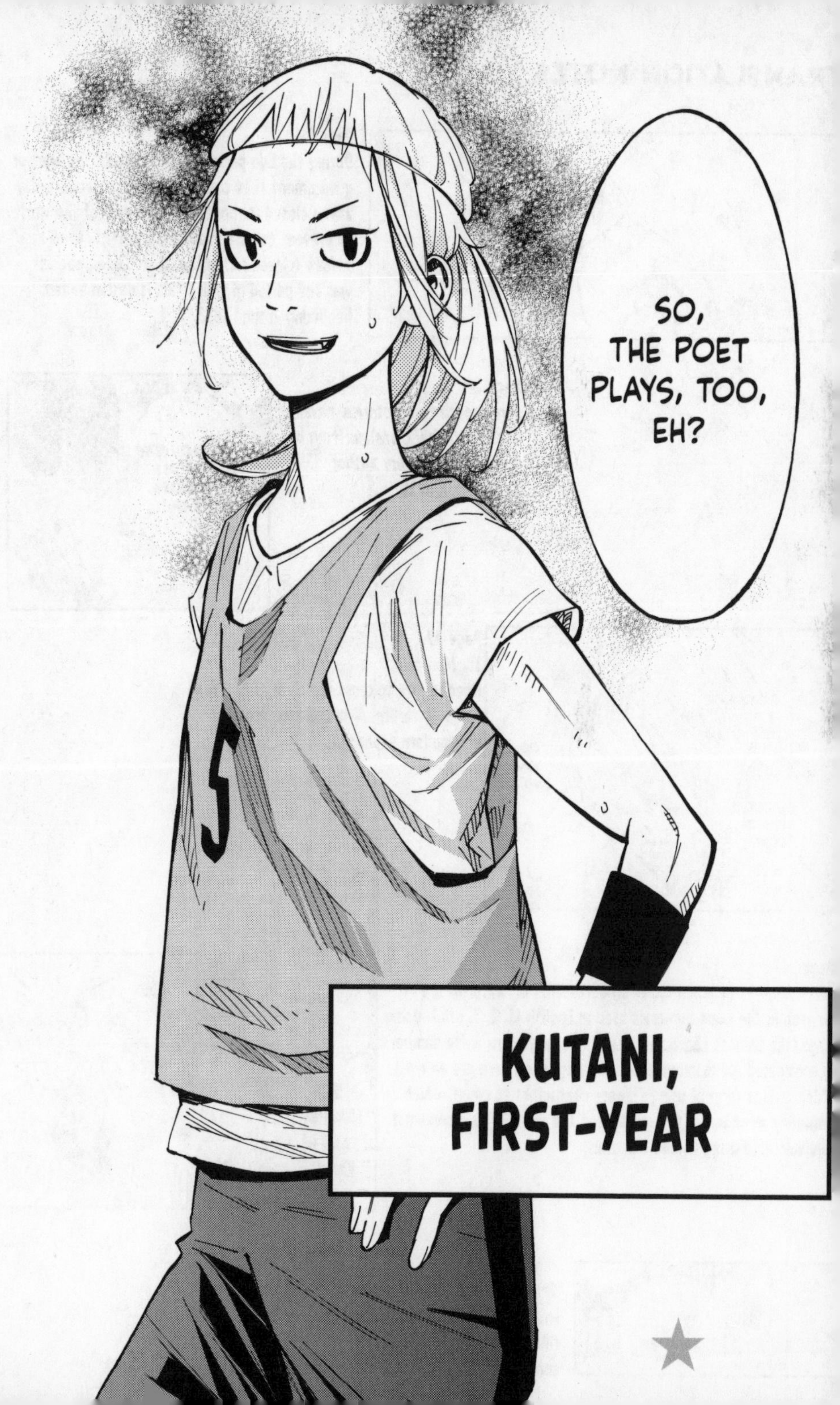
SO, THE POET PLAYS, TOO, EH?
KUTANI, FIRST-YEAR

TRANSLATION NOTES

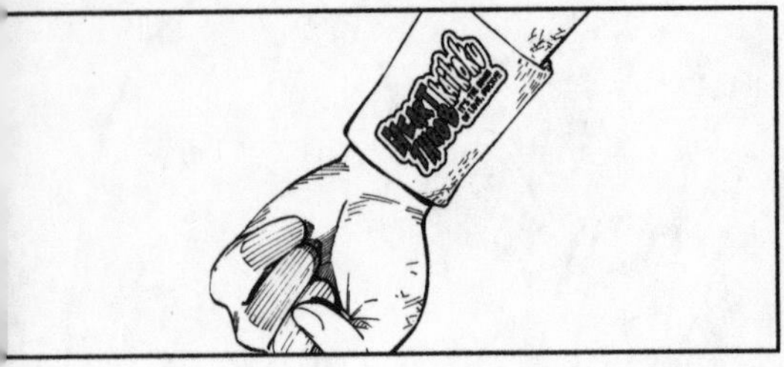

Page 11
During the Edo period (1600 - 1863), the warrior government that controlled most of modern-day Japan closed its borders to the rest of the world to prevent colonial invasion, a period called *sakoku* (closed nation). *Kaikoku* (open nation) was the period in which this isolation ended, beginning around 1853.

Page 27
A reference to a historical novel entitled *Unmei* (*Fate*), written by turn-of-the-century author Koda Rôhan in 1919.

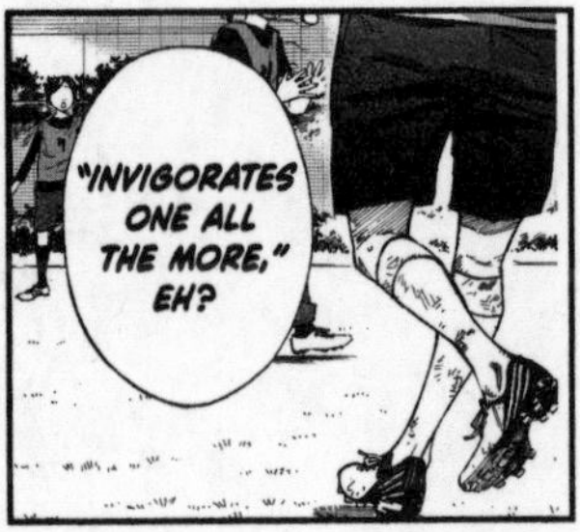
"INVIGORATES ONE ALL THE MORE," EH?

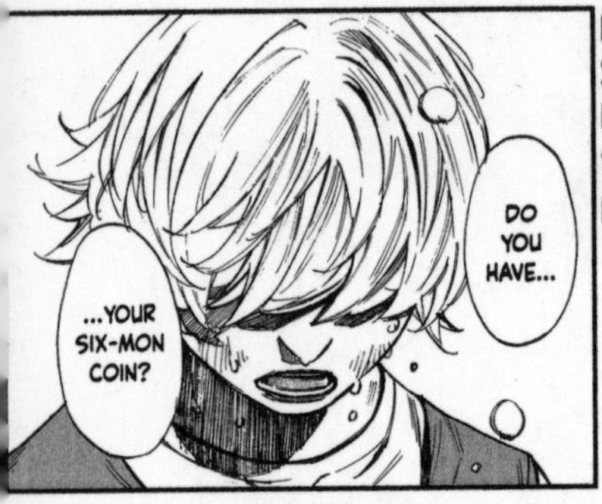
DO YOU HAVE...
...YOUR SIX-MON COIN?

Page 47
Six-Mon coin
Needed fare to cross the river of the dead to the afterlife. *Mon* was a currency in pre-modern Japan.

Page 142
Most numbers in Japan today on documents or uniforms are written in the same numerals used in English (1, 2, 3, etc.). Using *kanji* (the Chinese characters used in Japanese) to write numbers is considered old-fashioned, and the *kanji* used here are an even older variant form of using Chinese characters to count, which generally went out of fashion around the mid 1900's—somewhat equivalent to using Roman numerals.

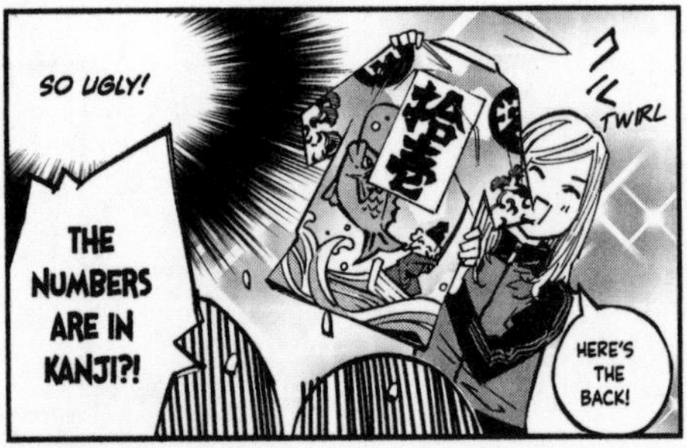
TWIRL
SO UGLY!
HERE'S THE BACK!
THE NUMBERS ARE IN KANJI?!

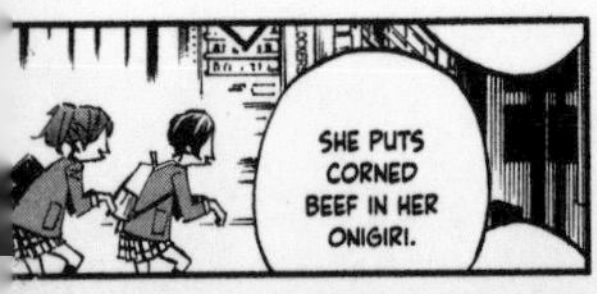
SHE PUTS CORNED BEEF IN HER ONIGIRI.

Page 163
***Onigiri* are hand-held rice balls, wrapped in seaweed and often filled with tuna or vegetables, commonly eaten as lunch in Japan.**

Farewell, My Dear Cramer

A Kodansha Comics Trade Paperback Original
Sayonara, Football 4 copyright © 2017 Naoshi Arakawa
English translation copyright © 2021 Naoshi Arakawa

Published in the United States by Kodansha Comics, an imprint of Kodansha USA Publishing, LLC, New York.

Publication rights for this English edition arranged through Kodansha Ltd., Tokyo.

First published in Japan in 2017 by Kodansha Ltd., Tokyo as *Sayonara watashi no Cramer*, volume 2.

ISBN 978-1-63236-985-7

Original cover design by Asakura Kenji

Printed in the United States of America.

www.kodanshacomics.com

9 8 7 6 5 4 3 2 1
Translation: Devon Corwin
Lettering: Allen Berry
Additional Layout and Lettering: Belynda Ungurath
Editing: PJ Hruschak
YKS Services LLC/SKY Japan, INC.
Kodansha Comics edition cover design by Adam Del Re

Publisher: Kiichiro Sugawara

Director of publishing services: Ben Applegate
Associate director of operations: Stephen Pakula
Publishing services managing editor: Noelle Webster
Assistant production manager: Emi Lotto, Angela Zurlo
Logo and character art ©Kodansha USA Publishing, LLC